The End of Corruption and Impunity

The End of Corruption and Impunity

Stuart S. Yeh

LEXINGTON BOOKS
Lanham • Boulder • New York • London

Published by Lexington Books
An imprint of The Rowman & Littlefield Publishing Group, Inc.
4501 Forbes Boulevard, Suite 200, Lanham, Maryland 20706
www.rowman.com

86-90 Paul Street, London EC2A 4NE, United Kingdom

British Library Cataloguing in Publication Information Available

Library of Congress Cataloging-in-Publication Data

Names: Yeh, Stuart S., author.
Title: The end of corruption and impunity / Stuart S. Yeh.
Description: Lanham : Lexington Books, [2022] | Includes bibliographical references and index. | Summary: "The End of Corruption and Impunity argues that it is feasible to limit the corruption that plagues developing regions of the world by implementing an international treaty designed to combat dysfunctional criminal justice systems and restore human rights"—Provided by publisher.
Identifiers: LCCN 2021048325 (print) | LCCN 2021048326 (ebook) | ISBN 9781793655097 (cloth) | ISBN 9781793655103 (epub)
Subjects: LCSH: Corruption—Law and legislation. | Corruption—Prevention.
Classification: LCC K5261 .Y44 2022 (print) | LCC K5261 (ebook) | DDC 345/.02323—dc23/eng/20211028
LC record available at https://lccn.loc.gov/2021048325
LC ebook record available at https://lccn.loc.gov/2021048326

Contents

List of Figures and Tables

FIGURES

TABLES

Preface

This book is addressed to those who are concerned about the billions of people who suffer extreme violence, poverty, and violations of their basic human rights. The focus is a model international treaty that I have authored. The treaty would establish a body of criminal inspectors who would be empowered to investigate allegations of corruption in states that are parties to the treaty. Inspectors would hand cases to dedicated domestic anticorruption courts. The treaty includes provisions to vet the selection, and ensure the accountability, of prosecutors and judges serving those courts. Each chapter addresses issues raised by the model treaty, building on the content of the previous chapters.

The model treaty seeks to solve many of the most difficult challenges in fighting corruption. In particular, the treaty includes innovative provisions that give States Parties the power to regulate activities by distant trust or company service providers located in bank secrecy havens that currently aid and abet money laundering. The treaty includes provisions to enforce those regulations through criminal penalties. The provisions seek to deter money laundering that permits criminals to hide the proceeds of illicit activities from investigators. Treaty provisions designed to reveal the true beneficial owners of these funds would make it extremely difficult to evade skilled criminal investigators and would pose a significant deterrent to criminals who currently have little difficulty hiding illicit assets.

The model treaty incorporates numerous additional provisions designed to fight corruption and impunity. Significantly, the model treaty includes provisions designed to ensure that the treaty is implemented as intended and corrupt parties are unable to evade, elude, or defy prosecution. No other strategy to fight corruption incorporates these elements.

Introduction

The End of Corruption and Impunity advances a novel idea: it is feasible to end the corruption and impunity that plagues the efforts of nongovernmental organizations (NGOs) and activists to end poverty and restore human rights in regions of the world where corruption and impunity prevail. The book details a solution that has been overlooked by activists, involving implementation of a powerful international institution designed to restore accountability in dysfunctional domestic criminal justice systems. The book offers what may be the most direct, effective strategy that could be adopted by the international community.

The End of Corruption and Impunity proposes the implementation of an international treaty, in the form of an Anticorruption Protocol to the United Nations Convention against Corruption (APUNCAC), that would establish a body of United Nations (UN) inspectors who would be authorized to conduct investigations into allegations of corruption. Parties to the treaty would voluntarily agree to facilitate these investigations and prosecute offenders.

The book reviews a growing body of evidence and precedents suggesting that this proposal is feasible, practical, and sensible. The book reviews evidence suggesting that implementation of this proposal would have an enormously positive effect in addressing the impunity that prevails in developing nations—impunity that undermines the best efforts to reduce poverty, promote development, and restore human rights. Significantly, rule of law institutions including the criminal justice system are the most important institutions for generating economic development, accounting for 57 percent of a nation's wealth.[1]

The methods are analytic, evaluative, and synthetic. The book analyzes the problem of corruption and specific factors contributing to corruption, drawing upon qualitative descriptions of mechanisms and processes, as well as quantitative evidence regarding the causal effects of corruption. The methods involve a mix of best-evidence synthesis, evaluative analysis, statistical analysis, feasibility analysis, legal analysis, and case analysis. The book evaluates evidence and precedents indicating that the provisions of the proposed treaty are feasible, practical, and sensible. Specific treaty provisions are analyzed in detail. These provisions were adapted over the past decade in response to critical review and analysis by dozens of experts versed in international public law and anticorruption law.

The book details special provisions of the treaty designed to break the stranglehold of corrupt elites who dominate domestic power structures and undermine reform. These provisions include the American Racketeer Influenced and Corrupt Organizations Act (RICO) to fight racketeering, as well as a model campaign finance law and a model law deterring conflicts of interest. Significantly, the treaty incorporates innovative provisions designed to address money laundering, the practice of hiding illicit funds in offshore tax havens, and the use of attorneys and financial service professionals to hide illicit revenues derived from crime—revenues that reward and drive violent criminals. The treaty incorporates provisions designed to address corruption in the sale of state assets, the use of loans to conduct illicit transactions, facilitation payments, and transfer pricing.

The Introduction introduces the book's thesis and sets the stage for the remainder of the book.

Chapter 1, "The Locust Effect," focuses on the catastrophic violence that is destroying the lives of billions of poor people. Gary Haugen, founder of the International Justice Mission (IJM), is the protagonist of this story. Haugen's experiences in developing nations reveal the cause—corruption, the absence of a functioning public justice system to enforce the rule of law, and the need to establish accountability for key actors in the criminal justice system. This points directly to the need to implement a powerful institution that would strengthen the rule of law by giving every member of the public justice system powerful incentives to perform his or her statutory duties.

Chapter 2, "Ending Corruption," explains why an international treaty is needed. The first section of the chapter suggests that a lack of effective checks and balances against corruption is the primary factor undermining the rule of law, the protection of human rights, and economic growth in sub-Saharan Africa. The second section reviews the experiences of Uganda, Tanzania, and Hong Kong in fighting corruption, and draws three conclusions about how to end corruption in Africa. The third section describes a scheme involving independent UN inspectors who would assist local prosecutors in prosecuting corruption. Under the draft protocol, parties to APUNCAC would establish a system of courts and prosecutors dedicated to the adjudication and swift resolution of charges of corruption. The UN Commission on Crime Prevention and Criminal Justice would ensure that dedicated courts and prosecutors have regular and adequate funding to perform their responsibilities, would conduct periodic reviews to evaluate the performance of dedicated courts and prosecutors, and would redirect funding based upon these evaluations. Dedicated courts and prosecutors would prioritize charges submitted by UN inspectors or their surrogates, would ensure the swift resolution of resulting cases, and would not tolerate delays that pervert the course of justice. The fourth section of the chapter concludes with an analysis suggesting that the process through which NGOs influenced the ratification of the Rome Statute provides a roadmap for obtaining ratification of the proposed treaty. Importantly, it is not necessary to rely on purely voluntary acquiescence. Instead, ratification would be obtained through a coordinated international effort, involving pressure exerted by influential international organizations such as Amnesty International. Framed as a moral issue, signature and ratification of APUNCAC would provide a public litmus test for leaders around the world who would be compelled to support the treaty or risk public condemnation and loss of office.

Chapter 3, "Ending Impunity," explores reasons for the failure of domestic anticorruption units, drawing upon the experience of Nigeria's Economic and Financial Crimes Commission (EFCC). The analysis suggests that this type of domestic anticorruption unit can only be successful if it is protected. A promising strategy involves the implementation of APUNCAC, similar to the bilateral treaty that established Guatemala's Commission against Impunity in Guatemala (CICIG). This type of institution, establishing UN inspectors, could provide the type of protection that is needed by domestic anticorruption units. This chapter offers a detailed explanation of the proposal to implement an international treaty establishing UN inspectors empowered to investigate allegations of corruption. The chapter walks the reader through a discussion of each barrier that may arise and explains how those barriers would be addressed. The chapter analyzes prospects for ratification and issues raised by the proposal. The precedent established by the Rome Statute, where 123 nations previously agreed to permit intrusive criminal investigations, suggests reason for optimism.

Chapter 4, "Corruption and the Drug War," applies the proposal to implement APUNCAC, establishing UN inspectors, to the problem of fighting drug trafficking and the violence associated with drug trafficking and suggests that this could be effective in deterring corruption that fuels the violence. The chapter suggests that the Rome Statute and CICIG offer models for the establishment of this type of treaty. The chapter analyzes numerous issues that are raised by this proposal. The chapter concludes that APUNCAC is feasible and is a promising approach for addressing what appears to be an insoluble problem.

Chapter 5, "Corruption and Insurgency," applies the proposal to implement an international treaty establishing UN inspectors to the problem of fighting insurgency and the violence associated with insurgency and suggests that this could be effective in deterring corruption that fuels insurgency. This chapter suggests the need to address corruption proactively through the implementation of APUNCAC, an international treaty modeled after the Rome Statute establishing international inspectors who would deter corruption among government officials around the world and thereby address a root cause of dissatisfaction that gives life to insurgency. In this view, the most effective way to inoculate the world against the scourge of violent extremism is to aggressively combat government corruption. The chapter appraises issues raised by APUNCAC, evaluates the case for pursuing an international agreement, and suggests that the United States and its allies are likely to be supportive of the proposed treaty as a means of addressing government corruption in developing nations that promotes resentment, extremism, and terrorism.

Chapter 6, "Six Theories," seeks to place APUNCAC in the context of current thinking regarding "what works" in promoting economic and social development in developing countries. Chapter 6 suggests that while the proposal to implement UN inspections is logical, sensible, and well aligned with current thinking, existing theorists overlook this option, focusing instead on tangential factors. Chapter 6 begins by reviewing evidence suggesting the importance of governance and institutions in explaining differences in per capita income across countries. The first section of the chapter reviews literature suggesting that the most important factor influencing economic growth is governance, defined as institutions and policies that influence the rule of law, property rights, and economic freedom. The second section reviews literature suggesting that the primary factor undermining the rule of law, property rights, and economic freedom in Africa is uncontrolled corruption and suggests the need to establish a powerful international institution with the capacity to investigate and deter corruption. The third section analyzes current theories of the failure of Africa to develop and suggests that these theories overlook the need to establish a powerful international institution to fight corruption. The fourth section addresses key objections that might be raised regarding the establishment of a strong institutional capacity to fight corruption. This section reiterates that the Rome Statute provides a powerful legal precedent for establishing this type of capacity.

Chapter 7, "The World Bank/IMF View," examines the views of the World Bank and IMF. The first section of the chapter examines statements by senior World Bank and IMF economists and statements published on official World Bank and IMF websites. The second section reviews the origin, nature, and scope of corruption in Africa to suggest why domestic law enforcement institutions are completely overmatched by corruption in

Africa, why the rule of law is weak, and why World Bank/IMF reliance on privatization and economic liberalization is misplaced. The third section illustrates the problem through a case study of Sierra Leone. The final section analyzes the problem and concludes that the monopoly on political and economic power that is exercised by African leaders fatally undermines domestic efforts to control corruption, requiring an international response involving vigorous investigations led by UN inspectors into allegations of corruption.

Chapter 8, "Systemic Corruption," describes APUNCAC provisions designed to neutralize the type of systemic corruption that permits corrupt elites to dominate economic and political activity, subvert reform, and perpetuate large-scale criminal violence. APUNCAC incorporates provisions from American "RICO" laws that fight racketeering, as well as model campaign finance laws, model conflict of interest laws, and model laws to deter bid-rigging. Significantly, APUNCAC incorporates innovative provisions designed to address money laundering, the practice of hiding illicit funds in offshore tax havens, and the use of attorneys and financial service professionals to hide illicit revenues derived from crime—revenues that reward and drive violent criminals. APUNCAC incorporates provisions designed to address corruption in the sale of state assets, the use of loans to conduct illicit transactions, facilitation payments, and transfer pricing. Chapter 8 explains that the United States and Organisation for Economic Co-operation and Development (OECD) Member States could be expected to seek ratification of APUNCAC because it would plug a major gap in the international sanction regime against money laundering and terrorist financing.

Chapter 9, "Ending Money Laundering," focuses on the problem of money laundering and explains how APUNCAC would seek to deter money laundering. The United States and its allies are likely to be attracted by innovative APUNCAC provisions that would permit States Parties to trace international flows of funds into and out of bank secrecy havens such as the British Virgin Islands (BVI), the Cayman Islands, and Panama and would permit investigators to follow and prosecute funding of terrorism, transnational criminal organizations, and criminal activities of corporations and executives that currently go unpunished. These provisions would be attractive to the United States and its allies because their efforts to halt terrorist financing have been stymied by the ability of terrorists to hide their funds in offshore havens. Chapter 9 explains why a global registry of companies is impractical and unlikely to be effective, and why the proposed strategy to identify beneficial ownership would be more effective. Chapter 9 illustrates the intended and expected ripple effects of APUNCAC through examination of likely responses by legitimate business owners, banks, and bank clerks who are currently permitted by lax regulatory regimes to aid, abet, and facilitate money laundering.

Chapter 10, "Six Case Examples," illustrates the application of APUNCAC regarding six case examples that span the range and complexity of money laundering: Danske Bank Estonia, the Vancouver Model, Liberty Reserve, the hawala system, online gaming, and Lightning. These case examples explain how APUNCAC would be implemented across a range of contexts where existing anti-money laundering (AML) regulation has failed to control money laundering and explain why the beneficial owner reporting requirements are feasible, practical, and sensible. The first section of the chapter describes the six case examples. The second section describes the APUNCAC strategy for obtaining accurate beneficial ownership information whenever funds are paid, deposited, transferred, or exchanged. The third section illustrates the application of APUNCAC regarding each of the six case examples.

Chapter 11, "Treble Damages," focuses on APUNCAC provisions that permit private parties to file civil actions to recover damages related to corruption. Chapter 11 focuses on the treble damages provision of RICO, which has been described as "the litigation equivalent of a thermonuclear device." This provision allows private litigants to institute a RICO action and recover three times the amount of their damages. APUNCAC retains this provision. Significantly, APUNCAC inserts four bases, relating to corrupt acts, for instituting a RICO action that are not included in the original RICO language.

Chapter 12, "Treaty Management," focuses on the problem of ensuring that APUNCAC is implemented as intended. The first section of the chapter describes Article 8, which creates dedicated anticorruption courts, with special procedures designed to ensure an independent, untainted process for selecting, retaining, and ensuring the accountability of competent judges to serve those courts.

The second section describes Article 11, which empowers the United Nations Commission on Crime Prevention and Criminal Justice to appoint entities to monitor domestic compliance with the terms of APUNCAC, with special emphasis on cooperation, responses to obstruction of justice, and the privileges, immunities, and protection of inspectors, staff, and surrogates. Monitors may include national or international human rights institutions, or any other entities deemed by the Commission on Crime Prevention and Criminal Justice to be duly qualified for the purpose of monitoring domestic compliance with the protocol. The Commission on Crime Prevention and Criminal Justice would ensure that designated monitors have regular and adequate funding to perform the responsibilities described in Article 11, would conduct periodic reviews to evaluate the performance of designated monitors, and would redirect funding based upon those evaluations. Designated monitors would "not seek nor act on instructions from any source." States Parties would provide access to all reports and information requested by designated monitors for the purpose of formulating an opinion regarding domestic compliance with the terms of APUNCAC, including materials deemed relevant by UN inspectors.

The third section describes Article 10, which makes obstruction of justice an offense that may be investigated by a UN inspector. Significantly, a UN inspector may seek a judicial opinion from a judge in the state where the investigation is conducted regarding any alleged act involving obstruction of justice.[2] The UN inspector may recommend charges or disciplinary actions to the appropriate prosecuting authorities or disciplinary bodies.[3] UN inspectors would file reports that would be published online by Transparency International.[4] The reports would be submitted to the appropriate prosecutorial, disciplinary, or oversight bodies.[5]

The fourth section describes Article 14, which provides a mechanism where a UN inspector may, when obstruction of justice has occurred or when cooperation is inadequate, file a request for censure; Article 15, which provides a mechanism where the World Bank and IMF would reduce aid and credits in response to the magnitude and frequency of acts of noncooperation with UN inspectors; and Article 16, which makes the Commission on Crime Prevention and Criminal Justice the final arbiter of disputes regarding the actions of the Commission, ICAC, the Anti-Money Laundering Debarment Office, FINCEN, and each State Party Conflicts of Interest Board and Fair Political Practices Commission.

The fifth section describes Article 70, which establishes a system where the institutional bodies established by APUNCAC may promulgate rules, regulations, and procedures to implement APUNCAC, adapt APUNCAC as needed, and resolve conflicts. Article 70 establishes a system of administrative law judges (ALJs) to adjudicate disputes about those rules, regulations, and procedures.

Chapter 13, "Complementarity," compares and contrasts the approach adopted by APUNCAC with the approach adopted by the Rome Statute establishing the International Criminal Court (ICC). The Rome Statute includes complicated provisions intended to avoid situations where the ICC usurps genuine proceedings conducted by domestic criminal justice systems. These provisions are based on the principle of "complementarity," meaning that the ICC is intended to complement, rather than replace, existing domestic systems. The provisions seek to ensure that the independent prosecutor only proceeds when a State Party's domestic system is *unable* to prosecute an accused person, manifestly takes *no action*, is *unwilling*, or the proceedings are *not genuine*. If this condition is fulfilled and prosecution is in the interest of justice, then a case is *admissible*, meaning that the independent prosecutor may proceed with an investigation and prosecution. However, the evaluation of this condition is fraught with difficulty. Evaluation of the degree to which a domestic criminal justice system is truly unable to prosecute, determination of whether in fact no action has been taken, and assessment of a state's willingness to prosecute or the degree to which proceedings are genuine is a complicated undertaking involving multiple points where knowledgeable observers may disagree.

In comparison, APUNCAC dispenses with these issues because it establishes a clear division of labor. Under APUNCAC, a UN inspector may only investigate a case. Upon completion of an investigation, the case is handed over to an appropriate prosecuting authority. There is no duplication of prosecutorial or judicial functions. Chapter 13 explains how APUNCAC would ensure accountability and ensure that the appropriate prosecutorial, disciplinary, or oversight bodies would act on reports by UN inspectors regarding obstruction of justice, or risk investigation and public exposure for corruption and obstruction of justice.

Chapter 14, "Why Would Leaders and States Agree?", explains that it is not unusual for political leaders to experience strong pressure to sign and implement agreements to fight corruption. Leaders—even those who may be corrupt—may feel compelled, for political reasons, to sign and implement international anticorruption agreements. This explanation is framed within an analysis of Judge Mark Wolf's proposed International Anti-Corruption Court (IACC) because the IACC proposal highlights the issue and raises two additional issues. One issue is that the IACC presupposes the existence of criminal investigators armed with powerful investigative tools. Chapter 14 suggests that this issue may be addressed by combining the APUNCAC and IACC proposals. A second issue is that Wolf proposes to compel submission to the jurisdiction of the IACC through coercive measures that have been criticized as unworkable and possibly counterproductive. Chapter 14 suggests that this concern may be addressed by dropping the coercive elements of Wolf's proposal and, instead, relying upon APUNCAC's positive features to incentivize potential States Parties to sign and ratify the combined proposal.

The Conclusion of the book reiterates that the international community could address poverty, underdevelopment, and basic human rights through implementation of a powerful international institution designed to restore accountability in dysfunctional domestic criminal justice systems. This path offers a promising strategy that could be adopted by the international community. This book suggests that the Rome Statute and the bilateral treaty establishing Guatemala's CICIG are strong precedents for the type of international treaty that I have proposed—a treaty that would establish the same type of powerful investigative capacity that is effective in all modern democracies in fighting corruption, addressing impunity, and ensuring effective domestic public justice systems. This offers a promising solution to seemingly insoluble problems—corruption, poverty, underdevelopment, and human rights. What is needed is an accurate understanding of the availability of an option that has not previously been considered, and the will to pursue it.

Chapter 1

The Locust Effect

Chapter 1 explains why APUNCAC is needed. Gary Haugen, founder of the IJM, has described a silent catastrophe of violence that is destroying the lives of billions of poor people. He traces the cause to the absence, in much of the developing world, of a functioning public justice system to enforce the rule of law. What is missing is accountability for key actors in the criminal justice system. This suggests a need to implement a powerful institution that would strengthen the rule of law by giving every member of the public justice system powerful incentives to perform his or her statutory duties.

> This plague of predatory violence is different from other problems facing the poor; and so, the remedy to the locust effect must also be different. In the lives of the poor, violence has the power to destroy everything—and is unstopped by our other responses to their poverty.[1]

The problem remains largely unrecognized:

> Perhaps the highest profile statement of the world's most fundamental priorities for addressing global poverty were set forth by the UN in its Millennium Development Goals—eight economic development goals endorsed by 193 nations at the UN's Millennium Summit in 2000 as *the* framework for galvanizing the world to attack global poverty. And yet, in that monumental document, addressing the problem of violence against the poor is not even mentioned.[2]
>
> This is particularly tragic because . . . the data is now emerging to confirm the common-sense understanding that violence has a devastating impact on a poor person's struggle out of poverty, seriously undermines economic development

> in poor countries, and directly reduces the effectiveness of poverty alleviation efforts.[3]
>
> Poor people are relentlessly ambushed by violence . . . productive capabilities lost . . . earning potential stolen . . . well-being devastated by trauma . . . resources ripped away [in a] massive sinkhole of violence.[4]
>
> Perhaps even more surprising than the failure to prioritize the problem of violence against the poor is the way that those who do appreciate the problem ignore the most basic solution—and the solution they rely upon most in their own communities: law enforcement . . . the poor in the developing world endure such extraordinary levels of violence because they live in a state of de facto lawlessness.[5]
>
> Law enforcement systems in the developing world are so broken that global studies now confirm that most poor people live outside the protection of law. Indeed, the justice systems in the developing world make the poor poorer and less secure. It's as if the world woke up to find that hospitals in the developing world actually made poor people sicker—or the water systems actually contaminated the drinking water of the poor.[6]
>
> Tragically, the world has neither woken up to the reality nor responded in a way that offers meaningful hope for the poor. It has mostly said and done nothing . . . the failure to respond to such a basic need—to prioritize criminal justice systems that can protect poor people from common violence—has had a devastating impact on two great struggles that made heroic progress in the last century but have stalled out for the poorest in the twenty-first century: namely the struggle to end severe poverty and the fight to secure the most basic human rights.[7]
>
> Indeed, for the global poor in this century, there is no higher-priority need with deeper and broader implications than the provision of basic justice systems that can protect them from the devastating ruin of common violence.[8]

Haugen draws upon his own experience and the experience of IJM staff to illustrate ways in which wealthy and powerful people in poor communities aggressively use the broken and corrupt criminal justice system to protect their violent abuse of the poor—either by affirmatively using the authorities as their instruments of abuse, or by proactively purchasing official protection of their abuses through bribes. He explains that

> Poor people—*by virtue of their poverty*—are not only vulnerable to hunger, disease, homelessness, illiteracy, and a lack of opportunity; they are also

vulnerable to violence. Violence is as much a part of what it means to be poor as being hungry, sick, homeless, or jobless . . . violence is frequently the problem that poor people are most concerned about. It is one of the core reasons they are poor in the first place, and one of the primary reasons they stay poor. Indeed, we will simply never be able to win the battle against extreme poverty unless we address it.[9]

Progress will depend on whether the world is ready to finally address the epidemic of ordinary terror that swallows up many of our well-intentioned attempts to assist them in sustainably improving their lives.[10]

A three-volume World Bank study titled, *Voices of the Poor*, involving tens of thousands of personal accounts, affirmed that the poor are victims of violence and the reality of their powerlessness.[11] All of this violence is against the law in nearly all of the countries where it occurs, but the laws are simply not enforced. The transcript of an IJM interview with the owner of a brick kiln in southern India illustrates the depth of corruption:

I get the police to beat my laborers . . . just give 100 rupees to a policeman and ask him to come and beat your laborers and he will come and beat them. . . . If I just give them a call, they will immediately come here.[12]

The reality is that

to be poor means you are never safe. . . . You are not safe at the bus station, in the market, on the way to school, at the well, in the fields, in the factory, in the alleyways. Most terribly, you are not safe in your own home.[13]

The poor are subject to forcible eviction from abusive corporations, unscrupulous developers and criminal gangs. Such forces are often supported by corrupt government authorities, or it may be the government itself that is initiating the forced displacement.[14]

For the global poor, forced removals and land grabbing joins forced labor and forced prostitution as another massive category of violence that is driven by powerful economic incentives—and against which the poorest have no defender.[15]

The institutions of law enforcement in the developing world that are meant to be the primary solution to violence are actually *adding* to the violence.[16]

The World Bank study concluded:

> Perhaps one of the most striking revelations of the study is the extent to which the police and official justice systems side with the rich, persecute poor people and make poor people *more insecure, fearful and poorer*. Particularly in urban areas, poor people perceive the police not as upholding justice, peace and fairness, but as *threats and sources of insecurity*.[17]

Police regularly abuse their powers:

> Throughout the developing world, poorly paid police use their coercive powers to continuously extort money from those who are most vulnerable. There are even well-established systems by which the money extorted by low-level officers makes its way up the chain of command to high-ranking officers overseeing a vast syndicate of extortion across the entire city or jurisdiction.[18]

In countries such as Nigeria, "a majority of police officers [use] the police uniform [as] a tool for generating income. They make money by extorting law-abiding citizens."[19]

Despite this abuse, judges typically accept police accounts at face value. For example, two apparently innocent Kenyan men were seized by police and accused of stealing a TV from a hotel. The judge relied entirely on the officers' accusations. No evidence was presented by the officers or demanded by the court. The men were imprisoned indefinitely while awaiting trial.

Police use their powers to arbitrarily arrest individuals who lack the financial resources to hire attorneys to contest the injustice. A global study found that "pretrial detention centers are populated almost entirely by poor people."[20] To elicit bribes, police use the threat of pretrial detention in overcrowded, filthy, disease-ridden facilities where crude mortality rates are comparable to those encountered by the International Committee of the Red Cross in war zones.[21]

Whether a detainee is guilty or innocent, pretrial detention can have devastating consequences:

> You have left prison sick and diseased (maybe with HIV) and your family can't afford medical care. You have lost your job because you didn't show up for work for a year and a half (and who will hire someone who has been in prison for all that time?). Your children have had to quit school because you couldn't afford to send them, are now way behind, and you can afford it even less. You have been evicted from your home because you could not pay for it or hold it, and it has been sold and occupied by someone else.[22]

Pretrial detention is often used as an opportunity to apply torture in an effort to obtain confessions. "In many countries around the world, torture remains a routine part of police work to extract confessions or other information from suspects who refuse to 'cooperate'."[23] "When pressure for conviction is combined with endemic corruption within the police culture, the result is a prevailing sense that a confession coerced by torture is the easiest and perhaps only way of convicting a suspect."[24] The vast majority of torture victims are poor people in the developing world who are tortured in pretrial detention.[25] They are victimized because they are powerless—they do not have the financial resources to hire the best attorneys; they do not have powerful connections to influential people; and they do not understand how to effectively negotiate the legal system. "Most of the victims of arbitrary detention, torture, and inhuman conditions are usually ordinary people who belong to the poorest and most disadvantaged sectors of society."[26]

When ordinary people are victimized by a dysfunctional legal system, robbed of their rights, and tortured into false confessions, the injustice is complete. A Zambian attorney observed that "when the state subjects people to such treatment, who are merely suspected of having done something wrong, the state itself becomes the worst of all criminals."[27] Haugen notes that "for many common poor people in the developing world, the police are just another armed, predatory gang in the community that steals, rapes, extorts from, and assaults them."[28] Haugen concluded: "The most pervasive criminal and predatory presence for the global poor is frequently their own police force."[29]

> Billions of the poorest people live in contexts where law enforcement not only fails to protect them from epidemics of sexual violence, forced labor, and violent land seizures—but affirmatively ravages its way through the community as a source of devastating and rapacious violence among the poor.[30]

In developing nations, "the expected norm" is that police will extort bribes.[31] Police extort bribes from the guilty, who are set free, and also from the innocent, who are forced to purchase their freedom from arbitrary detention. "Law enforcement" is twisted and perverted until it becomes unrecognizable: police officers refuse to chase a suspect who runs away from them, refuse to fill out a criminal complaint on behalf of a victim, refuse to visit a crime scene, refuse to interview a witness eager to provide testimonial evidence, refuse to show up in court when ordered to testify, or refuse to leave the police station to arrest a suspect.[32]

> Once corruption becomes endemic in the police forces, the entire concept of "law enforcement" becomes inverted to serve the money-making enterprise. Every law and regulation ceases to be seen as an authorization to restrain a socially hurtful behavior and is seen instead as an opportunity to extract money

> from the public. Police even come to use the cloak of "law enforcement" to initiate and run their own criminal enterprises such as sex trafficking, drug smuggling, illegal mining, or logging operations. Police provide muscle and intimidation for criminal enterprises, and gathering intelligence for gangs; and they act as hitmen, assassinating and threatening those whom they are charged with protecting.[33]
>
> In poor communities in the developing world where "law enforcement" has been disconnected from the law by corruption and dysfunction, the exercise of police power no longer works to elevate and protect those who are weak and vulnerable. Rather, law enforcement works to reinforce the subordination, abuse, and exploitation of those who are weak in the community. Instead of being motivated by an ethos of heroic protection of the weak underdog, the police are co-opted by the powerful and put to work oppressing and bullying the most vulnerable.[34]

In developing nations, the symptoms and effects of corruption are visible throughout the legal system. In India, a man convicted of holding scores of men, women, and children in slavery for years was sentenced by the judge to detention "until the rising of the court," that is, until the judge declared a short recess for any reason at all, including to take a bathroom break.[35] In Uganda, where a penniless widow expended great effort and incurred significant expense to travel to the court where she sought justice for the theft of her land, the magistrate failed to show up for trial—not once, not twice, but *nine* times, all without any consequence.[36] And in the Philippines, after the completion of a sex-trafficking trial, a court inexplicably withheld judgment for three years, without consequence.[37]

In developing nations, the poor may appear before judges and magistrates who are utterly unfamiliar with relevant passages of the criminal code; who declare from the bench that they "don't care" what the law says, or say that particular perpetrators are too powerful to have the law enforced against them, or explain that the rights in the law are written in books and therefore cannot be enforced for the illiterate; or who, in fits of punitive capriciousness, threaten to throw out a child rape case when the victim fails to appear in court because she has been hospitalized for severe trauma.[38]

What about the Universal Declaration of Human Rights, which prohibits torture, arbitrary arrest, slavery, and servitude?[39] The drafting of the Universal Declaration of Human Rights included among the universal entitlements "the right to an effective remedy by the competent national tribunals for acts violating the fundamental rights granted him by the constitution or by law."[40] Pursuant to the Universal Declaration, the International Covenant on Civil and Political Rights requires all parties to implement legislation affirming the right to physical integrity, the right to life and freedom from torture and slavery, the right to personal security and freedom from arbitrary detention, the right to a fair and impartial trial, and an effective legal remedy when those rights are violated.[41] Why, then, are these rights not enforced?

> For victims of common criminal violence around the world, the tragic problem is that the protection of their rights under national law was placed in the hands of dysfunctional national law enforcement institutions. That is, vindication of basic human rights was left in the hands of local police, prosecutors, magistrates, social welfare administrators, councils, and courts that simply do not enforce the law. As a result, for the hundreds of millions of the world's poorest people who live outside the protection of the rule of law, the principal reason they suffer abuse is often not the absence of good laws, but the absence of a functioning public justice system to enforce those laws.[42]

> As a result, after six decades, many victims of criminal violence in the developing world have not enjoyed the benefits won during the first two stages of the human rights movement. Without a credible deterrent, poor people by the hundreds of millions are relentlessly subjected to assault, rape, imprisonment, extortion, enslavement, theft, dispossession, and removal.[43]

> Absent an effective enforcement mechanism, the great work of the first two generations of the modern human rights movement will deliver to the world's poorest citizens only empty parchment promises.[44]

As a consequence:

> The brokenness of public justice systems in the developing world renders the promise of that movement largely undelivered to victims of common criminal violence across the globe. . . . More than a half century after the miracle of the Universal Declaration of Human Rights, billions of the world's poorest people remain in a state of de facto lawlessness.[45]

> The failure to build effective public justice systems in the developing world means that there is no system that can actually provide the protections that the human rights revolution promised.[46]

> We must . . . confront the way our failure to provide basic law enforcement for the poor has not only undermined their struggle to escape poverty but has left some of the most basic promises of the human rights revolution bitterly unfulfilled.[47]

What is the source of the problem?

> Many of the institutions in the developing world with names like "police," "prosecutors," and "courts" do almost none of the things you and I think those institutions should do or in the way we would expect them to be done. In most instances, these institutions in the developing world were set up by colonial or authoritarian regimes with purposes, mandates, missions, structures, procedures, and cultures that were completely different from those [in modern democracies].[48]

In Africa, for example, there are incentives for police in many countries to maintain the power of dominant political parties and wealthy land-owning and industrial groups by detaining and intimidating opponents, rigging election results, and focusing on crowd control.[49] Corrupt elites benefit from a broken public justice system where police, prosecutors, and judges may be bribed to cover up the criminal activity that is the source of elite wealth. Corrupt police, prosecutors, and judges quickly realize that they can earn extra income by not performing their duties as police, prosecutors, and judges: "Predatory elites actually need to keep [the criminal justice system] broken to secure their exploitive dominance over the poor."[50]

Significantly, this type of systemic corruption is not unique to Africa or any other developing region. Instead, investigative commissions exposed the same pattern of systemic corruption in nearly every major American city during the nineteenth and early twentieth centuries:

> The police were part of a larger criminal justice system that was essentially a form of systematic racketeering. The attractions of positions of authority lay primarily in the opportunities they offered for business ventures.[51]

In the 1890s, for example, the Lexow Commission exposed a massive system of corruption within the New York City police force that generated millions of dollars in revenue for the police chief and huge payouts for everyone down the chain of command, including payoffs from illicit businesses, extortion, and racketeering.[52]

In every society, there are corrupt political bosses, police, landowners, sex traffickers, industrialists, tenement owners, criminal gangs, and racketeers who advance their interests through violence. However, it is significant that systemic corruption and associated high levels of violence have largely been eliminated in major cities throughout the G7 nations.[53] This demonstrates that the problem of systemic corruption is not insoluble. Instead, the solution is within reach. It involves the application of a single basic principle: there must be real accountability for every member of the criminal justice system. Where accountability is missing, an institution must be created that enforces accountability. When strong accountability is enforced, the results are dramatic.

In Cincinnati, Ohio, for example, quick and effective reform of police and government corruption was achieved after a nonpartisan Committee of One Hundred was formed to clean up corruption. The committee pressured the state legislature to place the Cincinnati police under a Board of Commissioners appointed by the governor, rather than local political bosses.[54] The Board dismissed 80 percent of the police force and installed a new police chief who pursued aggressive reforms.[55]

Because of aggressive action, the pace of police reform across America during the early part of the twentieth century was dramatic:

> In no other branch of government have such remarkable changes been made as those made in the field of police organization and administration during the last quarter of a century. . . . One can hardly believe that such great advances could be made in so short a time.[56]

POINT OF DEPARTURE

This chapter builds heavily on work by Gary Haugen and IJM. I have quoted at length from *The Locust Effect* because Haugen and IJM have performed the spadework necessary to understand the nature and significance of the problem of violence in the developing world. This work gives the reader a full understanding of the scope and depth of the problem and offers a genuine rationale for the solution that is proposed and described in the rest of this book.

At this point, however, it is important to distinguish my proposed solution from Haugen's proposed solution. Haugen's approach is not inconsistent with what I propose, but may, instead, be viewed as a parallel strategy that could—and in my view should—be pursued on a parallel track. Haugen proposes interventions customized to each local context. In the Philippines, for example, IJM sought to catalyze a coalition of community forces to transform the corrupt and ineffective local law enforcement system so that the police, prosecutors, courts, and social service agencies would work to effectively protect poor children from sex trafficking.[57] IJM succeeded beyond all expectations. IJM increased local law enforcement's rescue of sex-trafficking victims by about 1,000 percent, obtained the release of over 250 victims of trafficking, and secured criminal charges against over 100 suspected sex traffickers.[58] After four years, external auditors documented a 79 percent reduction in the availability of children in the commercial sex trade.[59] This success indicates that IJM's approach works and should be expanded.

Significantly, however, IJM found that a major problem was corruption. Corruption obstructed enforcement of the law against child sex traffickers: "The very people who needed to be champions to end [sex trafficking] had become the reason that the problem was so entrenched."[60] For example, after rescuing 15 confirmed victims of trafficking, police officers let the powerful owner of the brothel escape.[61] Haugen concluded:

> Perhaps the most discouraging obstacle to the transformation of criminal justice systems in the developing world is corruption. As we have seen, many criminal justice systems in the developing world are indeed "criminal" because they relentlessly and routinely commit crimes of corruption against poor people—extorting money from poor people under threat of false arrest or false charges, or accepting money from wealthy people in order to *not* enforce the law when they commit crimes against poor people. Moreover, corruption of the law enforcement system is different than corruption of other public systems because it is the system specifically tasked with fighting the crime of corruption in every other system. So if your corruption-fighting system is corrupt, you are stuck in a closed loop of criminality that may appear impossible to break out of. Indeed, such corruption is perhaps the chief reason that people have given up on trying to reform broken public justice systems in the developing world.[62]

Significantly, systemic corruption can be successfully, dramatically reduced on a national basis. For example, prior to 2003, the former Soviet republic and now independent nation of Georgia was one of the most corrupt nations in the world. According to Transparency International, it ranked 124th among nations in the world on a scale of freedom from corruption (worse than Kenya, India, Bolivia, and the Congo).[63] Police corruption and abuse were particularly egregious—surveys indicated that police demanded bribes in more transactions (7 out of 10) than just about any other police force in the world.[64] According to a World Bank report, "corruption permeated nearly every aspect of life in Georgia."[65] "Corruption was at the core of Georgia's policing system."[66] By 2010, however, Transparency International ranked Georgia *first* in the world in reducing corruption and ranked the government's effectiveness second in the world in fighting corruption.[67] By 2010, Georgia's police were viewed as less corrupt than the most respected police forces in Europe, including Germany, France, and the United Kingdom (UK).[68] Reform was achieved by prioritizing and attacking corruption in the criminal justice system: the entire police force was replaced and a system of accountability was installed that ended impunity, allowed zero tolerance for

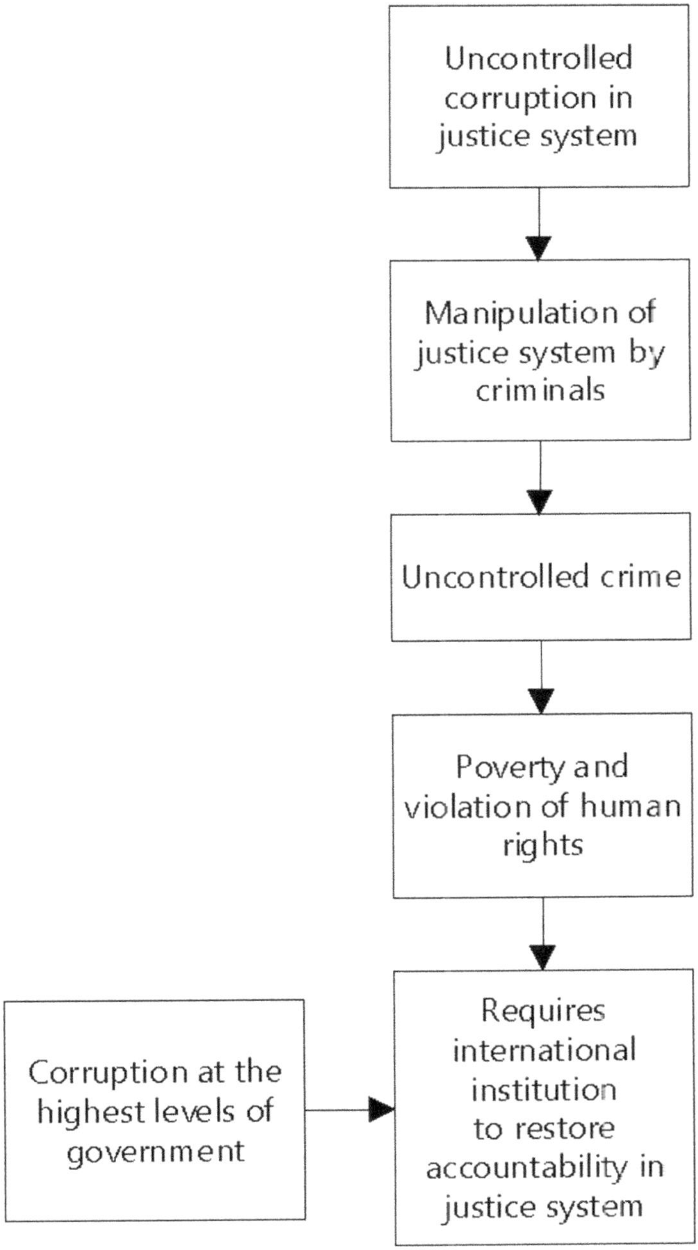

Figure 1.1 An International Institution Is Needed to Restore Accountability in Domestic Justice Systems. *Source*: Figure created by author.

corruption, and vigorously prosecuted corrupt officials.[69] Police officers who were caught taking bribes were fired.[70]

In the Philippines, IJM sought to catalyze a coalition of community forces to transform the corrupt and ineffective local law enforcement system. While the strategy was successful, IJM found that catalyzing community forces is laborious. IJM concluded that systemic corruption in criminal justice systems is a generalized feature blocking reform around the world.

The thesis of this book is that systemic corruption can—and should—be addressed through a specific global intervention that directly implements a strong international institution designed to restore accountability in dysfunctional criminal justice systems worldwide (figure 1.1).

This thesis flows directly from Haugen's analysis and key principles for reform:

1.) Direct solutions that attack the core problem work best.
2.) The core problem is corruption.
3.) What is missing is accountability for key actors in the criminal justice system.

While the implementation of a global intervention may seem utopian, the remainder of this book seeks to persuade the reader that it is indeed feasible, practical, and sensible. An international treaty establishing a powerful investigative capacity may be the only effective strategy to address the impunity that exists when domestic government leaders who are ultimately responsible for correcting abuses fail to perform their statutory duties.

Chapter 2

Ending Corruption

Econometric evidence suggests that corruption has a strong corrosive effect on economic growth, especially in African countries.[1] Chapter 2 reviews evidence suggesting that checks on corruption in the form of domestic laws and institutions have been ineffective, suggesting a need to consider an international treaty that would establish an ICAC, involving UN inspectors to investigate and prosecute corruption. A range of evidence reviewed in this chapter suggests that pressure from constituents as well as international organizations could ultimately be effective in compelling African leaders to sign this type of protocol.

This chapter reviews literature suggesting that a lack of effective checks and balances against corruption is the primary factor undermining the rule of law, the protection of human rights, and economic growth in sub-Saharan Africa. The chapter reviews the experiences of Uganda, Tanzania, and Hong Kong in fighting corruption and suggests three conclusions about how to end corruption in Africa. The chapter introduces a scheme involving independent ICAC inspectors to assist local prosecutors in prosecuting corruption. The chapter concludes with an analysis suggesting how African leaders might be induced to sign APUNCAC, an international agreement establishing independent inspectors.

A LACK OF EFFECTIVE CHECKS AND BALANCES

Historically, the International Monetary Fund (IMF) and the World Bank have traced poor economic growth in sub-Saharan Africa to misguided dirigisme—the practice of directing economic activity through central planning—and have tied structural adjustment conditions to their loans in an attempt to restructure African economies in the mold of Western industrialized countries.[2] Thus, senior IMF and World Bank directors and economists favor privatization, structural adjustment, economic liberalization, and democratization as the most effective means to remove the distortions introduced by the government, minimize opportunities for corruption, and maximize economic growth in countries previously characterized by dirigisme.[3] A strong private sector is expected to demand governmental accountability and economic reform, and strengthened civil institutions are expected to institute checks and balances. These improvements in governance are, in turn, expected to lay the foundation for vibrant economic competition, an efficient business sector, and strong economic growth. Direct prosecution of corruption is viewed as helpful but tangential to the core problem of dirigisme. In this view, corruption will fade away with time as the role of government is reduced and the private sector and civil society grow stronger.

In contrast, prominent African political economists identify the core problem as uncontrolled corruption—the abuse of governmental power for personal gain—rather than dirigisme, and explain that the preoccupation with dirigisme is itself misguided and leads to counterproductive policy prescriptions.[4] These scholars suggest that corruption in Africa has its origin in colonial practices; has been deeply ingrained as a self-reinforcing, self-perpetuating institution; and has fundamentally captured governmental institutions in African countries in a way that insulates corrupt practices from ordinary reforms.[5] Colonial administrators dismantled traditional checks and balances to centralize power in their own hands and the hands of a small number of local chiefs, colonial appointees, and acculturated elites shaped by the colonial educational system.[6] Local chiefs became accustomed to the exercise of absolute rule, without judicial restraint, as long as they enjoyed the confidence of the colonial administrator. Thus, colonial practices institutionalized favoritism, self-aggrandizement, and despotic rule, essentially training African elites in the methods of favoritism, the exercise of unbridled power, and personal enrichment.[7]

After independence, the transfer of this power to African heads of state had disastrous results. Africa's ruling elites quickly discovered that they could use their combined economic and political power to direct economic activity, enrich themselves, reward political supporters, punish political rivals, and crush opposition to their rule.[8] Political supporters were rewarded with government positions that permitted them to invent bureaucratic hurdles and then extract artificial license charges and fees to expedite requests through the bureaucracy, effectively throttling economic activity.[9] The power to direct economic activity and to dispense government positions allowed ruling elites to extract rents, build personal fortunes, and dispense patronage to buy political support.[10] The economic and political power invested in African heads of state was systematically abused for personal gain in one state after another, resulting in enormous personal fortunes.

Thus, Africa's dilemma is that

> The centralization of both economic and political power turns the state into a pot of gold that all sorts of groups compete to capture. Once captured, power is then used to amass huge personal fortunes, to enrich one's cronies and tribesmen, to crush one's rivals, and to perpetuate one's rule in office.[11]

The ruling elite take over and subvert every key institution of government: the civil service, judiciary, military, media, and banking.[12] Key positions in these institutions are handed over to the president's tribesmen, cronies, and loyal supporters.[13] As a result, meritocracy, rule of law, property rights, transparency, and administrative capacity vanish.[14] Suspicious of plots to overthrow them, strategic positions in the police and military are filled with personally loyal relatives and tribesmen.[15] Economic reforms that would strip out state controls and eliminate scarcity are opposed because the controls are the source of the rents that are extracted by the ruling elites. Since political defeat could mean exile, jail, starvation, and the confiscation of all property and wealth, ruling elites refuse to relinquish or share political power.[16] Those who are excluded from power resort to violence, insurgency, and civil war.[17]

The source of the problem of corruption in Africa is the colonial policy of dismantling traditional checks and balances on the power of rulers. Colonial governments used their power to extract wealth from their colonies, then transferred this power to African rulers upon independence, where it was abused on a grand scale: "With no effective restraints on government behavior, corruption became widespread."[18]

The primary catalyst for corruption is a lack of accountability among the ruling elite, who use their monopoly on unchecked discretionary power for personal economic and political gain. Corruption persists because "public officials have no fear of being held accountable for their actions."[19] Despite public outrage, "corruption in Africa has reached cancerous proportions."[20] Elites have turned state institutions into instruments for self-enrichment; thus, "corruption . . . has become, in almost all African countries, a common and routine element of the functioning of the administrative and para-administrative apparatus, from top to bottom," leading to enormous losses in state revenue—in some cases as much as 60 percent.[21] Corruption in Africa is "pandemic," "a way of life" and remains one of the continent's most enduring institutions.[22] Corruption is not only caused by a lack of checks and balances but also serves to prevent the emergence of the institutional reforms necessary to create checks and balances. In the majority of African countries, corruption pervades the institutions that normally provide checks and balances:

the police, judiciary, and the legal system. Thus, it is not possible to rely on those institutions to fight corruption.

Elites sabotage the development of transparent, participatory, democratic accountability structures to preserve their lucrative monopolies on governmental services and privileges. Despite free elections, African leaders continue to resist IMF reforms that would undermine the patrimonial system that keeps them in power, and have delayed and reshaped reform policies in ways that make them less threatening and, in some cases, even profitable, when state assets are "privatized" at fire sale prices to the president's cronies, with hefty fees going to government ministers.[23] Thus, democratization, privatization, and IMF-style reforms are not panaceas and do not provide effective checks and balances against the abuse of governmental power. Instead, "the control of corruption . . . is a fundamental condition for the sustainable transition to a market-oriented economy."[24] Harvard economist Robert Barro summarized the evidence and concluded that

> Even if a poor country could beat the odds and sustain democratic institutions, there is no reason to believe that this accomplishment would help much in the quest to escape poverty. . . . An increase in democracy is less important than an expansion of the rule of law as a stimulus for economic growth and investment. In addition, democracy does not seem to have a strong role in fostering the rule of law. Thus, one cannot argue that democracy is critical for growth because democracy is a prerequisite for the rule of law. . . . If a poor country has a limited amount of resources to accomplish institutional reforms, then they are much better spent in attempting to implement the rule of law . . . Even if democracy is the principal objective in the long run, the best way to accomplish it may be to encourage the rule of law in the short run.[25]

The persistence of Africa's problems despite democratization, privatization, and IMF reforms is puzzling except when viewed as the logical outcome of a lack of checks and balances. Recurring fiscal and balance of payments crises are predictable consequences of corruption, uncontrolled expenditures, and rent-seeking, which drains revenue from government coffers, causing revenue to lag behind expenditures. A continued lack of transparency, accountability, and honest, highly efficient civil servants may be understood as the logical outcome when ruling elites are permitted, through a lack of checks and balances, to use patronage networks to stay in power and, therefore, take every opportunity to subvert good governance. The continued pursuit of disastrous economic policies that would normally be disciplined by their consequences may be understood as the logical outcome when massive amounts of foreign aid provide the resources that allow ruling elites to sustain those policies. Without checks and balances, aid is wasted, and aid donors unwittingly undermine true reform, the development of strong institutions, and the rule of law.[26]

In this view, corruption is the core problem underlying Africa's poverty. What is required is a powerful institution to restore checks and balances against corruption, ensure the rule of law, and protect human rights. Only then will economic liberalization and privatization be effective in producing sustained economic growth. From this perspective, IMF and World Bank policies that focus on economic liberalization and privatization, without vigorous investigation and prosecution of corruption, are simply inadequate and will not achieve the desired results.

LESSONS FROM UGANDA, TANZANIA, AND HONG KONG

The experiences of Uganda, Tanzania, and Hong Kong in fighting corruption suggest three conclusions. First, in Africa, the establishment of domestic anticorruption agencies has not been sufficient to fight corruption because those institutions do not operate independently of African leaders. Second, in Hong Kong, the establishment of investigators operating independently of domestic leaders rapidly reversed endemic corruption. Third, ending corruption in Africa requires the establishment of inspectors who are independent of domestic leaders.

Uganda

Since the 1960s, Ugandan laws have provided police and prosecutors with the legal power to deal with corruption. The Prevention of Corruption Act (PCA) of 1970 calls on the Directorate of Public Prosecutions (DPP) to investigate and prosecute corruption and bribery, and authorizes the DPP to search, seize, arrest, and interrogate suspects.[27] The Office of Inspector General of Government (IGG) was established in 1988 with extensive powers to investigate and prosecute corruption and abuse of public office. A code of conduct was established for all civil servants, requiring leaders to annually disclose their income, assets, and liabilities to the IGG. However, despite the establishment of extensive anticorruption laws, codes of conduct, and potentially powerful agencies, a joint World Bank/Transparency International review team found that corruption remains rampant at all levels of Ugandan society.[28] As of July 2020, Uganda continues to rank poorly on Transparency International's CPI. A consistent pattern of corruption and unethical practice permeates the judicial system, with judges failing to vigorously apply the full power of the law.

The failure to apply existing laws and powers to prosecute corruption is not due to a lack of public support: the review team noted significant public support for more vigorous prosecution.[29] Instead, failure stems from inadequate checks and balances against the influence of the president and loyal elites. The review team made several recommendations, including the rotation of judges throughout the East African region to isolate them from political pressures, and the establishment of an agency similar to the Independent Commission Against Corruption in Hong Kong that would be insulated from political pressure, with extensive powers to investigate and prosecute corruption at all levels of government. In contrast, the Ugandan IGG is appointed by and serves at the pleasure of the president, substantially weakening its authority to investigate and prosecute corruption that may involve the president and loyal elites.

Tanzania

Corruption is endemic in Tanzania, despite the existence of anticorruption laws and institutions, and continues to rank poorly on Transparency International's CPI.[30] Civil servants are prohibited from giving or accepting personal benefits or gifts. The 1971 PCA, amended in 2002, increased the fines for violations and stiffened penalties from 7 to 10 years imprisonment. The Office of Controller and Auditor General has authority to audit accounts, appropriations, and spending to ensure compliance with government rules and regulations and sound accounting practices. The Permanent Commission of Inquiry (PCI) has authority to investigate acts involving arbitrary arrest, negligence, or omission in the performance of duties, improper use of discretionary powers, nepotism, decisions made with malice or unreasonable delays, and unjust or oppressive decisions. Tanzania's Prevention of Corruption Bureau (PCB) has extensive powers to investigate and prosecute corruption in the civil service and parastatals, including the power to enter and search premises and to arrest suspects. Despite this legal and institutional capacity, corruption has reached epidemic proportions, especially in the Ministry of Finance (which collects taxes), parastatal banks, customs, traffic police, magistrate courts, immigration, the Ministry of Lands Office, and the Dar es Salaam City Council (which allocates land and processes title deeds).

Competitive multiparty elections brought President Benjamin Mkapa to power in 1995. He immediately initiated several reforms, including the Public Leadership Code of Ethics Act, which required new cabinet ministers as well as top civil servants to declare their assets and sign a code of ethics, and stipulated that any property or asset acquired by a public official after the initial declaration of assets and not attributable to income, gift, or loan would be deemed to have been acquired in breach of the code, unless proven otherwise.

Despite these changes, corruption remains a problem in Tanzania. All political parties and many candidates for public office have been tainted by corruption, and bribery of potential voters remains widespread. In 1996, President Mkapa appointed a commission to examine the problem. The commission's report stated that the laws on corruption were full of loopholes and the public institutions charged with wiping out corruption, including the judiciary, were themselves corrupt. The report prompted significant changes. It did not, however, lead to reforms that would make the PCB entirely independent of the executive branch by placing it under the authority of parliament. Instead, the PCB was located within the Office of the President of Tanzania, its director general (DG) was appointed by the president, and it was only accountable to the president.[31] In July 2007, the PCA was abolished and replaced by the current Prevention and Combating of Corruption Act which renamed the PCB the "Prevention and Combating of Corruption Bureau" (PCCB). The PCCB reports directly to the Office of the President.[32] The president has the power to appoint and remove the DG.[33] This compromises the independence of the PCCB and its ability to perform its functions.[34] Of 5,450 cases, only 473 convictions had been secured by the end of June 2014, representing a mere 8.6 percent of all completed cases.[35] Similarly, the PCI is appointed by the president, operates at the pleasure of the president, and depends entirely on the president for actions on its recommendations. The Office of Controller and Auditor General is underfunded, and its budget is subject to executive approval.

The experiences of Uganda and Tanzania suggest that domestic anticorruption agencies cannot be effective when they lack independence and are dominated by the executive branch of the national government. There is a need to establish a powerful anticorruption agency with complete independence from the executive branch.

Hong Kong

Hong Kong's experience suggests that the establishment of a powerful anticorruption agency can make the fight against corruption effective. Prior to the anticorruption campaign initiated in 1974, syndicated corruption in Hong Kong "existed in a primal state" where "corruption infected not only the police, a classic source, but all government departments that provided any opportunity for its occurrence."[36] At that time, the eradication of corruption in Hong Kong seemed as hopeless as the eradication of corruption in Africa. Yet, within a few short years, Hong Kong achieved "spectacular success" in arresting corruption to the point where it scored higher than Germany, Belgium, and the United States on Transparency International's CPI,[37] and consistently higher than the average for OECD countries on 11 measures of governance, including freedom from corruption.[38] Hong Kong is now one of the five richest economies in the world.[39] This is directly attributable to a bureaucratically clean, predictable, investment-friendly environment.[40]

The key to Hong Kong's success was the establishment of the Independent Commission Against Corruption in 1974, which quickly proved to be embarrassingly successful.[41] The Independent Commission Against Corruption was established as an independent agency dedicated to fighting corruption, free from political interference, separate from the police force and the civil service, with adequate funding and resources. Salaries are high, attracting highly qualified individuals, and selection criteria were stringent. Once hired, staff are subject to a strict disciplinary code and anticorruption checks by an internal monitoring group. Consequently, the Independent Commission Against Corruption attracts and retains dedicated, highly competent individuals. The Independent Commission Against Corruption is authorized to prevent suspects from disposing of their property, to seek court orders preventing suspects from leaving Hong Kong, to examine bank accounts and safe deposit boxes, to require suspects to provide details of their finances, to search their premises, and to pursue any related offenses that are revealed during an investigation. The authority of the Independent Commission Against Corruption is backed by potent laws against corruption. Civil servants who possess unexplained property or maintain a standard of living in excess of that which can be financed by their official salaries are considered to be guilty of corruption unless they can provide a satisfactory explanation to the court as to how the wealth was acquired.

Since the transfer of sovereignty in 1997, the commissioner of the Independent Commission Against Corruption is appointed by the State Council of the People's Republic of China, on the recommendation of the chief executive of Hong Kong. Prior to the transfer, the commissioner and deputy commissioner were appointed by the governor of Hong Kong. The commissioner reported to the governor and appointed all other staff. While this reporting structure is very similar to the reporting structure for Uganda's IGG and Tanzania's PCCB, the Independent Commission Against Corruption has, with one major exception, operated with complete independence.[42] An obvious question is why the Independent Commission Against Corruption was able to operate independently and was more effective than either the IGG or PCCB in fighting corruption. An important difference was that Hong Kong's chief executive lacked the all-encompassing political and economic power possessed by African presidents. Thus, the chief executive could not simply roll back or undermine anticorruption campaigns in the same way that President Kabbah engineered the reversal of reform strategies and countermanded dismissals of corrupt government officials in Sierra Leone, or the way the head of Zambia's anticorruption task force was purged after his zealous investigation of former president Frederick Chiluba.

If strong institutional checks and balances within African states are missing—in large part, because of the legacy of colonial rule—a logical implication is that the international community bears responsibility for creating, funding, and implementing an appropriate agency that would provide checks and balances against government power and would perform a role analogous to Hong Kong's Independent Commission Against Corruption.

AN INTERNATIONAL COMMISSION AGAINST CORRUPTION

Hong Kong's experience suggests that a truly independent anticorruption commission, with the same powers as the Independent Commission Against Corruption, can be extremely effective in fighting corruption. However, the experiences of Uganda and Tanzania suggest that African leaders are far too powerful to permit the establishment of truly independent anticorruption commissions. This implies a need for the international community to establish and support an ICAC, with powers analogous to the powers of Hong Kong's Independent Commission Against Corruption, to investigate corruption and refer cases to local prosecutors. Only an international institution can be truly independent of powerful African presidents and loyal elites. The challenge is to craft an institution that performs the role of Hong Kong's Independent Commission Against Corruption but addresses concerns about national sovereignty and effectively elicits the consent and compliance of African governments.

Securing Consent and Compliance

Participation in an international version of the Independent Commission Against Corruption would ultimately require the approval and support of African leaders who may resist the idea. However, domestic pressure from constituents and international pressure from powerful organizations such as the IMF, World Bank, UN, and African Union (AU) can ultimately compel leaders to sign treaties that would otherwise be unpalatable, when the alternative is to risk removal at the next election. It is this pressure that can make a leader willing to sign an unpalatable treaty.

There are numerous examples of international treaties that have been signed by African leaders because of pressure from constituents and international organizations. In each case, these laws compel African leaders to comply with restrictions on their ability to act in corrupt ways. Significantly,

49 African leaders or their representatives have already signed the United Nations Convention against Corruption (UNCAC) and the African Union Convention on Preventing and Combating Corruption (AUCPCC). Both are international laws committing the signatories to create and enforce domestic laws against corruption and to extend cooperation in investigating and prosecuting corruption.

Significantly, 33 African nations have ratified the Rome Statute of the ICC. The Rome Statute created an international body of criminal investigators and endowed them with the same broad powers to conduct independent investigations on domestic territory that are envisioned for UN inspectors under an ICAC. The primary difference is that the Rome Statute focuses on crimes of war, aggression, genocide, and crimes against humanity, whereas the UN inspectors would focus on corruption. However, crimes of war, aggression, genocide, and crimes against humanity also involve the misuse of governmental power, often for personal gain, and thus constitute an extreme form of corruption. The Rome Statute compels all parties, including leaders and powerful elites, to submit themselves to independent investigators with the power to arrest, detain, try, and convict offenders in a court of law. Thus, the Rome Statute establishes a precedent whereby domestic sovereignty is surrendered in cases where government officials place themselves above the law. Importantly, it was not necessary to rely on voluntary acquiescence by African leaders to achieve adherence to the Rome Statute: pressure from constituents and the international community forced those leaders to sign the treaty or risk removal at the next election.

The key to this breakthrough was that the Rome Convention created a public litmus test of the willingness of leaders to sign an international treaty establishing the ICC. Leaders evidently found that the pressure to sign overcame any concerns they had about the challenge to their power and domestic sovereignty. The same process by which the Rome Statute was established provides a model for establishing a UN inspectorate through a similar public litmus test. The UN General Assembly established a committee that drafted the ICC Statute, which was subsequently adopted by 120 nations in 1998 and ratified by 111 nations by March 2010. The same process could be pursued to establish a UN inspectorate. Table 2.1 compares key features of the ICC and the proposed ICAC, suggesting that the ICC provides a suitable model and precedent for the powers that are envisioned for UN inspectors.

Thus, there is ample reason to think that leaders may be compelled to sign a protocol that would expand the scope of the UNCAC, create the ICAC and, upon ratification, create the legal duty to comply with investigations led by UN inspectors. Failure to sign such a protocol would open a leader to an electoral challenge at the next election. Opponents would almost certainly cite the

Table 2.1 Comparison of International Criminal Court and Proposed International Commission Against Corruption

ICC	*ICAC*
UN General Assembly establishes committee that drafts ICC Statute, leading to adoption by 120 nations in 1998 and ratification by 111 nations by March 2010	Same process
Signature and ratification create legal duty to comply	Same
Requires full cooperation of States Parties	Same
Authority to make determinations of noncooperation	Same
Prosecutor has complete independence; shall not seek or act on instructions from any external source	Same
Prosecutor shall be person of high moral character	Same
Prosecutor appoints staff investigators	Same
Prosecutor and staff enjoy immunity from prosecution under local law	Same
Salaries and expenses paid by States Parties, UN funds, and contributions	Same
Prosecutor endowed with investigative and prosecutorial powers	Only investigative powers
Independent court with power to convict and imprison	Domestic courts
Power to arrest, convict, imprison, impose fines, and property forfeiture	Power to arrest
Power to conduct on-site investigations, make arrests, gather evidence, take statements and testimony, prevent absconding, and (where permitted by law) conduct wiretaps and surveillance	Same
Power to order State Party to execute arrests	Same
Dedicated courts to prosecute the accused	Same
Power to enter into agreements to facilitate cooperation of states and persons	Same
Power to take steps to preserve evidence	Same
Crimes of war, aggression, genocide, crimes against humanity	Corruption only
Crimes involving corruption of justice, including bribery, retaliation, intimidation of witnesses, or court officials	Included
Criminal responsibility for those who order, solicit, induce, aid, or abet a crime	Same
Jurisdiction where crime is committed in state, or accused is national of state, that is party to the Statute	Same
Admissibility of a case or the jurisdiction of the court may be challenged only once	Same
Prosecutor may initiate investigations *proprio motu* (independently)	Same
Prosecutor does not proceed unless reasonable basis for allegation	Same
Prosecutor does not proceed unless in the interest of justice	Same
Investigation must pursue both incriminating and exonerating evidence	Same
Prosecutor must respect procedural rights of the accused against coercion and arbitrary arrest, and rights to remain silent and of assistance to counsel	Same
Preserves confidentiality of investigations	Same

(*Continued*)

Table 2.1 Comparison of International Criminal Court and Proposed International Commission Against Corruption *(Continued)*

ICC	*ICAC*
Limits information provided to states, to protect persons and evidence	Same
Applies national laws of States that would normally exercise jurisdiction, provided that those laws are not inconsistent with the Statute	Same
Applies equally to all, including heads of state, members of government or parliament, and military commanders, regardless of immunity under national law	Same
No statute of limitations	Same
Orders by superiors do not relieve the accused of criminal responsibility	Same

Source: Created by author.

failure as a clear indication that the incumbent condones corruption and is unwilling to abide by an international treaty designed to fight it aggressively. It is unlikely that an incumbent could survive this challenge, especially in Africa, since corruption is a perennial issue that often decides elections.

Public outrage regarding corruption creates enormous pressure to create laws and institutions that restrict it. Until now, however, incumbents have been able to escape serious reforms because changes have always been limited to domestic initiatives that they are able to circumvent. Only an international treaty, akin to the Rome Statute, can compel leaders to choose between the establishment of an independent force of UN inspectors and the likelihood of electoral defeat.

There is ample evidence that African leaders can be pressured to sign laws establishing institutions that are empowered to investigate misconduct by government officials. Significantly, 26 African countries have already created institutions such as the Ombudsman in Malawi and the Public Complaints Commission (PCC) in Nigeria that investigate citizen complaints regarding government officials.[43] Approximately 30 African countries have created dedicated anticorruption agencies modeled on Hong Kong's Independent Commission Against Corruption.[44] The creation of these institutions, whose role is similar to that proposed for UN inspectors, resulted either from the election of a reform-oriented president or pressure from reform-oriented civil groups seeking to install checks and balances to counter official misconduct. The popularity and growth of these institutions throughout Africa suggests that it may be difficult even for reluctant African leaders to resist pressure to sign a protocol permitting UN inspections. At the same time, widespread acknowledgment that the effectiveness of domestic anticorruption institutions has been undermined by the executive branch suggests why reform-oriented groups may wish to exert pressure to sign a protocol permitting UN inspections.

Oona Hathaway's theory of international law may be applied to the question of why leaders might commit themselves to an international agreement establishing an ICAC.[45] Central to Hathaway's theory is the recognition that state behavior is the result of complex interactions among political actors at the domestic level. These actors respond to an array of conflicting incentives and pressures exerted from many quarters: the electorate; interest groups; powerful elites, including appointed and elected officials; legislators; the legal and judicial system, including police, prosecutors, and anticorruption units; the media and public perceptions created by the media; competitors and potential successors; tribal kin; multinational corporations; international financial institutions including the IMF and the World Bank; the UNCAC; the AUCPCC; Transparency International; and other international organizations.

In general, patrimonial networks create incentives and pressure to resist an anticorruption commission, while international corporations, international financial institutions, States Parties to conventions against corruption, Transparency International, the media, the electorate, the G7 countries, and honest members of law enforcement and the legal system may be expected to support the accountability that would be exerted by an independent ICAC. Thus, a leader's commitment to a future ICAC depends on a complex calculation of the political benefits and costs. For example, a corrupt leader might judge that the media, IMF, and World Bank would turn against him—that it would be politically costly, and the electorate would oust him at the next election—if he did not sign an agreement permitting investigations under the auspices of an ICAC. Since African leaders routinely compete for electoral support based on promises to fight corruption, history suggests that support for an ICAC is likely to become a prominent election issue, forcing the incumbent as well as his challengers to declare their support for this type of anticorruption measure.

There is also another reason why African leaders may commit their countries to an ICAC. African leaders, acknowledging the failure of public institutions that have been captured by elites to serve narrow personal interests, resulting in corruption, a lack of accountability, and poor governance, have agreed to subject their countries to peer review.[46] The African Peer Review Mechanism (APRM) is being used to assess the performance of African countries with regard to compliance with the Declaration on Democracy, Political, Economic and Corporate Governance approved by the AU Summit in July 2002.[47] This Declaration commits the Member States of the AU to improve accountability and governance, to "undertake to combat and eradicate corruption," and to participate in the APRM process.[48] The significance of this commitment to the APRM process is that it suggests how and why

African countries might embrace changes that improve accountability and governance, perhaps including intrusive ICAC inspections.

As of October 2019, 38 countries had formally joined the APRM by signing the APRM Memorandum of Understanding: Algeria, Angola, Benin, Botswana, Burkina Faso, Cameroon, Chad, Côte d'Ivoire, Djibouti, Egypt, Equatorial Guinea, Ethiopia, Gabon, Gambia, Ghana, Kenya, Lesotho, Liberia, Malawi, Mali, Mauritania, Mauritius, Mozambique, Namibia, Nigeria, Republic of Congo, Republic of Niger, Rwanda, São Tomé and Príncipe, Senegal, Sierra Leone, South Africa, Sudan, Tanzania, Togo, Tunisia, Uganda, and Zambia. By October 2019, 23 countries had been peer reviewed.

Through the peer-review assessments, African countries have agreed to fight corruption, strengthen their institutions, adopt market-oriented policies, respect human rights and the rule of law, and spend more on the needs of the poor.[49] These commitments have been reinforced by the commitment of G8 countries, through the G8 Africa Action Plan, to provide substantial financial support through trade, aid, investment, and debt relief. For example, the Millennium Challenge Corporation (MCC) disburses $900 million in U.S. development aid based on performance criteria, including the control of corruption, accountability, and government effectiveness.[50] Furthermore, it is expected that private capital flows are attracted by APRM member commitments that reduce the risk of investing in Africa. Thus, there are substantial tangible benefits of participating in the APRM process and abiding by APRM review team recommendations. African leaders who refuse to abide by those recommendations cause their countries to lose valuable aid and investment. Opposition candidates would use the adverse publicity to unseat corrupt incumbents.

Thus, the APRM process provides a powerful mechanism to pressure African leaders to agree to ICAC investigations. An APRM review team recommendation to ratify APUNCAC and permit UN investigations would be difficult to refuse. Refusal of such a recommendation, or attempts to delay or undermine ICAC inspectors, would trigger adverse publicity that would threaten valuable MCC aid and private capital investment, and present an easy target for opposition candidates. If ICAC inspectors were permitted to conduct inspections, they would provide the ammunition needed by prosecutors to root out corruption across each branch and at every level of government. The APRM provides leverage to open the door to ICAC inspectors, who would then vigorously investigate corruption.

Surveys of African citizens routinely find strong support for the fight against corruption and new leaders are frequently elected based on promises to fight corruption.[51] Thus, it should not be difficult to make APUNCAC an election issue that would compel incumbents and opposition candidates to declare their support publicly. Failure to follow through on these commitments would risk public censure and loss of office. Significantly, a natural experiment tested the effect of an anticorruption program in Brazil and found that a one standard deviation (SD) increase in mayoral corruption, disclosed through random audits of municipal expenditures and posted on the internet, reduced the likelihood that an incumbent mayor would be re-elected by 25 percent.[52] The creation of an ICAC that published reports regarding corrupt practices might be expected to have a similar influence on elections in Africa.

The East Asian experience suggests that peer pressure is effective in eliciting commitments by member countries to perform the required corrective actions.[53] States are much more inclined to comply with stipulations when they know their implementation is monitored.[54] Compliance with the APRM process confers international recognition, raises the domestic legitimacy of governments, and increases the political risk attached to corrupt practices. Thus, there is ample reason to think that African leaders may feel pressure to agree to intrusive ICAC inspections, if recommended by an APRM review team, and reason to think that leaders would either comply with inspectors or face severe erosion of public and international support.

The implementation of ICAC inspections conducted by truly independent, competent UN inspectors may be expected to have the same salutary effect that was achieved in Hong Kong, where the initial corps of inspectors drew heavily upon experienced British criminal investigators.[55] Until the advent of the Independent Commission Against Corruption, Hong Kong's police force was notoriously corrupt. The introduction of the Independent Commission Against Corruption ensured, for the first time, that no corrupt policeman could feel safe from exposure. There would be no tip-off of a raid, inspection, or investigation, and no chance to hide or destroy evidence. The calculus of the benefits and costs of corruption changed dramatically.

In the same way, independent ICAC investigators could ensure that corrupt police, prosecutors, judges, and staff of anticorruption units never feel safe from exposure. By exposing every member of the law enforcement community, every prosecutor, every judge, and every investigator in an anticorruption unit to the threat of investigation, independent investigators serve to deter corruption in the institutions that society depends upon to fight corruption. Police are compelled to collect evidence, prosecutors are compelled to present evidence, and judges are compelled to cite evidence, or risk investigation and prosecution themselves for favoritism and corruption. When faced with the prospect of incarceration or removal, it becomes much easier for potentially corrupt police, prosecutors, and judges to turn down bribes and to behave ethically.

At the same time, it becomes easier for honest police, prosecutors, and judges to advance themselves through competent work. By deterring corruption and crime among crime fighters, independent investigators multiply the effectiveness of their own efforts to fight crime.

While numerous African countries have established anticorruption units, they lack the necessary independence from strong African leaders to be effective. A prerequisite is that any successful anticorruption unit must be international and, thus, completely independent of influence from corrupt leaders. A second prerequisite is the endowment of independent investigators with strong investigative powers that are adequate to the task of fighting corruption. A third prerequisite is the establishment of procedures that maximize the probability that honest members of the law enforcement and legal system can overcome the predations of dishonest members working in consort with criminal attempts to hide and destroy evidence and subvert justice.

APUNCAC would, upon entry into force, empower the UN to create an ICAC to investigate allegations of corruption.[56] The preamble justifies the protocol by citing Articles 3, 10, 13, 43, 46, 48, and 62 of the UNCAC. Article 62 of the UNCAC provides the legal basis for employing the resources of the UN, and Articles 3, 10, 13, 43, 46, 48, and 62 provide the legal basis to augment the capabilities of the police, law enforcement, and anticorruption agencies in developing countries to combat corruption. Furthermore, the UNCAC provides the legal authority for law enforcement personnel of Member States to act on behalf of the law enforcement personnel of a requesting state. Specifically, Article 46 of the UNCAC specifies that parties "shall afford one another the widest measure of mutual legal assistance in investigations, prosecutions[,] and judicial proceedings" in relation to corruption-related offenses,[57] including:

a) taking evidence or statements from persons;
b) effecting service of judicial documents;
c) executing searches and seizures, and freezing assets;
d) examining objects and sites;
e) providing information, evidentiary items, and expert evaluations;
f) providing originals or certified copies of relevant documents and records, including government, bank, financial, corporate or business records;
g) identifying or tracing proceeds of crime, property, instrumentalities, or other things for evidentiary purposes;
h) facilitating the voluntary appearance of persons in courts or administrative bodies of the requesting state party;
i) any other type of assistance that is not contrary to the domestic law of the requested state party;
j) identifying, tracing, and freezing proceeds of crime in accordance with the provisions of the UNCAC;
k) the recovery of assets, in accordance with the provisions of the UNCAC.

Finally, Article 62 of the UNCAC created a mechanism that could be used to fund the proposed ICAC through contributions by the World Bank, IMF, parties to the UNCAC, and the G7 countries, which have already agreed to commit substantial financial resources to fight corruption and ensure accountability and government effectiveness.

Thus, legal authority and a funding mechanism have already been established that would permit (a) the establishment of a UN-funded ICAC; (b) the use of ICAC inspectors to augment the capabilities of the police, law enforcement, and anticorruption agencies in developing countries; and (c) the employment of inspectors and law enforcement personnel of Member States, through the ICAC, to act on behalf of the law enforcement personnel of a requesting state to conduct investigations, involving all of the powers enumerated in Article 46, listed above. What is needed is not legal authority, but rather a UN protocol that spells out the details of how this would work in practice. Thus, APUNCAC is framed as a protocol that supplements the UNCAC.

APUNCAC specifies procedures. Any individual may submit an allegation of corruption. After receiving a request for an investigation, the ICAC, under the auspices of the UN Commission on Crime Prevention and Criminal Justice, would review the merits of, and prioritize, each request. The commission would designate a UN inspector who would lead and supervise every aspect of the investigation, ensuring that the investigation is conducted in a manner that respects and abides by the laws and law enforcement procedures of the state where the investigation is conducted. Inspectors, their staff, and their surrogates would be immune from arrest or detention, and their papers, documents, and personal baggage would enjoy the inviolability accorded to diplomatic envoys in conformity with Article VI of the United Nations Convention on Privileges and Immunities, but their conduct and the propriety of all investigations would be monitored by an Operations Review Committee, with members nominated by parties to the protocol. The Operations Review Committee would refer cases of criminal misconduct by inspectors or their surrogates for prosecution under the laws and judicial system of the state where the inspectors or surrogates maintain citizenship.

UN inspectors would exercise their powers through production of a written authorization showing their identity and position, together with documentation indicating the subject matter and purpose of the on-the-spot check, inspection, or investigation. Individuals served with these documents would be required to comply under the same terms as would be required by the police, law enforcement, and anticorruption units of the state where the investigation is conducted. Failure to comply would have the same consequences as failure to comply with investigations by the police, law enforcement, and anticorruption units of the state where the investigation is conducted. Under APUNCAC, inspectors may, without advance notice:

a) conduct on-the-spot inspections on the premises of potential witnesses and suspects who may have knowledge or involvement, direct or indirect, regarding the irregularity in question;
b) interrogate potential witnesses and suspects who may have knowledge or involvement, direct or indirect, regarding the irregularity in question;
c) seize and impound travel documents to prevent the flight of suspects;
d) arrest and detain suspects who may have knowledge or involvement, direct or indirect, regarding the irregularity in question, until the suspects are charged in accordance with the law enforcement procedures of the jurisdictional state and handed over to the law enforcement authorities of the jurisdictional state, or a period not to exceed 14 days;
e) seize evidence, including electronic files, that is relevant to the irregularity in question;
f) copy relevant documents;
g) conduct surveillance, including wiretapping and electronic surveillance, that is necessary to collect evidence regarding the irregularity in question;
h) freeze assets and prevent the flight of assets obtained through corruption, until the completion of legal proceedings;
i) undertake any other actions consistent with the laws and law enforcement procedures of the state where the investigation is conducted, as needed.

Where witnesses or suspects resist an on-the-spot check, inspection, interview, or investigation, the police, law enforcement, and anticorruption units of the state where the investigation is conducted, acting in accordance with national rules, would give UN inspectors assistance as needed to allow them to discharge their duty in carrying out an on-the-spot check, inspection, interview, or investigation. It would be for the police, law enforcement, and anticorruption units of the state where the investigation is conducted to take any necessary measures, in conformity with national law, to enforce cooperation. In cases where an inspector believes that adequate and timely assistance has not been provided by the requisite police, law enforcement, judicial, and anticorruption units, the inspector may file a request for censure by the Commission on Crime Prevention and Criminal Justice. The commission would review the request and may subpoena evidence or interview witnesses. The commission would decide, by a majority vote, to approve or disapprove the motion for censure no later than 21 days after receiving a request for censure.

Under APUNCAC, the World Bank and the IMF would develop and implement a system of reducing aid and credits in response to the magnitude and frequency of noncooperation with UN inspectors and their surrogates. Parties to APUNCAC agree to abide by the judgment of the Commission on Crime Prevention and Criminal Justice regarding the magnitude and frequency of any noncooperation, and with regard to the commission's recommendations for implementing reforms of the police, law enforcement, judicial, and anti-corruption units of the state where the investigation is conducted.

Under APUNCAC, inspectors would hand over disposition of each case to the appropriate prosecuting authority upon completion of the investigation. Each inspector would submit reports to the commission every 30 days following assignment to an investigation, until the investigation is completed, and the case is handed over to the appropriate prosecuting authority. When the case is handed over to the prosecuting authority, copies of the final report would be submitted to Transparency International, in addition to the relevant prosecuting authorities, to ensure that the reports are not ignored through the machinations of corrupt officials. Transparency International would publish updates regarding the disposition of the case every 30 days, until the case is dismissed by the appropriate prosecuting authority or court, or a final verdict is reached by the appropriate court.

The reports and all supporting documents would constitute admissible evidence in administrative or judicial proceedings of the UN Member State in which their use proves necessary, in the same way and under the same conditions as administrative reports drawn up by national administrative inspectors. They would be subject to the same evaluation rules as those applicable to administrative reports drawn up by national administrative inspectors and would be of identical value to such reports.

Under APUNCAC, parties to the treaty would establish a system of courts and prosecutors dedicated to the adjudication and swift resolution of charges of corruption. The Commission on Crime Prevention and Criminal Justice would ensure that dedicated courts and prosecutors have regular and adequate funding to perform their responsibilities, would conduct periodic reviews to evaluate the performance of dedicated courts and prosecutors, and would redirect funding based upon these evaluations. Dedicated courts and prosecutors would prioritize charges submitted by UN inspectors or their surrogates, would ensure the swift resolution of resulting cases, and would not tolerate delays that pervert the course of justice.

Under APUNCAC, parties to the treaty would establish national judicial councils vested with responsibilities to select judges and prosecutors of the utmost integrity, ensure adequate staffing of dedicated courts, develop and implement streamlined adjudication procedures, ensure the swift resolution of corruption charges, evaluate the performance of judges and prosecutors, and censure and remove judges and prosecutors whose performance is substandard. The membership of national judicial councils would be restricted to duly qualified judges and prosecutors of utmost integrity. National judicial councils would nominate individuals who would then be vetted by the Commission on Crime Prevention and Criminal Justice. Upon a majority vote, the commission could veto the nomination of an individual to serve on a national judicial council, veto the nomination of a judge or prosecutor to serve a dedicated court, or recommend the censure or removal of a judge or prosecutor serving a dedicated court whose performance is alleged to be substandard.

To ensure the safety of witnesses, victims, and UN inspectors under the violent conditions that exist in many developing countries, APUNCAC specifies that UN inspectors would determine the measures necessary to protect their own safety and the safety of ICAC staff, witnesses, victims, and all individuals who assist with ICAC investigations. The state where the investigation is conducted would implement measures requested by UN inspectors and their surrogates, including the use of armored vehicles, secure buildings, special plain-clothes guards, and measures to protect their identity. In addition, it may be necessary to implement witness protection measures, including laws that permit closed trial sessions, the use of pseudonyms, voice distortion technology to shield the identity of witnesses while in court, and the use of confidential witness interviews. These measures have been employed to protect witnesses and victims testifying before the ICC and other international tribunals.[58] It may be necessary to negotiate agreements with G7 countries for the relocation of protected witnesses. The necessary provisions may be written into APUNCAC or may be established through separate agreements. While these provisions could not eliminate the threat of violence, the threat could be managed, as indicated by the success of Guatemala's CICIG, operating under similarly violent conditions. Despite the possibility of intimidation, there is ample precedent from Guatemala that witnesses and victims are willing to provide testimony and inspectors are willing to lead investigations, even under the violent conditions that prevail in Guatemala.

APUNCAC specifies that attempts to arrest, interfere with, or harm witnesses, victims, or inspectors, contrary to the wishes of UN inspectors, would constitute obstruction of justice (figure 2.1).

An improper attempt to delay or thwart the effort of a UN inspector to obtain a warrant for arrest, or a prosecution or judicial proceeding that is substantially irregular, violates accepted norms and practices, and perverts the course of justice, would constitute obstruction of justice. These actions would trigger new ICAC investigations. UN inspectors would submit reports to be published online by Transparency International. They would recommend charges to the appropriate prosecuting authorities or disciplinary agencies

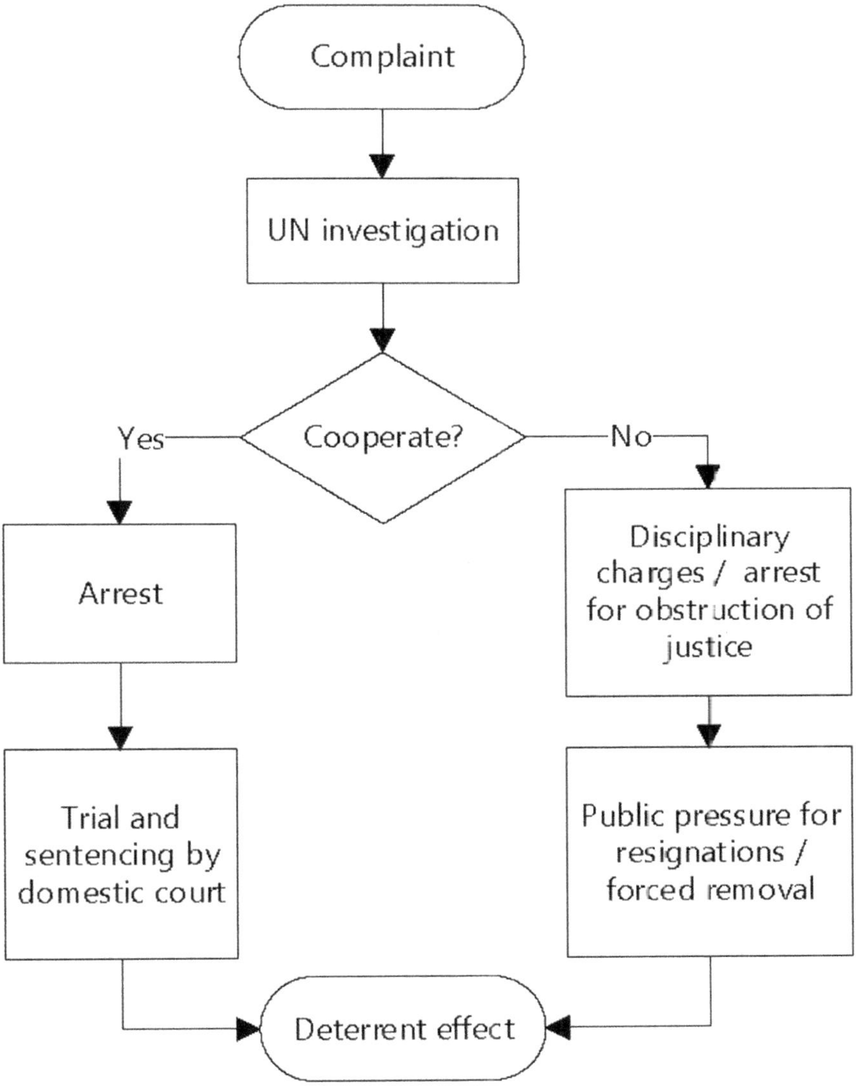

Figure 2.1 Lack of Cooperation Would Constitute Obstruction of Justice. *Source*: Figure created by author.

and those agencies would, under the proposed treaty, enforce sanctions in accordance with agency practices and domestic law. If a UN inspector believes that obstruction of justice has occurred, or adequate and timely cooperation, assistance, or protection has not been provided by requisite police, law enforcement, judicial, anticorruption, or government agencies, he or she could file a request for censure by the UN Commission on Crime Prevention and Criminal Justice. Under APUNCAC, the World Bank and IMF would reduce aid and credits in response to the magnitude and frequency of acts of obstruction or noncooperation.

CONCLUSION

APUNCAC would effectively provide an independent means of investigating corruption, and would do so under the existing legal authority of the UN, according to the provisions of UNCAC. Under APUNCAC, any individual could submit a request for an investigation. The UN Commission on Crime Prevention and Criminal Justice, through the ICAC, would assess the validity of each charge and would provide a check against politically motivated investigations. Importantly, the ICAC would have the authority to investigate counterclaims that a given investigation was politically motivated. The ICAC would serve as an independent arbiter of conflicting charges of corruption. The ICAC would have the authority to conduct multiple investigations simultaneously to sort out conflicting claims and would have the authority to recommend charges against multiple parties.

At the same time, trials would be conducted by domestic courts, unless cases were to be referred to the ICC. Thus, the ICAC would have no power to convict, sentence, and imprison (other than the temporary detention of suspects before they are handed over for trial). This separation of powers has been effective in Hong Kong in ensuring that the powers of investigation are not abused. At the same time, the lack of power to convict and sentence suspects is a potential weakness that could be exploited by corrupt leaders. However, any interference with prosecutions and the courts would itself be a major crime subject to investigation as an act of corruption. Repeated instances would be brought to the attention of the international community through ICAC reports filed with Transparency International, and this could be expected to adversely affect Transparency International and African Peer Review ratings, triggering financial sanctions by donors, the World Bank, and the IMF; flight of foreign investment; adverse publicity through the media; and erosion of electoral support that could unseat corrupt incumbents.

While it may seem unlikely that merely investigating corruption can stop it, this is exactly what happened in Hong Kong. The Hong Kong Independent Commission Against Corruption did not have the power to convict, sentence, or imprison suspects, yet was very successful in halting corruption.[59] The presence of independent investigators has a powerful effect on corrupt officials across all branches of government. When officials know that their telephones may be tapped, that any meeting might be recorded, and that any colleague may provide evidence to prosecutors, the scope for corruption is drastically reduced. However, this is only the case when there is a truly independent body of inspectors who are perceived as incorruptible. This is what is needed in Africa but has yet to be established by the international community.

Perhaps the greatest challenge is to induce leaders to approve a protocol that threatens their authority. However, the act of signing a law to fight corruption is not a purely voluntary act. If it were, there would be few laws or agencies to fight corruption anywhere in the world, because few leaders would voluntarily approve the creation of a law or agency that threatens their authority. The existence of effective anticorruption laws and agencies in Western countries is the consequence of concerted public pressure to fight corruption, rather than voluntary acquiescence by benevolent leaders.

While Western governments are relatively clean, this was not always the case. Government corruption was endemic in sixteenth- and seventeenth-century England and in America during the late nineteenth and early twentieth centuries.[60] Public pressure for reform ultimately forced political leaders to adopt checks and balances against corruption.[61] The fact that effective checks and balances currently exist in Western countries is not an indicator that Western leaders are more benevolent than African leaders, only that pressure in Western countries has been exerted more effectively, and at an earlier period, to restrict the freedom of Western leaders to misuse power.

There is substantial evidence that African leaders can be pressured to sign anticorruption laws that restrict their authority. African leaders have signed the UNCAC, the AUCPCC, the laws establishing 30 dedicated African anticorruption agencies, the Rome Statute establishing invasive investigative powers, and the agreement to subject their countries to invasive APRM reviews, with recommendations that are tied to MCC funding and the willingness of the G7 countries to maintain concessions regarding aid, trade, and debt relief. These laws restrict the authority of domestic leaders. In the case of the Rome Statute, domestic leaders who commit certain crimes are now subject to arrest, trial, and imprisonment under the authority of the independent prosecutor of the ICC, who operates independently of the authority of domestic leaders. These laws must necessarily have been signed into law by African leaders, despite their resistance. The explanation involves pressure from constituents fed up with corruption, along with pressure from powerful international agencies such as the IMF, World Bank, AU, and UN that compels leaders to sign laws that they may perceive as unpalatable.

A book-length analysis found that international NGOs created a powerful coalition and were influential in obtaining passage and ratification of the Rome Statute.[62] Organizations such as Amnesty International were particularly effective because of the recognition by domestic leaders that these organizations could mobilize voters, thereby threatening the survival of any leader opposed to the statute. NGOs such as Amnesty International set the terms of the debate, framed the passage of the statute as a moral issue, and compelled domestic leaders to adopt the statute or face public condemnation.

NGOs initially focused on securing signatures to the statute rather than full ratifications because signatures had few immediate consequences. Consequently, signatures were obtained from 120 nations on July 17, 1998. This overwhelming endorsement immediately created pressure to ratify the treaty. To lobby for ratification, international NGOs coordinated their actions with local NGOs that had direct access to domestic political leaders. By obtaining early ratifications from a coalition of nations that favored the Rome Statute, pressure was brought to bear on those that were reluctant, who then became more willing to ratify because their neighbors were doing so. For example, Uganda resisted ratification but finally ratified the treaty on June 14, 2002, as a direct result of pressure from other governments, human rights NGOs, and humanitarian relief organizations to improve Uganda's record on human rights.[63] Ugandan government officials believed that this action would improve Uganda's reputation within the international community and would maintain international support for concessions regarding aid, trade, and debt relief.[64]

The process through which NGOs influenced the ratification of the Rome Statute provides a roadmap for obtaining ratification of the proposed treaty. Importantly, it is not necessary to rely on purely voluntary acquiescence. Instead, ratification would be obtained through a coordinated international effort, involving pressure exerted by influential international organizations such as Amnesty International. Framed as a moral issue, signature and ratification of the treaty would provide a public litmus test for leaders around the world who would be compelled to support the treaty or risk public condemnation and loss of office.

Chapter 3

Ending Impunity

Corruption takes a variety of forms. Significantly, the UNCAC specifies that corruption includes "the abuse of functions or position, that is, the performance of or failure to perform an act, in violation of laws, by a public official in the discharge of his or her functions" as well as giving any person "an undue advantage" resulting from the abuse by a public official of his or her influence.[1] One hundred eighty-seven nations ratified the UNCAC, signaling their support for this definition of corruption.[2]

The persistence of corruption is associated with a culture of impunity. Individuals who engage in corrupt behavior presumably do so because they believe that the risk of punishment is low relative to the reward. This suggests a need to identify what is missing from the environment surrounding these individuals that leads them to believe that the risk of punishment is low. If an institutional structure is missing, what is that structure? For example, one type of structure is a dedicated domestic anticorruption unit. However, while many countries have created this type of unit, results have been disappointing.

Chapter 3 explores the reasons for this failure by drawing upon the experience of Nigeria's EFCC. The analysis suggests that this type of domestic anticorruption unit can only be successful if it is insulated from interference by powerful domestic elites who benefit from the continuation of corruption. Chapter 3 suggests that APUNCAC—an international treaty establishing UN inspectors empowered to investigate allegations of corruption—is a promising strategy. In this respect, APUNCAC is similar to the type of international treaty that established the CICIG. The treaty establishing CICIG established UN-supported inspectors. UN-supported inspectors might provide the type of protection that is needed by domestic anticorruption units.

This chapter analyzes prospects for ratification, walks the reader through a discussion of each barrier that may arise, explains how those barriers would be addressed, examines issues raised by the proposal, and suggests that the precedent established by the Rome Statute, where 123 nations previously agreed to permit intrusive criminal investigations, offers reason for optimism.[3] The implementation of this type of international treaty could have a profound effect on the culture of impunity that prevails wherever corrupt individuals feel that the risk of punishment is low.

NIGERIA'S ECONOMIC AND FINANCIAL CRIMES COMMISSION

The experience of Nigeria's EFCC is instructive. The EFCC was established in 2002, after the election of President Olusegun Obasanjo, with a mandate to investigate and prosecute a range of financial crimes, including governmental corruption.[4] In 2005, the EFCC investigated all of the country's 36 powerful state governors and asserted that almost all were corrupt.[5] By November 2006, five had been charged with corruption and were impeached.[6] By April 2008, the EFCC had recovered $5 billion in stolen public funds and secured 250 convictions, including a chief of police, a governor, and a minister.[7]

The EFCC's director, Mallam Nuhu Ribadu, moved aggressively to institutionalize the EFCC; he obtained a $5 million grant from the World Bank, permitting the EFCC to target political corruption at the highest levels without fear of the financial consequences to his agency.[8] He established international links between the EFCC and INTERPOL, the United Kingdom's Metropolitan Police, the U.S. Federal Bureau of Investigation, the Canadian Mounted Police, and South Africa's Scorpions, extending the EFCC's capacity to investigate corruption.[9] Through his efforts, a coalition of civic groups agreed to mobilize 500 lawyers, including 25 senior advocates, to support EFCC prosecutions of corrupt officials.[10]

However, these dedicated efforts were insufficient to protect the EFCC. Powerful elites had already begun to strike back. In August 2007, Attorney General Michael Aondoakaa announced that the independent prosecutorial powers granted to the EFCC were unconstitutional, and that all future prosecutions would need to be vetted by his office.[11] This blocked the EFCC's prosecution of former governors Joshua Dariye and Orji Uzor Kalu.[12] In December 2007, the EFCC arrested former governors Ayodele Fayose and James Ibori, a well-connected, powerful supporter of President Yar'Adua.[13] The government struck back by announcing that the EFCC, the Independent Corrupt Practices Commission (ICPC), and the Code of Conduct Bureau would merge, followed by a second announcement that Ribadu had been reassigned to attend a one-year policy and strategic studies course in central Nigeria.[14] Within a year, Ribadu was demoted along with 139 other police officers, then dismissed and driven into exile.[15] An EFCC official told Human Rights Watch that these moves were intended to undermine "the independence of the EFCC and halt the investigation and prosecution of former governors."[16]

The case of Nigeria's EFCC illustrates how domestic anticorruption units are neutralized by powerful elites who benefit from the continuation of corruption and seek to thwart domestic anticorruption agencies. However, this case suggests that these units can be very effective if they are insulated from interference. Is it possible for the international community to install an institution that would provide such insulation?

GUATEMALA'S CICIG

A promising approach involves the type of bilateral treaty between the UN and Guatemala that established the CICIG.[17] This treaty authorized the creation of a body of international, UN-supported inspectors to lead criminal investigations in Guatemala.[18] The rationale is that domestic agencies, weakened by corruption, are no match for powerful criminal organizations.[19]

Guatemala has experienced high levels of corruption and violence.[20] For example, in 2007, Vice President Eduardo Stein conceded that organized crime cartels had gained effective control of 6 of Guatemala's 22 departments.[21] According to Human Rights Watch,

> Guatemala's weak and corrupt law enforcement institutions have proved incapable of containing the powerful organized crime groups and criminal gangs that contribute to one of the highest violent crime rates in the Americas. . . . [I]mpunity remains the norm.[22]

Illegal armed groups and criminal gangs operate death squads and employ violence and intimidation, supporting their activities through drug trafficking.[23] Guatemalan law enforcement institutions are unable to address this rampant violence due to intimidation, corruption, and infiltration of the police and judiciary by criminal organizations.[24] In a notorious case, three members of the Central American Parliament were killed by senior members of Guatemala's police force, including the head of the organized crime unit.[25] Leadership and pressure from Guatemalan and international human rights groups, pressure exerted by the UN to monitor and verify Guatemala's commitments to the 1994 Human Rights Accord, and political calculations by Presidents Alfonso Portillo and Óscar Berger, led Guatemala and the UN to create the CICIG via a treaty-level bilateral agreement.[26] CICIG sought to address the infiltration of government institutions by criminal organizations and the operation of violent death squads operating beyond the control of the Guatemalan state.[27] CICIG was the first instance of a UN investigative body whose jurisdiction focused on corruption and organized crime, rather than human rights violations.[28]

CICIG employed international and local staff members to conduct independent investigations and produce reports that were submitted to Guatemalan prosecutors.[29] The agreement with the UN specified:

> The Government of Guatemala shall provide CICIG with all the assistance necessary for the discharge of its functions and activities . . . and shall ensure, in particular, that its members enjoy:
>
> a) freedom of movement without restriction throughout Guatemalan territory;
> b) freedom of access without restriction to all State locations . . . without prior notice . . .
> c) freedom to meet and interview any individual . . . whose testimony is deemed necessary for the discharge of its mandate;
> d) free access to information and documentary material that has a bearing on its investigations . . . whether civilian or military.[30]

Furthermore,

> The Government of Guatemala shall take such effective and adequate measures as may be required to ensure the security and protection of [CICIG personnel]. . . . International personnel shall enjoy . . . immunity from personal arrest or detention.[31]

CICIG investigators had extraordinarily broad freedom to conduct independent investigations into any person, official, or entity, and to present criminal charges to Guatemala's Public Prosecutor.[32] However, CICIG was not empowered to enforce cooperation or impose penalties for noncompliance.[33]

CICIG's activities during its first four years suggest that this type of international investigative body can quickly achieve success, despite having limited enforcement tools and no independent ability to prosecute. CICIG's investigations led to the indictment of powerful individuals including ex-president Alfonso Portillo for corruption; ex-defense minister Eduardo Arévalo Lacs for corruption; Senior Prosecutor Álvaro Matus for obstruction of justice and destruction of evidence; General Enrique Ríos Sosa, son of former Guatemalan general Efrain Rios Montt, and five other ex-military officials for embezzlement; the kidnappers of Gladys Monterroso, wife of the Human Rights Ombudsman; and four members of the National Civilian Police who engaged in extortion and assault.[34] "In all eight cases, the accused [were] directly and visibly connected to government institutions, politicians[,] or drug-trafficking organizations."[35] In 2015, CICIG's investigations forced the resignations of President Otto Pérez Molina and Vice President Roxana Baldetti.[36] Molina was indicted and imprisoned for four years.[37] Baldetti was sentenced to more than 15 years in prison.[38]

When Judge Irma Leticia Valenzuela issued a ruling that protected ex-president Portillo, CICIG appealed to Guatemala's Supreme Court, forcing Judge Valenzuela to resign from the case.[39] CICIG also forced multiple resignations of public prosecutors for corruption or obstruction of justice, including Attorney General Juan Luis Florido, Senior Prosecutor Álvaro Matus, and Administrative Crimes Prosecutor Patricia Lainfiesta.[40] CICIG's investigations also led to a purge of 1,700 allegedly corrupt police officers.[41] These results suggested that CICIG was effective despite its inability to discipline or prosecute individuals, and despite the risk of violence to its investigators. CICIG's success suggests that this type of investigative body can be successful even under conditions where criminal gangs, death squads, and powerful individuals appear to operate with impunity—conditions that characterize many developing countries.

Lessons from CICIG's experience include the need to dedicate significant resources to witness and staff security.[42] Unless witnesses and victims feel sufficiently protected, they are unlikely to provide crucial information and the necessary cooperation for a successful investigation. Consequently, CICIG created a witness protection program by negotiating an agreement with Spain for the relocation of protected witnesses, training 48 police officers to create an elite group of agents responsible for protecting witnesses, and successfully pressuring Guatemala to implement legislative reforms enhancing identity protection for witnesses in organized crime cases.[43]

However, after the commission opened an investigation into President Jimmy Morales, his brother, and son, he declined to renew CICIG's mandate, effectively ending the commission after 12 years of operation and over 400 convictions, and despite public opinion polls demonstrating that over 70 percent of Guatemalans support CICIG.[44] This outcome underlines the importance of establishing a permanent international institution insulated from domestic tampering and dedicated to the investigation of corruption.

Despite these challenges and setbacks, CICIG suggests a way forward that has not previously been explored. Had Nigeria established a comparable agreement with the UN, Ribadu potentially could have filed a complaint with UN investigators, leading to an investigation of his demotion and dismissal as acts that fall within the UN definition of corruption because they were intended to protect corrupt government officials.[45] The mere threat of investigation and prosecution for corruption might have deterred Attorney General Michael Aondoakaa from acting in a way that blocked the EFCC's prosecution of former governors Joshua Dariye and Orji Uzor Kalu, and might have deterred government officials from demoting and dismissing Ribadu.[46] Under APUNCAC, UN investigators would have likely determined that these actions involved obstruction of justice—crimes subject to prosecution and punishment under Nigeria's laws.[47] Having made that determination, and after referral of the case to domestic prosecutors, Aondoakaa and his corrupt colleagues would have faced a legitimate risk of punishment. At a minimum, public condemnation might have forced Aondoakaa's resignation in the same way that the CICIG forced the resignations of public prosecutors in Guatemala for corruption or obstruction of justice.[48]

The experiences of Guatemala suggest that it is feasible to implement an international treaty that involves intrusive criminal investigations led by UN investigators even in a country where the rule of law is extremely weak, where powerful and violent criminal cartels have gained control of several government departments, where impunity prevails, and where the prospects for implementing an international treaty are less than favorable. Guatemala's experience also provides reason to believe that barriers to the implementation of a treaty establishing UN investigators can be overcome through the leadership of international and domestic human rights organizations, pressure exerted by the World Bank, the IMF, and other nations, as well as realist political calculations by domestic leaders that the political benefits outweigh the political costs. Finally, Guatemala's experience suggests the need for a permanent UN institution that does not depend on renewal of its mandate by domestic officials, is insulated from interference by domestic officials, and is dedicated to the investigation of corruption.

AN INTERNATIONAL TREATY

A promising strategy for fighting corruption involves the implementation of APUNCAC, a multilateral treaty similar to the treaty that established CICIG.[49] Instituting a treaty that would establish UN inspectors empowered to investigate allegations of corruption might provide the type of protection needed by domestic anticorruption units from interference by powerful elites who benefit from the continuation of corruption. APUNCAC would require signatory parties to establish a system of courts and prosecutors dedicated to the adjudication and swift resolution of corruption charges. These dedicated courts would be funded by the UN and would include checks and balances to ensure they are only served by honest, competent judges and prosecutors. The dedicated courts would prioritize charges submitted by UN inspectors and would ensure the swift resolution of resulting cases.

However, the proposal also raises numerous issues. For example, it might be argued that Nigeria would never ratify the type of agreement that established CICIG. This argument presumes (a) conditions for ratifying this type of agreement were more favorable in Guatemala than in Nigeria, (b) the influence of reform-oriented elements of society is stronger in Guatemala than in Nigeria, and (c) the rule of law is stronger in Guatemala than in Nigeria. However, the violent circumstances within Guatemala suggest that conditions for ratification were not more favorable.[50] Instead, it may be argued that the creation of the EFCC and its apparent successes in investigating all 36 of Nigeria's governors, indicting 5 governors for corruption, recovering $5 billion in stolen public funds, and securing 250 convictions, including a chief of police and a governor, are evidence that the rule of law in Nigeria is stronger than that of Guatemala.[51] Thus, it appears that conditions in Nigeria are more, rather than less, favorable for the ratification of the same type of agreement that established CICIG.

Significantly, Nigeria has ratified both the UNCAC[52] and the AUCPCC.[53] Both are international laws committing the parties to create and enforce domestic laws against corruption, and to extend cooperation in investigating and prosecuting corruption.[54] These ratifications suggest that Nigeria might also ratify an international agreement similar to CICIG.[55]

While it might be argued that CICIG goes far beyond the UNCAC and the AUCPCC by permitting intrusive inspections by UN inspectors, Nigeria has also ratified the Rome Statute, which established the ICC and permits intrusive inspections similar to CICIG.[56] The Rome Statute created an international body of criminal investigators endowed with broad powers to conduct independent investigations on domestic territory, similar to the investigations permitted by CICIG.[57] The primary difference is that the Rome Statute focuses on crimes of war, aggression, genocide, and crimes against humanity,[58] whereas UN inspectors would focus on corruption. However, crimes of war, aggression, genocide, and crimes against humanity also involve abuse of functions or position by public officials, and thus constitute an extreme form of corruption. The Rome Statute compels every citizen of a party to the treaty, including the president and powerful elites, to submit to independent investigators who have the powers of arrest, detention, trial, and conviction through the ICC.[59] Thus, the Rome Statute establishes a precedent of surrendering domestic sovereignty in cases where government officials place themselves above the law.

Importantly, it was not necessary to rely on voluntary acquiescence by leaders to achieve adherence to the Rome Statute: pressure from constituents and the international community forced those leaders to sign the treaty or risk removal at the next election.[60] The key to this breakthrough was that the Rome Statute created a public litmus test of a leader's willingness to sign an international treaty establishing the ICC. Leaders evidently found that the pressure to sign was greater than any concerns they had about the challenge to their power and domestic sovereignty.[61] The same process by which the Rome Statute was established provides a model for establishing a UN inspectorate, involving a similar public litmus test. The UN General Assembly established a committee that drafted the ICC Statute, which was subsequently ratified by 122 nations.[62] The same process could be pursued to establish a UN inspectorate.

While it might be argued that international inspectors would be viewed as an unwanted intrusion into domestic affairs, international treaties are by definition voluntary agreements.[63] Only voluntary nations would accede to such a treaty. Pressure from the international community might expedite passage, but no leader would sign a treaty and no parliament would ratify a treaty without the support of their constituents. Significantly, public opinion polls indicate that Africans have grown tired of failed promises from domestic authorities claiming they will address corruption and are ready to embrace the type of international intervention represented by the ICC.[64] For example, 61 percent of Kenyans prefer ICC trials while only 8 percent prefer to have domestic courts deal with the perpetrators of the post-2007 election-related violence.[65] This evidence suggests that Africans may prefer international criminal inspectors for the same reasons that Kenyans prefer ICC trials: they might be persuaded that the only realistic hope to establish accountability is international inspectors who are beyond the government's influence. They want more international intervention, not less.[66] Thus, leaders may be forced by public opinion to sign a protocol that would expand the scope of the UNCAC to permit investigations, led by UN inspectors, of alleged acts of corruption committed by public officials.[67] The reasons that leaders would sign such a protocol are the same reasons that previous leaders signed the UNCAC: public outrage regarding corruption and pressure to create laws and institutions that restrict it.[68] There is nothing unusual about political leaders signing laws that restrict their own powers: every existing law restricting power must necessarily have been signed into law by previous leaders, albeit in response to pressure from their constituents.

The broad adoption by 123 nations of a treaty permitting intrusive inspections suggests that there is reason to believe that a similar agreement to establish UN inspectors might be ratified by many nations where levels of corruption are high and the rule of law is weak. The list of parties to the Rome Statute includes many nations that rank poorly on Transparency International's Corruption Perceptions Index (CPI).[69] Despite high levels of corruption and weak rule of law, these nations ratified a treaty permitting intrusive inspections and agreed to execute arrest warrants for all citizens charged by the ICC prosecutor.[70] Significantly, autocracies with weak rule of law were at least as likely to ratify the ICC Statute as high rule of law countries.[71] Thus, governments that were arguably at the highest risk of ICC action were most likely to ratify the Rome Statute. Therefore, there is reason to think many of these nations may also agree to permit UN inspections and may agree to execute warrants for the arrest of citizens who are charged with corruption. Significantly, 187 nations are parties to UNCAC,[72] and 44 African nations have ratified the AUCPCC,[73] evidencing broad acceptance of international laws designed to fight corruption.

The reasons why the least accountable governments were most likely to ratify the Rome Statute are worth exploring in more detail. Simmons and Danner suggest that in weak rule of law countries, internal conflicts are rife, rebel groups unleash attacks, government forces retaliate, violence abounds, and many parties suffer, including the party in power as well as opposition parties.[74] Thus, there may be bipartisan support and strong motivation to ratify a treaty that binds all parties in a way that reduces the risk of genocide, war crimes, and crimes against humanity, even at the cost of giving up traditional sovereign rights regarding the prosecution of individuals accused of those crimes. In other words, the perceived benefits of ratification for both the governing and opposing parties may exceed the costs. Once the treaty is ratified, the threat of prosecution for those crimes becomes very real, causing all parties to restrain themselves out of fear of prosecution. Similarly, there may be bipartisan support for an anticorruption protocol if multiple parties believe that their rivals are corrupt and need to be restrained. Once a protocol is ratified, the threat of prosecution would become real, causing all parties to restrain themselves.

While it might be argued that even if this type of agreement was ratified, domestic authorities would resist cooperation with UN inspectors and would resist the execution of arrest warrants for domestic officials; any nation that ratifies APUNCAC would voluntarily accede to the requirement to cooperate and to execute arrest warrants.[75] APUNCAC specifies procedures that require the cooperation of domestic authorities, including the cooperation of local police in executing arrest warrants, and specifies penalties for instances of noncooperation.[76] Once APUNCAC is ratified, these provisions would bind all domestic authorities.

APUNCAC includes built-in provisions for monitoring domestic compliance with the terms of the treaty.[77] APUNCAC specifies that the UN Commission on Crime Prevention and Criminal Justice would appoint one or more entities to monitor compliance, including national human rights institutions or any other entities deemed by the commission to be duly qualified to monitor compliance. States Parties would agree to give designated monitors access to all reports and information necessary to formulate a judgment regarding the degree of compliance, including information deemed relevant by UN inspectors. Refusal by domestic authorities to provide access to requested reports and information would constitute a failure of cooperation and an obstruction of justice. Designated monitors would possess standing to bring suit in domestic courts to compel the production of relevant reports and information. Monitors would publish regular reports regarding compliance, and Transparency International would publish these reports online. The reports would be admissible as evidence in administrative or judicial proceedings in the same way and under the same conditions as administrative reports drawn up by national administrative inspectors.

It might be argued that ratification would be purely symbolic and would not affect behavior; however, the available evidence does not support this conclusion. Ratification of the Rome Statute influenced behavior: the least democratic governments were almost eight times more likely to terminate a violent conflict if they had ratified the ICC Statute, apparently because of the real threat of prosecution for war crimes.[78] Thus, "the idea that ratification is purely symbolic does not square with the facts."[79] Ratification was not a symbolic action by leaders who could presume they would be unaffected.[80]

While it might be argued that domestic authorities lack the capacity and willingness to execute arrest warrants, domestic authorities have already demonstrated a basic level of capacity and willingness. Nigeria's EFCC recorded 603 convictions between January 2015 and May 2018, including convictions of judges and top military officers for corrupt enrichment.[81] Over 1,000 individuals have been convicted of economic and financial crimes, including a chief of police and a governor.[82] Jolly Nyame, former governor of Taraba State, was sentenced to 14 years in prison on 27 counts of corruption involving US $4.5 million.[83] In April 2018, a senior advocate of Nigeria, Joseph Nwobike, was convicted on 12 counts of attempting to pervert the cause of justice, including the payment of a US $2,071 bribe to Justice Mohammed Yinusa.[84] Even in one of the most corrupt nations in the world, it is possible to obtain convictions. The issue is how to improve the rate of prosecution and conviction in every state so that corrupt individuals cannot act with impunity. In every state where the rule of law is weak, the introduction of independent investigators, with the capacity to illuminate corrupt police, prosecutors, and judges, would potentially plug leaks in the judicial system that occur when corrupt police, prosecutors, and judges believe they can engage in corruption without being discovered and tried in the court of public opinion.

Regarding the Rome Statute, the ICC has been effective in conducting successful investigations, indicting alleged criminals for committing mass atrocities, executing arrest warrants with the assistance of domestic authorities, and bringing suspects to trial. The ICC's success demonstrates that it is not a paper tiger, and adoption and ratification are not empty gestures by politicians to placate the international community. The ICC is bringing criminals to justice in cases covering Uganda, the Democratic Republic of the Congo, Darfur/Sudan, and the Central African Republic.[85] The court convicted Thomas Lubanga, the founder of the United Congolese Patriots, of war crimes, including kidnapping and forcing children to participate in armed conflict.[86] The court convicted Germain Katanga, former leader of the Patriotic Resistance Force in Ituri, of war crimes and crimes against humanity.[87] The court convicted Bosco Ntaganda, the third-ranking official in the Patriotic Force for the Liberation of the Congo, of war crimes and crimes against humanity.[88] Sudanese president Omar al-Bashir, the first sitting head of state to face ICC charges, was indicted for war crimes and crimes against humanity in Darfur,[89] and was arrested.[90] He was convicted of corruption and money laundering and sentenced to two years of detention by a Sudanese court.[91] Sudan has agreed to hand al-Bashir to the ICC to face genocide and war crimes charges.[92] The evidence suggests that international investigators can be effective and can obtain the cooperation and assistance of domestic authorities in executing arrest warrants, even in nations characterized by high corruption and weak rule of law.

However, it might be argued that, irrespective of APUNCAC provisions requiring cooperation with UN inspectors and regardless of the success of the ICC, UN inspectors would not possess the legitimacy and capacity necessary to enforce the execution of domestic arrest warrants. What prevents local police from refusing to cooperate?

UN inspectors would not be completely powerless. They could obtain and present an arrest warrant to the local police and request their assistance in its execution. Under APUNCAC, if local police attempt to delay or refuse to cooperate when presented with a valid warrant, they would be subject to investigation and arrest by UN inspectors for obstruction of justice—specifically, the failure to execute a valid arrest warrant. There would be real consequences. For example, Nigeria's criminal code makes the failure to execute a valid arrest warrant a felony: "Any person who conspires with another to obstruct, prevent, pervert, or defeat the course of justice is guilty of a felony, and is liable to imprisonment for seven years."[93] Thus, the failure to execute a valid arrest warrant would be an act of corruption, as it is an "abuse of functions" involving a "failure to perform an act" that is required of local police when presented with a valid arrest warrant.[94] Furthermore, the Nigerian Police Code of Conduct requires cooperation with, for example, UN inspectors in the event that Nigeria ratifies the proposed treaty: "Police officers will cooperate with all legally authorized agencies and their representatives in the pursuit of justice."[95] The Code of Conduct instructs Nigerian police to cooperate with legally authorized inspectors.[96] This code, in combination with the APUNCAC requirement to cooperate with UN inspectors and to provide any assistance needed to execute warrants for arrest, would obligate local police to assist in executing valid arrest warrants. UN inspectors would obtain and present a warrant to arrest the corrupt police and would seek the assistance of honest, competent police to execute the warrant.[97] Even in the most corrupt nations in the world, there are many honest, competent police officers, as demonstrated by the hundreds of arrests and convictions obtained by the EFCC in Nigeria. The conviction of a chief of police and a governor suggests that powerful individuals are not immune to arrest and prosecution.[98] The threat of arrest for obstruction of justice would be a powerful deterrent to any local police. Furthermore, the police would know that UN inspectors could not be bribed or corrupted in the same way as their corrupt domestic counterparts. The danger of arrest and conviction would be real.

Since the salaries of UN inspectors would be funded by the UN and the careers of UN inspectors would depend on the propriety of their investigations, they could not be manipulated or pressured in the same way that police or investigators from a domestic anticorruption unit could be manipulated and pressured. Unlike domestic police and domestic members of anticorruption units, UN inspectors would be insulated from the power exerted by domestic authorities over jobs and careers. As a result, UN inspectors could not be subjected to the same pressure to tip-off suspects, tip-off local police, or give corrupt officials opportunities to arrange with local officials to obstruct investigations and arrests. UN inspectors would arrive unannounced, giving corrupt officials no time to react. When presented with an arrest warrant, the local police would have the choice of either cooperating with UN inspectors and executing the warrant or obstructing the investigation in the hope that corrupt protectors would quash any attempt by UN inspectors to execute arrests for obstruction of justice. But when there is a real threat of arrest for obstructing justice, even corrupt police may decide that cooperation with UN inspectors is the wisest course of action.

The same logic applies across the entire system of criminal justice. It might be argued that corrupt prosecutors and judges would block investigations by UN inspectors, perhaps by releasing suspects, refusing to prosecute, refusing to hear a case, delaying judgment, or manipulating the outcome of a case. Under APUNCAC, however, those prosecutors and judges would be subject to investigation by UN inspectors for corruption and obstruction of justice. The UNCAC defines corruption to include "the abuse of functions or position, that is, the performance of or failure to perform an act, in violation of laws, by a public official in the discharge of his or her functions," as well as giving any person "an undue advantage" resulting from the abuse by a public official of his or her influence.[99] APUNCAC defines the crime of obstruction of justice, a procedure whereby UN inspectors may request an opinion from a domestic judge, and a process whereby reports of obstruction would be published online by Transparency International in a way that would publicly identify individuals accused of obstructing justice and would expose these individuals to the court of public opinion.

Under APUNCAC, any attempt to delay or thwart the effort of a UN inspector to obtain or execute a warrant for arrest, in excess of the discretionary authority of the court that receives the request for a warrant, would constitute an obstruction of justice. Any attempt to delay or thwart the lawful prosecution, trial, disciplinary hearing, or oversight hearing of an individual accused of corruption or obstruction of justice, in excess of the discretionary authority of the prosecutor, judge, disciplinary body, or oversight agency exercising jurisdiction over the relevant case, would constitute an obstruction of justice. A prosecution, trial, disciplinary hearing, or oversight hearing regarding an individual accused of corruption or obstruction of justice that is substantially irregular; violates accepted prosecutorial, judicial, disciplinary, or oversight norms and practices; and perverts the course of justice would constitute an obstruction of justice.

These actions would also trigger new UN investigations. Since opinions about what falls within the discretion of a prosecutor, judge, or disciplinary body may differ, APUNCAC specifies that UN inspectors may seek a judicial opinion from a domestic court regarding an allegation of an obstruction of justice. Domestic courts are in the best position to formulate a judgment about whether a prosecutor or judge exceeded his or her discretionary authority. Since domestic judges are familiar with domestic norms and practices, they are unlikely to censure a prosecutor or fellow judge without compelling evidence that corruption or obstruction of justice has occurred. The provision for obtaining judicial opinions is intended to respect domestic norms and places judgments about criminality in the hands of individuals who are constitutionally vested with the role of deciding criminality.

APUNCAC specifies that UN inspectors would submit reports to be published online by Transparency International. This provision is analogous to the unsealing of an indictment by a U.S. prosecutor. The intent of this provision is to illuminate corruption and obstruction of justice in a way that would be maximally embarrassing and very difficult to ignore, while still preserving the legitimate discretionary authority of honest prosecutors and judges. APUNCAC seeks to maintain that authority while addressing gross abuses engineered by powerful domestic elites that currently exploit countries where the rule of law is weak and impunity abounds.

It is likely that UN reports would receive attention from the media, especially if they include judicial opinions that obstruction of justice has occurred. The adverse publicity would be difficult to ignore. UN inspectors would recommend charges to the appropriate prosecuting authorities or disciplinary agencies, and those agencies would, under APUNCAC, enforce sanctions in accordance with agency practices and domestic law. These provisions are intended to ensure that any prosecutor or judge who attempts to obstruct justice would be forced from office in the same way that the CICIG forced the resignations of public prosecutors in Guatemala for corruption, including Attorney General Juan Luis Florido, Senior Prosecutor Álvaro Matus, and Administrative Crimes Prosecutor Patricia Lainfiesta.[100]

Nigeria offers case examples illustrating how this could be accomplished. In February 2014, Nigeria's National Judicial Council (NJC) forced two high court judges to retire, reprimanded an appeals court justice and two high court justices, and issued warning letters to two high court justices for various acts of corruption, gross misconduct, and low productivity.[101] The process employed by the NJC suggests how accountability over corrupt judges may be enforced when judges attempt to manipulate outcomes (figure 3.1). These cases suggest the process that may be employed to suppress any temptation to thwart investigations by UN inspectors.

The NJC is comprised of the following:

> (a) the Chief Justice of Nigeria . . . [;] (b) . . . [a] senior Justice of the Supreme Court . . . ; (c) the President of the Court of Appeal; (d) five retired Justices selected by the Chief Justice . . . ; (e) the Chief Judge of the Federal High Court; (f) five Chief Judges of States . . . ; (g) one Grand Kadi . . . from the Sharia Courts of Appeal . . . ; (h) [the] President of the Customary Court of Appeal . . . ; (i) five members of the Nigerian Bar Association . . . [; and] . . . . (j) two persons [who are not] legal practitioners.[102]

The Council is constitutionally vested with the responsibility of exercising disciplinary control over Nigeria's judicial officers and recommending the removal of officers for misconduct or poor performance.[103] The Judges' Performance Evaluation Committee of the NJC assesses and evaluates the performance of all judicial officers and formulates recommendations regarding disciplinary actions.[104] Any individual, including a UN inspector, may file a complaint against any judge, triggering a hearing and possible disciplinary sanctions.[105]

The Council ordered Federal High Court Justice Gladys Olotu to retire after delaying judgment for 18 months in a case that consumed a total of 7 years, in violation of constitutional provisions that require judgment within a period of 90 days.[106] The NJC found that Justice Olotu "forgot" to deliver a ruling.[107] In a second case, she failed to deliver a judgment twice, and in a third case, was guilty of reopening a matter in the absence of legal authority to do so.[108] Investigative reports by the EFCC revealed that she possessed assets exceeding NGN 2 billion (equivalent to US $12,388,000) that were almost certainly obtained through corruption.[109] Similarly, the NJC ordered Federal High Court Justice U. A. Inyang to retire after finding that he had engaged in numerous deliberate, irregular, prejudicial actions.[110] The NJC issued letters of reprimand to Presiding Appeals Court Justice Dalhatu Adamu, High

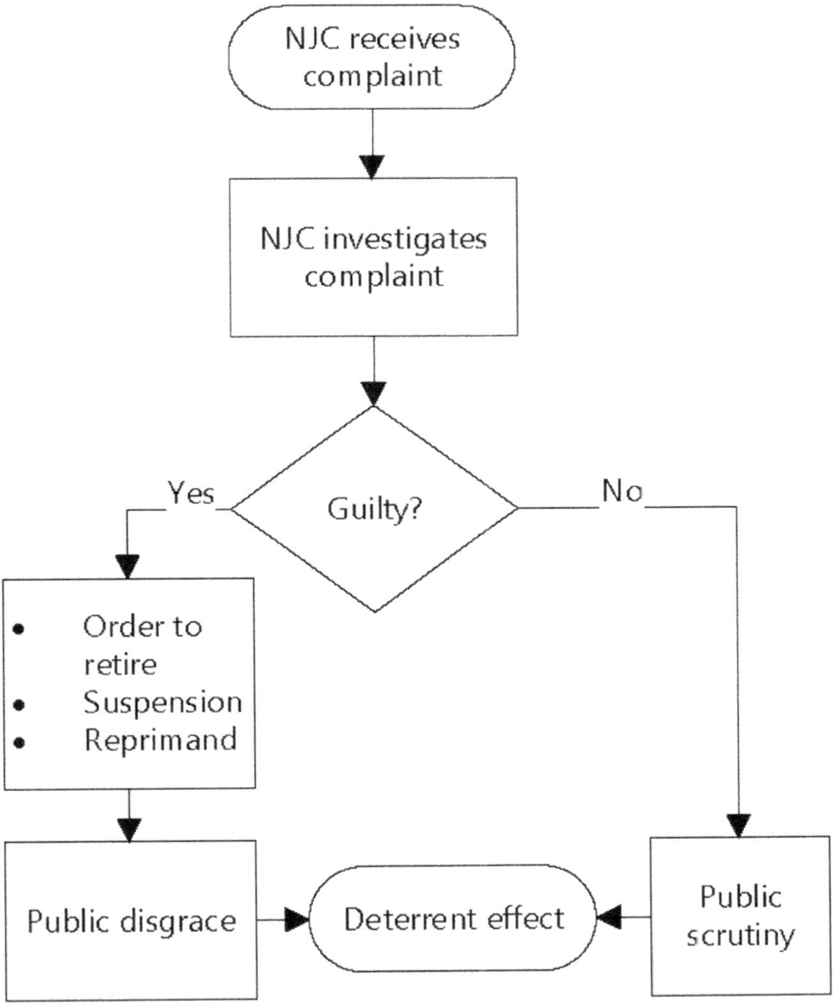

Figure 3.1 NJC Process for Establishing Accountability over Corrupt Judges. *Source*: Figure created by author.

Court Justice A. A. Adeleye, and High Court Justice D. O. Amaechina for misconduct and poor performance.[111] The NJC previously issued a reprimand to Federal High Court Justice Okechukwu Okeke, forcing his retirement.[112] In 2013, the NJC suspended Federal Justice Abubakar Talba for 12 months without pay as a result of an investigation into his role in a police pension case involving John Yusuf, an assistant director in the Police Pension Office.[113] Justice Talba had engineered a reduction in the charges against Yusuf and a concomitant reduction in the associated recommended sentence of 14 years to 2 years of jail time; Talba then gave Yusuf the option of paying a fine of NGN 250,000 (US $1,549) for each charge instead of imprisonment.[114] The egregious nature of the complaints against these judges led several members of the Nigerian legal profession to call for criminal prosecutions.[115]

The preceding examples from Nigeria suggest that UN investigations and referrals to disciplinary bodies such as the NJC would have real consequences for corrupt judges. Even in one of the most corrupt nations in the world, immoral judges are not immune to public opinion. A UN investigation and referral to a disciplinary body could trigger suspension, an order to retire, or forced retirement as a consequence of pressure exerted by the stain of a letter of reprimand.[116] The stain of a UN investigation and a charge of corruption—especially a charge that is sustained by a judicial opinion—would be difficult to ignore and would undermine the legitimacy of a corrupt prosecutor or judge, causing erosion of public support. Without public support, corrupt prosecutors and judges may be forced from office, even in the most corrupt nations in the world. When faced with a real threat of vigorous investigation by independent investigators who are perceived to be incorruptible, even corrupt police, prosecutors, and judges may decide that virtuous behavior is the wisest course of action.

CONCLUSION

The evidence from Guatemala and Nigeria suggests that UN investigations and referrals to disciplinary bodies could trigger the removal of corrupt prosecutors, judges, and government officials. They are not immune to public condemnation and can only survive if their crimes are hidden from public view. UN inspectors would serve to pull back the veil and expose corruption for the world to see. UN inspectors who act independently of the ethnic, tribal, and class rivalries endemic to Nigeria and other nations may possess a level of legitimacy not possessed by domestic police and domestic anticorruption units.

APUNCAC seeks to multiply the power of public opinion by including a provision specifying that periodic updates regarding the progress of each case would be posted by Transparency International on a publicly accessible website. Thus, any individual with access to the internet could check the progress of cases as they wind through the domestic court system. While internet access is limited, as of March 2020, over 526 million Africans now have access,[117] including most journalists in major African cities. When printed, their stories are widely accessible to the public. In addition, citizen journalists, using mobile phones with internet access, are emerging as a powerful phenomenon across Africa.[118] Furthermore, significant news, including news about corrupt elites, is disseminated orally.[119] Through these channels, and despite limited internet access, the online publication of UN investigative reports would ensure that efforts to thwart justice would become widely known. The referral of charges regarding corruption or obstruction of justice to disciplinary bodies such as the NJC would likely trigger letters of reprimand, inflame public opinion, and create intense pressure to resign. This process may force the resignations of powerful individuals in the same way that CICIG forced Attorney General Juan Luis Florido, Senior Prosecutor Álvaro Matus, and Administrative Crimes Prosecutor Patricia Lainfiesta,[120] and the NJC forced Federal High Court Justice Okechukwu Okeke, to resign.[121]

While it may seem unlikely that mere investigations can stop corruption, this is exactly what happened in Hong Kong. The Hong Kong Independent Commission Against Corruption did not have the power to convict, sentence, or imprison suspects, yet was very successful in halting corruption.[122] Until the advent of the Independent Commission Against Corruption, Hong Kong's police force was notoriously corrupt.[123] However, the introduction of the Independent Commission Against Corruption ensured for the first time that no corrupt police officer could feel safe from exposure.[124] There would be no tip-off of a raid, inspection, or investigation, and no chance to hide or destroy evidence. The calculus of the benefits and costs of corruption changed dramatically.[125]

In the same way, independent UN investigators could ensure that corrupt police, prosecutors, judges, legislators, and staff of anticorruption units never feel safe from exposure. By exposing every member of the law enforcement community, prosecutor, judge, legislator, and investigator in an anticorruption unit to the threat of investigation, independent investigators deter corruption in the very institutions that normally fight corruption. Police are compelled to collect evidence, prosecutors are compelled to present evidence, judges are compelled to cite evidence, and legislators are compelled to investigate evidence of corruption, or risk investigation and prosecution themselves for favoritism and corruption. When faced with the prospect of incarceration or removal, it becomes much easier for potentially corrupt police, prosecutors, judges, and legislators to decline bribes and to behave ethically. At the same time, it becomes easier for honest police, prosecutors, judges, and legislators to advance themselves through competent work. By deterring corruption and crime among crime fighters, independent investigators multiply the effectiveness of their own efforts to fight crime and restore the powers of the police, judiciary, and anticorruption units.

The experience of the Independent Commission Against Corruption suggests that the presence of independent investigators has a powerful effect on corrupt officials across all branches of government.[126] When officials know that their telephones may be tapped, that any meeting might be recorded, and that any colleague may provide evidence to prosecutors, the potential for corruption is drastically reduced. However, this is only the case when there is a truly independent body composed of inspectors that are perceived to be incorruptible. This is what is needed but has yet to be established by the international community.

The proposal to create a body of UN inspectors may be distinguished from the many failed attempts to create strong anticorruption units modeled after the Independent Commission Against Corruption. The difference is that UN inspectors would be protected from the ability of domestic ruling elites to manipulate the jobs and careers of domestic investigators. UN inspectors could not be removed in the same way that Mallam Nuhu Ribadu, the director of Nigeria's EFCC, was removed.[127] UN inspectors would have the authority to investigate any instances where corrupt police, prosecutors, or judges attempted to obstruct justice. This would include the authority to obtain and execute arrest warrants for corrupt police and the ability to aggressively investigate corrupt prosecutors and judges. This capacity would distinguish UN inspectors from domestic anticorruption units that can be easily manipulated and thwarted by powerful ruling elites.

The proposal for APUNCAC, modeled on the treaty authorizing the CICIG, was presented at the Symposium on Institutional Capacity, Corruption, and Development sponsored by the Rule of Law Collaborative on April 11, 2014, at the University of South Carolina School of Law. The spirited discussion at the symposium suggested the need to write this chapter. Numerous issues have previously been addressed in articles published in *International Affairs*,[128] the *International Public Policy Review*,[129] the *International Criminal Justice Review*,[130] and the *Journal of African Policy Studies*.[131] The interested reader is urged to read those articles, begin a serious examination of APUNCAC, and consider the possibility that UN inspectors could have a profound effect on the culture of impunity that prevails wherever corrupt individuals feel the risk of punishment is low.

Chapter 4

Corruption and the Drug War

Mexico is a major source and transit country for heroin, marijuana, and synthetic drugs destined for the United States and a main transit country for cocaine from South America.[1] The crime and violence associated with drug trafficking caused the U.S. military's Joint Forces Command to issue a warning that Mexico might collapse: "the government, its politicians, police, and judicial infrastructure are all under sustained assault and pressure by criminal gangs and drug cartels."[2] The 2017 National Drug Threat Assessment report declared that the "Mexican Transnational Criminal Organizations remain the greatest criminal drug threat to the United States."[3] The drug war has now claimed over 100,000 lives since December 2006.[4]

While the severity of the threat is now recognized, there is no consensus regarding the solution. The United States has focused on policies that assist the Mexican government with supply interdiction, enforcement, and security measures. However, the murder rate continued to rise and reached a new high in 2019, driven by the violence associated with drug trafficking.[5]

A Strategic Studies Institute analysis titled "Mexico's Narco-Insurgency and U.S. Counterdrug Policy" suggests that U.S. narcotics policy is failing because it ignores government corruption.[6] The analysis suggests that the drug cartels have informants and protectors at every level of government who ensure that the cartels are always a step ahead of law enforcement.[7]

If corruption sabotages law enforcement, the implication is that an effective deterrent against corruption is necessary. In the United States, vigorous prosecution by investigators who are resistant to corruption deters corruption. This chapter suggests that corruption in Mexico may be addressed by establishing a comparable deterrent: a body of independent, UN-supported inspectors, established through APUNCAC, empowered to investigate corruption at every level of government.

The approach adopted here focuses on dissection of the mechanics of trafficking: how traffickers operate under the protection of police and government officials, with a view toward understanding the potential role of independent investigators in disrupting this protection and restoring the type of deterrence that discourages criminal behavior.

CARTELS AND CORRUPTION

The Mexican drug cartels essentially operate under license from Mexican municipal, state, and federal government officials and police forces through an organized network of corruption.[8] Until the fall of the Institutional Revolutionary Party (PRI) in 2000, geographical areas along the U.S.-Mexico border were carved into drug smuggling territories controlled by subdivisions of the Sinaloan mafia. The mafia paid the police or military units commanding jurisdiction of those areas for their protection and cooperation.[9] In return, the mafia informed the police of freelance and rival operators so that the authorities could arrest them and give the impression of an authentic enforcement operation.[10] While control of these territories is now contested, this system continues to the present.[11]

Types of Corruption

Information obtained from arrests of high-level Mexican antidrug officials offer details explaining how the drug cartels can operate with impunity. In many cases, key police and military officials leaked information about government investigations to the drug cartels in exchange for bribes. For example, Noe Ramirez Mandujano, the former antidrug chief and head of SIEDO (Mexico's elite organized crime unit), leaked information to the Beltrán Leyva and Zambada drug cartels in exchange for $450,000 a month in bribes.[12] General Jesus Gutierrez Rebollo, Mexico's top antinarcotics officer under President Zedillo, gave drug trafficker Amado Carrillo Fuentes access to all of Mexico's classified drug enforcement information, police records, and names of informants.[13] Ricardo Gutierrez Vargas, head of Mexico's Interpol office from 2003 through 2008, leaked confidential information to the Sinaloa cartel in exchange for money.[14] Ivan Reyes Arzate, Mexican federal police officer and commander of the Mexican Federal Police's Sensitive Investigative Unit, was trusted for years with the most sensitive information surrounding U.S. investigations of dangerous drug traffickers, including notorious Sinaloa cartel boss Joaquin "El Chapo" Guzmán and the Beltrán-Leyva cartel. The cartels paid Reyes Arzate $3 million to leak information about informants to targets of the investigations.[15] U.S. attorney Richard P.

Donoghue stated, "By choosing to align himself with drug traffickers instead of the people of Mexico that he was sworn to protect, Reyes Arzate's corruption ensured the safe passage of massive quantities of illegal narcotics into the United States."[16] Former Guzmán lieutenant Miguel Angel Martínez testified in U.S. District Court that Guillermo González Calderoni, the chief of Mexico City's federal police, received millions of dollars from Mr. Guzmán.[17] In return, Calderoni provided Mr. Guzmán with secret information on an almost daily basis, including an invaluable tip in the early 1990s that the U.S. government had built a radar installation on the Yucatán Peninsula to track his drug flights from Colombia.[18]

Another form of collaboration involved the appointment of government officials who were willing to ignore or actively support cartel activities. For example, Rodolfo de la Guardia García, the second most senior official in the elite Federal Investigation Agency (AFI) from 2003 to 2005, received a monthly payment of $10,000 to appoint regional leaders who were sympathetic to the Sinaloa cartel.[19] The attorney general for the Mexican state of Nayarit conspired to manufacture, distribute, and import heroin, cocaine, methamphetamine, and marijuana worth $250 million into the United States.[20] Mexican authorities arrested Javier Duarte, governor of Veracruz, on charges of corruption and organized crime involving the diversion of $3 billion for himself and his cronies.[21]

A third form of collaboration involved the active manipulation of police forces that would otherwise interfere with cartel activities. For example, Victor Gerardo Garay Cadena, chief of Mexico's Federal Police, protected the Sinaloa cartel by ordering the withdrawal of police on two separate occasions after they had surrounded the leader of the cartel, Arturo Beltrán Leyva.[22] Genaro Garcia Luna, secretary of Public Security under President Felipe Calderón, forced the release of Victor Gerardo Garay Cadena while allegedly receiving payments from Arturo Beltrán Leyva's cartel.[23] Jesús Zambada, a top lieutenant in Joaquin "El Chapo" Guzmán's Sinaloa cartel, testified that the cartel paid off a host of top Mexican officials to ensure the Sinaloan drug business ran smoothly.[24] Zambada testified that the drug traffickers paid García Luna $50 million in protection money to ensure the appointment of corrupt officers to head police operations.[25] Zambada testified that he gave the money to García Luna in briefcases full of cash.[26] Mexican ex-governor Tomás Yarrington was assigned eight state policemen as bodyguards between July and December 2016, a period when Yarrington was being sought by Mexican federal police on charges of drug trafficking and corruption.[27] Mexico's federal security agencies received notification that the police officers were acting as bodyguards to Mr. Yarrington.[28]

A fourth form of collaboration involved the participation of corrupt police in protecting cartel activities by actively kidnapping and killing rival cartel members and honest policemen. For example, almost 1,500 members of the AFI, created to fight corruption and organized crime, were themselves suspected of corruption, including kidnapping and killing while on the payroll of Joaquin "El Chapo" Guzmán, leader of the Sinaloa cartel.[29] Interviews with Pablo Acosta Villarreal, the most powerful drug lord of the central border area, detailed the protection provided by the state and federal police, politicians, and the army to the Acosta syndicate during the 1980s.[30] Corrupt police continue the masquerade throughout Mexico, participating in killings, drug trafficking, and cartel activities.[31] Nationwide, drug cartels pay corrupt police $100 million in bribes every month.[32] A report by the International Crisis Group described a "de facto merger of regional and local police forces with organised criminal groups."[33] "The Secretariat of Public Security (SSP) . . . became an authoritarian-criminal enclave . . . [and a] key mechanism to facilitate and shield organised criminal activity."[34]

Corruption at the Highest Level

Corruption extends to the highest level. A U.S. Department of Justice (USDOJ) lawsuit implicated Mexican ex-president Carlos Salinas de Gortari in drug trafficking operations as a member of a group headed by his father and protected by the former Mexican deputy attorney general, Mario Ruiz Massieu, in cooperation with drug lords, including Juan Garcia Abrego, Miguel Angel Felix Gallardo, the Arellano Felix brothers, and Amado Carrillo.[35] The ex-president's brother, Raul Salinas, collected $150 million monthly payments from the drug mafias, may have amassed $2 billion,[36] and was convicted but later acquitted of ordering the 1994 assassination of a leading politician, Jose Francisco Ruiz Massieu.[37] Raul Salinas's wife controlled an $84 million Swiss bank account.[38] The U.S. Department of Justice charged that former Mexican deputy attorney general Mario Ruiz Massieu engaged in drug trafficking and money laundering,[39] tortured witnesses, and suppressed evidence to conceal the role of Raul Salinas in the plot to kill Ruiz Massieu's brother Jose Francisco.[40] Adrian Carrera Fuentes, the imprisoned former head of Mexico's national police, testified that he collected nearly $2 million in drug bribes in 1993 and 1994 and turned the money over to Mario Ruiz Massieu.[41] The USDOJ charged that Mexican government officials entered into a conspiracy and used their positions to assist members of drug trafficking gangs, and that Mario Ruiz Massieu was a member of this conspiracy.[42]

The web of corruption involved the Procuraduría General de la República (PGR) Ministerio Público Federal federal prosecutor, who was generally the intermediary between the drug traffickers, the PGR/Policía Judicial Federal (PJF) hierarchy, and the military.[43] Suitcases filled with money and gifts from the cartels were collected by the PGR/PJF "plaza" holders throughout

Mexico, then disbursed to their superiors in the PGR/PJF and ultimately to President Salinas.[44]

Mexico's Dirección Federal de Seguridad (DFS) intelligence service was also corrupted by the drug cartels. In the 1970s and 1980s, DFS personnel tortured and killed hundreds of Mexicans while participating in the drug trade.[45] The head of the DFS, Jose Antonio Zorrilla Pérez, ordered the killing of Mexican newspaper reporter Manuel Buendía after he began publishing details of the drug traffickers' connections to high-level police, politicians, and businessmen.[46]

Mexico's secretary of defense was also implicated in activities supporting the drug cartels. According to a U.S. Drug Enforcement Agency (DEA) informant, a consortium of traffickers including Rafael Caro Quintero, Juan Esparragoza Moreno, Jaime Figueroa Soto, Manuel Salcido, and Juan Quintero Paez paid $10 million for protection to the Secretary General Juan Arevalo Gardoqui, in a videotaped transaction.[47]

On October 15, 2020, former Mexican defense minister Salvador Cienfuegos, nicknamed "The Godfather," was arrested by U.S. authorities on charges of conspiring with the H-2 cartel in Mexico to smuggle thousands of kilos of cocaine, heroin, methamphetamine, and marijuana while he was defense secretary.[48] According to the U.S. indictment, "In exchange for bribe payments, [Cienfuegos] permitted the H-2 Cartel—a cartel that routinely engaged in wholesale violence, including torture and murder—to operate with impunity in Mexico."[49] The evidence against General Cienfuegos included thousands of Blackberry messages between Cienfuegos and H-2 cartel members that were intercepted by the authorities.[50] U.S. prosecutors said intercepted messages showed that Cienfuegos accepted bribes in exchange for ensuring that the Mexican military did not take action against the cartel and that operations were initiated against its rivals.[51] One month later, however, U.S. attorney general William Barr and his Mexican counterpart Alejandro Gertz Manero announced, in a surprise decision, that the United States would drop drug trafficking and money laundering charges against General Cienfuegos.[52] The announcement stated that the charges against General Cienfuegos would instead be investigated by Mexican authorities.[53] The announcement stated that "sensitive" foreign policy considerations outweighed the interest in pressing the case.[54] However, after Cienfuegos was returned to Mexico, the Mexican government declined to prosecute him.[55]

The evidence of high-level government protection is significant because it is impossible to move tons of cocaine, launder billions of dollars, and maintain a clandestine organization of several hundred armed persons without a system of political and police protection.[56] Without this protection, large-scale, blatant violations of the law extending over decades cannot persist. Discipline is enforced by selectively removing the protection and ordering assassinations. This suggests that an effective strategy must address high-level corruption and corruption among the federal police, military, and anticorruption units.

Institutionalization of Corruption

Corruption in Mexico cannot be attributed to a few isolated bad apples. Instead, it has become institutionalized in a way that is difficult for honest members of law enforcement to resist. The political economy of corruption ensures that individuals who might otherwise seek to act independently are faced with a potent mix of carrots and sticks wielded by the drug cartels and embedded throughout the Mexican law enforcement system.

During the 1990s, offices within the PGR/PJF system were sold to criminals who used control of the offices to facilitate drug trafficking. The sale of offices within the PGR/PJF was accomplished through a deputy attorney general who was purposely selected by the PRI hierarchy and named by Mexico's president.[57] A former PGR delegate (who functions like a U.S. district attorney) reported that he was bluntly informed by a deputy attorney general that the drug plaza he was taking over would cost $3 million, plus a payment of $1 million per month rent to the PGR hierarchy, and that he should pay up front.[58] The drug mafias would provide the funds; he would be responsible for funneling much of this to his superiors who, in turn, would channel it to President Salinas's private secretary, where the monies would be placed in secret accounts to be used as the president or the PRI hierarchy saw fit.[59] Organized crime figures were only arrested to appease the United States, for example, in the weeks prior to the annual "certification" by the United States of Mexico's cooperation with drug control efforts.[60]

Starting in 1992, the military, the PGR/PJF, and state judicial police officials began providing "limousine service" protection for drug shipments to the border area; roadblocks were implemented by the military, the PGR/PJF, or the local authorities to safeguard rather than detect the contraband shipments.[61] Through intermediaries, the "plaza" holder was notified when a drug shipment was expected and instructed to set up the checkpoints, facilitate and supervise the operation, and ensure the safe shipment of the "merchandise" through his/her area.[62]

To maintain high-level protection from law enforcement officials, protected drug traffickers assisted the police by informing on rival traffickers.[63] This permitted the police to record arrests, gain credit and promotions, and permitted Mexican government officials to demonstrate progress to their American counterparts in the fight against the drug cartels, thereby maintaining the flow of U.S. money and support to Mexico (e.g., through the Merida initiative).

Starting in 1997, however, the PRI lost its majority in the Cámara de Diputados (Chamber of Delegates). This erosion of power reduced the ability of the PRI to exert control over the drug cartels. Drug-related violence is now uncontrolled, as rival cartels battle for territory. They have seized the opportunity to go after their competitors and are assassinating the police officers and prosecutors who do go after them.[64] Honest policemen will not investigate because it is better to delay an investigation than face assassination by one's own police comrades.[65] Corruption of the judicial system means that honest prosecutors and policemen are undercut in their efforts to fight crime. Through intimidation, coercion, and bribery of judges, serious charges against major criminals are dismissed, allowing them back on the street to continue their criminal activities.[66]

In December 2006, newly elected president Felipe Calderón began the large-scale introduction of Mexican Army soldiers into the fight against the drug cartels, marking the start of the Mexican Drug War between the government and the drug traffickers. However, after a decade in which over 100,000 lives were lost, there is little evidence of success. Instead, rampant drug-related violence continues. Corruption within the PGR continues.[67] Wholesale, institutionalized corruption within the Mexican government and law enforcement system continues.[68] In December 2017, former state officials described a "nationwide plan to funnel tens of millions of dollars in public money" for illicit purposes.[69] According to Mexican anticorruption activist Juan Pardinas, "the system isn't broken. It's actually working perfectly to allow impunity."[70] Audacious corruption continues to pervade the government at high levels. Numerous Mexican state governors have lost their positions, now face charges, and have been arrested or are being sought.[71] At the time he was president of Mexico, Enrique Peña Nieto's wife received a $7 million home from a business group linked to lucrative government contracts.[72] Emilio Lozoya, the former head of Pemex, Mexico's state oil company, implicated Peña Nieto in a multimillion dollar bribery scheme.[73] Alex Cifuentes Villa, a Colombian drug lord who described himself as El Chapo's "right-hand man," testified in U.S. District Court that after taking office in 2012, Peña Nieto accepted a $100 million bribe from El Chapo in return for ending a manhunt for the drug cartel kingpin.[74] According to Jeffrey Lichtman, one of El Chapo's lawyers, Dámaso López Núñez, who was one of El Chapo's top lieutenants, had placed Mexican Marines, intelligence officers, and local politicians on his payroll: "There is no part of the Mexican government or law enforcement apparatus that Dámaso did not control."[75]

If the drug war is being lost, the ultimate reason may be corruption. The evidence of Mexican corruption suggests *how* corrupt authorities protect the traffickers from honest members of law enforcement, *why* government authorities have been unable to control narcotics trafficking and the associated violence, and *why* it has become nearly impossible for honest members of law enforcement to prevail. Governmental offices are sold to criminals who use control of these offices to facilitate drug trafficking. State judicial police, the military, and government authorities are induced to ensure the safe shipment of contraband drugs. Political leaders provide protection for drug traffickers by manipulating the judicial system. All of this suggests that honest members of law enforcement confront a web of corrupt actors who thwart their efforts to fight trafficking and the associated violence.

Enforcing Agreements

The business of drug trafficking involves all the problems of a conventional business. Agreements must be enforced. Enforceable agreements permit the business to expand; lack of enforcement causes the business to fail. Drugs will not be supplied if payment is unreliable. Payment will not be made if deliveries are short of the agreed-upon quantity or quality.

Unlike a conventional business, however, drug traffickers cannot rely on the legal system to enforce their agreements. Instead, traffickers employ sicarios—contract killers—to kill cheaters and to enforce discipline. In the words of one assassin: "What they needed to make things run smooth was enforcement."[76] In the absence of enforcement, cheating would be rife. Lacking the ability to enforce agreements through the legal system, the threat of violence is perhaps the main factor that prevents suppliers from cheating on quantity or quality, or prevents delivery personnel from skimming or stealing the product, or prevents street-level distributors from failing to pay for the drugs that are delivered to them, or prevents informants from reporting criminal activity to authorities who would prosecute criminals. Without the enforcement of agreements and intimidation of potential informants, large-scale organized drug trafficking would not be possible because both supply and payment would be unreliable. This type of activity depends on the ability of the drug cartels to enforce business agreements and intimidate potential informants through violence.

To deter cheating, a special brand of violence is used: torture, mutilation, and graphic messages left with headless bodies prominently displayed on bridges, highway overpasses, and other public areas.[77] The purpose is to terrorize everyone who might resist the traffickers—potential informants, honest members of law enforcement, and eyewitnesses to the crimes committed by traffickers—and to demonstrate the absolute control of the narco-traffickers and the futility of challenging them.

Enforcement is needed to deter honest law enforcement agents and discipline potential informants working for law enforcement. For example, when federal army troops arrested one of the founding commanders of Los

Zetas in November 2008 and confiscated 428 guns (including 288 assault weapons), antiaircraft missiles, 287 grenades and bombs, and half a million rounds of ammunition, Los Zetas retaliated by torturing and executing a Mexican Army general and two associates.[78] This type of crime is abetted by corrupt authorities: within a week, federal agents arrested Cancún's chief of police, Francisco Velasco, and six other officers, for their alleged roles in the general's murder.[79] Federal prosecutors estimated that as many as 1,700 of Velasco's officers in Cancún's police force were working for Los Zetas.[80]

To conduct its operations, including an audacious prison break that freed 40 prisoners affiliated with the Gulf cartel, Los Zetas obtained police and commando uniforms as well as military weapons and ammunition that were likely purchased from corrupt police and soldiers with access to those items.[81]

EL SICARIO

To enforce agreements, the cartels recruit paid assassins from the ranks of the police and army. In an 80-minute documentary by Gianfranco Rosi, "El Sicario: Room 164," a contract killer, who served as a commander in the Chihuahua state police while kidnapping, torturing, and murdering individuals targeted by the Mexican drug cartels, provided a firsthand account of how the system worked. This account suggests the significance of corruption in facilitating the crime associated with drug trafficking and, therefore, the significance of developing an effective deterrent to corruption.

According to this commander, all Mexican law enforcement academies serving the various police forces, the investigative police, the military police, and the army have been co-opted and used by the narco-trafficking organizations to train their future employees. The drug cartels lavished monthly cash payments of $1,000, drugs, and women on young cadets who had few prospects in life and only received the equivalent of $12.75 per month in government salary.[82] In this way, the cadets were recruited by the traffickers, who prized the skills taught in the academies, such as the use of weapons and surveillance techniques.[83] The assertion that narco-traffickers use law enforcement and military academies to train their personnel is supported by Craig Deare, the former commander of the U.S. 7th Special Forces Group at Ft. Bragg, North Carolina, who also served as country director in the Office of the U.S. Secretary of Defense and is now a professor at the U.S. National Defense University. According to Deare, some of the Gulf and Zeta cartels' initial members were elite Mexican troops, trained in the early 1990s by U.S. Special Forces based at Ft. Bragg.[84] They were given standard Special Forces training, including map reading, communications, and training with machine guns, automatic weapons, and other firearms.

According to the state police commander, 50 of the 200 cadets in his Chihuahua state police academy graduating class were recruited and placed on the payroll of the narco-traffickers.[85] The 50 graduates were distributed throughout Juárez, Chihuahua City, Parral, and Ojinaga so that when an offer was received to traffic drugs from Durango, Sonora, or Coahuila into Chihuahua, state policemen were already committed to the traffickers at each port of entry into the state and could ensure easy circulation of the drugs. In many cases, official police vehicles were used to transport drugs. In other cases, drugs were hidden in trucks that were approved by the police. Marijuana was stacked in boxes on flatbed trailers and driven through checkpoints.

To foil law enforcement, individual policemen were assigned by the narco-traffickers to specific roles: guarding safe houses, surveillance, kidnapping of individuals who owed money or who switched to work for rival gangs, execution of those individuals, and burial of those who were executed.[86] The kidnapper delivered the victim to the executioner, who delivered the body to the person who buried it. The separation of roles ensured that no single person could give information to police investigators that would directly link the traffickers with the entire sequence of criminal actions required to kidnap and execute an individual and dispose of the body.

Policemen using official patrol cars were recruited and assigned to shadow victims before they were kidnapped or killed.[87] On the day that the kidnapping or assassination was scheduled, the director of the police was notified and told to call a 45-minute meeting, so that all police were cleared off the streets and the kidnappers or assassins could operate freely. The police dispatcher was also bribed so that policemen would not be dispatched to the scene until after the kidnappers or assassins were finished.

According to the commander, officers who might otherwise decide to "retire" from their service with the narco-traffickers were compelled to carry out their orders or be killed.[88] Discipline among the criminals was enforced through the same tactics.

In addition to the involvement of the police, the commander described the involvement of military officers in organized assassinations, including an individual known as "El Cora de Sinaloa" who commanded a group that executed people for the Sinaloa cartel.[89] This specialized group of assassins operated throughout Sinaloa, Durango, Torreón in Coahuila, Chihuahua, and Sonora, allegedly in collaboration with ranking military officers.

The commander and his team of 90 men, trained by the military, were recruited to kill high-level police commanders, including commanders of the state judicial police.[90] This team employed all the advantages of being actual police officers who had been tracking the daily schedules of each target in the course of their official roles as investigators. This included the use of devices to intercept and record cell phone calls. In his official role, the commander maintained direct communication with numerous other security agencies, including municipal police, state judicial police, federal judicial police, ministerial police, and the special police, who purposely or inadvertently supplied information that assisted in tracking the targets.

The commander described the ease of working in Juárez, Chihuahua, Sinaloa, and Durango, with every step facilitated by corruption:

> All we had to do was arrive at an airport, get on a plane, and go. It was not a problem. Arms and cash were also transported by private planes. In the airport, everything was arranged such that the private flights—small Cessnas—were taken care of in all of the airports by elements of the army. The commercial flights were taken care of by the federal preventive police, and everything was arranged for us. . . . We would travel to these states to find people who owed money, and our job was to execute them. . . . For some time, six to eight months or more, I was working inside the police, kidnapping people and then handing them over to other people. The advantage of being a policeman while also working for the narco-trafficking organizations is that you can play both sides. Supposedly, you are working to protect people and society, but at the same time, you are getting paid a lot of money to do jobs required by the narco-traffickers, to deliver people to them.[91]

This account is consistent with contemporaneous reports in 2004 that U.S. and Mexican officials believed that at least 20 officers in the Chihuahua State and Ciudad Juárez police departments doubled as enforcers and traffickers for the Juárez drug cartel.[92] According to an International Crisis Group report:

> Through coercion from superiors and organised crime groups, as well as payoffs offered to officers, the resources of the State Police were refitted to serve criminal purposes. One way was to adopt a passive response to crime. Officers were explicitly instructed to reject citizens' requests of help and assistance, to arrive late at crime scenes, to not report sightings of suspicious vehicles and armed individuals or groups, and to stay clear of ongoing armed confrontations, according to a former police officer. "Our order was to simulate action and do nothing," he said. Active participation in criminal operations, including kidnappings-for-ransom and forced disappearances, formed another part of police operations. An informal "elite squad," composed of former members of the armed forces, was employed for the "dirty work," he said. This group was provided with cloned patrol cars, distributed throughout the state and used to lure victims.[93]

The evidence suggests that the control exerted by cartel leaders depends on the ability of the cartels to recruit contract killers from individuals who are trained at government-run police and military training academies and who masquerade as police and soldiers. The recruitment of these contract killers permits the cartels to enforce discipline among police who might otherwise quit the business of trafficking and become informants; this discipline permits large-scale drug trafficking and high drug profits.

The commander's account suggests that narco-traffickers have infiltrated, corrupted, and hijacked the resources of the Mexican law enforcement system for their own purposes, permitting them to operate with impunity and to kill any member of law enforcement who opposes them. The institutions that are intended to fight crime have been co-opted. According to the commander, most of the cartels' work is managed from inside the Mexican prison system. Executions are ordered by individuals who are in prison, and prisons are used as manufacturing centers and packing houses for drugs that are shipped to the United States.[94] In one case, a prison director released prison inmates at night to carry out executions using rifles originally issued to prison guards, including the massacre of 17 people at a party outside the city of Torreón on July 18, 2010.[95]

Because of corruption, members of the police and the government essentially participate with and assist the narco-trafficking organizations, rather than fighting them. At every level, corrupt police and army soldiers essentially work under the command of the narco-trafficking cartels as puppets, manipulated and controlled for the convenience of cartel bosses. Control is exerted through the power to assassinate any policeman or soldier who opposes the cartels.[96]

The preceding analysis suggests that the crux of the problem is corruption. In the absence of corruption, police cadets could not be enticed to work for the traffickers as enforcers; without enforcement, it would be difficult for traffickers to control police who might otherwise quit the business of trafficking and become informants; without control over potential informants, it would be difficult for the traffickers to operate. The issue is, therefore, how to establish a powerful deterrent to corruption, a deterrent that is resistant to corruption by the traffickers and resistant to control by corrupt domestic officials.

DETERRENCE

As described in chapter 3, Guatemala's CICIG offers an intriguing model involving international, UN-supported inspectors who led criminal investigations in Guatemala, one of the most violent countries in Latin America. Illegal armed groups and criminal gangs operate death squads and employ violence and intimidation, supporting their activities through drug trafficking.[97]

Guatemalan law enforcement institutions are unable to address this rampant violence due to intimidation, corruption, and infiltration of the police and judiciary by criminal organizations.[98] In response, Guatemala and the UN created CICIG via a treaty-level bilateral agreement.[99]

CICIG employed international and local staff members to conduct independent investigations and submit reports to Guatemalan prosecutors.[100] The agreement with the UN specified that Guatemala would cooperate with CICIG-led investigations.[101] Guatemala agreed to ensure the security and protection of CICIG personnel and immunity from personal arrest or detention.[102] CICIG investigators had extraordinarily broad freedom to conduct independent investigations into any person, official, or entity, and to present criminal charges to Guatemala's Public Prosecutor.[103]

As described in chapter 3, CICIG's activities during its first four years suggest that this type of international investigative body can quickly achieve success, despite having limited enforcement tools and no independent ability to prosecute. The results suggest that CICIG was effective despite its inability to discipline or prosecute individuals, and despite the risk of violence to its investigators. CICIG's success suggests that this type of investigative body can be successful even under conditions where criminal gangs, death squads, and powerful individuals appear to operate with impunity—conditions that characterize Mexico, as well as Guatemala.

Corruption among the police, military, customs and border agents, and government officials means that the same authorities who are society's primary bulwark against crime serve, instead, to actively facilitate and promote the type of large-scale, organized drug trafficking and wholesale violence that has developed along the U.S.-Mexico border. The starting point of any effective strategy to reduce drug trafficking and the associated violence is to establish a credible capacity to investigate, prosecute, and deter corruption among police, military, and government officials.

If corruption among the police, military, and Mexican government officials can be controlled in the same way that it is controlled in Western developed nations, and if corrupt individuals are replaced with honest, competent officials, then honest, competent policemen could do their jobs effectively. If the police arrest those responsible for drug trafficking, kidnapping, and murder, instead of participating in those activities, criminals and corrupt individuals would have a reason to fear arrest and would be deterred from committing crime. In Colombia, for example, kidnappers operated with impunity until reforms purged the police force of corrupt officers; as a result, Colombia made significant gains in reducing the kidnapping rate.[104] The former president of Colombia, César Gaviria Trujillo, stated: "kidnapping is a problem of bad policing. Because good police can always catch kidnappers."[105]

APUNCAC

The depth and scope of corruption in Mexico suggests the need for an institution to fight corruption that operates independently of the control of senior domestic officials—in other words, an international institution (figure 4.1).

This type of institution is needed not only in Mexico but in many states around the world. While the notion that the international community could effectively deter corruption may seem utopian, this book seeks to explain why it is not. As described in chapters 2 and 3, the implementation of APUNCAC would establish a body of UN inspectors who would be empowered to investigate allegations of corruption, then refer cases to dedicated, UN-funded, domestic anticorruption courts for trial.[106] Significantly, both Mexico and the United States are parties to UNCAC and, thus, have already signed and ratified a legally binding international treaty requiring them to implement and enforce laws against corruption. APUNCAC would, upon ratification, require all parties to cooperate with UN inspectors to enforce those laws.

All Western developed countries deter corruption through aggressive, independent investigators. Since corruption in Mexico and many other nations extends to the highest level, it is necessary for the international community to establish a body of inspectors—it is not possible to rely on domestic leaders to implement the necessary changes.

As described in chapter 2, Hong Kong offers perhaps the clearest evidence of the impact of independent investigators on corruption. Prior to the anticorruption campaign initiated in 1974, syndicated corruption in Hong Kong "existed in a primal state" where "corruption infected not only the police, a classic source, but all government departments that provided any opportunity for its occurrence."[107] Yet, within a few short years of introducing independent inspectors, Hong Kong achieved "spectacular success" in arresting corruption.[108]

Investigators from the ICC have demonstrated that many of the most notorious, seemingly untouchable perpetrators of war crimes can be arrested and brought to trial even in the most lawless African states, where the rule of law is no stronger than in Mexico.[109] Arrests were made despite the possibility that the investigators might themselves be harmed. This challenges the notion that Mexico is somehow a special case where corrupt officials cannot be brought to justice by international investigators.

As described in chapters 2 and 3, the Rome Statute of the ICC offers a powerful precedent suggesting how and why nations may be induced to surrender domestic sovereignty in cases where government officials place themselves above the law. Importantly, it was not necessary to rely on voluntary acquiescence by autocratic leaders to achieve adherence to the Rome Statute: pressure from constituents and the international community forced

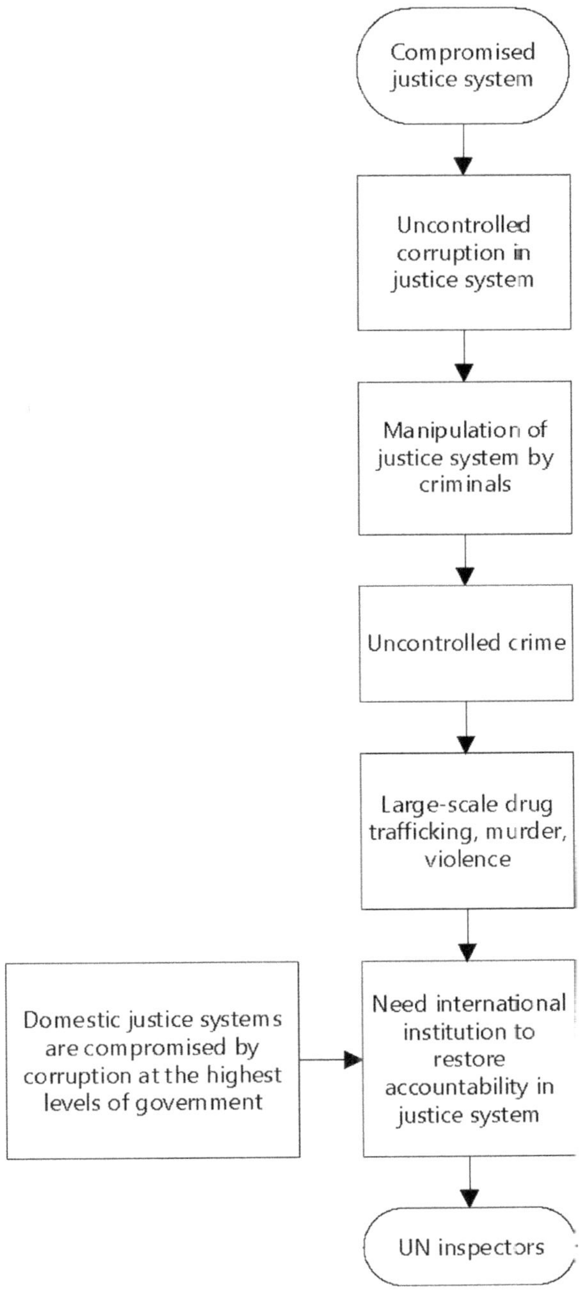

Figure 4.1 Domestic Justice Systems Are Compromised at the Highest Levels. *Source*: Figure created by author.

those leaders to sign the treaty or risk removal at the next election. A similar process might be used to implement APUNCAC, authorizing the creation of an international body of criminal investigators endowed with broad powers to conduct independent investigations on domestic territory.

The Rome Statute provides a model of the process through which domestic leaders may be compelled, through international pressure, to sign and ratify an anticorruption protocol that would expand the scope of the UNCAC, create the ICAC and, upon ratification, create the legal duty to comply with investigations led by UN inspectors that would accompany ratification. After an international treaty has been signed and ratified, domestic leaders may attempt to obstruct investigations and warrants issued to arrest powerful figures. However, the examples cited in chapter 3 suggest that the ICC has been remarkably successful in bringing powerful individuals to justice, despite the dominance of domestic leaders over the legislative and judicial branches in autocratic nations. Even in the most corrupt nations in the world, the experience of the ICC suggests that independent investigators can complete their work, domestic officials can execute arrest warrants, and powerful figures can be brought to justice. The experience of the ICC gives reason to think that the proposed ICAC might be equally effective.

Several provisions aim to discourage perfunctory compliance with APUNCAC. In addition to the provisions that permit UN inspectors to file requests for censure and require the World Bank and IMF to institute sanctions for noncooperation, APUNCAC contains provisions designed to foster transparency. Reports would be available online. Refusals by domestic prosecutors to prosecute would become apparent. Refusals to prosecute egregious cases would arouse public condemnation. Public pressure may force resignations, just as CICIG forced the resignations of corrupt prosecutors. UN inspectors may have the same success as CICIG, operating under equally violent conditions.

The presence of corruption-resistant UN inspectors would discourage the recruitment of police by drug cartels. If UN inspectors are as successful as similar investigators in Guatemala and if the expectation of impunity is broken, whistleblowing may increase, the risk of arrest and incarceration may increase, private calculations of the relative benefits and costs of crime would change, and fewer police would be tempted to participate in corrupt schemes.

CONCLUSION

APUNCAC would effectively provide an independent means of investigating corruption and would do so under the existing legal authority of the UN under the provisions of UNCAC. Under APUNCAC, the UN Commission on Crime Prevention and Criminal Justice would assess the validity of each charge and would provide a check against politically motivated investigations.

Importantly, the ICAC would have the authority to investigate counterclaims that a given investigation is politically motivated. The ICAC would serve as an independent arbiter of conflicting charges of corruption. The ICAC would have the authority to conduct multiple investigations simultaneously to sort out conflicting claims and would have the authority to recommend charges against multiple parties.

Mexican citizens who are outraged at the violence and seeming impunity of cartel assassins may embrace UN-led investigations and may choose to cooperate with UN inspectors. Mexican citizens may see UN-led investigations as a credible alternative to the strategy initiated by former president Felipe Calderón of using military troops to fight the drug cartels. To the extent that APUNCAC is viewed as a credible alternative to Calderón's strategy, APUNCAC may receive popular support. A campaign to gain public support could emphasize the success of Guatemala's CICIG and suggest that a similar approach may be effective in Mexico.

If APUNCAC is posed as a public litmus test regarding a leader's willingness to fight corruption, it would be difficult to ignore. Upon ratification, APUNCAC would create an institution supporting aggressive investigators that would be difficult for criminals to control. CICIG's success in forcing the resignations of prosecutors and judges who obstruct justice demonstrates that this type of institution is not easy to manipulate. UN inspectors, paid generously out of UN funds, would operate independently. Career advancement would depend on the probity of their investigations, rather than rewards controlled by corrupt leaders. This insulation from domestic influence distinguishes the proposed ICAC from existing domestic law enforcement agencies and is the reason why the ICAC would be more effective than domestic agencies.

While domestic leaders might balk at signing a protocol authorizing UN inspections, it might be difficult for them to refuse if the protocol is framed as a public litmus test of their commitment to fight corruption, and in the face of strong public pressure. Are Mexican citizens entitled to freedom from the assassination, mutilation, kidnapping, and extortion that accompanies drug trafficking? Are they entitled to assistance from international inspectors in conducting vigorous investigations of corrupt police, military, and government officials? Mexican leaders have repeatedly promised aggressive action to combat corruption and drug-related crime.[110] Political leaders may choose to support APUNCAC for political reasons. Events in Tunisia, Egypt, and Libya demonstrate that leaders who resist change are not immune to public pressure for political reform.

The proposal to create a body of UN inspectors and endow them with investigative powers raises numerous issues. However, APUNCAC offers a way forward that has not previously been suggested—a way that arguably addresses a root problem not only in Mexico but anywhere in the world where corrupt police and government officials facilitate criminal activity.

Chapter 5

Corruption and Insurgency

In 2009, Frank Ledwidge, former justice adviser to the UK Provincial Reconstruction Team in Helmand Province, Afghanistan, wrote:

> Recent counter-insurgency doctrine has largely ignored the justice sector. . . . This is a serious mistake. . . . For the people of Afghanistan, justice is the single most important issue.[1]

Under the guise of fighting militants, Afghan security forces armed, trained, supported, sponsored, and overseen by the U.S. Central Intelligence Agency kidnap, torture, assault, and murder innocent men, women, and children, then burn their homes.[2] According to a provincial government official, "there is absolutely no justice."[3] Widespread, persistent atrocities and unlawful killings, conducted with near impunity, leave a trail of abuse and anger.[4] This anger translates into support for the Taliban and threats to take up arms against the government.[5] The contradiction is profound. It is impossible to fight militancy through an approach that relies upon corrupt, out-of-control government forces whose behavior creates anger, resentment, and support for the Taliban.

This chapter builds upon evidence that corruption generates resentment and beliefs that certain groups are favored over other groups, driving insurgency.[6] This chapter argues that the establishment of APUNCAC would deter corruption among government officials around the world, address a root cause of dissatisfaction that gives life to insurgency, and inoculate the world against the scourge of violent extremism.

THE THEORY OF COUNTERINSURGENCY

David Kilcullen, formerly the senior counterinsurgency adviser to General David Petraeus in Iraq and adviser to General Stanley McChrystal in Afghanistan, is the author of *Counterinsurgency*, a section of which was adapted and included in the U.S. Army and Marine Corps counterinsurgency field manual, *FM 3-24 Counterinsurgency*.[7] I draw upon Kilcullen's analysis to describe the theory of counterinsurgency:

> We can drive the insurgents away from the population, and then introduce local security forces, protective measures, governance reforms, and economic and political development, all designed to break the connection between the insurgents and the population, undermine the insurgents' mass base, and thereby "hardwire" the enemy out of the environment—excluding them permanently and preventing their return.[8]

According to this theory, American military intervention can be applied in a way that restores local security, permits local security forces to take over, and permits local governance reforms and the economic and political development that would give the local population reason to support the local government, rather than the insurgents.[9] In this view, military intervention is only required temporarily. However, Kilcullen acknowledges a flaw in the theory: "An expeditionary force fights at a critical disadvantage because everybody—allies and opponents alike—knows it will leave once the fighting ends, making it by definition an unreliable long-term or postconflict ally."[10]

U.S. forces were ordered to be completely withdrawn from Afghanistan no later than the end of 2014, raising concern that the Taliban would take over once the withdrawal was completed.[11] With the knowledge that the U.S. military would eventually leave Afghanistan, insurgents could simply wait for the inevitable withdrawal. Furthermore, the local populace, knowing that the U.S. military would eventually withdraw, and the insurgents would eventually resume control, had every reason to avoid cooperating with the U.S. military in ways that would antagonize the insurgents and incur reprisals. An Afghan civilian stated the issue explicitly: "If we have contact with coalition or government forces, the Taliban will shoot us."[12] An American commander acknowledged, "They think we're going to come in here and leave."[13] By early 2012, according to a classified NATO report, Afghan civilians were already bracing themselves for the eventual return of the Taliban.[14] This explains the lack of cooperation among the local populace in assisting U.S. forces to identify insurgents and the difficulty in reducing the level of insurgent attacks.

Kilcullen's analysis suggests that corruption is the source of discontent in Afghanistan:

> Afghanistan is experiencing a cycle of increasing instability and violence, with four key drivers: (1) *corruption* in the government, in the societal elites, and in the international assistance effort, which enables and encourages (2) *bad behavior by government officials and power brokers*, which in turn creates (3) *popular rage and disillusionment*, which empowers (4) the *insurgency*. The war against the insurgents in turn creates further opportunities and incentives for corruption and criminality, driving the cycle onward.[15]

Figure 5.1 illustrates the cycle of corruption and violence. The analysis pinpoints government corruption as the source of discontent that empowers insurgency and suggests that a direct attack on corruption before insurgency gains strength could potentially forestall the conditions that later develop into insurgency. While insurgents may be inspired by radical interpretations of Islam and resentment of the American military presence in Afghanistan, they cannot thrive without the support of the populace.[16] That support depends directly on discontent that is driven by government corruption. Corruption generates resentment and beliefs that government officials abuse their power at the expense of those who are not in power, promoting insurgency.[17] Thus, the control of corruption is essential to the success of counterinsurgency efforts. However, previous analyses implicitly assumed that corruption is primarily a domestic matter that the international community is ill-equipped

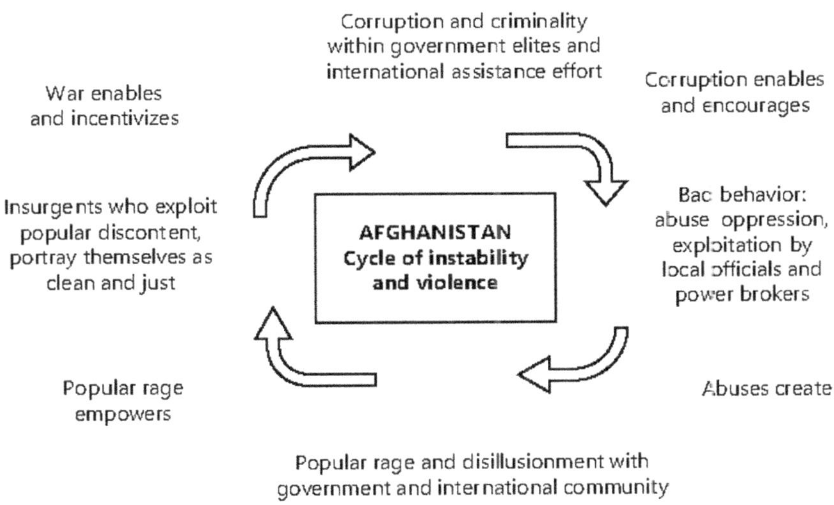

Figure 5.1 Corruption Foments Discontent Which Is Exploited by Insurgents. *Source*: Kilcullen, David (2010). *Counterinsurgency*. New York: Oxford University Press.

to address. Consequently, the U.S. government fails to adequately address the problem of corruption and instead continues to focus on the collection of intelligence about impending terrorist acts, efforts to arrest or assassinate terrorists, and military intervention to destroy terrorist bases, rather than addressing the basic causes of discontent.[18]

Kilcullen explained that American military commanders tended to use force in a way that exacerbated the problem while neglecting its causes, which he identified as unemployment and government corruption:

> Since insurgents kill our people daily while unemployment and corruption do not . . . most military commanders prioritize kinetics (fighting the insurgents). . . . In doing so, they tend to treat, or even exacerbate, the symptoms of instability while neglecting its causes.[19]

While Kilcullen's analysis was embraced within the U.S. military, the emphasis on killing insurgents remained unchanged, primarily because military commanders were not able to address unemployment and corruption, but also because commanders remained optimistic about the efficacy of military force. If, however, the Afghan populace was outraged by government corruption and if insurgents were aligned against corrupt government officials, then U.S. military attacks on insurgents were inevitably viewed as an unpopular defense of corrupt officials. The United States was viewed as propping up a corrupt government, much as it did in Vietnam. Popular outrage was fanned whenever U.S. forces swept through neighborhoods; broke into homes; and cuffed, interrogated, and imprisoned anyone who seemed suspicious. Incidents where U.S. forces mistakenly killed innocent civilians generated fury that inspired brothers, cousins, and tribal kin to take up arms against American soldiers. The Taliban insurgency, previously contained in southern and eastern Afghanistan, spread into the north and west, with Taliban shadow governors operating in all but one of the country's 34 provinces.[20]

In December 2019, the *Washington Post* published a confidential trove of government documents revealing that senior U.S. officials failed to tell the truth about the war in Afghanistan throughout the 18-year campaign. More than 400 insiders, including generals, diplomats, aid workers, and Afghan officials, offered unrestrained criticism of what went wrong in Afghanistan. General Douglas Lute, who served as the White House's Afghan war czar during the Bush and Obama administrations, admitted: "We were devoid of a fundamental understanding of Afghanistan—we didn't know what we were doing."[21]

AFGHANISTAN

The international community failed to grasp the central importance of law enforcement and justice sector reform in restoring the rule of law and addressing underlying causes of popular discontent in Afghanistan that alienated the local population and caused the population to embrace the Taliban. Corrupt misuse of power by local officials was blatant and intolerable.

> During the civil war in the 1990s police stations were nothing more than an extension of the power of local commanders and warlords, and they continued to be so under [President Hamid] Karzai. Justice was rarely meted out, and the police—lacking salaries or facilities—lived off the land by exploiting the public rather than serving it. They were heavily involved in the drug trade, land grabbing, kidnapping, and extortion. The Ministry of Interior, which ran the police after 9/11, became a center for drug trafficking, with police posts in opium-growing regions being auctioned to the highest bidder—sometimes for as much as $100,000 for a job that had a salary of $70 a month.[22]

In August 2006, Secretary of Defense Donald Rumsfeld received a classified report stating that "enormous popular discontent is building" against the Afghan government because of its corruption and incompetence.[23] In December 2010, Transparency International rated Afghanistan as the second most corrupt country in the world.[24] Thus, corruption "is rampant at every level of Afghan society."[25] The Kabul government "quickly evolved into a criminal enterprise, siphoning tens of millions of Western dollars and, later, enriching itself from the booming trade in opium."[26] Thus, corruption in Afghanistan is pervasive and overwhelming. It undermined the counterinsurgency effort. It is despised by ordinary Afghans and may constitute the single largest factor that drove them into the arms of the Taliban.[27] Afghan district officials candidly observed that "The people of Afghanistan keep losing their trust in the government because of the high amount of corrupted government officials. . . . The general view of the Afghans is that the current government is worse than the Taliban."[28] Weary of the extortion suffered at the hands of corrupt officials, the local population eagerly embraced the Taliban.

PAKISTAN

The insurgency in Afghanistan was also driven by Islamic extremists who operated with the support of Pakistan's corrupt president Pervez Musharraf. Musharraf maintained his power by co-opting political elites through offices and patronage. He co-opted the army through lucrative plots of land parceled out at nominal prices to officers throughout their careers and at retirement, permitting the officers to sell the plots at market rates, generating profits of 50–100 times their investment.[29] In addition, every general who retired from the army was promised a civilian job.[30]

Musharraf routinely flouted the nation's constitution. In 2002, he called a referendum to illegally extend his power for five years, manipulated the results of the referendum by ordering army and government employees to vote for him multiple times, and manipulated parliamentary elections.[31] In August 2002, Musharraf issued an unconstitutional order that amended the constitution and made him president for the next five years.[32]

Ultimately, Musharraf's support eroded to the point where he was forced to resign in August 2008. However, his record of corrupt rule suggests the possibility that the existence of international inspectors, operating with the support of honest members of parliament and law enforcement, might have compiled damning reports that could have been used to accelerate democratic change. Events in Tunisia, Egypt, and Libya demonstrate that even the most authoritarian rulers are not immune to public pressure for political reform. Detailed reports of corruption would likely inflame public sentiment and create intense pressure to resign.

What would have been the effect? Consider the changes that occurred after Musharraf was forced from office. Until 2008, Pakistan was "perhaps the world's most active sponsor of terrorist groups."[33] However, Musharraf's ouster resulted in a significant decline in support. While the Taliban's Haqqani network appears to maintain a haven in Quetta, the country is no longer the same haven for other elements of the Taliban. Taliban commanders and fighters who formerly roamed Quetta, in Pakistan, went underground.[34] Members of the Taliban refused to talk on their telephones for fear that they would be identified and targeted for assassination.[35] In February 2011, three powerful Taliban commanders, leaders of units fighting in the southern Afghan province of Helmand, were killed in Quetta.[36] Several senior Taliban commanders were arrested by Pakistani security forces.[37] After suffering heavy losses, the Taliban struggled to find recruits and were reluctant to return to Afghanistan to continue fighting.[38] Whether the Taliban were being targeted by covert American assassination teams with the tacit cooperation of Pakistan's ISI or directly by the ISI itself, Pakistan's civilian government began to prosecute elements that formerly roamed freely.

In September 2013, Prime Minister Nawaz Sharif convened a meeting of his senior ministers.[39] He ordered the paramilitary Rangers into Karachi and gave them unlimited powers to root out terrorists.[40] As a consequence of aggressive action, 919 militants were arrested.[41] Violence fell by 75 percent.[42] In Karachi, killings declined from 2,789 in 2013 to 592 in the first 11 months of 2016.[43] Over the same period, terrorist bomb blasts declined from 51 to 2. Cases of extortion declined from 533 to 133.[44]

Sharif ordered the Pakistani Army into North Waziristan, the Taliban stronghold on the Afghanistan border.[45] In January 2015, following a massive military offensive that triggered Taliban atrocities, including the killing of 140 children, Pakistan implemented the National Action Plan, which established special military courts and outlawed terror groups that had previously been given latitude by the state.[46] At the same time, the army stepped up its operations, resulting in the killing of 3,500 Taliban fighters, the destruction of 992 hideouts, and clearance of 3,600 square kilometers of territory.[47]

Consequently, Pakistan is no longer the safe haven for the Taliban that it was under Musharraf.[48] The Pakistani Taliban are "experiencing a precipitous decline" and operational degradation due to a massive onslaught by the Pakistani Army in both urban and rural areas.[49] This has significantly undermined Tehrik-i-Taliban Pakistan enclaves, infrastructure, and recruitment ability. These efforts resulted in a significant decline in terrorist attacks across Pakistan.[50] Pakistan's terrorism-related fatalities declined 94 percent from 2009 through 2018.[51] Presumably, the same effect could have been achieved much earlier if reform elements, armed with reports of corruption, had been able to arouse public opinion and raise a challenge to Musharraf's corrupt rule.[52]

The existence of an institutional capacity to root out corruption might be expected to foster the type of democratic government that would promote the rule of law and prevent the use of Pakistan (or any other nation) as a base for violent extremists. To the extent that an effective anticorruption agency fosters the rule of law and secures the cooperation of existing government, military, and police units in enforcing the rule of law, it could promote peace and security by jailing militant extremists.

CONCLUSION

If corruption among Afghan government officials had been controlled in the same way that it is controlled in Western developed nations, if corrupt individuals were replaced with honest, competent officials, if the police had arrested those responsible for land grabbing, extortion, and kidnapping, instead of participating in those activities, Afghans would have had reason to support the police and American soldiers who sought to identify and arrest insurgents and other criminals. Similarly, if corruption among Pakistani government officials had been controlled in the same way that it is controlled in Western developed nations, and if honest, competent Pakistani government leaders had sought to identify and arrest violent extremists, instead of arming and supporting them, a major driver of the insurgency in Afghanistan would have been neutralized.

The Taliban have demonstrated that courts and the rule of law are not only consistent with local culture but elicit tremendous popular support. This challenges the notion that Western forms of justice are somehow alien or rejected by Afghans and challenges the notion that local culture poses a barrier to APUNCAC. What Afghans reject is the corrupt application of the government system of justice—not the idea that justice should be meted out by courts following rules that define punishments.

Bribery of UN staff would be difficult because UN staff would be paid generously out of UN funds and career advancement for international investigators would depend on the probity of their investigations, rather than rewards that are controlled by corrupt domestic leaders. This insulation of UN inspectors from the control of domestic leaders is what sets the proposed ICAC apart from domestic law enforcement agencies and is the reason why it would be potentially much more effective than domestic agencies.

The evidence from Hong Kong, Singapore, and Guatemala suggests that independent investigators, established through APUNCAC, could dramatically reduce corruption; promote good governance; promote the rule of law and property rights; foster economic, social, and political development; and defuse resentment that leads to extremism and terrorism. However, a range of objections might be raised regarding APUNCAC:

- It might be argued that APUNCAC is not workable. However, the fact that 123 nations are parties to the Rome Statute establishing the ICC demonstrates that 123 nations agree that international inspections are in fact workable. Those nations emphatically voted to permit international inspections. While political obstacles may obstruct ratification of APUNCAC, those obstacles were previously overcome in 123 nations. It might be argued that APUNCAC would not achieve wide acceptance, but 123 nations have demonstrated their support for this type of international response, suggesting that it is a legitimate response to impunity. All 123 nations agree that international inspections are logical, sound, workable, acceptable, and legitimate. This does not guarantee that the same nations would ratify APUNCAC, but a strong legal precedent has been established.
- It might be argued that the success of the ICC has been limited because the ICC struggles to bring wanted suspects to account. But justice is notoriously slow in every Western developed nation. Cases wind their way through the courts for years. The record of the ICC is arguably no worse than the record of courts in Western nations.
- It might be argued that there is no reason to think that domestic authorities would cooperate with UN inspectors, but they clearly cooperated in every

instance cited in chapter 3 where arrest warrants were issued and executed, and the accused were brought to trial.

- It might be argued that the mere existence of international inspectors would not be sufficient to establish a global anticorruption norm. However, 187 nations have already ratified the UNCAC and, thus, 187 nations have agreed to a legally binding agreement to fight corruption. The norm already exists. What is needed is capacity to enforce the norm.
- It might be argued that the anticorruption norm is "new" and securing international cooperation would be difficult. However, the Rome Statute broke a 1,000-year-old pattern that—with few exceptions—reserved prosecution of criminals for domestic courts. The Rome Statute established a powerful legal precedent for the creation of international agreements that permit international prosecutors to step forward when impunity prevails. From this point forward, the 187 nations that are parties to UNCAC can point to the Rome Statute as a model for an international agreement to fight corruption. The anticorruption norm may be relatively "new" but there is now a powerful legal precedent for APUNCAC.
- It might be argued that corrupt elites will have every incentive to block cooperation with UN inspectors. But those elites have every incentive to block ICC inspectors as well. While they have delayed the progress of ICC inspectors, they have been unable to stop inspectors from arresting the suspects in the cases cited in chapter 3.
- It might be argued that few states suffer from insurgency and, thus, it is not reasonable to subject large numbers of states to anticorruption inspections. However, APUNCAC would be voluntary, not imposed by some external force. Only voluntary nations would be subjected to anticorruption inspections.
- It might be argued that states where the rule of law is strong would not be willing to submit themselves to supranational supervision, leaving only weak rule of law states as parties to APUNCAC, undermining the legitimacy of inspections. However, inspections could never be "imposed" on unwilling nations because international treaties are voluntary agreements. Only willing nations would sign and ratify APUNCAC. They would do so only if their citizens believe APUNCAC is a legitimate approach for reducing corruption.
- It might be argued that local leaders may mobilize nationalistic arguments against an agreement permitting international inspectors. However, citizens who are fed up with government corruption might see international inspections as a welcome antidote to corrupt rule.
- It might be argued that a weakness of APUNCAC is that it relies on domestic prosecutors and courts to try and convict individuals arrested for corruption. However, as described in chapter 3, international inspectors in

> Guatemala were successful in exposing corrupt prosecutors and judges and forcing their resignations. APUNCAC would require signatory parties to establish a system of courts and prosecutors dedicated to the adjudication and swift resolution of corruption charges. These dedicated courts would be funded by the UN and would include checks and balances to ensure they are only served by honest, competent judges and prosecutors. The dedicated courts would prioritize charges submitted by UN inspectors and would ensure the swift resolution of resulting cases. APUNCAC seeks to multiply the influence of public pressure through provisions where periodic updates would be published by Transparency International. Prosecutors and courts that seek to thwart justice and the rule of law would be exposed and tried in the court of public opinion.

APUNCAC would establish a mechanism where parties to the treaty would be compelled to prosecute corrupt government officials or face public condemnation. The United States and its allies may support APUNCAC as a means of addressing government corruption in developing nations that promotes resentment, extremism, and terrorism. The establishment of international inspectors who would aggressively combat corruption among government officials around the world would serve to address a root cause of dissatisfaction that gives life to insurgency. APUNCAC offers a promising strategy to address corruption; neutralize the bitterness, resentment, and conflict that leads to violent extremism, terrorism, and insurgency; and reduce the need to employ U.S. military forces to fight unpopular wars in distant lands.

Chapter 6

Six Theories

Chapter 6 seeks to place APUNCAC in the context of current thinking regarding "what works" in promoting economic and social development in developing countries. Chapter 6 suggests that while APUNCAC is logical, sensible, and well aligned with current thinking, existing theorists overlook this option, focusing instead on tangential factors.

The analysis begins by reviewing evidence suggesting the importance of governance and institutions in explaining differences in per capita income across countries. The most important factor influencing economic growth is governance, defined as institutions and policies that influence the rule of law, property rights, and economic freedom. The primary factor undermining the rule of law, property rights, and economic freedom in Africa is uncontrolled corruption, suggesting the need to establish a powerful international institution with the capacity to investigate and deter corruption. Chapter 6 analyzes current theories of the failure of Africa to develop, suggests that these theories overlook the need to establish a powerful international institution to fight corruption,[1] and addresses key objections that might be raised regarding the establishment of a strong institutional capacity to fight corruption.

THE RULE OF LAW, PROPERTY RIGHTS, AND ECONOMIC FREEDOM

Harvard economist Robert Barro analyzed major factors hypothesized to influence economic growth in a panel of 87 countries, using data from the Penn World Tables and the World Bank.[2] His regression model strongly predicted the economic growth rates of the top 20 and bottom 20 countries. The low-performing group included 18 African countries. The results strongly suggest the importance of the rule of law. Significantly, the rule of law appears to be more important than democracy. Barro concluded that

> Even if a poor country could beat the odds and sustain democratic institutions, there is no reason to believe that this accomplishment would help much in the quest to escape poverty. . . . An increase in democracy is less important than an expansion of the rule of law as a stimulus for economic growth and investment. In addition, democracy does not seem to have a strong role in fostering the rule of law. Thus, one cannot argue that democracy is critical for growth because democracy is a prerequisite for the rule of law. . . . If a poor country has a limited amount of resources to accomplish institutional reforms, then they are much better spent in attempting to implement the rule of law. . . . Even if democracy is the principal objective in the long run, the best way to accomplish it may be to encourage the rule of law in the short run.[3]

Barro links the rule of law to property rights: "The assumption is that an improvement in the rule of law . . . implies enhanced property rights and, therefore, an incentive for higher investment and growth."[4] In addition, Barro found that his variables measuring economic freedom were significant: government consumption as a proportion of gross domestic product (GDP), international openness, and inflation.[5] Thus, Barro's results suggest the influence of the rule of law, property rights, and economic freedom on economic growth rates.[6]

On average, countries where the rule of law predominates, property rights are protected, and economic freedom is high outperform countries with weak rule of law, weak protections, and limited economic freedom.[7] The reason is that economic performance is determined mostly by the structure of the incentives that face entrepreneurs, which depends "on the legal systems that enforce contracts and protect property rights and on political structures, constitutional provisions, and the extent of special-interest lobbies and cartels."[8] When property rights are protected and the scope of economic freedom is high, entrepreneurs can exploit market opportunities that would otherwise be unexploited. Rapid exploitation of available opportunities generates wealth that creates demand for products and services, expands market opportunities for other entrepreneurs, and fosters economic growth.

Thus, the critical issue is to identify the policies that are most effective in promoting the rule of law, protection of property rights, and expansion of economic freedom. The next section presents an analysis of the problem of corruption in Africa. This analysis suggests that domestic law enforcement systems have been compromised, implying that an effective intervention must involve international inspectors.

THE NEED FOR A TREATY

The interested reader will find voluminous accounts of the corruption that has characterized African states since independence.[9] As described in chapter 2, the primary catalyst for corruption is a lack of accountability among the ruling elite, who use their monopoly on unchecked discretionary power for personal economic and political gain. Corruption persists because public officials have no fear of being held accountable for their actions. In many African countries, corruption pervades the institutions that normally provide checks and balances: the police, judiciary, and the legal system.[10] Thus, it is not possible to rely on those institutions to fight corruption.

Previous studies regarding the political economy of corruption in Africa suggest that governance institutions that would normally fight corruption are corrupted by a "shadow" state operating through a web of personal and political relationships, informal concessions, and negotiated privileges. In many countries, government has become little more than a system of organized crime.[11] In countries such as Nigeria, those in power have used the machinery of the state both to enrich themselves personally and to aid the groups that support them.[12] Thus, rent-seeking by officials at the highest levels of government has now become a prime suspect in explaining disappointing economic growth.[13] The power exercised by the shadow state overwhelms conventional strategies for fighting corruption. Nigeria has laws against corruption, but they have had little impact, and history suggests that removal of a head of state is not sufficient to generate meaningful reform, implying that the introduction of democratic elections is not a panacea.[14] Africa's ruling elites co-opt structural adjustment programs and economic and political reforms mandated by the World Bank and IMF in ways that serve to reinforce neopatrimonialism and channel resources to leaders and their supporters.[15]

Political conflict has become an all-or-nothing struggle to gain access to and exclude others from state resources.[16] This suggests why conventional, purely domestic reforms are inadequate—they fail to address the powerful symbiotic relationships that eviscerate domestic checks and balances against corruption and fail to address the misuse of power exercised by Africa's ruling elites over the distribution of economic and political resources.

Africa scores dramatically lower than any other region of the world on measures of corruption and property rights, suggesting that failures in these areas are indeed binding constraints on economic development in this region.[17] Econometric evidence suggests that corruption has a strong corrosive effect on economic growth.[18] The best econometric evidence, employing statistical techniques to control for reverse causation, suggests that a one SD decrease in the incidence of corruption would cause the growth rate of per capita GDP in African countries to increase by 1.29 to 1.30 percentage points, accounting for the direct effect of corruption on economic growth as well as the indirect effect operating through reduced investment.[19] Thus, "corruption has a large negative and statistically significant impact on the growth rate of income in African countries."[20]

What is debatable is not whether corruption has occurred, or whether it has undermined the rule of law, property rights, economic freedom, and growth, but the nature of the policy that would be most effective in countering corruption. One strategy is exhortation, such as former U.S. president Barack Obama's plea that corrupt countries "have an obligation" to reform themselves.[21] A second strategy is to exhort corrupt countries to implement national integrity systems, involving comprehensive reforms in laws, institutions, and policies that minimize the scope for corruption.[22] A third strategy is to exhort corrupt countries to implement privatization and economic liberalization, in the hope that this will minimize the scope for corruption. In this view, corruption will fade away with time as the role of government is reduced and the private sector and civil society strengthen:

> A major thrust of any effective strategy to reinvigorate the public sector will be to reduce the opportunities for corruption by cutting back on discretionary authority. Policies that lower controls on foreign trade, remove entry barriers for private industry, and privatize state firms in a way that ensures competition—all of these will fight corruption.[23]

As recently as February 2013, the World Bank's own anticorruption website emphasized anticorruption strategies based on economic policy liberalization and enhanced competition:

> Deregulation of prices or other aspects of production or trade are important steps toward reducing opportunities for corruption. Implicit price subsidies, in the form of tax and utility arrears, provide politicians and bureaucrats with discretionary power that is highly subject to abuse. . . . Enhancing competition, especially in concentrated sectors, by lowering barriers to entry, requiring competitive restructuring, and clarifying ownership structures are important elements toward creating a vibrant and corruption free private sector.[24]

However, the continuation of rampant corruption in Africa suggests that these strategies have been ineffective (figure 6.1). The essential problem is that domestic checks and balances on corruption have been compromised. Conventional measures are inadequate largely because the tremendous concentration of political and economic power among African elites has been repeatedly abused for personal enrichment. When faced with investigations led by domestic authorities, this power has been used to purge recalcitrant

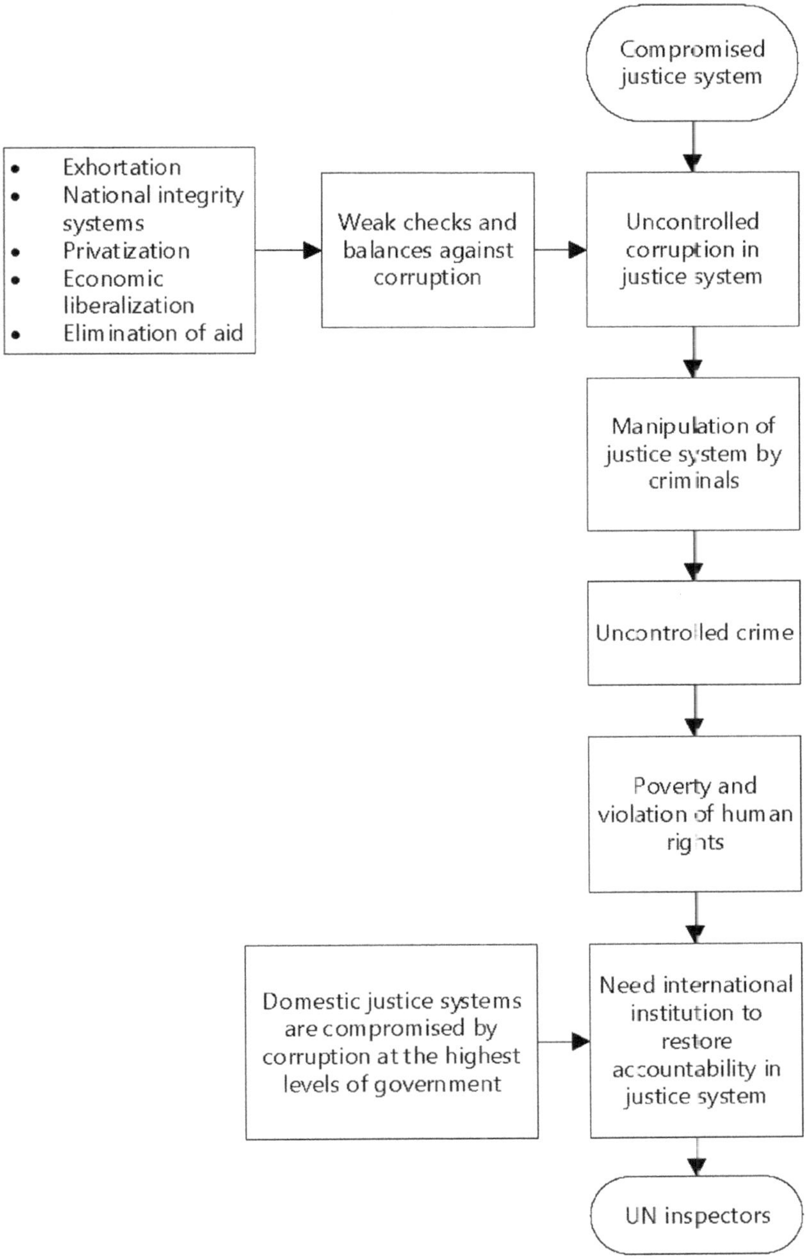

Figure 6.1 Existing Anticorruption Strategies Are Weak Checks against Corruption.
Source: Figure created by author.

officials, such as the purge of the head of Zambia's anticorruption task force after his zealous investigation of former president Frederick Chiluba.[25]

This suggests the need for a different approach. In states where Africans are weary of the ability of corrupt domestic elites to avoid accountability, it may be possible to elicit support for an international treaty that would establish independent UN inspectors who would be empowered to investigate allegations of corruption at the highest levels of government and would be largely immune to pressure exerted by domestic officials. As described in chapters 2 and 3, APUNCAC would establish an ICAC, modeled after Hong Kong's highly successful Independent Commission Against Corruption. APUNCAC would empower UN inspectors to respond to requests by any African citizen to investigate alleged corruption, under the existing legal authority of the UN and the provisions of the UNCAC.[26] APUNCAC aims to provide an independent means of investigating corruption.

SIX THEORIES OF UNDERDEVELOPMENT

While various standards could be used to evaluate theories of underdevelopment in Africa, the standard that I have selected is *usefulness to policymakers*. Thus, the focus is on the practical implications of the theories. While theories are also useful in illuminating alternative ways of viewing issues related to development, policymakers ultimately require concrete recommendations. Theories that lack useful policy guidance may be of interest to academic researchers but are not helpful to policymakers.

A useful theory may be defined as a theory that provides *actionable* recommendations based on a *persuasive* explanation of the *limiting constraint* on development. "Actionable" means actions that are within the control of national or international policymakers. This criterion excludes theories such as Jared Diamond's theory that emphasizes geographic destiny as the determining factor in economic development.[27] "Persuasive" means that the explanation that is offered by the theorist adequately addresses key counterarguments. This criterion requires critical analysis and review of the key counterarguments. The focus on limiting constraints reflects Harvard economist Dani Rodrik's point that there are many potential constraints on economic development but, in regard to a specific state or region at a specific time, there is likely to be only one or two constraints that are truly limiting.[28] If relaxation of the constraint in question would have a strong effect on development, then the constraint is defined as limiting, otherwise it is not limiting. In the absence of an explicit policy experiment where the constraint in question is relaxed, indirect evidence may be deduced from econometric analyses, controlling for reverse causation (such as the research cited above), or from qualitative analyses that persuasively describe the causal process through which the factor in question is believed to constrain output and income, including evidence that the process in question potentially affects a large proportion of the population in a significant way.

A judgment about whether a given theory offers actionable recommendations that would relieve limiting constraints ultimately involves a meta-theory about the range of actions that are possible and whether they would be effective. Thus, it is necessary to go beyond correlations between sets of independent and dependent measures. There may be a strong correlation between "Washington Consensus" policies and economic development in Western democracies, but this information may be useless to policymakers seeking to improve conditions in African states where corrupt officials subvert privatization and economic liberalization to channel wealth to their pockets. Policymakers who attempt to implement Washington Consensus policies in African states are constrained by the existence of corruption.

It may be useful to develop meta-theories about changes in international regimes and policies that would address weaknesses that are inherent in national laws, institutions, and policies. Thus, current theorists agree on the importance of controlling corruption as a prerequisite for the successful implementation of Washington Consensus policies, yet existing research regarding approaches for controlling corruption has focused on changing national, rather than international policies. There is an emphasis on developing "integrity systems" that involve a laundry list of changes in national laws, institutions, and policies, but little research regarding changes in *international* laws, institutions, and policies.[29] The significance of this failure is that changes in national laws, institutions, and policies have not been effective in controlling corruption, largely because corruption in African states routinely involves the highest levels of leadership. Presidential power is routinely used to undermine and subvert integrity systems and anticorruption units. Thus, the evidence suggests a need for international intervention, in the form of changes in international laws, institutions, and policies, to deal with systemic corruption in a way that adequately accounts for the existence and misuse of presidential power in African states. While some may dispute the notion that international action would be more feasible than national-level action, this chapter presents an analysis suggesting why international action may be feasible and why it may be substantially more effective than previous changes in domestic laws, institutions, and policies designed to fight corruption.

With few exceptions, existing theories of underdevelopment in Africa acknowledge the role of corruption in undermining the rule of law, property rights, and economic freedom, contributing to the economic stagnation, poverty, and underdevelopment that has characterized Africa. However, these theories tend to place equal, if not greater emphasis, on other factors. Is it possible to reconcile these theories with the evidence presented above regarding the significance of corruption?

Moyo

Dambisa Moyo has written an influential book that has been sympathetically received by a growing number of development planners and policymakers, including former UN secretary-general Kofi Annan, co-recipient of the 2001 Nobel Peace Prize. Moyo argues that African countries are poor precisely because they have received enormous amounts of foreign aid: "aid is the problem."[30] Moyo argues that aid encourages corruption and conflict because aid is the predominant source of financial resources for much of the African continent, yet it is easy to steal:

> With aid's help, corruption fosters corruption, nations quickly descend into a vicious cycle of aid. Foreign aid props up corrupt governments—providing them with freely usable cash. These corrupt governments interfere with the rule of law, the establishment of transparent civil institutions and the protection of civil liberties, making both domestic and foreign investment in poor countries unattractive. Greater opacity and fewer investments reduce economic growth, which leads to fewer job opportunities and increasing poverty levels. In response to growing poverty, donors give more aid, which continues the downward spiral of poverty.[31]

Moyo argues for the following set of policies: (a) the aid taps should be permanently shut off, (b) African governments should follow the example of Asian countries by raising funds through the international bond market, (c) African governments should encourage the type of large-scale direct investments in infrastructure that the Chinese have pursued in Africa, (d) African governments should press for free trade in agricultural products, and (e) African governments should foster the spread of microfinance institutions.[32] Moyo also argues that poor countries need decisive benevolent dictators to implement the needed reforms, rather than multiparty democracies.

While there is little doubt that aid undermines institutional checks and balances and fosters corruption, an alternative view is that the source of the problem is unchecked corruption, rather than too much aid. If corruption is checked, the downward spiral of poverty that Moyo has described ends.[33] The existence of effective checks on corruption would imply that corrupt individuals could not steal aid; therefore, aid would not be available to prop up corrupt governments. Effective checks on corruption imply that aid could not be diverted for corrupt purposes and could not serve as a source of wealth for corrupt individuals. Presumably, effective checks on corruption would put corrupt individuals in jail or chase them out of office, and would provide a powerful competitive advantage to honest, competent officials, creating the type of good governance that Moyo argues is so important: "Good governance trumps all."[34]

Moyo argues, instead, that the elimination of aid would produce good governance: "a world of good governance . . . will naturally emerge in the absence of the glut of aid."[35] However, there is an inconsistency in this view. From the perspective of a corrupt official, there is nothing about the elimination of aid that would deter corruption. While a corrupt official would have to generate wealth from some other source, such as bribery, kickbacks, and misappropriation of other public funds, a lack of checks and balances against corruption implies that corruption and bad governance would continue, unchecked. Thus, it appears that unchecked corruption is the problem, rather than too much aid.

Moyo argues that African governments should raise funds through the international bond market but notes that "Of the 35-odd African countries that had issued bonds in the international capital markets [by the mid-1990s], virtually all of them defaulted; and in the subsequent thirty years, none of them have returned."[36] This record is overlooked when Moyo recommends that African governments replace foreign aid with bond offerings.[37]

Moyo recommends that African governments encourage large-scale direct investment in infrastructure.[38] However, she also notes that African governments need to strengthen moribund legal and regulatory systems to protect and promote investment: "who would want to invest their money in aid-ridden states where it is easy for others to take property away, either at gunpoint or through corruption."[39] This implies the need for effective checks and balances against corruption and the crime that occurs when police, prosecutors, judges, and anticorruption staff are bribed to look the other way.

Moyo recommends that African governments press for free trade, yet free trade agreements do not address impassable roads, unreliable trains, power blackouts, and spotty telecommunication networks that result when officials give government contracts to their cronies in return for kickbacks and ignore deficiencies in the products and services that are delivered.[40]

Moyo recommends that African governments support microfinance institutions, noting that "entrepreneurs . . . are the life-blood of any economy, and the crucial emerging private sector in poor countries is the engine for private-sector-led growth."[41] While microfinance can be helpful, "entrepreneurs need a receptive and user-friendly environment within which to thrive."[42] In other words, an environment where good governance and the rule of law prevails, where corruption is effectively checked and honest, competent officials are rewarded and promoted.

Moyo argues that African countries "must enforce rules of prudence and not live beyond [their] means," yet the imprudence that has characterized African governance is due to corruption.[43] If officials are corrupt, it seems odd to urge them to enforce rules of prudence.

Acemoglu, Johnson, and Robinson

In 2005, Massachusetts Institute of Technology economist Daron Acemoglu received the John Bates Clark medal, awarded to the most accomplished economist aged under 40.[44] Acemoglu and his coauthors, Simon Johnson and James Robinson, trace underdevelopment to colonial influences: "Extractive systems of production [in many European colonies] concentrated power in the hands of the elite, and built a state apparatus designed to use coercion against the majority of the population."[45] Acemoglu, Johnson, and Robinson (hereafter, "AJR") emphasize the importance of property rights as the institution that has the greatest influence on economic growth, because property rights create incentives to invest in both physical and human capital, to adopt efficient technologies, and to generate wealth.[46] Their conclusions are consistent with IMF and World Bank policies emphasizing privatization and economic liberalization as a means of nurturing the economic power of entrepreneurs so that they may gain the political power necessary to enforce their property rights, and as a means of limiting the rents extracted by corrupt elites:

> First, political institutions that place checks on those who hold political power, for example, by creating a balance of power in society, are useful for the emergence of good economic institutions. This result is intuitive; without checks on political power, power holders are more likely to opt for a set of economic institutions that are beneficial for themselves and detrimental for the rest of society, which will typically fail to protect property rights of a broad cross-section of people. Second, good economic institutions are more likely to arise when political power is in the hands of a relatively broad group with significant investment opportunities. The reason for this result is that, everything else equal, in this case power holders will themselves benefit from secure property rights. Third, good economic institutions are more likely to arise and persist when there are only limited rents that power holders can extract from the rest of society, since such rents would encourage them to opt for a set of economic institutions that make the expropriation of others possible.[47]

Thus, AJR suggest that checks on political power are important and argue that effective checks arise when the economic power of entrepreneurs has grown to the point where entrepreneurs achieve the political power necessary to enforce their property rights against rent-seeking bureaucrats and politicians. AJR support their view by citing the example of Kenyan farmers: "[In Kenya], large farmers . . . have secured public policies that are highly favorable by comparison to those in other nations."[48] AJR conclude that the distribution of political power in society is crucial in determining whether economic institutions are good or bad:

> Commercial interests in England and the Netherlands acquired significant de facto political power as a result of their improving economic fortunes. . . . These commercial interests used their de facto power to reform (or revolutionize) political institutions so as to acquire de jure political power and solidify their gains.[49]

Notably, AJR stop short of making any recommendations at all, concluding that it is premature to offer practical guidance to policymakers:

> Though social science research is of intrinsic interest, one would hope that a convincing fundamental theory of comparative growth based on institutions would lead to policy conclusions that would help us improve the institutions and thus the lives and welfare of people in poor countries. It should be obvious that, at the moment, we are a long way from being in a position to draw such conclusions.[50]

While it might be argued that building the economic power of entrepreneurs is as important as investigating and prosecuting corruption, case studies of Sierra Leone suggest that privatization and economic liberalization are simply ineffective when corrupt elites operate outside the law.[51] If the greatest barrier to economic development in Africa is that corrupt elites operate outside the law to channel wealth to their own pockets, then privatization and economic liberalization, in the absence of vigorous investigation and prosecution of corruption, may simply become additional tools used by elites to amass wealth.

Rodrik

Harvard economist Dani Rodrik suggests that development economists often make specific policy recommendations without considering whether the constraint that is addressed through those recommendations is a truly binding constraint:

> One of the professional deformations of economists is to see an economy's problems almost exclusively from the perspective of their own area of specialty. A trade theorist will turn to developing economies and see lack of openness to

> trade as the key obstacle to growth. A financial market economist will identify imperfections in credit markets and lack of financial depth as the main culprit. A macroeconomist will worry about budget deficits, levels of debt, and inflation. A political-economy specialist will blame weakness in property rights and other institutions. A labor economist will point to labor-market rigidities. Each of them will then advocate a demanding set of institutional and governance reforms targeted at removing the presumed defect. . . . Rarely will the advisor ask whether the problem at hand constitutes a truly binding constraint on economic growth, and whether the long list of institutional reforms on offer are well targeted at the economy's present needs. But governments are constrained by limits on their resources—financial, administrative, human, and political. They have to make choices on which constraints to attack first and what kind of reforms to spend political capital on. What they need is not a laundry list, but an explicitly diagnostic approach that identifies priorities based on local realities.[52]

Rodrik draws a distinction between universal *principles* of sound economic management and the set of specific "Washington Consensus" *policies* that are frequently advocated.[53] In Rodrik's view, the universal principles of sound management include *property rights* and the *rule of law*, but these objectives can be achieved in many ways, some of which are inconsistent with the specific policies that are labeled "Washington Consensus."[54] Policies in East and Southeast Asian countries such as Japan, China, India, South Korea, and Taiwan departed significantly from Washington Consensus policies emphasizing privatization and economic liberalization, yet those countries experienced remarkable increases in GDP over four decades.[55] As a result, "Few are now convinced that liberalization, deregulation, and privatization on their own hold the key to unleashing economic growth."[56] Rodrik argues that a reasonably competent and noncorrupt government is an essential prerequisite for the success of market-oriented reform strategies.[57] To the extent that corruption is rampant in Africa, undermining property rights and the rule of law, corruption may constitute a binding constraint on economic growth in this region and policies targeting this constraint may be especially important.

Easterly

Former World Bank economist William Easterly suggests that "Lack of feedback is one of the most critical flaws in existing aid."[58] "The needs of the poor don't get met because the poor have little money or political power with which to make their needs known and they cannot hold anyone accountable to meet those needs."[59] Thus, he suggests a menu of piecemeal, decentralized reforms emphasizing accountability to the poor. For example, GlobalGiving .com is an internet website and company that matches social entrepreneurs proposing projects to help the poor with donors who wish to fund those projects and individuals and institutions that wish to provide technical assistance.[60] Easterly suggests a system where projects could compete for funds from potential donors based on their merits and the prior performance of project leaders. This approach might avoid manipulation and corruption of aid by recipient governments. In addition, Easterly suggests a second approach, involving the use of vouchers that the poor could redeem at any aid agency for any development good they desired, such as vaccinations, life-saving drugs, a health worker's visit, an improved cook stove, textbooks, seeds, fertilizer, or food supplements.[61]

> Since the poor would be choosing which agency would deliver the goods, the agencies would feel competitive pressure to deliver results. . . . Any agency that was not delivering what the poor wanted would see its budget go down. . . . The poor would be firmly in charge, giving feedback on what they did and did not want from the aid agencies.[62]

It seems likely that both approaches could improve outcomes. However, neither approach would eliminate corruption. Even if aid is channeled in a way that bypasses corrupt officials, they could simply turn to other avenues to amass wealth. Approaches such as GlobalGiving.com and voucher programs may help to insulate aid from corrupt officials but would not obviate the need to combat corruption.

Sachs

Columbia University economist Jeffrey Sachs is a special adviser to UN secretary-general António Guterres on the UN's Sustainable Development Goals and author of *The End of Poverty*. Sachs argues that a massive infusion of aid is needed to push poor countries out of a poverty trap:

> When people are . . . utterly destitute, they need their entire income, or more, just to survive. There is no margin of income above survival that can be invested for the future. This is the main reason why the poorest of the poor are most prone to becoming trapped with low or negative economic growth rates. They are too poor to save for the future and thereby accumulate the capital that could pull them out of their current misery.[63]

Few economists would disagree with the assertion that widespread poverty hinders growth. In the poorest African countries, much of the population scratches out a subsistence living on small rural farms. These farmers have low savings rates, limiting investment and economic growth, and are unable to provide an adequate source of demand for products and services in the nonfarm sector. However, most economic models of growth (and most poor countries) include a small modern sector that generates savings, investment, and growth that draws workers from the subsistence sector. Thus, there is in principle no reason why even very poor countries cannot escape widespread poverty.

Easterly tested Sachs's hypothesis that a poverty trap keeps poor countries poor.[64] Contrary to this hypothesis, Easterly found that the poorest fifth of countries in 1950 increased their incomes by a factor of 2.25, statistically indistinguishable from the growth of the other four-fifths, which increased by a factor of 2.47 over the same period.[65] Easterly tested and rejected the assumption that the income of the poorest countries stagnates at a low level.[66] This result holds even after controlling for the level of foreign aid: "Poor countries without aid had no trouble having positive growth."[67] Most telling, Easterly points out that 11 of the 28 poorest countries in 1985 were not in the poorest fifth back in 1950: "They got into poverty by declining from above, rather than being stuck in it from below, while others escaped," which is inconsistent with the hypothesis of a trap.[68] Finally, economists Aart Kraay and Claudio Raddatz found that data regarding the savings rate in poor countries is inconsistent with the hypothesis of a poverty trap.[69] Easterly found, instead, that

> When we control both for initial poverty and for bad government, it is bad government that explains the slower growth. We cannot statistically discern any effect of initial poverty on subsequent growth once we control for bad government. This is still true if we limit the definition of bad government to corruption alone. The recent stagnation of the poorest countries appears to have more to do with awful government than with a poverty trap, contrary to the UN/Sachs hypothesis.[70]

Thus, the binding constraint on economic growth appears to be bad government, that is, corruption, rather than poverty. Easterly concluded that the hypothesis that poor countries are poor because they are stuck in a poverty trap from which they cannot emerge without a big push from foreign aid is not supported by the empirical evidence.[71]

Collier

Economist Paul Collier previously served as director of the World Bank's development research group and has written an influential book regarding the failure of poor countries to develop.[72] Collier focuses on the "bottom billion" of the poor, the vast majority of whom are in Africa, and argues that poor countries tend to fall into four traps.

The first trap is military conflict. Collier uses statistical data to argue that civil war is much more likely to break out in low-income countries, controlling for reverse causality.[73] He suggests that "Wars and coups keep low-income countries from growing and hence keep them dependent upon exports of primary commodities. Because they stay poor, stagnant, and dependent upon primary commodities they are prone to wars and coups."[74] Thus, poor countries become trapped in a cycle of conflict and poverty. However, the reasoning appears somewhat circular: poverty causes conflict, which causes the continuation of poverty. Without a theory about how to reduce poverty or how to reduce conflict, this view does not offer actionable recommendations about ways that policymakers could reduce poverty or reduce conflict to break out of the trap. If conflict arises when uncontrolled corruption sabotages equitable distribution of the economic pie, then a root cause of conflict may be corruption, suggesting the importance of reforms aimed at controlling corruption.

Collier's second trap is the "natural resource" trap, which has also been labeled a "resource curse": "The heart of the resource curse is that resource rents make democracy malfunction."[75] In this view, wealth from natural resources is easily misused by leaders to bribe voters, fostering corruption that hinders economic growth. However, the implication is that the natural resource trap ends with the implementation of effective checks that prevent the use of national wealth to steal votes. This implies that the underlying problem is uncontrolled corruption, not natural resource wealth. According to this view, the natural resource curse would be eliminated once effective checks against corruption are installed. If so, the second trap is more accurately labeled "uncontrolled corruption" rather than a "natural resource" trap. Interestingly, Collier presents evidence that supports this interpretation: stronger checks and balances on political power significantly improve the effect of resource rents on economic growth.[76] Thus, his own evidence supports the interpretation that the problem is uncontrolled corruption rather than a "natural resource" trap.

Collier's third trap is "landlocked with bad neighbors."[77] Collier gives the example of Uganda, which depends on Kenya's transport system for access to seaports.[78] However, this thesis is contradicted by the historical record. In the period surrounding independence, between 1960 and 1965, Uganda's booming exports of coffee, cotton, and tea led the state to the highest per capita growth rate in East Africa.[79] The new prime minister, Milton Obote, quickly abrogated the constitution and installed himself as president, endowed with enormous powers which he used to crush opposition to his rule. Idi Amin's coup in 1971 led to eight years of death squads, 250,000 deaths, plundering of the state treasury, and expulsion of 50,000 Asians who represented a large proportion of the nation's doctors, bankers, managers, and technicians and were responsible for much of the state's trade and industry.[80] The result was a 40 percent reduction in state revenues. Uganda was left ravaged, lawless, and bankrupt. Obote regained power through disputed elections, plunging Uganda into civil war, resulting in 300,000 civilian deaths, and making the state among the poorest in the world.[81] This record suggests that corrupt misuse of power was the cause of Uganda's dramatic collapse from economic prosperity into poverty, which is inconsistent with Collier's thesis of a trap due to geographic location.

Collier's fourth trap is "bad governance in a small country." He argues that "terrible governance and policies can destroy an economy with alarming speed."[82] Few would disagree with this assessment. Collier advocates the establishment of new international laws to provide reformers "with an instrument with which to berate poor governance."[83] But what is needed are vigorous measures to investigate and deter corruption, rather than instruments to "berate poor governance."

DISCUSSION

The views of the six development theorists examined here are consistent with the notion that bad governance plays a key role in explaining why poor countries remain poor. Moyo traces the problem to aid-fueled corruption.[84] AJR trace the problem to a lack of effective checks and balances on the abuse of power.[85] Rodrik argues that a reasonably competent and noncorrupt government is an essential prerequisite for the success of market-oriented reform strategies and, furthermore, that property rights and the rule of law are essential for sustained economic growth.[86] Easterly concludes that after controlling both for initial poverty and for bad government, it is bad governance that explains slower growth.[87] Collier argues that bad governance is one of four traps that keep poor countries poor.[88] And, while Sachs argues that initial levels of poverty create a trap that is difficult to escape, Easterly's data demonstrate that it is bad governance—not poverty—that explains slower growth.[89]

African countries are especially vulnerable to corruption because economic and political power is concentrated in the head of state.[90] Checks and balances against the misuse of power were largely removed or negated by colonial authorities prior to independence.[91] This unbalanced power structure was then transferred to African leaders.[92] The significance is that—unlike in Western developed countries—it is not possible to rely on domestic law enforcement agencies to provide effective checks on corruption. Domestic agencies are dominated by the power exerted by African leaders and elites. Since political and economic power in African states has been concentrated in a way that overwhelms domestic law enforcement, the implication is that only international investigators who are resistant to pressure from powerful African elites can provide an effective check on African corruption. Since the UN is the only international institution with sufficient moral authority, resources, and the ability to field a large force of independent investigators who are resistant to pressure from powerful African elites, the UN arguably must create the capacity to conduct independent investigations. Viewed from this perspective, the UN can play an important role in reducing the corruption that is at the heart of bad governance in Africa.

It is useful to critique the six theories of underdevelopment discussed above. Arguably, these theories overlook the potential of independent criminal investigations as an effective check against corruption. Moyo's theory of aid-fueled corruption overlooks the possibility that effective criminal investigations would check corruption and end the downward spiral she describes, regardless of the presence of aid.[93] Arguably, corruption would continue in the absence of effective criminal investigations, even if all aid is discontinued to poor countries. AJR agree that checks and balances against the abuse of power are essential, but their emphasis on the role of the private sector suggests that, in their view, the most effective check on corruption may be the development of a powerful bloc of commercial interests to enforce property rights.[94] Rodrik argues that economists typically fail to identify the binding constraint with regard to the countries in question, but he does not identify corruption as a binding constraint with regard to Africa nor does he offer suggestions for fighting corruption.[95] Easterly concludes that bad governance explains slow growth in this region, and Collier concludes that bad governance is one explanation for slow growth, but they neglect the possibility that international institutions might provide an independent body of inspectors to curb corruption, preserve property rights, and promote economic freedom.[96] Sachs omits the connection between bad governance and slow growth, which Easterly's analysis demonstrates is more important than any connection between poverty and slow growth.[97]

Why have development theorists overlooked the possibility of international investigations? First, there is a perception that this would infringe on national sovereignty and would not be permitted. The presumption of national sovereignty over law enforcement appears to preclude consideration of international investigations. Second, African leaders would have to agree to investigations. If it is true that corruption frequently infects the highest levels of government in Africa, there would have to be powerful countervailing factors motivating African leaders to accept investigations.

However, chapter 2 described the precedent set by the Rome Statute of the ICC. The Rome Statute created an international body of criminal investigators and endowed the investigators with the same broad powers to conduct independent investigations on domestic territory that are envisioned for UN inspectors. The process by which the Rome Statute was established provides a model for establishing a UN inspectorate. The UN General Assembly established a committee that drafted the Rome Statute, leading to adoption and ratification by 123 nations. The same process could be pursued to establish a UN inspectorate.

Chapters 2, 3, and 5 addressed a range of objections that might be raised regarding the proposed treaty. A major question is whether African leaders could be persuaded to agree to international investigations. However, surveys of African citizens routinely find strong support for the fight against corruption and new leaders are frequently elected based on promises to fight corruption.[98] Thus, it may not be difficult to make a commitment to participate in international investigations an election issue that would compel incumbents and opposition candidates to publicly announce their support. Failure to follow through on these commitments would risk public censure and removal at the next election.

Once inspectors are permitted to investigate allegations of corruption, public officials may find it difficult to survive published reports of their misdeeds. Significantly, a natural experiment tested the effect of an anticorruption program in Brazil and found that a one SD increase in mayoral corruption, disclosed through random audits of municipal expenditures and posted on the internet, reduced the likelihood that an incumbent mayor would be re-elected by 25 percent.[99] The implementation of a system of UN investigations and the publication of reports regarding corrupt practices might be expected to have a similar influence on elections in Africa.

At present, however, the discourse regarding development in Africa is dominated by theorists who overlook the possibility of international investigations. Perhaps the challenges appear daunting, but it is useful to recall that the ICC was a utopian idea when it was first proposed. While international investigations raise issues of legality and coordination with domestic law enforcement agencies, the Rome Statute provides a powerful precedent suggesting how those issues may be resolved. If so, it may be useful to reorient the discourse to examine these issues and to consider expansion of the UN's role to include the vigorous investigation of corruption.

Chapter 7

The World Bank/IMF View

It is not controversial to assert that corruption is deeply engrained and undermines development in Africa. What is debatable, however, is the most effective approach for addressing corruption. This chapter examines the views of the World Bank and the IMF, as revealed in statements by senior World Bank and IMF economists. While the World Bank and IMF do not formally take a stance on the topic of corruption, a remarkably consistent stance may be inferred by explicit statements that have been made by senior officials and statements published on official World Bank and IMF websites. This stance emphasizes privatization and economic liberalization as the most effective means of reducing corruption.

If the World Bank and IMF had little influence on African countries, the views of their senior economists would primarily be of academic interest. However, these institutions have assumed a dominant—some would say hegemonic—role in dictating conditions that produced wrenching economic and social changes throughout Africa. These conditions were tied to massive World Bank and IMF loans necessary to keep poverty-stricken nations from sliding into destitution and famine.

For these reasons, it is important to examine the assumptions upon which the views of senior World Bank and IMF economists are based. If the assumptions are incorrect, and if World Bank and IMF policies are based on incorrect assumptions, then there may exist an alternative set of policies that would be more effective in addressing the underdevelopment that has characterized Africa for the past 50 years.

At the core of this argument is the observation that all Western developed countries deter corruption through vigorous investigation and prosecution, rather than privatization and economic liberalization. It is apparent that investigation and prosecution must be central to any strategy for controlling corruption. However, while Western countries rely on domestic institutions to investigate and prosecute corruption, the concentration of unchecked political and economic power in African states neuters domestic capacity to control corruption. There is a need for an international institution to assume this role. Since the UN is the only international institution with sufficient moral authority, resources, and ability to field a large force of independent investigators who are resistant to pressure from powerful African elites, a logical conclusion is that the UN must create the capacity to conduct independent investigations.

This chapter begins with an examination of the views of the World Bank and the IMF, as revealed in statements by senior World Bank and IMF economists and statements published on official World Bank and IMF websites. The chapter reviews the origin, nature, and scope of corruption in Africa, and suggests why domestic law enforcement institutions are overmatched by corruption, why the rule of law is weak, and why World Bank/IMF reliance on privatization and economic liberalization is misplaced. The chapter illustrates the problem through a case study of Sierra Leone and concludes that the monopoly on political and economic power that is exercised by African leaders fatally undermines domestic efforts to control corruption, requiring an international response involving vigorous investigations led by UN inspectors into allegations of corruption.

THE WORLD BANK/IMF VIEW

Historically, the IMF and the World Bank have traced poor economic growth in Africa to misguided dirigisme—the practice of directing economic activity through central planning—and have tied structural adjustment conditions to their loans in an attempt to restructure African economies in the mold of Western industrialized countries.[1] This view is exemplified by a special World Bank publication devoted to the role of the state, as well as the view of Martin Wolf, former senior economist at the World Bank for 10 years:

> Most developing countries in Asia, the Middle East, and Africa came out of the colonial period with a strong belief in state-dominated economic development. The state would mobilize resources and people and direct them toward rapid growth and the eradication of social injustice. State control of the economy, following the example of the Soviet Union, was central to this strategy. . . . By the 1960s states had become involved in virtually every aspect of the economy, administering prices and increasingly regulating labor, foreign exchange, and financial markets. By the 1970s the costs of this strategy were coming home to roost.[2]

> Working as an economist (of the World Bank) on east Africa between 1972 and 1974 and then on India between 1974 and 1977, I learned first-hand of the damage done by dirigiste, inward-looking economic policies. This was not only because of the grotesque inefficiency, but also because of the epidemic of corruption they caused. Throughout my ten years at the Bank, I was principally engaged in arguing for greater reliance on the market mechanism and trade.[3]

In contrast, prominent African economists identify the core problem as uncontrolled corruption—the abuse of governmental power for personal gain—rather than dirigisme and explain that the preoccupation with dirigisme is itself misguided and leads to counterproductive policy prescriptions.[4]

The IMF and the World Bank acknowledge the existence of corruption but view it as an unintended consequence of earlier experiments with centralized economic planning.

> The transition from socialism . . . [has been marked by administrative corruption and] has introduced scope in some nations for powerful interests to influence the structure of state institutions and the formulation and implementation of economic policy to their own advantage. This ingrained tendency toward state intervention . . . creates the potential for corruption.[5]

> This paper views corruption largely as a *symptom* of weaknesses in economic structures and institutions, considered to be the *origin* of much of what is perceived as corruption in the public sector. Furthermore, the paper finds that once these weaknesses are defined and somehow "measured," they tend to provide a stronger link to economic performance than do measures of real or perceived corruption. Thus although corrupt behavior should always be addressed head-on by administrative means, the design of economic policies to deal with the phenomenon called "corruption" is best pursued through structural and institutional reform.[6]

In this view, corruption will fade away with time as the role of government is reduced and the private sector and civil society strengthen:

> A major thrust of any effective strategy to reinvigorate the public sector will be to reduce the opportunities for corruption by cutting back on discretionary authority. Policies that lower controls on foreign trade, remove entry barriers for private industry, and privatize state firms in a way that ensures competition—all of these will fight corruption.[7]

The World Bank's own anticorruption website emphasized anticorruption strategies based on economic policy liberalization and enhanced competition:

> Deregulation of prices or other aspects of production or trade are important steps toward reducing opportunities for corruption. Implicit price subsidies, in the form of tax and utility arrears, provide politicians and bureaucrats with discretionary power that is highly subject to abuse. . . . Enhancing competition, especially in concentrated sectors, by lowering barriers to entry, requiring competitive restructuring, and clarifying ownership structures are important elements toward creating a vibrant and corruption free private sector.[8]

In the World Bank's view, good governance and strong institutions are best developed through economic liberalization and competition, regulatory reform, improvements in transparency, instruments for increased voice, and transnational cooperation to fight corruption, because fundamental economic reforms remove the conditions that give rise to corruption in the first place and, therefore, are believed to be most effective over the long run:

> The ability of powerful economic interests to capture the state can be constrained by: (i) economic policy liberalization; (ii) introducing greater competition, especially in concentrated sectors, by lowering barriers to entry, requiring competitive restructuring, and clarifying ownership structures; (iii) regulatory reform at all levels; (iv) a stronger and more transparent framework for corporate governance; (v) instruments of voice for business associations, trade unions, and concerned parties; and (vi) transnational cooperation.[9]

IMF policies are aligned with the policies of the World Bank and reflect the World Bank's views. For example, senior IMF directors George Abed and Sanjeev Gupta examined the relationship between governance, corruption, and economic growth. A section of their report, titled "The Role of the IMF," states that the IMF's policy is to fight corruption by implementing economic liberalization and structural reforms (i.e., privatization of state assets):

> The IMF is contributing to strengthening governance in member countries through various means. The first is by *supporting economic policies and structural reforms* that limit the scope for ad hoc decision making, for rent seeking, and for preferential treatment of individuals or organizations. This approach is founded on the IMF's mandate to promote macroeconomic stability, and limits its role to those aspects of governance that could have a significant macroeconomic impact. . . . Increasing the reliance on market-based pricing and creating a sound regulatory environment should help in lowering corruption. . . . The IMF's emphasis on deregulation, liberalization, privatization, and its technical assistance aimed at strengthening the budgetary process and institution building, help improve economic governance and reduce opportunities for rent-seeking behavior.[10]

Abed and IMF economist Hamid Davoodi assert that economic performance is fundamentally dependent on economic liberalization and privatization, rather than direct prosecution of corruption:

> It is the hypothesis of this paper that . . . economic performance . . . is related fundamentally to the achievement of these structural and institutional reforms and only incidentally to the degree to which corruption may have been reduced. Indeed, this paper claims that corruption per se (as measured by the widely used corruption perception indices) has much weaker explanatory power than variables measuring structural and institutional reforms.[11]

In May 2016, Christine Lagarde, the former managing director of the IMF, published an essay denying what is now voluminous quantitative evidence regarding the negative effect of corruption on economic growth:[12]

> In this essay, I would like to share the IMF's perspective on the economic impact of corruption and our experience in helping countries design and implement strategies to address it. . . . Clearly, causation is difficult to establish and, in quantitative analysis, a significant effect of corruption on growth has not been found (Svensson 2005).[13]

Lagarde reiterated the IMF position that the source of corruption is overregulation and, therefore, economic liberalization is an effective strategy to reduce corruption:

> Because an over-regulated economy provides opportunities for regulators to demand bribes, corruption creates a strong incentive to delay economic liberalisation and innovation. . . . Wherever discretion is granted to an official regarding the approval of an economic activity, there is a risk that this discretion will be abused. Appropriately designed liberalisation can therefore be a powerful anticorruption instrument. As part of its core mandate, the Fund has been actively engaged in encouraging liberalisation of trade, price and financial systems.[14]

Thus, senior IMF and World Bank directors and economists favor privatization, structural adjustment, and economic liberalization as the most effective means to remove the distortions introduced by government, minimize opportunities for corruption, and maximize economic growth in countries previously characterized by dirigisme.[15] A strong private sector is expected to demand governmental accountability and economic reform, and strengthened civil institutions are expected to institute checks and balances.[16] These improvements in governance are, in turn, expected to lay the foundation for vibrant economic competition, an efficient business sector, and strong economic growth. Direct prosecution of corruption is viewed as helpful but tangential to the core problem of dirigisme.

ORIGIN AND NATURE OF CORRUPTION IN AFRICA

In contrast to the views of IMF and World Bank economists, Africa specialists suggest that corruption in Africa has its origin in colonial practices; has been deeply ingrained as a self-reinforcing, self-perpetuating institution; and has fundamentally captured governmental institutions in African countries in a way that insulates corrupt practices from ordinary reforms.[17] Colonial administrators dismantled traditional checks and balances to centralize power in their own hands and the hands of a small number of local chiefs, colonial appointees, and acculturated elites shaped by the colonial educational system.[18] Local chiefs became accustomed to the exercise of absolute rule, without judicial restraint, as long as they enjoyed the confidence of the colonial administrator:

> It is the chief who has the right to make a bylaw governing his locality, who assesses the value of your petty property and therefore how much tax you must pay, who comes to collect that tax, who fines you if you fail to pay that tax, who jails you if you fail to pay the tax and the fine, who decides where you labor when in jail, and who releases you upon termination of the sentence. The chief is the petty legislator, administrator, judge, and policeman all in one. Every moment of power—legislative, executive, judicial and administrative—is combined in this one official.[19]

This system invited abuses. A chief could requisition the third child of every subject as personal servants.[20] Women were ruthlessly appropriated.[21] Forced tribute was systematically extorted from the entire population under each chief's control, for personal enrichment.[22] Thus, colonial practices institutionalized favoritism, aggrandizement, and despotic rule, essentially training African elites in the methods of favoritism, the exercise of unbridled power, and personal enrichment.[23] This legacy was to have disastrous results in the postcolonial period when the same elites replaced colonial administrators and re-applied well-learned lessons about the exercise of power.[24]

The central fact of postcolonial Africa is the tremendous concentration of economic and political power in each head of state. This concentration of power is a legacy of the French and British colonial practice of centralizing governmental power in the colonial head and his trusted elites.[25] The transfer of this power to African heads of state had disastrous results upon independence.[26] After the transfer of power, Africa's autocrats quickly discovered that they could use their combined economic and political power to direct economic activity, enrich themselves, reward political supporters, punish political rivals, and crush opposition to their rule.[27]

This view suggests that the source of the problem of corruption in Africa is the colonial policy of dismantling traditional checks and balances on the power of rulers. Colonial governments used their power to extract wealth from their colonies, then transferred this power to African rulers upon independence, where it was abused on a grand scale.

The primary catalyst for corruption is a lack of accountability among the ruling elite, who use their monopoly on unchecked discretionary power for personal economic and political gain. Corruption is not only caused by a lack of checks and balances but also serves to prevent the emergence of the institutional reforms necessary to create checks and balances. In many African countries, corruption pervades the institutions that normally provide checks and balances: the police, judiciary, and the legal system. Thus, it is not possible to rely on those institutions to fight corruption.

Elites sabotage the development of transparent, participatory, democratic accountability structures to preserve their lucrative monopolies on governmental services and privileges. Thus, democratization, privatization, and IMF-style reforms are not panaceas and do not provide checks and balances against the abuse of governmental power. Instead, "the control of corruption . . . is a fundamental condition for the sustainable transition to a market-oriented economy."[28] Barro summarized the evidence and concluded that

> If a poor country has a limited amount of resources to accomplish institutional reforms, then they are much better spent in attempting to implement the rule of law . . . Even if democracy is the principal objective in the long run, the best way to accomplish it may be to encourage the rule of law in the short run.[29]

The persistence of Africa's problems despite democratization, privatization, and IMF reforms is puzzling except when viewed as the logical outcome of a lack of checks and balances. Without checks and balances, aid is wasted, and aid donors unwittingly undermine true reform, the development of strong institutions, and the rule of law.[30]

In this view, corruption is the core problem underlying Africa's poverty. Checks and balances against the abuse of governmental power are inadequate. Consequently, privatization, elections, deregulation, and the introduction of competition are frequently manipulated by those in power in ways that reward allies and punish rivals. The reforms that are required by the IMF and World Bank are often twisted in ways that undermine, rather than promote, the private sector and civil society, and undermine the fight against corruption and underdevelopment. Paradoxically, IMF and World Bank economists continue to advocate privatization, deregulation, and the introduction of competition as the primary means of fighting corruption and promoting economic development in Africa.

THE CASE OF SIERRA LEONE

To illustrate how corrupt leaders subvert privatization, elections, deregulation, and competition to reward allies and punish rivals, I draw upon William Reno's detailed studies of Sierra Leone.[31] These studies illustrate the dynamics of corruption and explain why the IMF's and World Bank's focus on privatization, economic liberalization, and competitive elections is likely to reinforce patrimonialism, exacerbate corruption, and undermine the goals of economic reform and growth. The interested reader will find similar studies for each of the major African countries.[32] In essence, the mechanisms whereby civil society and the mass of private citizens hold leaders accountable in Western democracies and ensure that privatization, economic liberalization, and competitive elections promote good governance are broken in countries such as Sierra Leone. The problem is not weakness that can be strengthened through economic and political liberalization, but the complete domination and manipulation of the rules of the game by those who are in power. This domination requires a different response than has previously been offered by the international community.

The Political Economy of Indirect Rule

Colonial rulers sought to maximize the profits that were extracted from their colonies by establishing systems of indirect rule, where colonial dictates were implemented by local chiefs, who commanded the loyalty of their subjects, to minimize administrative payroll costs. However, the loyalty of the chiefs had to be purchased and enforced by colonial rulers. Over time, rewards and sanctions had to be increased to ensure loyalty. Any disloyalty or inefficiency would increase the time, effort, personnel, and cost required to implement the system of indirect rule. While the costs of the payoffs became substantial, they were outweighed by the profits obtained by colonial rulers. Furthermore, rulers could contain those costs by resorting to harsh sanctions. Thus, powerful incentives drove the development of a system of payoffs linked to despotic rule.

For the same reasons, local chiefs replicated this system of payoffs and despotic rule regarding their subjects. Each chief sought to maximize his current and future stream of profits by selectively allocating privileges to individuals who displayed their loyalty by performing tasks that reinforced the chief's power. This included the use of force to enforce sanctions when subjects strayed. Essentially, the colonial practice of indirect rule institutionalized the use of payoffs and despotism to extract profits from the populace. African chiefs learned the required attitudes and skills at the feet of their masters, then applied the same attitudes and skills on a grand scale after independence.[33]

Controlling Diamond Profits

The raison d'être for establishing African colonies was to extract wealth from natural resources—diamonds, in the case of Sierra Leone. Typically, a colonial government awarded contracts to private firms that extracted, processed, and sold the natural resources, then split the revenue with the government. Thus, in 1932, England awarded a 99-year monopoly on diamond mining to the Sierra Leone Selection Trust (SLST), a subsidiary of DeBeers, in exchange for a 27.5 percent tax on net profits.[34] However, revenues were threatened by illicit miners, whose sales were not taxed and, therefore, eroded the revenue base for the colony. Thus, the SLST monopoly was extended to the entire country and enforced by government laws designed to prevent the establishment of competing operations.[35] Faced with declining state revenues, the Freetown government authorized SLST to field a force of 35 armed men to patrol the mining areas.[36]

The SLST lease clashed with the customary rights of local chiefs, who accepted rents from "illicit" tenant miners in exchange for protection. Believing that chiefs controlled the influx of illicit miners, SLST initiated informal payments of £50 to each chief who agreed to withhold settler rights, beginning a policy of payoffs that expanded over time.[37] To ward off SLST patrols, illicit miners armed themselves with swords and machetes, while local chiefs parlayed their fortunes to finance personal armed forces.[38] In response to these threats, the government implemented the Native Authority Scheme (NAS) of 1937. Local chiefs were enticed to become paid agents of the government through salaries aimed at replacing the "customary" rents that chiefs traditionally received from illicit miners and merchants, with the goal of securing the loyalty and active cooperation of the chiefs in stamping out illicit mining.[39] The NAS greatly increased the chiefs' legal incomes from about £500 per year in the 1930s to enormous amounts (by West African standards) approaching £10,000 by the late 1940s.[40]

Even at this early stage, neither the Freetown government nor the local chiefs desired economic or political competition. Economic and political competition from more actors would have exacerbated the problem of control that each actor faced. The government wished to control the country's diamond industry and maintain the associated stream of tax revenues by paying off the smallest number of chiefs possible, while local chiefs had no interest in splitting their power bases with any other actor. From the perspectives of the key actors, competition in either sphere would simply increase costs and/or reduce revenues and profits. This, in a nutshell, is the reason why IMF and World Bank reform policies are doomed to fail. Reforms designed to increase economic and political competition can only succeed if they benefit the actors who must enact them. If economic and political competition serves instead to undercut the livelihoods of these actors, there is every incentive for these actors to undermine the reforms by intensifying the corrupt arrangements that maximize their profits.

Expansion of Corruption

The Mining Area Development Administration program, ostensibly to channel diamond mining revenues into local development, expanded corruption by channeling enormous £10,000 payments to compliant chiefs for maintaining social order as well as turning out Sierra Leone People's Party (SLPP) voters and harassing Kono Progressive Movement supporters, who were critical of government restrictions on "illicit" diamond mining.[41] With the approval of District Commissioners, chiefdom treasuries increasingly turned state resources over to the chiefs' personal uses in order to buy their support for the colonial government and its policy of stamping out illicit mining.[42] These expensive accommodations drained the treasuries of funds that could otherwise have been invested in development projects, causing Kono citizens to stop paying taxes.[43] The government resorted to vigorous police and SLST security force attacks on illicit miners to collect revenue.[44] The illicit diamond dealers and miners responded by organizing 50-member youth gangs, structured like police riot units, to defend illicit mining operations.[45] Dealers bought food and tools for the miners, paid rents to local chiefs, and gave the miners stakes in return for a share of revenues.[46] Dealers supported the All Peoples Congress (APC) in exchange for APC-organized assaults and intimidation of chiefs attempting to stamp out illicit mining.[47]

After independence, corruption and strong-arm tactics expanded into parliamentary politics, dominated by local chiefs and their descendants seeking to protect the political and economic privileges upon which they had built their power.[48] For example, Paul Dunbar armed a 50-man "action group" to intimidate SLPP rivals and used his family ties to three Kono chieftain ruling houses to mobilize support for Dunbar's candidates for state and chiefdom offices.[49] Once elected, these individuals defended Dunbar's political and economic privileges in Kono.

After consolidating power in 1968, President Siaka Stevens transformed SLST into a new state-owned mining company, the National Diamond

Mining Company (NDMC), so that taxes on profits would flow directly to his control, bypassing state revenue collectors who were siphoning the money for their own uses.[50] Stevens gained control over revenues as well as control over new NDMC administrative positions that he could award to loyal allies. By 1981, at least 10 of Kono's 12 chiefs had been awarded lucrative NDMC management positions.[51]

The creation of NDMC effectively nationalized the distribution of patrimonial resources. Stevens used the authority of the Ministry of Mines to selectively issue licenses to dealers loyal to him, undercutting the loyalty of dealers to local chiefs. Dealers and chiefs quickly learned the consequences of failure to support Stevens. Using these tactics, Stevens isolated recalcitrant strongmen and imposed his control. To unseat the chief of Gbense, at the political heart of Kono, Stevens launched a commission of inquiry to investigate allegations of corruption.[52] When Dunbar mobilized his political network around a candidate opposed to Stevens's choice, Yafenneh Toli, Stevens declared a state of emergency, then issued preventative detention decrees that were used to intimidate campaigns for the rival candidate.[53] Once Toli was elected, he was quickly appointed to an NDMC management position, which he used to raise money to campaign for candidates supporting Stevens.[54]

Stevens installed his allies in key positions and subcontracted the collection of revenues to them, thereby expanding the sources and amounts of revenue. Revenue was no longer limited to the formal collection of the state share of NDMC profits but now included rents paid by diamond dealers (and, thus, a portion of rents paid by illicit miners to diamond dealers). Thus, Stevens co-opted nearly every category of Sierra Leone's economically important strata—illicit miners, diamond dealers, local chiefs, and parliamentary members—to align them in support of his presidency.

Local chiefs now had powerful incentives to cooperate with governmental efforts to control both illicit and legal mining to maximize government revenues and, thus, the resources available for distribution by Stevens. Compliant chiefs were rewarded with lucrative positions on the NDMC board, along with governmental police and paramilitary protection that could be used to extract rents from illicit and legal diamond dealers and miners.[55] Increasingly, chiefs became dependent on revenues and protection that emanated from Stevens, rather than illicit miners and dealers. As a result, the chiefs became allies of Stevens in prosecuting uncooperative illicit miners and dealers.

The 1973 elections were rigged by Stevens and his supporters to rid the APC Party of radicals who posed a threat to Stevens's rule, using the same strategies that he used to elect Toli.[56] Stevens used his ability to control dealer licenses and prosecute out-of-favor dealers to dispense resources to favored allies, undercut and isolate recalcitrant opposition leaders, and impose discipline that few dared to challenge.[57] In cases where these methods proved to be insufficiently persuasive, such as diamond poaching, Stevens utilized the NDMC's paramilitary Internal Security Unit, tagged "I Shoot You" by its victims.[58]

Neither Stevens nor the dealers and politicians who benefited from Stevens's favor had any desire to introduce the type of free market reforms favored by the IMF and World Bank as a device for improving output and income. More competition would have diluted the monopolistic profits of favored dealers who had acquired licenses at great cost, diluting the value of the licenses and, thus, Stevens's ability to control dealers through his monopoly on the issuance of dealer licenses.

Politicians competed for Stevens's favor to gain access to lucrative dealer licenses, mining plots, and NDMC management positions. By 1982, 12 of Kono's 14 chiefs held dealer licenses along with plots for diamond mining, 10 chiefs held NDMC management positions, and all 6 of Kono's members of parliament held licenses or plots.[59] A license enabled the average dealer to gross approximately $500,000 in one mining season, from January to June.[60] Importantly, dealer licenses permitted chiefs and politicians not only to make money but also to convert the money, along with rents collected through exploitation of their official positions, into purchases of diamonds.[61] The proceeds of diamonds sold abroad for foreign currency could then be deposited in foreign bank accounts, safe from the possibility of confiscation in the event of a fall from favor.[62]

Erosion of Checks and Balances

The exploitation of official positions extended to the court system. Gbense merchants complained that the paramount chief maintained "star chamber courts," where his relatives were appointed to adjudicate and impose fines on litigants.[63] This revenue was split between the chief and his relatives. Thus, gross violations of the law and blatant misuse of power eroded the system of checks and balances that Western democracies rely upon to counter corrupt individuals.

The introduction of elections, rather than instilling democratic control by the populace over its elected leaders, merely served as another tool in Stevens's arsenal to discipline and control rivals as well as supporters. Stevens used his powers to control the process of nominating and electing candidates for office. To maintain a level of job insecurity for every elected official that reinforced compliance with his desires, Stevens used the same tactics that were effective in deposing the chief of Gbense and assuring Toli's election. Selective prosecutions for corruption were orchestrated to remove recalcitrant officials and replace them with allies.

The police and security forces were corrupted as well. These highly coveted positions were awarded to Stevens's supporters, who took advantage of lucrative opportunities to set up roadblocks and checkpoints where identity documents were "checked" and bribes were extracted as the price of avoiding further delay, imprisonment, or worse.[64]

Nearly every citizen was subjugated to a position of obligation regarding Stevens and his network, with few alternatives and no easy exit.[65] He granted attractive tax incentives to Sierra Rutile to expand rutile mining in the home area of one of his rivals, which destroyed all plant cover, polluted water supplies, and created stagnant water ponds that bred malarial mosquitoes.[66]

At the core of Stevens's power was his monopoly on the use of force to label unsanctioned activities as "crimes."[67] He used threats of prosecution and confiscation to ensure that rivals were unable to establish their own bases of power. He also entangled international banks, the IMF and the World Bank in a web that threatened multilateral banks, ensuring that he would be treated gingerly by the international community.[68] He financed patrimonial spending and revenue shortfalls through loans procured by his loyal network of dealers and collateralized by illicit diamond exports.[69] These highly profitable loans, carrying high interest rates, bound private creditors tightly to Stevens in a symbiotic relationship.[70] However, these loans were insufficient to bridge growing shortfalls, inducing the IMF and World Bank to extend increasing amounts of credit in order to avoid domino-like defaults that could damage large multilateral banks and the international banking system. A standby arrangement with the IMF for special drawing rights (SDR) of 17 million in 1979 quickly expanded to SDR 186 million by 1981.[71] In return, the IMF required Sierra Leone to privatize many state-run enterprises and institute currency restrictions.[72] However, privatizations were rigged and steered to allies of Stevens on extremely favorable terms, while the currency restrictions were used to selectively allocate scarce currency to Stevens's supporters.[73] Most shocking, Bank of Sierra Leone governor Sam Bangurah was murdered after criticizing arrangements to direct $200 million in patrimonial expenditures to Stevens's allies and refusing to authorize foreign exchange allocations directed by Stevens.[74]

Sierra Leone failed to meet IMF-mandated reforms and conditions regarding repayment yet received an additional SDR 20.7 million in 1983 and SDR 50.2 million in 1984 from the IMF and World Bank.[75] Official IMF and World Bank credits provided 45–55 percent of Sierra Leone's deficit financing from 1980 through 1983.[76] This support permitted Stevens to continue using state resources for political purposes.[77]

Stevens expanded the scope of corruption and sources of revenue by rigging IMF-mandated privatization in import-export trading, fisheries, agricultural marketing, banking, oil, construction materials, and consumer goods imports, essentially reducing the state of Sierra Leone to a gigantic personal network of corrupt associates and dependents.[78] Stevens eventually amassed a personal fortune estimated at $500 million.[79] This diversion of state revenues starved and destroyed the effectiveness of most state institutions.[80] State spending on health and education fell by 60 percent between 1980 and 1987.[81]

Changes in Leadership

Sierra Leone fared no better after changes in leadership. In 1986, the new president, Saidu Momoh, announced a "New Order" of sweeping reforms aligned with IMF recommendations to attack corruption and greatly reduce governmental involvement in the economy, but applied privatization, economic liberalization, and reform as weapons to discipline rivals and build his economic and political power base.[82] In 1992, Valentine Strasser overthrew Momoh, promised reform and commitment to IMF conditions supporting divestiture, private enterprise, and foreign investment, but also succumbed to corruption.[83]

CONCLUSION

It is evident that senior IMF and World Bank economists assume that privatization, deregulation, economic liberalization, and restructuring will limit the scope for corruption. The evidence reviewed here suggests that this assumption is incorrect. The concentration of economic and political power in the heads of African states, due to colonial policies, effectively removed checks and balances against that power. Concentrated power is routinely used by African leaders and their loyal supporters to subvert purely domestic reforms—including privatization, deregulation, economic liberalization, and restructuring—to amass personal wealth and punish rivals.

IMF and World Bank economists attribute anemic economic growth and poverty in Africa to dirigisme: state ownership, price controls, and the manipulation of exchange rates and foreign trade to benefit entrenched elites. IMF and World Bank economists assume that privatization, deregulation, and economic competition will grow the economic power of entrepreneurs to demand efficient, ethical government leaders, thereby reversing the breakdown in law and order. The opening of African economies through currency devaluation and trade liberalization is believed to introduce pressure from international trading partners and creditors for efficient, honest governance.

Studies of Liberia, Sierra Leone, Congo, Nigeria, and Cameroon suggest, on the contrary, that privatization and economic liberalization inadvertently hasten the shift of state assets into the hands of corrupt politicians and their supporters, undermining the development of central governments responsible to their citizens.[84] Presidents use anticorruption tribunals to discipline associates as well as enemies.[85] A consequence of the corruption is the erosion of education, health, and social services as ruling elites cut the budget for teachers, health care workers, and other government workers who consume scarce resources but are not useful to elites seeking to strengthen their hold on power.[86] This pattern holds throughout Africa. In Congo, for example, state spending in these areas was practically reduced to zero.[87] In Zaire, President Mobutu Sese Seko cut state spending on health and education from 17.5 percent of the state budget in 1972 to 2.1 percent in 1990, reflecting the diversion of 95 percent of Zaire's budget for his own use.[88]

Paradoxically, the World Bank's and IMF's efforts to foster good governance through privatization and economic liberalization provide the cover under which corrupt ruling elites dismantle and destroy individuals and institutions that could threaten their power.[89] Donors inject funds that effectively support corrupt ruling elites. Conditioned on austerity measures, cutbacks in spending, privatization, and economic liberalization, these funds are then manipulated by corrupt leaders to funnel resources away from enemies and toward loyal supporters. Budget cutbacks are selectively targeted to undermine political enemies. Violence is used to control commercial opportunities, the distribution of wealth, and the building of political alliances.[90]

As Reno explains, the president becomes a warlord who rules through violence and by selectively distributing wealth.[91] The president uses the power of his office to manipulate IMF-mandated privatization, economic liberalization, and austerity measures in ways that build his wealth and political support. The president is faced with competing, regional warlords who use violence and selective distribution of wealth to rule regional bastions carved out of the sovereign territory nominally ruled by the president.[92] Each warlord employs official and unofficial security forces funded through agreements that funnel state resources to them—access to diamonds, in the case of Sierra Leone.[93] African leaders are ultimately compelled to reject true political liberalization because this would merely serve to increase the independent access of opposing warlords to economic resources that would threaten the authority of the African leaders.[94] The development of civil society, favored by the IMF as a means of building a bulwark against unfettered government power, is accurately viewed by African leaders as a potential threat to their rule.[95] Thus, it is unrealistic to expect African ruling elites to prioritize good governance over the use of their power to instill discipline through violence and manipulation of government resources. Under these conditions, the economic liberalization and reforms favored by the IMF and World Bank paradoxically undermine good governance.

In contrast, the rule of law in Western democracies channels economic liberalization productively, creating wealth. It is this experience that leads IMF and World Bank economists to assume that Western-style economic and political liberalization may be exported to African countries with the same positive effects. However, the experiences of Sierra Leone, Congo, Nigeria, Cameroon, and their neighbors suggest that this assumption is incorrect. A prerequisite is to establish checks and balances to counter corruption and patrimonial networks.

The condition that permits patrimonial networks and embedded corruption is the uncontested capacity of ruling elites and warlords to apply unfettered control over any significant source of wealth from natural resources, foreign aid, and rent-extracting networks based on controlled production and prices. This lack of accountability is at the heart of Africa's poverty and slow growth. The ability of African ruling elites to militarize commerce and discipline associates and rivals through violence and intimidation allows them to perpetuate corrupt rule and counterproductive economic policies. In contrast, Western-style democracies have effectively eliminated this option, forcing politicians to operate within the law and to respond to demands from voting constituents to maintain power. In Africa, this mechanism is broken. Corrupt politicians selectively create, define, and apply laws to reward allies and punish rivals.

Officially, African states must adopt the reforms advocated by the IMF and World Bank to continue receiving aid. However, implementation is manipulated so that the reforms serve the dual purpose of keeping aid flowing while maintaining discipline among associates and rivals. IMF and World Bank support for competitive elections and political liberalization exposes African ruling elites to challenges from rivals, forcing those ruling elites to increase their reliance on patrimonial practices to maintain their grip on power. In an effort to control these practices, World Bank officials prescribe privatization along with deep cuts in civil service employment in order to expose bureaucrats to market discipline and promote efficiency, modeled on reforms in Côte d'Ivoire.[96] However, privatization through alliances with foreign firms can be initiated and ended in ways that reward allies and punish rivals, without arousing the violent opposition that would occur if domestic workforces were treated in the same cavalier manner. This tactic permits African ruling elites to continue corrupt rule and negates any need for ruling elites to become more responsive to their voting constituents. Commercial alliances allow ruling elites to dominate wealth created from state-owned resources and pay for security services contracted out to foreign firms, allowing ruling elites to jettison unreliable military officers who might otherwise seize power through a coup d'état. In sum, African ruling elites are not accountable to their citizens, breeding opposing warlords who contest the power of those elites through violence, which triggers even more repressive, dictatorial, self-aggrandizing behavior from those in power.

The evidence presented here suggests that the reliance of IMF and World Bank economists on privatization, deregulation, economic liberalization, and restructuring to fight corruption is naive. Instead of reducing corruption, these policies are manipulated by corrupt African leaders to shift state assets into the hands of their allies, enhance their revenue streams, and punish their rivals. This occurs because of the lack of effective checks and balances on their power. This lack of accountability cannot be fixed by requiring transparency, promoting competitive elections, bolstering the judiciary, passing local laws against corruption, or establishing domestic anticorruption agencies. These strategies have been tried and have failed. The reason is that they have been manipulated by corrupt leaders to reward allies and punish rivals. Reforms that are limited to local laws, regulations, agencies, and personnel are susceptible to the corruption that pervades African governments.

This analysis suggests a conclusion that has been overlooked by development specialists: the international community must create and implement an international check against corruption in Africa. The monopolization of domestic power by African heads of state for corrupt purposes implies that an effective intervention against corruption can only come from outside the state. The only plausible candidate is the UN, which is the only international institution with sufficient moral authority and resources.

Previous development specialists, almost without exception, have advocated reforms that rely on changes in domestic laws, regulations, policies, agencies, institutions, and leaders, but these domestic reforms are routinely subverted by powerful African elites.[97] Privatization, deregulation, economic liberalization, and restructuring are examples of changes that are necessarily implemented through changes in domestic laws, regulations, policies, agencies, and institutions and, therefore, are easily manipulated by corrupt African elites.

Furthermore, an effective intervention against corruption must be powerful. No Western developed country relies on privatization, deregulation, and economic competition to deter corruption. These are weak forces against corruption. Instead, corruption is held in check through aggressive investigation and prosecution. The primary examples of successful interventions against grand corruption are the establishment of the Independent Commission Against Corruption in Hong Kong and the Corrupt Practices Investigation Bureau in Singapore.[98] In these states, corruption was only effectively addressed after the establishment of truly independent bodies of inspectors.

In African countries, corrupt leaders manipulate the domestic police, anticorruption agencies, judiciary, legal system, laws, regulations, and policies to their own advantage. This suggests that the problem of corruption in Africa cannot be addressed through domestic reforms that are easily manipulated by corrupt elites. Instead, the international community must create and implement a system where international inspectors who are largely immune from pressure exerted by powerful African elites are empowered to respond to requests by African citizens to conduct impartial investigations.

If investigations must be conducted to deter future corruption, if those investigations must be conducted by independent investigators who are immune to pressure from powerful African elites, and if the UN is the only international institution with sufficient moral authority and resources, only UN inspectors could conceivably fulfill this requirement. What is needed is an independent body of UN inspectors to vigorously investigate corruption in Africa. Only the UN can field a large force of professional inspectors who are independent of domestic authorities and have no allegiance to powerful domestic elites.

This view contrasts sharply with the conclusions and recommendations of prominent development specialists.[99] However, if the analysis presented here is correct, the establishment of UN inspectors is potentially the most direct, effective strategy to address the problem of corruption and underdevelopment in Africa.

Chapter 8

Systemic Corruption

Chapter 8, "Systemic Corruption," describes provisions of APUNCAC designed to neutralize the type of systemic corruption that permits corrupt elites to dominate economic and political activity, subvert reform, and perpetuate poverty and violations of human rights. APUNCAC incorporates provisions from American "RICO" laws that fight racketeering,[1] as well as model campaign finance laws, model conflict of interest laws, and model laws to deter bid-rigging. APUNCAC incorporates provisions designed to address corruption related to facilitation payments, the use of loans to conduct illicit transactions, the sale of state assets, and base erosion and profit-shifting (BEPS). Significantly, APUNCAC incorporates innovative provisions designed to address money laundering, the practice of hiding illicit funds in offshore tax havens, and the use of attorneys and financial service professionals to hide illicit revenues derived from crime—revenues that reward and drive violent criminals.

One reason that corruption persists is that criminals use the international financial system to shift illicit funds in a way that is difficult to trace. To trace these funds, it is necessary for investigators to obtain mutual legal assistance from multiple jurisdictions. While many jurisdictions endeavor to provide mutual legal assistance upon request, the process is neither seamless nor swift. The challenges encountered when pursuing mutual legal assistance hinder efficient investigation and prosecution of corruption.

APUNCAC would address this issue. Each State Party would empower UN inspectors to conduct investigations involving: (a) nationals of the State Party wherever they may be found; (b) any person or entity within the territory of the State Party; and (c) conduct by any person or entity that has, or is intended to have, substantial effect within the territory of the State Party. Under APUNCAC, UN inspectors would have access to a centralized, online database of information compiled by FINCEN, modeled on the United States Treasury Department's Financial Crimes Enforcement Network (FinCEN). APUNCAC would require key actors throughout the international financial system to enter information into the FINCEN database that would assist UN inspectors in tracing illicit funds and investigating charges of corruption. The required information would include beneficial ownership information for each transaction in currency and each international wire transfer to or from the territory of a State Party in excess of $3,000. The establishment of this type of centralized, online database, in combination with APUNCAC's regime for enforcing the submission of accurate beneficial ownership information, would greatly facilitate efficient investigation and prosecution of charges of corruption, promoting deterrence. Chapter 9 offers a detailed explanation of this regime.

To trace illicit proceeds, it is frequently necessary to trace proceeds that are moved around the world through international wire transactions. However, the information that is needed by investigators to trace these proceeds is frequently missing. Beneficial ownership information is missing or is obscured through a complicated series of transactions engineered by criminals who use loopholes in the international financial system to hide information that would identify the criminals conducting the transactions.

APUNCAC would address this issue. Each State Party would require wire transmitters that handle an international funds transfer in excess of $3,000 on behalf of, or for the benefit of, a national of a State Party, or that are transmitted to or from the territory of a State Party, to obtain beneficial ownership information and to submit that information to FINCEN. APUNCAC requires beneficial ownership information to be conveyed to intermediary and recipient financial institutions and requires intermediary and recipient financial institutions to submit wire transaction reports to FINCEN. This regime ensures that FINCEN would have a complete record permitting an investigator to trace the entire path of a series of wire transactions.

APUNCAC implements two strategies to enforce this regime and discourage efforts to falsify information or avoid the reporting requirements. One enforcement strategy, described below, involves a requirement that a party who transfers funds offshore from a State Party must, as a condition of the transfer, obtain a guarantee from the recipient. The guarantee requires the recipient to observe the APUNCAC beneficial ownership reporting requirements whenever funds are retransmitted. The guarantee also requires the recipient to obtain an identical guarantee from the recipient of the retransmitted funds, establishing a chain of custody (figure 8.1). This would be enforced through civil damages specified in the guarantee and payable upon breach of the guarantee.

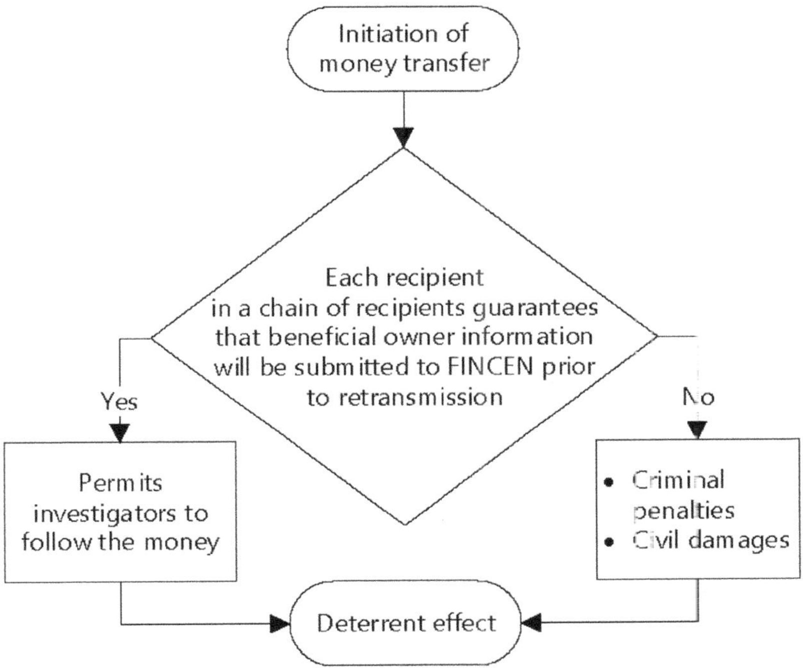

Figure 8.1 Establishes Chain of Custody. *Source*: Figure created by author.

A second enforcement strategy, described in chapter 9, involves a system of criminal penalties that would be applied to any transmitter (or re-transmitter) of funds originating from the territory of a State Party who fails to abide by the APUNCAC reporting requirement, or any front man who chooses to submit false beneficial ownership information. Failure to submit beneficial ownership information, or submission of false beneficial ownership information, would be punishable by debarment, fines, and criminal penalties. Chapter 9 offers a detailed explanation of this strategy.

RICO

Corruption is one of the most difficult crimes to investigate. In general, there is no crime scene. There are no fingerprints and no eyewitnesses. It is by nature a very secret crime and can involve just two satisfied parties, so there is no incentive to divulge the truth. Even if there are witnesses, they are often parties to the corruption themselves, with little incentive to cooperate with investigators. The offenders may be skillful in hiding their tracks. The offenders may be powerful and ruthless in enforcing a code of silence and may employ intimidation and violence to stymie investigators. Sophisticated offenders seek out loopholes in the law and employ the assistance of skilled professionals, including attorneys, accountants, and financial service professionals, to hide their activities and launder corrupt proceeds.

Perhaps the most difficult crime to investigate involves large-scale systemic corruption where corrupt government leaders acting like powerful mafia bosses command the loyalty of a vast network of individuals who have been co-opted through favors and either actively or passively cooperate and support corrupt activities. Chapter 7 illustrated this type of systemic corruption, drawing upon William Reno's book-length description and analysis of the web of corruption created by Sierra Leone president Siaka Stevens over an 18-year period.

While this type of corruption may seem irredeemable, it is instructive to review the experience of American prosecutors seeking to prosecute mafia bosses in the United States. For many years, American prosecutors were stymied by the difficulty of prosecuting mafia bosses because of the mafia's code of silence, use of violence and extortion, employment of highly skilled attorneys, accountants, and financial service professionals to launder corrupt proceeds, and the fact that organized crime involves a pattern of criminal activity extending over time. The difficulty of prosecuting mafia crimes prompted passage of the Racketeer Influenced and Corrupt Organizations Act, commonly referred to as the RICO Act.[2] RICO is a United States federal law that criminalizes a pattern of criminal activities that may include money laundering and misappropriation of assets. Significantly, RICO criminalizes any pattern of racketeering activity involving an "association-in-fact" enterprise. This language opened the door for prosecutions of peripheral figures including attorneys, accountants, and financial service professionals who were loosely affiliated with the mafia.

RICO enabled prosecutors to turn the tide in the fight against the mafia because it enabled prosecutors to use prosecutions of peripheral figures to obtain cooperation agreements and turn those individuals into witnesses against high-level mafia figures. The basic strategy was to compile cases against peripheral individuals, obtain cooperation through plea agreements, and use the cooperating witnesses to build cases against the mafia bosses. The strategy was highly successful and offers a playbook for prosecuting the type of protected, systemic corruption that is otherwise extremely difficult to prosecute.

Florida's RICO Act is an improved version of the federal RICO law.[3] For this reason, APUNCAC adapts and incorporates Florida's version of the RICO language.[4] In combination with independent UN inspectors and dedicated anticorruption courts, the RICO provisions would give prosecutors the legal tools needed to target peripheral figures including attorneys, accountants, and financial service professionals; obtain plea agreements and deferred prosecution agreements; turn the peripheral individuals into cooperating witnesses; and obtain convictions against powerful criminals (figure 8.2).

A key feature of RICO is the availability of civil remedies. RICO permits civil actions by private parties: "Any aggrieved person may institute a proceeding."[5] Private parties may pursue remedies consistent with domestic law regarding civil remedies: "relief shall be granted in conformity with the principles that govern the granting of injunctive relief from threatened loss or damage in other civil cases."[6] Prosecutors may obtain liens and pursue civil forfeiture.[7] These remedies permit prosecutors to seize and impound property obtained through illicit activities. Liens serve to freeze assets that might otherwise be sold or transferred. Criminals are quickly deprived of the use of their property. Forfeiture entails a relatively low evidentiary burden of

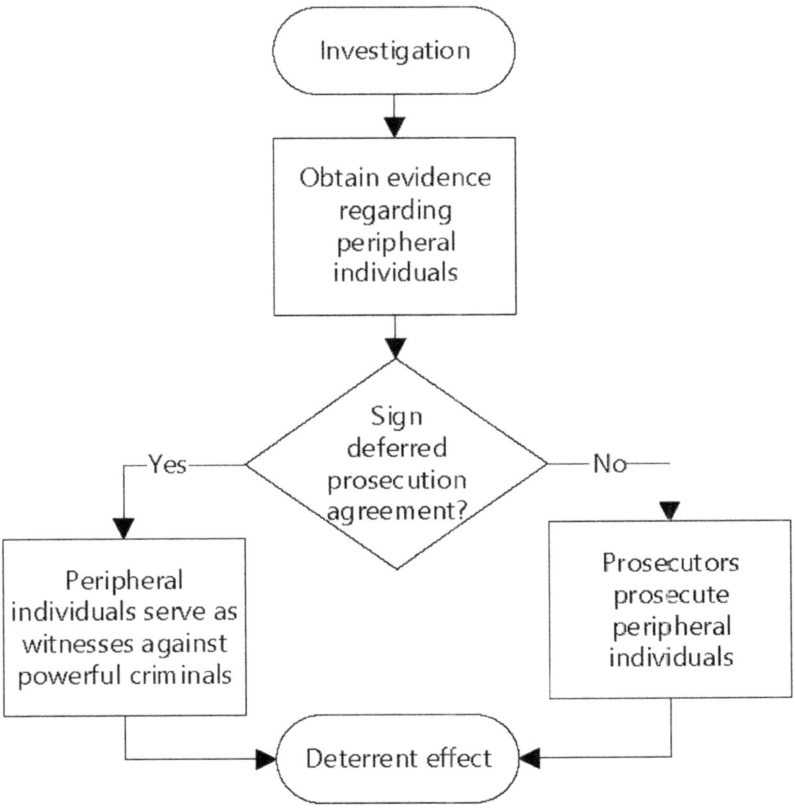

Figure 8.2 RICO Provisions Enable Prosecutors to Turn Peripheral Individuals into Cooperating Witnesses. *Source*: Figure created by author.

proof on prosecutors. This increases the likelihood that illicit activities will be punished. Both consequences are swift, enhancing deterrence.

CAMPAIGN FINANCE

APUNCAC adapts and incorporates a model campaign finance law developed by the Center for Governmental Studies, a nonprofit, nonpartisan organization that helps civic organizations and decision-makers to strengthen democracy and improve governmental processes.[8] The rationale for incorporating campaign finance provisions is that, in the absence of this type of provision, powerful politicians such as Sierra Leone president Siaka Stevens may manipulate elections to maintain their control.

The campaign finance provisions seek to reduce the negative influence of large contributions by limiting the size of campaign contributions and establishing a system where competitive candidates who can secure a large number of small contributions receive matching contributions from the public treasury. This effectively increases the resources available to popular candidates and limits the ability of wealthy individuals to outspend their opponents. The law seeks to encourage popular candidates to run against well-financed opponents, thereby serving to moderate the influence of wealthy individuals who may have obtained their wealth through corruption or may seek to preserve their wealth through corruption. APUNCAC defines penalties and sanctions.

CONFLICTS OF INTEREST

APUNCAC adapts and incorporates New York's highly successful conflict of interest and disclosure laws.[9] The rationale for incorporating these provisions is that in the absence of this type of provision, conflicts of interest would be rife and would give government officials incentives to misuse their positions and powers. Arguably, much of the corruption that occurs in developing nations occurs because of absent or inadequate controls regarding conflicts of interest.

APUNCAC establishes a conflicts of interest board for each State Party, defines the individuals who are covered by the disclosure and ethics provisions, requires all government officials to disclose conflicts of interest, and defines allowed and prohibited conduct with regard to the acceptance of gifts and favors; the use or disclosure of confidential information; use of positions for private advantage; the receipt of income from second jobs, businesses, and investments; gifts and favors between superiors and subordinates; volunteer activities; political activities; and post-employment activities. APUNCAC defines penalties and sanctions.

BID-RIGGING

Another source of corruption occurs when the bidding and/or contracting process for public contracts is manipulated and rigged in a way that favors selected associates of powerful government officials. This form of corruption is rife in developing nations and is used by powerful elites to reward loyal associates and maintain their economic, financial, and political domination over reform-oriented sectors of society. The rationale for incorporating provisions to control bid-rigging and tender-related corruption is that in the absence of this type of provision powerful individuals can maintain their control over the levers of economic and political power, thwarting reform and efforts to control corruption.

Germany is viewed as a benchmark for anticorruption-related legislation. Germany has adopted "integrity pacts" to deter tender-related corruption. APUNCAC adapts and incorporates language modeled on the agreement between the Berlin-Schönefeld Airport authority and the bidders/contractors associated with the development of the airport into the Berlin-Brandenburg International Airport.[10] This type of integrity pact agreement deters tender-related corruption by establishing commitments by the principal (e.g., the Berlin-Schönefeld Airport authority); the bidders and contractors; and an external, independent monitor to monitor the tender process and contract execution. The innovative aspect involves the establishment of an external, independent monitor who is granted access to all bid- and contract-related documents and meetings and is empowered to report his or her findings to the public prosecutor.

APUNCAC requires the implementation of integrity pacts for all public tenders with a value exceeding $1,000,000. The public tendering authority is required to identify, and establish an agreement with, a duly qualified civil society organization (CSO). The CSO appoints a duly qualified monitor and a monitoring committee of three duly qualified individuals who monitor the monitor and censure or replace the monitor as appropriate. The monitor is directed to act independently and objectively "without favor to any individual or entity." The monitor is retained by the tendering authority prior to substantive pretender planning, meetings and discussions, and is retained throughout the tendering and contracting process, ending 12 months after the last contract payment. The monitor is directed to investigate the compliance of the tendering authority, bidders, sub-bidders, contractors, subcontractors, and CSO regarding their obligations and commitments pursuant to APUNCAC, and to investigate behavior or actions that suggest or imply obstruction of the monitor's duties or evasion of the obligations and commitments of the tendering authority, bidders, sub-bidders, contractors, subcontractors, and CSO. Information and documents obtained by the monitor are to be shared upon demand with the state prosecutor's office, UN inspectors, the conflicts of interest board, authorized investigators, and the CSO to the extent that such communication is necessary to provide a full and complete evaluation of the compliance of the parties with their commitments.

In addition to integrity pacts and monitors, APUNCAC incorporates the language of the False Claims Act (FCA).[11] The FCA is an American law that imposes liability on individuals and companies that defraud the American government. It is the American government's primary legal means of combating fraud against the government.

Significantly, the FCA includes provisions that permit private individuals who have knowledge of fraud (but were not convicted of criminal conduct arising from their role in the violation) to file a *qui tam* suit, on behalf of the government, for violations of the FCA. If the government intervenes in the *qui tam* action, the person bringing the action (the "relator") is entitled to receive between 15 and 25 percent of the amount recovered by the government through the *qui tam* action. If the government declines to intervene in the action, the relator's share is increased to 25–30 percent. Under certain circumstances, the relator's share may be reduced to no more than 10 percent. If the relator planned and initiated the fraud, the court may reduce the award without limitation. The relator's share is paid to the relator by the government out of the payment received by the government from the defendant. If a *qui tam* action is successful, the relator is also entitled to receive legal fees and other expenses of the action from the defendant.

The *qui tam* provisions provide powerful financial incentives for whistleblowers to expose the type of bid-rigging and contract fraud that plagues developing nations and is a primary path through which powerful elites channel patrimonial rewards to loyal associates. The establishment of incentives for individuals who are most likely to become aware of fraud to expose that fraud is key to regaining control over the patrimonial system of rewards and punishments.

FACILITATION PAYMENTS

Article 49 explicitly prohibits bribery in the form of facilitation payments. In addition, Article 49 requires public officials to post specified information to a publicly accessible website regarding bid-related payments submitted to such officials:

> Information regarding payments, remuneration and any consideration submitted to any public official related to a bid, proposal, exploration, investigation, discussion or agreement regarding rights to a valuable state asset, as determined by rule of the board, shall be posted to a publicly accessible website designated by the board in a form and manner approved by the board.[12]

This provision is intended to improve transparency in tender-related bidding processes.

LOANS

APUNCAC includes provisions designed to close loopholes that currently permit the use of uncollected loans to reward loyal associates:

> A public servant who directly or indirectly makes or receives a loan in an amount exceeding $3,000 shall record the following information on a limited-access website designated by the board in a form and manner approved by the board . . .
>
> (d) the name, principal business address and title of each person who received the loan or, in the case of a business entity, the name, principal business address and title of each shareholder, partner or member owning 10 percent or more of the business entity;
>
> (e) a true, correct and complete description of any familial, marital, business or personal relationship between any person named in subparagraph (c) or subparagraph (d) and any public servant who directly or indirectly contributed or directed that contributions be made or received any principal, interest, payment, benefit or favor in relation to the corresponding loan;
>
> (f) a true, correct and complete description of any principal, interest, payment, benefit or favor received by any person having a familial, marital, business or personal relationship with any public servant who contributed, or directed contributions regarding, or received any principal, interest, payment, benefit or favor, in relation to the corresponding loan;
>
> (g) a true, correct and complete description of any contribution and direction regarding any contribution that was made, and any principal, interest, payment, benefit or favor paid, given or received by any public servant in relation to the corresponding loan.[13]

Article 19 explicitly prohibits the use of interest-free or nearly interest-free loans, weakly collateralized loans, or uncollected loans to evade the AML provisions of APUNCAC.[14]

STATE ASSETS

APUNCAC includes provisions designed to close loopholes that currently allow government officials to reward loyal associates through state asset sales at below-market prices:

> Public servants who sign agreements or cause agreements to be signed that offer, tender or convey valuable state assets or rights to valuable state assets, as defined by rule of the board, to any person or entity, must disclose these agreements by posting the following information to a publicly-accessible website designated by the board in a form and manner approved by the board . . . the name, principal business address and title of each person who received the right or asset or, in the case of a business entity, the name, principal business address and title of each shareholder, partner or member owning 10 percent or more of the business entity . . . a complete description of any consideration that was provided by the recipient other than the remuneration described in subparagraph (f).[15]

A major contribution of APUNCAC is that it includes provisions that require recipients of state assets to insert, in any future sale of those assets to subsequent parties, a requirement that those subsequent parties shall post to the same publicly accessible website the same identifying information about the beneficial party who receives the assets. These provisions would permit investigators to follow the trail of a complicated series of transactions that might otherwise permit criminals to hide the identity of the beneficial owner who ultimately receives state assets (figure 8.3). The provisions criminalize false reports that seek to hide the identities of the beneficial owners, closing existing loopholes that currently permit beneficial owners to hide their identities through complicated transactions involving nominee owners of accounts held by anonymous shell companies in offshore jurisdictions that currently serve to hide criminal activity.

BEPS

Base erosion and profit-shifting (BEPS) refers to the multinational corporation practice of manipulating reported production costs in a way that artificially minimizes the taxes owed to developing nations where the multinational extracts resources. For example, a multinational corporation might report that the production cost of copper extracted in Chile is 168 cents per pound when the true net cost of producing the copper, after subtracting

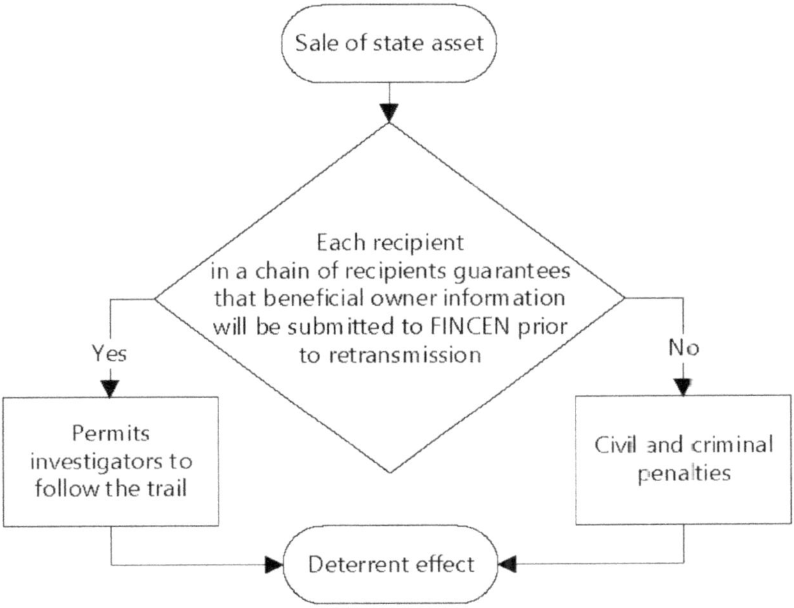

Figure 8.3 Reporting Requirements Allow Investigators to Trace Proceeds of State Asset Sales. *Source*: Figure created by author.

revenue from secondary products, is 126 cents per pound. By using the higher cost figure, the corporation would artificially minimize the amount of taxes on profits owed to the Government of Chile. The corporation may arrange to "sell" the copper at 168 cents per pound to a subsidiary located in a tax-haven jurisdiction that levies little or no taxes, where it is "processed" and sold on the global market at a retail price of 311 cents per pound. The result is that the multinational pays little or no taxes to any government (figure 8.4).

This trickery is possible because a single multinational corporation can negotiate a license to extract all copper from a given mine, while maintaining tight internal control of information about its true production costs in a way that is difficult or impossible for government auditors to penetrate. This deception serves to cheat developing nation treasuries of revenue that would otherwise be available for law enforcement, education, health, and human services for citizens of those nations.

BEPS is a well-understood practice. It is a major problem that affects developed nations as well as developing nations. Consequently, OECD developed rules that apply to multinational enterprises operating within OECD jurisdictions. APUNCAC includes provisions that require firms operating

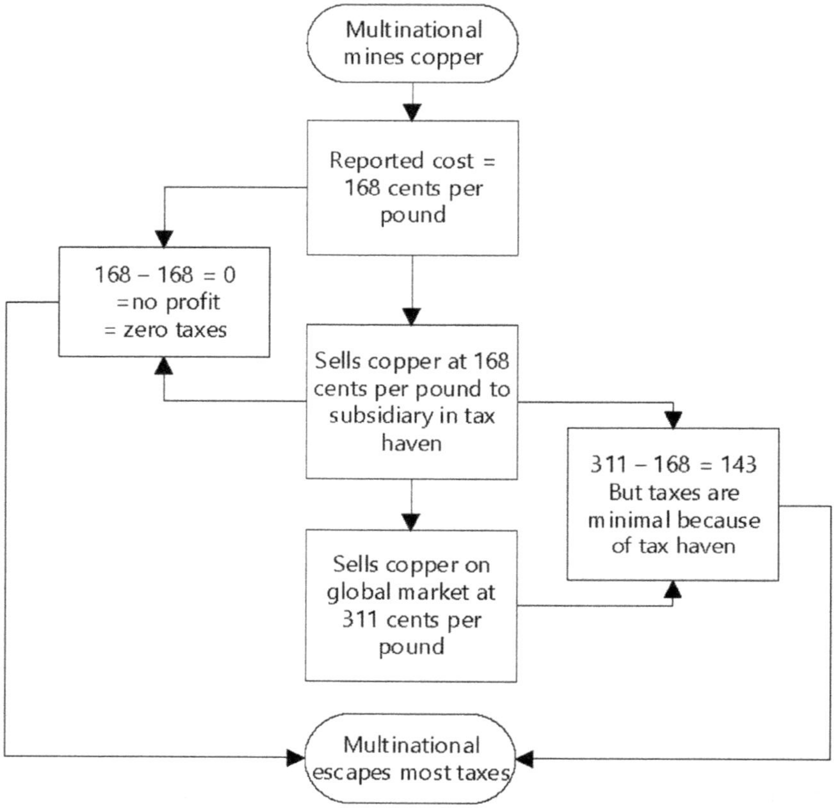

Figure 8.4 Multinationals Escape Taxes through Profit-Shifting. *Source*: Figure created by author.

within the territory of a State Party to conform to the OECD transfer pricing guidelines.[16] APUNCAC includes audit requirements:

> Firms that operate within the territory of the State Party shall submit audited reports documenting conformance with paragraph one to the board and to the requisite tax authorities and shall post copies of these reports to a publicly-accessible website designated by the board in a form and manner approved by the board.[17]

APUNCAC requires firms to pay their share of taxes:

> Firms that operate within the territory of the State Party shall pay the taxes due as indicated by the reports submitted in accordance with paragraph two. If taxes are not paid timely, such firms shall pay late penalties and double interest on the portion of taxes that are late, as determined by rule of the board.[18]

APUNCAC requires firms to specify in bid proposals and contract agreements the intercompany prices and pricing formulas, together with audited analyses of estimated revenues:

> Bids, proposals and agreements to extract natural resources within the territory of the State Party including but not limited to oil, gas and minerals shall specify the intercompany prices or formulas used to calculate those prices with regard to the intercompany purchase, sale, lease, cost-allocation, revenue-allocation, cost-sharing, and pricing agreements and arrangements that will likely govern and will significantly impact the revenue received by the State Party, and shall include independent, audited analyses estimating the revenue that would be received by the State Party assuming the most probable set of circumstances and conditions projected throughout the life of the proposed natural resource extraction agreement, as determined by the independent agency conducting the analysis and as certified by the auditing agency.[19]

These provisions are designed to close loopholes that currently allow multinational corporations to avoid paying their share of taxes. From the perspective of the citizens of developing nations, this failure to pay taxes is a form of corruption and abuse that involves misappropriation of valuable state assets.

MONEY LAUNDERING

A major reason that corruption is difficult to investigate is that criminals have become adept at using the international financial system to hide illicit proceeds of crime in offshore tax havens that encourage this activity through lax enforcement of controls against money laundering. In the absence of information regarding the beneficial owners of offshore accounts, it is difficult—in many cases impossible—to prosecute sophisticated forms of corruption because of the difficulty of following the money trail. Once funds are moved to offshore jurisdictions, the ability of a state party to demand information regarding beneficial ownership is severely limited. The lack of an enforcement mechanism is arguably the single greatest impediment to the prosecution of sophisticated forms of corruption. One of the most significant contributions of APUNCAC is the articulation of provisions that would create a powerful mechanism to peel away the anonymity that currently shields criminals who hide their proceeds in offshore tax havens.

These provisions would be enforced through two strategies. Chapter 9 describes a system where offenders would be debarred. APUNCAC limits the activities of debarred individuals and entities and imposes requirements intended to protect society. Issues of extraterritorial jurisdiction and enforcement are addressed in chapter 9. While many debarred individuals and entities may be expected to challenge debarment, APUNCAC includes provisions designed to preserve due process while handling a large volume of challenges.[20] This chapter, however, focuses on a second enforcement strategy, involving a system of contractual guarantees that would be required of all recipients of funds transferred offshore from an APUNCAC State Party. APUNCAC incorporates provisions that would employ the London Court of International Arbitration to adjudicate disputes regarding these guarantees.

FINCEN

Article 19 of APUNCAC establishes FINCEN, modeled on the U.S. FinCEN, for the purpose of safeguarding the international financial system from illicit use, to combat money laundering, to fight crime, and to promote international security through the cooperation of financial authorities and criminal investigators in collecting, analyzing, and disseminating financial intelligence that may be used to prosecute money laundering and other crimes.

Article 19 establishes a secure database for the purpose of collecting and centralizing information that identifies the beneficial owners and sources of funds originating within the territory of a State Party and facilitates the prosecution of crime, including money laundering. This information would be accessible and readily searchable upon demand by authorized financial regulators and criminal investigators via a secure web portal. The database and retrieval system would be designed to promote interoperability with other databases to facilitate the efficient investigation of allegations of corruption, money laundering, or other criminal activity. The database would include:

(a) a system that records the identities of individuals accessing the system, the dates and times the system was accessed, and information regarding the webpages that were viewed;
(b) a portal that permits authorized personnel to upload currency transaction reports pursuant to Articles 28, 29, and 30;
(c) a portal modeled on the U.S. Designation of Exempt Person e-file system operated by FinCEN to designate banking customers exempt from currency transaction reporting requirements, pursuant to Article 31;
(d) a portal that permits any individual to upload a copy of his or her passport and a searchable electronic copy of his or her tax return document;
(e) a portal that permits authorized trade, business, or financial institution personnel to view a database copy of an individual's passport, if available, and verify the existence in the database of a searchable electronic copy of an individual's most recent tax return, if available; such portal would indicate the taxpayer's name, last four digits of the tax identification number, date of the return document, and confirm that it is a searchable copy;

(f) a portal that permits any person to check the FINCEN debarment status of any individual or entity and view a copy of such individual's passport name, photo, and identification number;
(g) a portal that permits the Chief Debarment Officer to enter information regarding debarred individuals and entities, including the expiration of debarment, if applicable, pursuant to subparagraph (d) of paragraph six of Article 18;
(h) a portal that permits financial institution personnel to obtain checkbox affirmation by each customer of his or her responsibilities pursuant to Article 30;
(i) a portal that permits authorized financial institution personnel to e-file a Suspicious Activity Report (SAR) pursuant to Articles 33, 34, 35, 36, and 37;
(j) a portal that permits a person to file a report of foreign bank and financial accounts pursuant to Article 26;
(k) a portal that permits a financial institution to file a foreign transaction report pursuant to Article 27.

Article 19 permits the use of a dedicated software application approved by the Commission on Crime Prevention and Criminal Justice for the purpose of fulfilling APUNCAC's reporting requirements. Article 19 requires institutions that handle reportable currency transactions to:

(a) Contract with an approved independent auditing firm to perform annual audits if deposits into a recipient's account exceed specified amounts. If an audit finds insufficient documentation regarding the beneficial ownership or origin of a significant portion of all audited transactions, the account beneficiaries would be debarred.
(b) Cooperate fully with auditors, produce requested documentation promptly, maintain and file certified electronic copies of all audit reports, and cooperate fully with authorized financial regulators and criminal investigators, notwithstanding domestic laws regarding privacy.
(c) Maintain, and provide access upon demand to financial regulators and criminal investigators, electronic records of all funds transfers out of the receiving account, and report suspicious activity.
(d) Verify, record, and check against the debarment list the identity of the person handling receipt of such funds and the identities of persons who are beneficial owners linked to the account receiving the out-transfer and void the out-transfer if any of these individuals are on the debarment list.
(e) Prior to retransmission of such funds, involving amounts in excess of $3,000, secure a guarantee by the new receiving person and entity. The guarantor stipulates to certain facts: the intended beneficiaries of the

> guarantee are the States Parties to APUNCAC and nationals of such States Parties; the guarantor unconditionally agrees (i) to comply with certain requirements and prohibitions pursuant to APUNCAC; (ii) to assume liability for $100,000 in compensatory damages upon each failure to comply with APUNCAC requirements and prohibitions; (iii) to waive any objection to the judicial forum and governing law specified by the guarantee for resolving all disputes in relation to the guarantee; and (iv) to waive any objection to the jurisdiction, process, and venue of such forum, and to the effectiveness, execution, and enforcement of any order or judgment (including, but not limited to, a default judgment) of any such forum in relation to the guarantee.

Pursuant to the guarantee, the guarantor unconditionally agrees to the terms of APUNCAC as if the guarantor was a national of, or entity registered with or within, a State Party to APUNCAC. Significantly, the guarantor agrees, prior to retransmission of funds that are the subject of the guarantee, involving an amount in excess of $3,000, (i) to obtain and submit to FINCEN a subsequent guarantee by the new receiving entity, essentially identical to the first guarantee and incorporating all essential elements of the first guarantee, including the stipulation of facts, the commitments of the guarantor, and the provision that the guarantor unconditionally agrees to the terms of APUNCAC as if the guarantor was a national of, or entity registered within, a State Party to APUNCAC; and (ii) to obtain and submit to FINCEN certification of beneficial ownership by the beneficial owners of the sending and receiving accounts.

APUNCAC incorporates a safe harbor designed to minimize the administrative burden of securing a guarantee every time funds are retransmitted. An entity that would ordinarily be required to secure a guarantee prior to retransmission may satisfy the requirement through a one-time agreement with FINCEN, in a form and manner approved by FINCEN, that applicable funds would be segregated and no transmissions in excess of $3,000 would occur except to persons or entities that have previously stipulated to a guarantee that is essentially identical to the required guarantee, including the provision that the guarantor unconditionally agrees to the terms of APUNCAC as if the guarantor was a national of, or entity registered within, a State Party to APUNCAC.

A "Model Guarantee" is incorporated into and attached to APUNCAC. The Model Guarantee is tailored to resist legal challenges by requiring the guarantor to stipulate that the intended beneficiaries of the guarantee are the States Parties to APUNCAC, and by requiring the guarantor to waive objections to the judicial forum and governing law specified by APUNCAC.[21] The Model Guarantee specifies that disputes regarding the guarantee would be adjudicated by the London Court of International Arbitration.

These requirements would permit FINCEN investigators to follow the path of a complex series of transactions. Each successive entity would be required, by contract with the preceding entity, to record beneficial ownership of the source account and receiving account in the FINCEN database. By contractual agreement, each successive entity would accede to APUNCAC rules. By contractual agreement, each successive entity would explicitly stipulate that the intended beneficiaries of the guarantee are the States Parties to APUNCAC and nationals of such States Parties, and stipulate that the guarantee gives the States Parties and nationals of such States Parties the right to enforce the guarantee. By contractual agreement, such entities would submit to binding arbitration and accept the Rules of the London Court of International Arbitration to resolve all disputes regarding the guarantee. Therefore, a State Party to APUNCAC, or a national of a State Party, could bring a complaint before the London Court of International Arbitration regarding an alleged violation of APUNCAC or of any related State Party law by the new receiving person or entity. Since the Rules of the London Court of International Arbitration stipulate that the governing law is the law of the arbitral seat, and since the parties stipulate to the Rules, the parties stipulate that the governing law is the law of the arbitral seat. The Rules state that if the parties to the arbitration are unable to reach an agreement regarding the arbitral seat, the seat shall be London.

APUNCAC ends the chain of agreements when a penultimate receiving entity submits certification to FINCEN that the final beneficial recipient is a corporation publicly traded, on an exchange approved by rule of FINCEN, where no natural person(s) directly or indirectly, through any contract, arrangement, understanding, relationship, or otherwise (i) exercises substantial control or (ii) owns or controls not less than 25 percent of the ownership interests of the funds.[22] The rationale is that a publicly traded corporation is unlikely to be involved in money laundering, and it would be onerous and impractical to require corporations engaged in high-volume transactions with hundreds of counterparties to demand Article 19(4)(e) contract guarantees related to funds disbursed from accounts that received Article 19(4)(e) funds.

As a practical matter, the Article 19(4)(e) requirement, in combination with existing pressure from the United States, the UK, and OECD Member States to properly identify beneficial ownership, exemplified by increasingly specific, comprehensive, and onerous Financial Action Task Force (FATF) regulations regarding the submission of customer identity information and initiatives by the United States and the European Union (EU) to require submission of corporate beneficial ownership information, would likely force the majority of financial institutions worldwide to adopt and enforce a general rule that the beneficial owner of a given financial account must self-certify beneficial ownership of all received funds. This simple solution would greatly reduce the need to implement Article 19(4)(e) contracts. Financial institutions would likely adopt the rule to save time and reduce their administrative burden. While this type of rule could have been written into APUNCAC, it would only have applied to financial institutions and beneficial owners within the jurisdiction of the States Parties to APUNCAC. It would not have applied to institutions or beneficial owners not within the jurisdiction of States Parties. The Article 19(4)(e) requirement is necessary because it extends the APUNCAC beneficial owner reporting requirement to entities and beneficial owners in states that are not parties to APUNCAC but receive funds transferred from the jurisdiction of States Parties.[23]

Third Party Rights

Under the laws of the UK, the United States, and France, a third party may enforce a contract if such enforcement is expressly provided in the contract and the third party is an intended beneficiary.[24] This means that a State Party to APUNCAC that is the intended beneficiary of an Article 19 paragraph 4(e) contract between two money transmitters may enforce that contract, even though the State Party is not a contracting party. The State Party is not a contracting party, but it is the *intended beneficiary*—the sole purpose of the contract is to assist the State Party in controlling potential money laundering. French law specifically states that "one of the parties to a contract (the 'stipulator') may require a promise from the other party (the 'promisor') to accomplish an act of performance for the benefit of a third party (the 'beneficiary')," "the beneficiary is invested with a direct right to the act of performance against the promisor," and "the stipulator may himself require the promisor to perform his undertaking towards the beneficiary."[25] This is an exact description of the Article 19 paragraph 4(e) contract. The APUNCAC requirement would compel the promisor to obtain and record information regarding beneficial ownership of the source account and receiving account in the FINCEN database, or pay the damages spelled out in the guarantee. The promisor, having acceded to APUNCAC and related domestic law, would be bound by that law and the jurisdiction of the London Court of International Arbitration to render judgment regarding alleged violations of that law. Enforcement of civil judgments would proceed in the same way that civil judgments are currently enforced (chapter 9 spells out a second strategy for enforcing APUNCAC's beneficial ownership reporting requirements, involving criminal penalties).

There is nothing coercive in these provisions of APUNCAC. Parties would only choose to enter into Article 19 paragraph 4(e) agreements voluntarily. They would only do so if, and when, they judge that the benefits outweigh the potential costs. If they judge that the requirements are unacceptably onerous, they will decline to enter into the required agreements. Note that the promisor is only guaranteeing that he will obtain and record information regarding beneficial ownership of the source account and receiving account in the FINCEN database. The promisor is not guaranteeing that the information is correct. Instead, the beneficial owners of the source and receiving accounts must certify, under penalty of perjury, that the information they supply to the promisor is true and correct. If the information is false, they assume liability for penalties specified by APUNCAC. A person who is named as the beneficial owner who is in fact the beneficial owner would presumably have few qualms about certifying that he or she is in fact the beneficial owner. On the other hand, a person who is a nominee owner, in violation of APUNCAC, would have to think twice about whether it is worth the risk of "certifying" information that is false, thereby assuming liability for penalties specified by APUNCAC.

Choice of Law and Forum Selection Clauses

Significantly, international contract law permits a party to voluntarily accede to the authority of a foreign law or foreign court.[26] For example, under English common law, a foreign monetary judgment rendered by a foreign court can be enforced in England

> If the person against whom the judgment was given had before the commencement of the proceedings agreed, in respect of the subject matter of the proceedings, to submit to the jurisdiction of that court or of the courts of that country.[27]

"The effect of a party's submission to the jurisdiction is that he is precluded thereafter from objecting to the court exercising its jurisdiction in respect of such claim."[28]

The employment of a forum selection clause to specify a judicial forum for the resolution of disputes regarding an agreement is a standard feature of international contracts. A valid forum selection clause is nearly ironclad. Under U.S. law, the controlling legal case is *M/S Bremen*, decided by the U.S. Supreme Court in 1972.[29] The case involved a German petitioner and an American respondent. England had no interest in, or contact with, the controversy except for a forum selection clause stating that "any dispute arising must be treated before the London Court of Justice."[30] The U.S. Supreme Court held that forum selection clauses are "prima facie valid and should be enforced" unless the resisting party can show that enforcement would be "unreasonable and unjust, or that the clause was invalid for such reasons as fraud or overreaching."[31] "The choice of that forum was made in an arm's length negotiation by experienced and sophisticated businessmen, and, absent some compelling and countervailing reason, it should be honored by the parties and enforced by the courts."[32]

Subsequent court rulings adhere closely to this Supreme Court decision. Where neither plaintiff nor defendant was based in New York, a New York court rejected foreign defendant's due process argument ("[Defendent] knowingly signed the Agreement containing the forum selection clause. It willingly submitted itself to the jurisdiction of this Court. [Defendant] can claim neither surprise nor unfairness.")[33] Where neither plaintiff nor defendant was based in New York, a New York court held that voluntary submission to New York jurisdiction through a forum selection clause constituted a waiver of the right to object to such venue.[34]

A valid forum selection clause establishes sufficient contacts with the forum for exercise of personal jurisdiction over a nonresident defendant to satisfy constitutional principles of due process.[35] "In fact, the forum selection clause alone would constitute consent to personal jurisdiction."[36] Where a New York court accepted as true that defendants had no personal or financial contacts with the state of New York, the court held that voluntary submission to New York jurisdiction through a forum selection clause satisfied the constitutional due process requirement and constituted a waiver of the right to object to such venue.[37] Where a defendant voluntarily submits to a jurisdiction through a forum selection clause, satisfaction of due process does not require any contact by the defendant with the jurisdiction.[38]

The EU also recognizes the validity and enforceability of forum selection clauses. The primary source of law on forum selection clauses in the EU is Brussels Regulation No. 44/2001, which is binding on every Member State.[39] Article 23 provides for the possibility that parties domiciled in one of the Member States may elect a specific court or courts to have jurisdiction to hear a dispute, and such jurisdiction shall be exclusive unless otherwise agreed by the parties.[40] The primary source of law on choice of law clauses in the EU is Council Regulation 593/2008 on the Law Applicable to Contractual Obligations. This regulation, known as the Rome I Regulation, governs contracts among parties of EU Member States and requires an express choice of law clause to be respected even if the chosen law has no other connection with the contract.[41]

An "asymmetric" jurisdiction clause typically requires one party, but not both parties, to an agreement to sue in the courts of a specified jurisdiction. In February 2017, England's High Court held, in *Commerzbank Aktiengesellschaft v. Liquimar Tankers*,[42] that an asymmetric jurisdiction clause is valid under the Brussels Regulation (Recast) (the Brussels Recast) and qualifies as an exclusive jurisdiction clause for the purposes of the Brussels Recast's "anti-torpedo" protections.[43] The High Court held that the natural meaning of the language in Article 31(2), "an agreement [which] confers exclusive jurisdiction," includes asymmetric jurisdiction clauses.[44] Under the Brussels Recast, an asymmetric jurisdiction clause confers exclusive jurisdiction on the named EU Member State. The fact that it applies in respect of a claim by one party only does not change the analysis. The judge found support for this proposition in *Meeth v. Glacetal Sarl* in which the European Court of Justice held that a jurisdiction clause requiring a French party to sue in Germany and a German party to sue in France conferred exclusive jurisdiction on Germany in proceedings brought by the French party and exclusive jurisdiction on France in proceedings brought by the German party.[45]

Significantly, the European Court has upheld contracts concluded wholly or partly for the benefit of a third party, containing a jurisdiction clause which is also designed to benefit the third party.[46] This type of third party choice-of-jurisdiction clause is precisely the type of clause that is incorporated into the APUNCAC Article 19 paragraph 4(e) guarantee, which requires the guarantor "to waive any objection to the judicial forum and governing law specified herein for resolving all disputes in relation to this Guarantee," and to

> waive any objection to the jurisdiction, process and venue of such forum, and to the effectiveness, execution and enforcement of any order or judgment (including, but not limited to, a default judgment) of any such forum in relation to this Guarantee, to the maximum extent permitted by the laws of such forum or any enforcing forum, the laws of which might be claimed to be applicable regarding the effectiveness, enforcement or execution of such order or judgment (including, but not limited to, a default judgment).[47]

This language would permit a State Party plaintiff to obtain and enforce a monetary judgment regarding a guarantor (a money transmitter) that fails to submit required beneficial ownership information to FINCEN at the point of transmitting funds that originated from the territory of an APUNCAC State Party. The reason this language is needed is because such funds may be transmitted through a complex series of transactions, involving jurisdictions such as the BVI, the Caymans, or Panama, that may not be parties to APUNCAC and may otherwise serve to shield parties to such transactions from APUNCAC.

Both the United States and the EU have signed the Convention on Choice of Court Agreements, whose purpose is to promote international trade and ensure the effectiveness of forum selection clauses in international contracts.[48] Any other court that might be chosen by one of the parties in violation of the forum selection clause is required to dismiss the case.[49] Significantly, the Convention provides for the recognition of any judgment rendered by the selected court in any other jurisdiction.[50] This implies that a hypothetical

State Party to APUNCAC such as Kenya could potentially avail itself of a New York court to enforce a judgment rendered by the London Court of International Arbitration against a BVI money transmitter who maintains a bank account in New York.

Under UK law, the third-party beneficiary may be identified in the contract "as a member of a class" or "as answering a particular description."[51] The law does not require that the third-party beneficiary is an individual person identified by name. Under the APUNCAC contract guarantee system, the Model Guarantee language identifies the third-party beneficiary of each contract as "the States Parties to the Anticorruption Protocol to the United Nations Convention against Corruption (APUNCAC) and nationals of such States Parties."[52] UK law states that

> For the purpose of exercising his right to enforce a term of the contract, there shall be available to the third party any remedy that would have been available to him in an action for breach of contract if he had been a party to the contract.[53]

This gives a third party, such as a State Party to APUNCAC, the same enforcement rights as the contracting parties. Recall that under the Rules of the London Court of International Arbitration, the default location of the arbitral seat is London, and the governing law is therefore English law.

Criminalization of Deceptive Practices

Article 19 closes loopholes that currently permit criminals to evade prosecution:

> No person or entity shall act in a manner that seeks to evade or assists in evading the provisions of this protocol through the creation or use of pseudonyms, codes, initials, numbered bank accounts that hide the identity of the beneficial owner, legal entities involving nominee directors who assign power of attorney to the beneficial owners of such entities, blank letters pre-signed by nominee directors, blank power of attorney forms pre-signed by nominee directors, undated letters of resignation from nominee directors, agents acting on behalf of beneficial owners but shielding the identity of such owners, nominee beneficial owners, nominee shareholders, anonymous trusts, anonymous beneficiaries, orphan assets, anonymous foundations, anonymous bearer instruments, anonymous instructions, anonymous e-mails, false invoices, over-invoicing, under-invoicing, backdated transactions, interest-free or nearly interest-free loans, weakly-collateralized loans, uncollected loans, consulting agreements where no substantive services are provided, equity share options, performance failure fees, or any stratagem or deceptive practice that seeks to obscure, or

> obscures from an educated person, the true identities of beneficial owners linked to financial transactions as described in Articles 21, 22, 23, 24, 28, 29, 30, or 38 or the source of such funds described in Articles 21, 22, 23, 24, 28, 29, 30, or 38, or seeks to launder funds obtained through criminal activities or tax evasion.[54]

This provision criminalizes "any stratagem or deceptive practice" designed to evade APUNCAC. A prosecutor would have the burden of demonstrating that a given practice is deceptive and designed to evade APUNCAC. A court would decide whether the prosecutor had met that burden.

Restrictions on Debarred Persons

Paragraph 7 of Article 19 prohibits a debarred individual from receiving, depositing, or holding funds that originate from the territory of a State Party unless:

(a) the source of such funds is his or her:
  (1) wage and salary income from employment with an entity publicly traded on a national stock exchange;
  (2) wage and salary income from employment with a private entity not engaged in specified activities in such jurisdictions defined by rule of FINCEN and not engaged in illicit activity;
  (3) self-employment income not involving illicit activity, excluding specified activities in such jurisdictions defined by rule of FINCEN;
  (4) dividend and interest income from corporations publicly traded on national stock exchanges; or
  (5) capital gains from the sale of property not involving illicit activity.

(b) an audit was performed within the previous 12 months by a duly qualified independent auditor approved by FINCEN;

(c) the auditor examined documentation in accordance with subparagraph (a);

(d) the auditor submitted an audit report and an audit memorandum to the Chief Debarment Officer describing material observations leading to the auditor's conclusions and audit statement;

(e) the auditor provided an unqualified opinion that, to the best of his or her knowledge, the debarred individual derived the entire amount of his or her income from licit sources pursuant to subparagraph (a) and is in compliance with applicable anticorruption law and regulations;

(f) the debarred individual submitted documentation to the Chief Debarment Officer pursuant to subparagraph (a) that may include paystubs, income statements, dividend and interest statements, executed sale agreements, or statements filed with the national taxing authority to report partnership income or other income;

(g) the debarred individual annually certified under penalty of perjury that, to the best of his or her knowledge, no funds were received from employment with an entity involved in illicit activity, from self-employment involving illicit activity, or from the sale of property involving illicit activity.

The provisions are sufficiently onerous to discourage legitimate attorneys, bank clerks, or trust or company service provider (TCSP) personnel from engaging with individuals who have difficulty documenting the source of large currency deposits. The provisions balance the need to give debarred individuals a second chance and an opportunity to earn an honest living, while discouraging bad behavior and illicit activity that would trigger arrest and criminal penalties.

Article 19 prohibits a debarred individual from transmitting or retransmitting funds that originate from the territory of a State Party to a foreign destination. The rationale is similar—it is sufficiently onerous to deter legitimate attorneys, bank clerks, and TCSP personnel from engaging with money launderers, while giving debarred individuals one more opportunity to obey the law before incurring criminal penalties.

These provisions would make it difficult for debarred persons to serve as bank clerks or TCSP personnel in high-risk jurisdictions such as the BVI, the Cayman Islands, or Panama. The provisions would make it difficult for debarred persons to receive and hide illicit income. Debarred persons who are self-employed and engaged in opaque activities would presumably have difficulty obtaining an unqualified opinion from a FINCEN-approved auditor that they derived their entire income from licit sources and comply with applicable anticorruption law and regulations. The provisions would accomplish the goal of deterring bad behavior while giving debarred individuals an opportunity to obey the law and avoid criminal penalties. Chapter 9 addresses the issues of jurisdiction and enforcement.

Paragraph 9 of Article 19 prohibits a debarred entity from sending, receiving, depositing, holding, transmitting, or retransmitting funds that originate from the territory of a State Party unless:

(a) revenues and expenses of such entity have been audited within the previous 12 months by a duly qualified independent auditor approved by FINCEN;

(b) the auditor performed an audit of the entity's operations with the aim of determining whether the entity is in compliance with applicable anticorruption law and regulations;

(c) the audit examined possible improprieties involving:
(1) cash and financial transactions;
(2) use of funds for illicit purposes;
(3) procurement;
(4) payments to unauthorized persons;
(5) payments lacking supporting documentation;
(6) over-invoicing, under-invoicing, double-invoicing, or false invoicing;
(7) laundering of monetary instruments;
(8) falsification of receipts or other documents;
(9) bribery;
(d) the auditor submitted an audit report and an audit memorandum to the Chief Debarment Officer describing material observations leading to the auditor's conclusions and audit statement;
(e) the auditor provided an unqualified opinion that, to the best of his or her knowledge, the entity is operating in compliance with applicable anticorruption law and regulations; and
(f) All officers and directors (or equivalent) of the debarred entity have annually certified under penalty of perjury that, to the best of their knowledge, no funds were received by the entity from a person or entity involved in illicit activity, or from the sale of property involving illicit activity.

These provisions would make it difficult for a debarred entity to serve as a financial institution or TCSP in high-risk jurisdictions such as the BVI, the Cayman Islands, or Panama. The provisions would make it difficult for a debarred entity to receive and hide illicit funds for the benefit of criminals. Debarred entities that are engaged in opaque activities would presumably have difficulty obtaining an unqualified opinion from a FINCEN-approved auditor that the entity is in compliance with applicable anticorruption law and regulations. Chapter 9 addresses the issues of jurisdiction and enforcement.

Prohibition on Assisting Debarred Persons

Article 19 prohibits a person or entity from assisting a debarred person by sending, receiving, depositing, holding, transmitting, or retransmitting funds in excess of $3,000 that originate from the territory of a State Party at the behest, or for the benefit, of a debarred person, or with the cooperation of a debarred person, or for the purpose of a transaction with a debarred person, unless:

a. for an individual, the source of the funds is a source pursuant to subparagraph (a) of paragraph 7 of Article 19; or

b. for an entity, the entity meets the requirements of subparagraphs (a) through (f) of paragraph 9 of Article 19.

Article 19 prohibits a national of a State Party from transmitting funds in excess of $3,000 to or from, or for the benefit of, a debarred person, unless:

a. for an individual, the source of the funds is a source pursuant to subparagraph (a) of paragraph 7 of Article 19; or
b. for an entity, the entity meets the requirements of subparagraphs (a) through (f) of paragraph 9 of Article 19.

While the audit and reporting requirements may seem onerous and invasive, the intent is to halt activity that plainly serves to aid and abet criminals seeking to hide illicit funds. Innocent parties can avoid the audit requirements if they abide by APUNCAC's requirements to collect and report beneficial ownership information to FINCEN and observe APUNCAC's currency transaction and wire transaction reporting requirements. Only parties that refuse to obey the law would be subject to the audit requirements. These parties are likely to be involved in money laundering, either intentionally or unintentionally.

A precedent and model for this type of requirement is the UK's use of court-ordered financial reporting by individuals who are convicted of "obtaining a money transfer by deception," "obtaining property by deception," "obtaining a pecuniary advantage by deception," or money laundering.[55] A financial reporting order is not a penalty but a preventive measure intended to enable a court to control offenders who are likely to indulge in further criminal activity. Offenders are required to submit regular reports of "such particulars of his financial affairs relating to the period in question as may be specified" by the order and are required to "include any specified documents with each report" for a period that may last up to 15 years.[56] These reports may be used by law enforcement officers for "the prevention, detection, investigation or prosecution of criminal offences, whether in the United Kingdom or elsewhere."[57] A person who fails to comply may be fined and imprisoned for up to one year.[58]

Article 19 of APUNCAC prohibits a person from transmitting funds in excess of $3,000 originating from the territory of a State Party with the assistance of a debarred person. A national of a State Party is prohibited from sending, receiving, depositing, holding, transmitting, or retransmitting funds in excess of $3,000 with the assistance of a debarred person. A debarred person is prohibited from serving as a director, officer, partner, trustee, or equivalent of a legal entity. Debarred individuals and entities are prohibited from certifying information regarding the source of funds or the identities of beneficial owners. Auditors are required to report suspicious activity to the Chief Debarment Officer.

Extradition

Article 19 requires States Parties to cooperate, and to seek the cooperation of states with extradition agreements with States Parties, to arrest, extradite, and prosecute violators, notwithstanding preexisting limitations on extradition. Article 19 requires States Parties to cooperate, and to seek the cooperation of nonparty states through cooperative agreements, to enforce the fines levied in accordance with APUNCAC by seizing the assets of individuals and entities that fail to pay the fines. Half of the assets would be directed to compensate the State Party assessing the fines and half would be directed to the ongoing costs of enforcing APUNCAC.

Money Laundering

Article 20 of APUNCAC criminalizes money laundering. This language is adapted from the language of the U.S. Code.[59] Articles 21, 22, 23, and 24 of APUNCAC require banks, currency dealers, casinos, and financial institutions to maintain records of customer identities and customer transactions. This customer identity and transaction information is useful when investigating money laundering and other financial crimes. The language is adapted from the U.S. Code of Federal Regulations (CFR).[60]

Records and Reporting

Articles 21 and 22 require banks, money transmitters, and other financial institutions that transmit funds by wire to retain, and submit to FINCEN, information about customer identities and customer transactions that is useful when investigating money laundering and other financial crimes. Articles 21 and 22 specifically require banks, money transmitters, and financial institutions to obtain and submit to FINCEN information regarding the source and beneficial owner of wire source funds, and the beneficial owner of the receiving account. Individuals who assert beneficial ownership are required to certify this assertion under penalty of perjury. This provision would facilitate prosecution for false statements, deter false statements, and create leverage for prosecutors to obtain the cooperation of front men who may decide to cooperate in exchange for deferred prosecution or leniency in sentencing.

Articles 21 and 22 require banks, money transmitters, and financial institutions to pass information about a customer originating a wire transaction to intermediaries and require intermediaries to pass this information to receiving institutions when multiple institutions are involved in a wire transaction. In combination with Article 19, which prohibits any deceptive practice that seeks to obscure the true identities of beneficial owners linked to financial transactions, this rule, called the "travel rule," would help to ensure that sufficient information is available to financial crime investigators seeking to trace the route of a complicated series of wire transactions involving multiple intermediary institutions.

Transportation of Currency

Article 25 requires individuals who physically transport, mail, or ship currency or other monetary instruments in an aggregate amount exceeding $10,000, either into or out of the territory of the State Party, to file a report with FINCEN. This information is useful when investigating money laundering and other financial crimes because money launderers often transport currency across international borders for the purpose of money laundering. This language is adapted from the U.S. CFR.[61]

Foreign Financial Accounts

Article 26 requires individuals who maintain foreign financial accounts to file a report with FINCEN for each year during which such accounts are maintained. Article 27 requires specified financial institutions to file reports of certain transactions with designated foreign financial agencies. This information is useful when investigating money laundering and other financial crimes because money laundering frequently involves the use of offshore accounts. This language is adapted from the U.S. CFR.[62]

Currency Transaction Reports

Articles 28 and 29 require financial institutions and casinos to file currency transaction reports with FINCEN for each transaction in currency that exceeds $3,000. With the exception of individuals employed by banks that are exempted from currency transaction reporting requirements pursuant to Article 31, Article 30 requires any person doing business, whether or not on a regular basis or as an organized business concern, who provides remittance services or receives cash deposits or cash payments or converted negotiable instruments or bearer instruments to cash as a financial service, and handles a transaction in currency that exceeds $3,000, or handles a transaction in currency or involving a negotiable instrument, bearer instrument, bank draft, wire transfer, or money order with a value totaling $3,000 or more in specified high-risk jurisdictions such as the BVI, the Cayman Islands, or Panama, to file a report with FINCEN.

Article 30 requires that such individuals obtain and submit to FINCEN information regarding the source and beneficial owner of the source funds, and the beneficial owner of the receiving account. Individuals who assert beneficial ownership are required to certify this assertion under penalty of perjury. This could be accomplished using digital certificates, which are the digital equivalent of a passport or signature, using an electronic device such as a computer or smartphone. A digital certificate uses RSA encryption so it cannot be compromised or "cracked" by someone posing as the beneficial owner.[63] This provides assurance that the person asserting beneficial ownership is genuinely that person. A bank clerk would place a hold on funds that are deposited until the certification process is completed.

The requirement to obtain certification of beneficial ownership would facilitate prosecution for false statements, deter false statements, and create leverage for prosecutors to obtain the cooperation of front men who may decide to cooperate in exchange for deferred prosecution or leniency. Article 30, in combination with Articles 19, 21, 22, and 25, would permit investigators to follow the trail of cash that is transported internationally, deposited offshore, then wired to the BVI, the Cayman Islands, or Switzerland (figure 8.5).

Article 30 requires collection and reporting of information regarding each cash or bearer share contribution to the transaction amount by a customer of the person on whose behalf the transaction was conducted that exceeds $3,000. In addition, Article 30 requires submission of, or verification that FINCEN currently maintains, a searchable electronic copy of the most recent tax return for each such customer. The rationale for this requirement, and issues related to privacy and the reporting burden, are discussed in chapter 9.

The language of Article 30 is crafted to extend extraterritorial application of APUNCAC to bank clerks in offshore jurisdictions who previously aided and abetted money laundering by accepting large currency deposits without question. Article 30 is one of the most innovative features of APUNCAC. It seeks to close a loophole in the international regulatory regime that currently permits criminals to abscond with illicit funds and profit from criminal activity. The issue of jurisdiction is addressed in chapter 9.

Bank Currency Transaction Report Exemptions

Article 31 exempts banks, regarding certain customers, from filing currency transaction reports with FINCEN. The exemption includes any bank, any legal entity exercising governmental authority, any legal entity (other than a bank) whose common stock is listed on a national stock exchange as designated by FINCEN, and eligible "non-listed businesses," as defined by APUNCAC. The exemption seeks to reduce the reporting burden regarding established customers that are unlikely to be involved in money laundering. The language is adapted from the U.S. CFR.[64]

APUNCAC Requirements:

- Wire transmitters and recipients of cash deposits report beneficial owner of source funds, and beneficial owner of receiving account, if beneficial owner is State Party national
- Recipients must enter into contractual agreements to obey all APUNCAC rules and accede to State Party jurisdiction
- Records entered into FINCEN electronic database
- "No person or entity shall act in a manner that seeks to evade or assists in evading the provisions of this protocol"

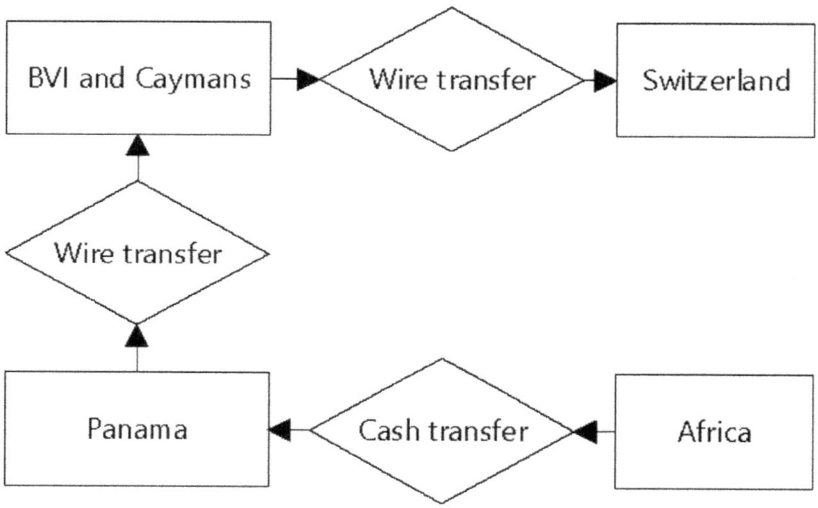

Figure 8.5 Beneficial Owner Reporting Requirements Permit Investigators to Follow International Transactions. *Source*: Figure created by author.

Structuring

Article 32 prohibits any person from causing or attempting to cause a financial institution or a nonfinancial trade or business to fail to file a required report or maintain a required record, or to cause or attempt to cause such institution or trade or business to file a report or maintain a record that contains a material omission or misstatement of fact, or structure or assist in structuring, or attempt to structure or assist in structuring, any transaction with one or more persons or financial institutions or nonfinancial trades or businesses, where "structuring" means an attempt to evade the reporting requirements of APUNCAC. The Article 32 prohibition is a key element in fighting financial crime because money launderers frequently employ sophisticated schemes designed to use the loophole in financial reporting rules that exempts small transaction amounts from the rules. The language of Article 32 is adapted from the U.S. Code.[65]

Suspicious Activity Reports

Articles 33, 34, 35, 36, and 37 require banks, saving associations and service corporations, money service businesses, casinos, and securities brokers and dealers to file SARs with FINCEN regarding any suspicious transaction relevant to a possible violation of law or regulation, if the transaction involves or aggregates funds or other assets beyond a certain minimum amount and the entity knows, suspects, or has reason to suspect that the transaction (or a pattern of transactions of which the transaction is a part):

i. involves funds derived from illegal activity or is intended or conducted in order to hide or disguise funds or assets derived from illegal activity (including, without limitation, the ownership, nature, source, location, or control of such funds or assets) as part of a plan to violate or evade any federal law or regulation or to avoid any transaction reporting requirement under federal law or regulation;
ii. is designed to evade any requirements of APUNCAC or associated regulations; or
iii. serves no business or apparent lawful purpose, and the entity knows of no reasonable explanation for the transaction after examining the available facts, including the background and possible purpose of the transaction.

SARs are among the most valuable sources of information for financial crime investigators. The language is adapted from the U.S. CFR.[66]

Cash Received in a Trade or Business

Article 38 requires a person who, in the course of a trade or business in which such person is engaged, receives cash, or receives cash for the account of another, or acts as an agent and receives cash from a principal in excess of $3,000, to file a report with FINCEN regarding the receipt of cash. Article 38 seeks to detect and deter money laundering that occurs when goods are purchased with illicit cash, then sold to obtain funds that appear to derive from legitimate sales. The language is adapted from the U.S. CFR.[67]

Article 38 requires collection and reporting of information regarding each cash or bearer share contribution to the transaction amount, by a customer of the person on whose behalf the transaction was conducted, that exceeds $3,000. In addition, Article 30 requires submission, or verification that FINCEN currently maintains, a searchable electronic copy of the most recent tax return for each such customer. The rationale for this requirement, and issues related to privacy and the reporting burden, are discussed in chapter 9.

Civil and Criminal Penalties

Article 39 describes civil penalties for violations of Articles 19 through 38 of APUNCAC. Article 40 describes criminal penalties for violations of Articles 19 through 38 of APUNCAC. Civil penalties involve a lower standard of proof and a simplified administrative adjudication procedure, facilitating prosecution. Criminal penalties involve a higher standard of proof and adjudication through the courts. Both civil penalties and criminal penalties involve debarment and fines, while criminal penalties include prison terms. Civil penalties and procedures are quicker and easier, facilitating prosecution. The language regarding fines and prison terms is adapted from the U.S. CFR.[68]

APUNCAC includes provisions that permit investigators to use the threat of debarment to negotiate agreements where peripheral figures such as front men and TCSP personnel would agree to cooperate with investigators in exchange for deferred prosecution:

> The Chief Debarment Officer may at any time enter into a deferred debarment agreement with a defendant who agrees to cooperate as a witness in a criminal investigation that may include but is not limited to allegations of corruption or financial crimes. Such agreement shall specify that debarment, or a determination of debarment, shall be suspended for the duration of such cooperation and shall be resumed at the discretion of the Chief Debarment Officer upon a finding of noncooperation or upon the end of such criminal investigation.[69]

Deterrence

In sum, APUNCAC includes provisions that would enable investigators to follow the trail of significant transfers of money from the territory of a State Party. APUNCAC debars individuals who violate the reporting provisions and criminalizes the act of employing debarred individuals to send, receive, deposit, hold, transmit, or retransmit funds that originate from the territory of a State Party. Enforcement would depend on whether an offender is found in, or travels to, a jurisdiction that is a State Party or has an extradition agreement with a State Party. The deterrent effect would, therefore, depend on the number and international significance of the States Parties. Ratification by OECD Member States would have a major deterrent effect.

Regardless, it may be expected that APUNCAC would have a deterrent effect regarding all but the most incorrigible offshore financial service professionals. If a potential customer has a choice between employing a debarred individual, thereby risking debarment and, upon repeat violations, risking extradition and imprisonment, or simply choosing not to employ a debarred individual, it is unlikely that a customer would voluntarily choose to assume those risks by employing a debarred individual.

Risk-averse customers would presumably choose to minimize their risk by selecting financial service professionals who are not debarred. This process of natural selection would steadily reduce the client base of debarred financial service professionals, driving down their revenues and profit (figure 8.6). This prospect would likely deter the type of violations that would result in debarment. In the absence of large numbers of financial service professionals who are willing to risk debarment, it would become more difficult to use financial service professionals to hide the proceeds of crime in offshore tax havens.

APUNCAC seeks to halt the facilitation of money laundering by banking and financial industry professionals. APUNCAC is expected to have minimal impact on individuals who handle legitimate banking transactions where "know your customer" (KYC) regulations already require verification of the identity of account beneficiaries. APUNCAC requirements are expected to have minimal impact on legitimate businesses conducting legitimate business transactions. Protocol requirements may be met by submitting genuine documentation of legitimate transactions for legitimate business reasons. However, anyone who submits questionable documentation for questionable funds would risk criminal investigation. The existence of APUNCAC requirements would effectively force money launderers to sign, certify, and submit documentation that is demonstrably false, subjecting money launderers and anyone who aids and abets their activities to enhanced risk of prosecution by national authorities.

A REGISTRY?

A popular idea for addressing money laundering involves the creation of a registry of all companies in the entire world.[70] It is believed that this would permit law enforcement agencies to disentangle complicated ownership structures created by criminals who seek to hide the identity of ultimate beneficial owners. However, there are three reasons why a registry of companies would be ineffective in halting money laundering.

- A registry cannot be effective if even a single jurisdiction declines to participate. Suppose, for example, that 99 out of 100 jurisdictions agree to

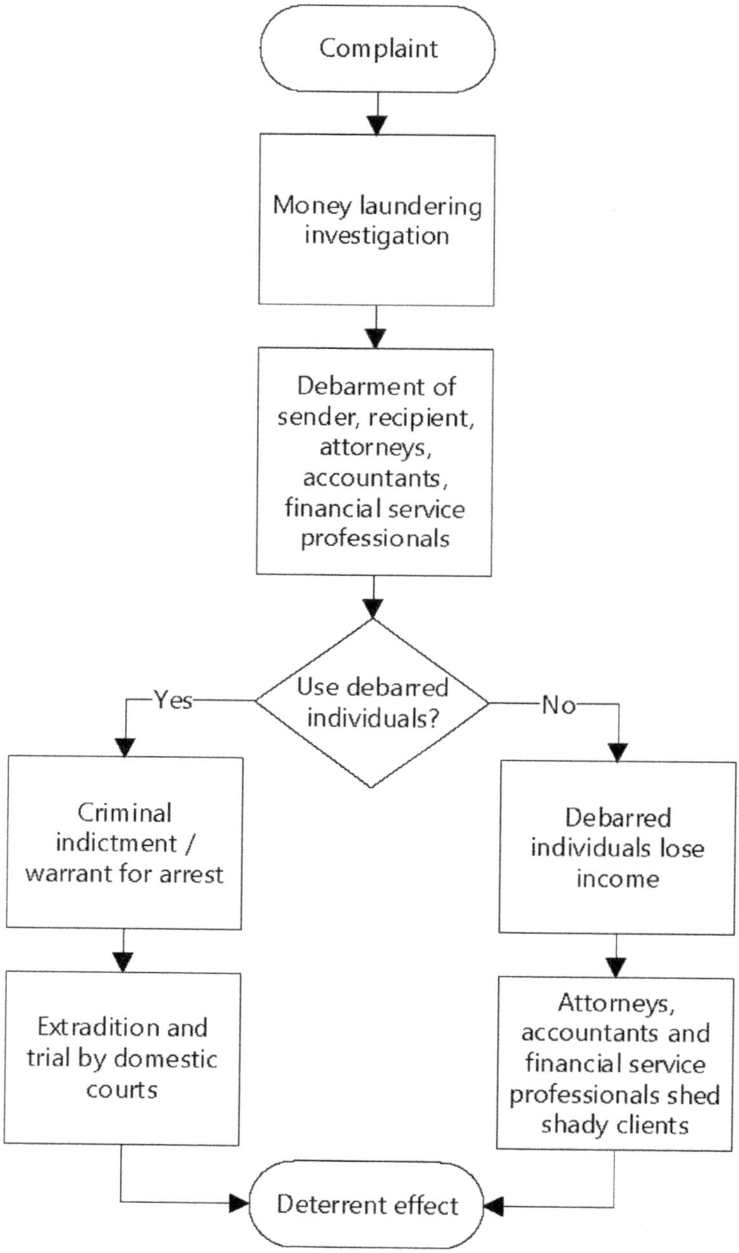

Figure 8.6 Incentives for Attorneys, Accountants, and Financial Service Professionals to Shed Shady Clients. *Source*: Figure created by author.

require beneficial owners to register their accounts. Criminals would simply shift their accounts to the one jurisdiction that does not require beneficial owners to register ownership of their companies with the registry. This would bypass the registry.

- A registry cannot be effective if criminals do not deposit their funds into an account that is owned by a company. Suppose, for example, that criminals transmit their funds to an offshore location but do not use any account that is subject to a registry. This would bypass the registry.
- A registry cannot be effective if a criminal chooses to employ a trusted confidant who agrees to be listed as the beneficial owner of a company account, and if there is no mechanism to punish the nominee owner. This would render the beneficial ownership information useless for the purpose of tracing money laundering. Currently, no nation has sought to criminalize the practice of naming a nominee owner if such nominee is not a national and is beyond the jurisdiction of that nation.

In sum, it is unlikely that a global registry would be effective (figure 8.7).

THE BENEFICIAL OWNER REPORTING REQUIREMENT

What I am proposing instead is an international treaty that would require each beneficial owner to name himself or herself as beneficial owner every time that cash is received or deposited, or funds are transmitted across borders to known offshore bank secrecy havens, in amounts equal to or exceeding $3,000. The proposed scheme would apply to money launderers worldwide who currently use money transmitters such as Western Union, MoneyGram, or InterCambio Express to transmit funds to bank secrecy destinations such as the BVI, the Cayman Islands, Guernsey, Hong Kong, Luxembourg, Panama, Singapore, or Switzerland. If a trusted confidant is induced to circumvent the law by agreeing to be listed as the beneficial owner, the trusted confidant would risk debarment. Each illicit transmission or receipt of funds by a debarred individual would be punishable by a fine of $100,000, five years in prison, or both. A debarred individual who is convicted of 10 instances of illicit transmission or receipt of funds would risk fines totaling $1,000,000 and 50 years of imprisonment. These penalties would apply even when such individuals are not nationals of States Parties to APUNCAC. In that case, arrests would not occur unless and until such individuals travel to a jurisdiction that is a State Party to APUNCAC, or to a jurisdiction with an extradition treaty with a State Party to APUNCAC. While this would blunt the threat of punishment, the deterrent effect would not be insignificant.

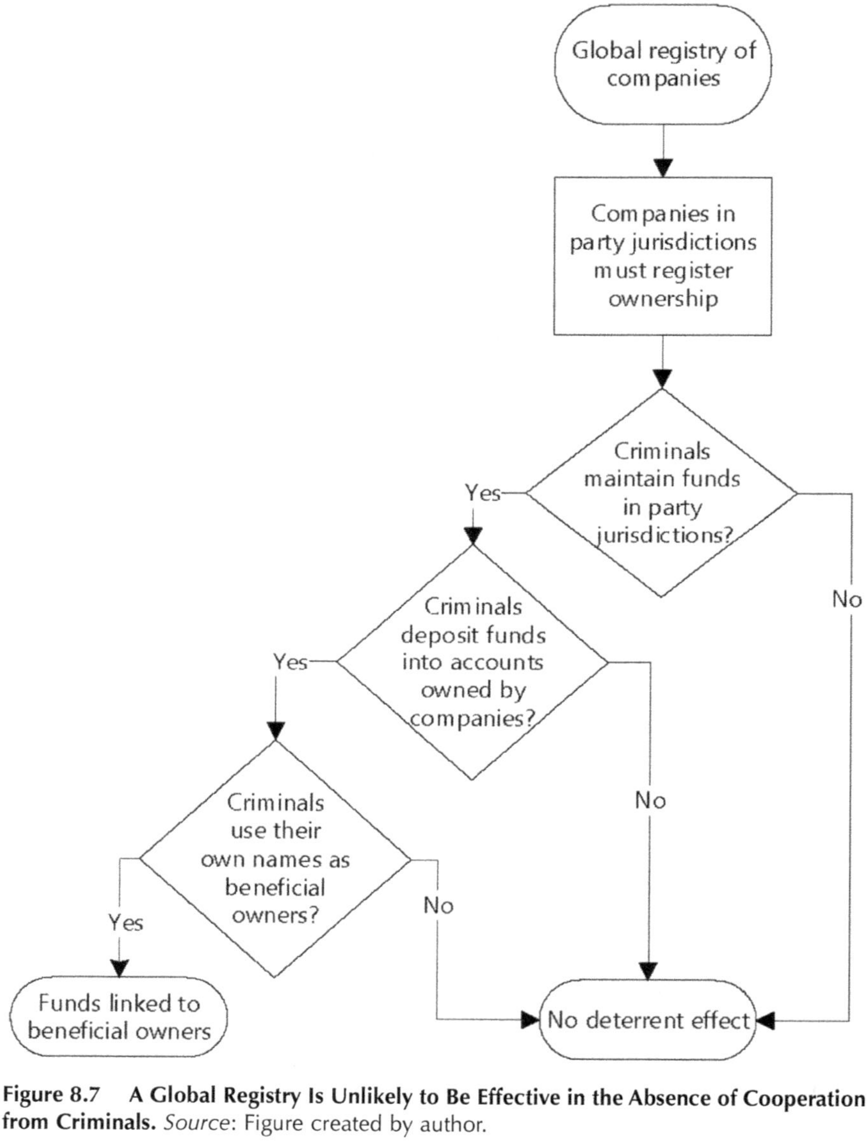

Figure 8.7 A Global Registry Is Unlikely to Be Effective in the Absence of Cooperation from Criminals. *Source*: Figure created by author.

It may be expected that the United States and OECD Member States would seek ratification of such a treaty because it would plug a major gap in the international sanction regime against money laundering and terrorist financing. Individuals for whom an arrest warrant has been issued could avoid arrest by avoiding travel to any jurisdiction where they could be arrested. However, this might require avoidance of travel to any of the OECD Member States.

The mere threat of arrest would tend to deter large numbers of individuals from the temptation to participate in any scheme where they might risk fines exceeding $1,000,000 and imprisonment for 50 or more years. This scheme may not deter hardened criminals who are unfazed by the prospect of lengthy prison terms but would deter the vast number of individuals who are currently willing to serve as nominee owners only because the threat of punishment is low. The proposed treaty would dramatically raise the potential cost, and significantly alter the perceived cost-benefit ratio, of participating in schemes that seek to hide the identities of true beneficial owners.

The proposed scheme could be implemented unilaterally and would bypass the need to secure the agreement of jurisdictions such as the BVI, the Cayman Islands, Guernsey, Hong Kong, Luxembourg, Panama, Singapore, or Switzerland. At the same time, money launderers who seek to use those jurisdictions to hide their cash could not do so without exposing bankers in those jurisdictions to significant criminal penalties. Consequently, bankers who previously operated with impunity to hide the money of criminals would be forced to make a choice: risk severe criminal penalties, avoid travel to OECD Member States, or decline the business of criminals and money launderers.

FATCA?

In 2010, the United States passed the Foreign Account Tax Compliance Act (FATCA), and in 2012 strengthened the Act, to compel foreign financial institutions (FFIs) that serve U.S.-based individuals to give the U.S. Internal Revenue Service (IRS) specified client account information linked to those individuals.[71] FFIs may either sign an agreement to submit account information directly to the IRS or sign an agreement where account information is submitted to domestic tax authorities who then make the information available to the IRS upon request. An FFI that refuses to sign an agreement triggers 30 percent withholding of all U.S. source income paid to the FFI. To implement this, the IRS issues rules requiring all domestic entities that remit such income to withhold 30 percent, pending FFI submission of the required client account information to U.S. authorities. This effectively drives away U.S.-based clients whose only incentive to bank at an offshore FFI is the prospect of evading taxes. By exerting control over domestic entities that fall within its jurisdiction, and by using the threat of income withholding, the IRS exerts control over FFIs that ordinarily would not be subject to IRS jurisdiction.

FATCA ingeniously targets FFIs that previously enabled U.S.-based individuals to hide and evade taxes on U.S. source income by parking those funds in secret offshore bank accounts. FATCA creates an onerous reporting and paperwork burden on institutions that previously aided and abetted tax evasion. The response from many of these institutions has been to abandon and refuse to serve American clients, rather than to submit to the FATCA requirements. However, to the extent that those clients were evading taxes, this development is, from the IRS's view, a desirable consequence.

FATCA reduces tax evasion and associated money laundering. However, it is a complex, indirect approach that has severe disadvantages. Since most FFIs choose to sign an agreement whereby they provide U.S.-based client account information to domestic tax authorities, and since these agreements only require that information be provided to the IRS after the IRS initiates a formal investigation of tax fraud, the IRS cannot employ software that would permit the IRS to quickly search a single database to efficiently identify suspicious accounts. Furthermore, FATCA does not address money laundering involving money transmitters that are not depository financial institutions. FATCA is not designed, and is ineffective, for the purpose of addressing money laundering that does not involve U.S.-based clients. Significantly, FATCA is ineffective in following the flow of money or in addressing money laundering involving clients who hide their identities by opening an account under the name of a trusted confidant.

ENDING IMPUNITY

In comparison, the approach that I propose would require all financial sector personnel who receive funds and are located in bank secrecy havens to register information about the beneficial owner and the source of the funds in a centralized, searchable database operated by FINCEN. If these personnel choose to flout the regulation, they will risk debarment. Anyone who agreed to be listed as a beneficial owner but is not in fact a true beneficial owner would risk debarment. Debarred individuals who violate APUNCAC would be subject to arrest, fines, and imprisonment if they traveled to any jurisdiction that is a State Party to APUNCAC, or to any jurisdiction that maintained an extradition agreement with a State Party to APUNCAC. Nominee (fake) beneficial owners would no longer be able to aid and abet money laundering without facing a genuine risk of imprisonment (figure 8.8).

The approach that I propose would criminalize behavior on the part of financial sector personnel and fake beneficial owners that is currently legal, unregulated or poorly regulated, and serves to aid and abet criminal activity. It would strongly discourage the cooperation of financial sector personnel and nominee owners—cooperation that is essential to the success of criminals who need to hide their identities and move the illicit proceeds of their

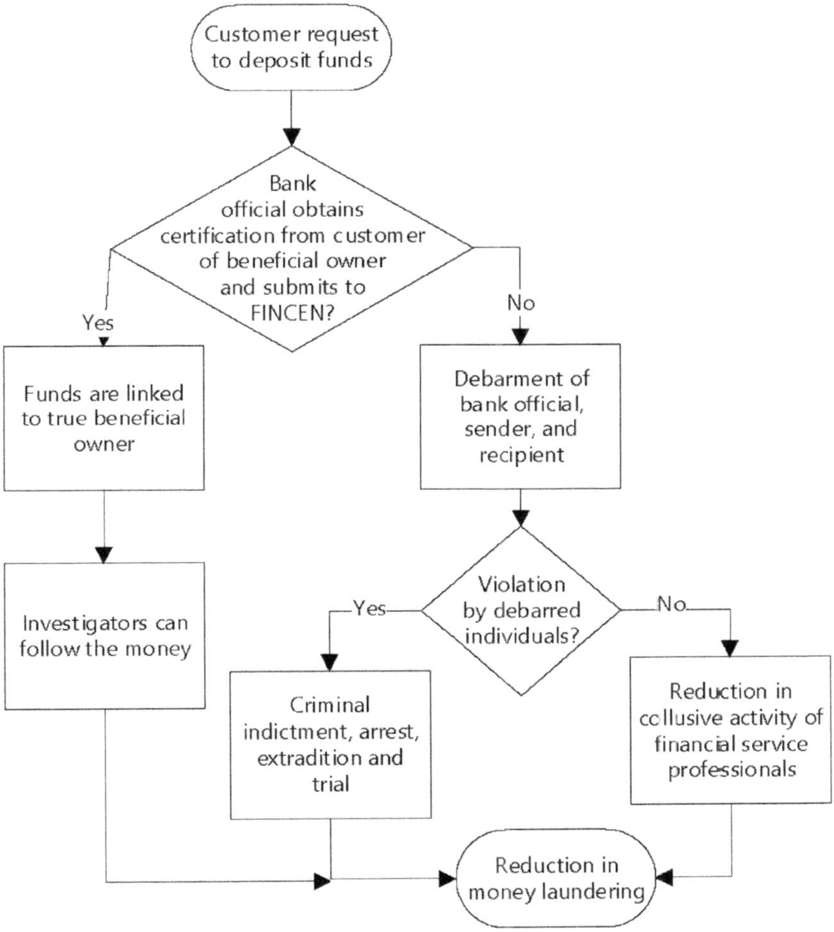

Figure 8.8 Sanction Regime Reduces Collusive Activity of Financial Service Professionals. *Source*: Figure created by author.

activities to hidden locations. In the absence of this cooperation, the identities of the criminals and the movement and location of these proceeds would become apparent.

Criminal prosecution of major criminals would be enabled because prosecutors would obtain agreements with low-level bank clerks, money transmitters, and nominee owners who would agree to cooperate and testify regarding the activities of major criminals in exchange for plea agreements or deferred prosecution of minor crimes. Low-level bank clerks, money transmitters, and nominee owners who, in the absence of a real threat of prosecution, currently welcome the business of individuals who deposit large amounts of cash and transmit the funds to bank secrecy destinations would, after the introduction of a law that criminalizes cooperation with criminals, be compelled to cooperate with investigators or risk imprisonment. Since money laundering typically involves the cooperation of bank clerks, money transmitters, and fake beneficial owners to transmit criminal proceeds to bank secrecy destinations, and since the limited jurisdiction of existing domestic laws prevents the prosecution of this behavior, it is necessary to develop a new type of law, in the form of APUNCAC, that would create a genuine threat of prosecution for all individuals who aid, abet, and participate in criminal activities.

CONCLUSION

In sum, APUNCAC draws upon existing model laws but incorporates innovative provisions designed to address the systemic corruption and impunity that occurs when criminals can hide illicit proceeds in offshore bank secrecy havens and hide behind nominees who pose as beneficial owners. These provisions distinguish APUNCAC from all other strategies that are designed to fight corruption. The analysis presented in this chapter explains why these provisions may be significantly more effective than a global registry of companies or provisions modeled on FATCA.

Chapter 9

Ending Money Laundering

While the FATF, FATF-Style Regional Bodies (FSRBs), and other intergovernmental institutions seek to develop and promote national and international policies to combat money laundering and terrorist financing, both money laundering and terrorist financing persist. Global banks defy U.S. crackdowns by serving oligarchs, criminals, and terrorists. According to documents obtained by the International Consortium of Investigative Journalists, trillions in tainted dollars flow freely through major banks, swamping a broken enforcement system.[1]

The FATF "40 Recommendations" involve a set of 40 policy recommendations urging nations to strengthen domestic AML laws and regulations, related domestic financial system regulations, and measures to improve international cooperation. Many of the recommendations have been recognized, endorsed, and adopted. However, the scope and persistence of money laundering suggest a need to consider stronger measures. An international treaty is one such measure. In comparison with policy recommendations, a treaty is binding on all parties to the treaty. It has the force of law. Adoption of policy recommendations is optional; adherence to a treaty is not.

The practice of adopting international treaties to fight corruption is not new. Among these treaties is the UNCAC,[2] the United Nations Convention against Transnational Organized Crime (UNTOC),[3] the United Nations Convention against Illicit Traffic in Narcotic Drugs and Psychotropic Substances (1988 Vienna Convention),[4] and the International Convention for the Suppression of Financing of Terrorism.[5] However, money laundering persists, suggesting a need to consider additional measures.

This chapter explains how the crime of money laundering could be addressed through APUNCAC, a model protocol to UNCAC that would seek to deter money laundering by criminalizing behavior that is currently not criminalized.[6] Innovative protocol provisions would permit investigators to trace international flows of funds into and out of bank secrecy havens such as the BVI, the Cayman Islands, and Panama and would permit investigators to follow illicit funds related to terrorism, transnational criminal organizations, and activities of corrupt individuals that currently go unpunished.[7] These provisions may be attractive to the United States and its allies because their efforts to halt terrorist financing have been stymied by the ability of terrorists to hide their funds in offshore havens. This chapter explains why a global registry of companies is impractical and unlikely to be effective, and why the proposed strategy to identify beneficial ownership would be more effective. This chapter illustrates the intended and expected ripple effects of APUNCAC through examination of likely responses by legitimate business owners, banks, and bank clerks who are currently permitted by lax regulatory regimes to aid, abet, and facilitate money laundering.

The model convention is posed as a protocol to UNCAC because UNCAC is the flagship international treaty against corruption. UNCAC has been adopted by 186 of the 193 UN Member States. It has achieved broad acceptance and is the law of the land in 186 UN Member States. It is difficult for any person who desires to seek an elected leadership position to challenge or reject UNCAC. For this reason, it is advantageous to pose APUNCAC as a protocol to UNCAC that seeks to fulfill the promise of UNCAC.

Unlike UNCAC and other anticorruption conventions, APUNCAC offers detailed language that seeks to demonstrate how changes in international law could be implemented in a way that would permit parties to the convention to exert extraterritorial control over distant offshore financial service personnel, identify beneficial owners whenever funds exceeding $3,000 are transmitted internationally, and provide leverage needed by financial crime investigators to secure the cooperation of distant offshore financial service personnel. The detailed language of APUNCAC seeks to preempt objections that it is not possible to exert extraterritorial control over distant offshore personnel, not possible to enforce these provisions, and not possible to implement this approach. The detailed language seeks to address all of the legal and practical challenges that would arise and provides a detailed model for the type of domestic conforming legislation that would be required upon ratification.

APUNCAC has been the topic of multiple articles published in scholarly journals.[8] These articles seek to address the many legal and practical issues raised by APUNCAC. The purpose of this chapter is to invite discussion of APUNCAC and the approach adopted by APUNCAC, and prepare the way for possible consideration by the International Law Commission. This chapter seeks to improve understanding of an approach that is arguably feasible, practical, and sensible.

To facilitate the discussion, the language of APUNCAC adopts terms that are familiar to readers. This includes the use of the term "FINCEN" to describe the financial crime intelligence agency established by APUNCAC. APUNCAC would create and establish FINCEN with the objective of maintaining a centralized database of information regarding beneficial ownership and related information that is useful in conducting investigations into allegations of money laundering and financial crime. The term "FINCEN" deliberately evokes the U.S. FinCEN. While the term may seem U.S. centric, and while it may be confusing that APUNCAC refers to "FINCEN" as well as "FinCEN," the use of the term "FINCEN" conveys the intended nature and purpose of the new agency.

While APUNCAC incorporates an array of provisions intended to fight corruption, including provisions already incorporated into existing treaties, model treaties, or model regulations, the focus of this chapter is innovative provisions that would require financial system personnel to collect and report information regarding the beneficial owner of funds that are sent and received internationally. The chapter focuses on high-risk jurisdictions that have traditionally been used by criminals engaged in financial crime. For illustrative purposes, certain jurisdictions are identified by name. However, the analysis applies to all jurisdictions where money laundering and financial crime occur. This includes the United States, OECD Member States, and all modern democracies, as well as countries where money laundering and financial crime are especially prevalent.

FRONT MEN

Corruption cannot persist in the absence of vehicles that permit criminals to hide illicit funds from investigators: "the flows of funds do not lie."[9] Investigators seek to penetrate these vehicles so that they can follow the money. Once illicit funds are traced, prosecutors have the evidence needed to convict.

Investigators invariably focus on the "front man" who purports to be the beneficial owner of the funds but is not the true beneficial owner. The corrupt party places formal control of the funds in the hands of this trusted confidant to hide the fact that the funds are ultimately controlled by the corrupt party. For example, in the Augusto Pinochet case, Pinochet's son, Marco Antonio Pinochet Hiriart, and his daughters, Inés Lucía Pinochet Hiriart and Maria Veronica Pinochet, served as front men for corporate vehicles, trusts, and bank accounts that were ultimately controlled by Augusto Pinochet.[10] In addition, Óscar Custodio Aitken Lavanchy, an attorney with close ties to Pinochet, controlled six other corporate vehicles that were involved in the scheme.[11]

In addition to these front men, financial crimes are wittingly or unwittingly aided and abetted by TCSPs that create, and provide administrative services for, corporate vehicles. A TCSP may be a single individual operating through a website, or a small law or accounting firm. TCSPs commonly act as intermediaries between their clients and the respective financial institution or bank where the customer wishes to establish a corporate account.

TCSP personnel are financial service professionals, attorneys, or accountants who profit by performing services needed to create and maintain corporate vehicles. Their services are needed by criminals who wish to use corporate vehicles to hide illicit funds. Criminals use TCSPs to deliberately create multiple corporate vehicles that are nested and administered in multiple jurisdictions in a way that hides the identity of the respective beneficial owners and is designed to thwart investigators. Consequently,

> solving a transnational corporate vehicle misuse scheme is like putting together a jigsaw puzzle, with investigators in different jurisdictions each holding separate pieces of the puzzle. To complete the puzzle, an investigator needs to have access to all the pieces.[12]

To start an investigation, an investigator must obtain information about the precise jurisdiction where each corporate vehicle is registered. If the registry information is not available online, investigators must travel to each respective jurisdiction, obtain access to the registry information, then examine the information for clues to the beneficial owner of the funds in question. If a criminal has created a dozen corporate vehicles, this may involve travel to the dozen jurisdictions where the vehicles are registered. Once investigators locate the registry office, however, they may find that relevant information regarding corporate directors and shareholders that provides clues to the beneficial owner is maintained at a location separate from the registry office. If the customer is located in a different country, the beneficial ownership information may be maintained by a TCSP that serves as an intermediary and is located in that country, necessitating additional travel to obtain relevant information.

In general, there is no simple way to examine a corporate registry and obtain a straightforward answer about the beneficial owner's identity. Since registries rarely require clients to state the identity of the true beneficial owner, investigators are forced to piece together clues from whatever source is available to build a case about the true identity of the beneficial owner. If a registry lists Pinochet's son and daughters as corporate directors, then an investigator might infer that the true beneficial owner is Augusto Pinochet. However, if Óscar Custodio Aitken Lavanchy is listed as the sole director, an investigator may have difficulty connecting control of the corporate vehicle to Pinochet. In practice, the identification of true beneficial owners is a laborious guessing game that consumes an enormous amount of an investigator's time and resources. Investigators will typically examine trust deeds, contracts that indemnify agents working for the beneficial owners, and power-of-attorney declarations whereby nominees agree to take legal possession of corporate shares or act as the directors of the company in question.[13] An investigator might seek to interview the front men who are listed as corporate directors and trustees and named on bank accounts, but the investigator has little leverage to compel them to provide useful information because the act of serving as a nominee is typically not illegal.

Similarly, an investigator might seek to interview TCSP personnel, but the investigator has little leverage to compel them to provide useful information. Criminals deliberately choose jurisdictions that tacitly permit and encourage TCSPs to operate in a non-transparent fashion. The laws and regulations in those jurisdictions are designed to be customer friendly and to encourage large flows of money to those jurisdictions. In many cases, the banking and financial transaction fees generated from those funds keep the local economy afloat. Tighter regulation would drive business away and depress the local economy. Therefore, there is little appetite for such regulation.

An investigator who wishes to solve a corruption case needs the cooperation of witnesses and documentary evidence that reveals the trickery. In general, however, the cooperation of front men and TCSP personnel is not forthcoming unless the investigator already has ample evidence documenting money laundering and can use this evidence to pressure the front men and TCSP personnel into plea agreements or deferred prosecution agreements where they agree to testify in exchange for probation, a fine, or deferred prosecution. However, since the evidence necessary to document money laundering is difficult to obtain without the cooperation of front men and TCSP personnel, the investigator is faced with a chicken-and-egg dilemma. In large part, this explains why the problem of corruption and impunity remains unaddressed.

APUNCAC, and the idea of creating a global registry of companies, are two alternative strategies for addressing corruption and impunity. This chapter compares, contrasts, and evaluates the efficacy of these strategies. Special attention is given to the potential efficacy of each strategy in addressing the chicken-and-egg dilemma that exists when front men and TCSP personnel have little incentive to cooperate with investigators. It may be argued that the potential success of any given anticorruption strategy will depend on the extent to which it untangles this knot.

UNTANGLING THE KNOT

APUNCAC solves the chicken-and-egg problem by establishing a system whereby the beneficial owner is identified and recorded in an online FINCEN database every time currency in excess of $3,000 is deposited anywhere in the world, or a check, bank draft, or money order is deposited or a wire transfer is received in specified high-risk jurisdictions in amounts exceeding $3,000, or funds in excess of $3,000 are transmitted internationally by wire, by a national of a State Party to APUNCAC.[14]

Failure to record the beneficial owner information is a violation of APUNCAC.[15] Individuals who flout the rule or aid and abet individuals who flout the rule are subject to debarment, fines, or imprisonment.[16] Debarred individuals who persist in violating the rule are subject to arrest, extradition, and criminal penalties.[17] The cooperation of any person, including any front man or TCSP personnel, in hiding the beneficial owner is punishable through fines and imprisonment.[18] The reason that this strategy would be effective is that no covered transaction would take place unless the true beneficial owner was identified and recorded, or unless the front man, posing as beneficial owner, chose to deliberately submit false beneficial owner information and risk criminal prosecution (figure 9.1).

Incentives

This strategy would be effective because it would create a strong risk of debarment and criminal prosecution for front men and TCSP personnel who submit false beneficial owner information. This risk would create strong incentives for front men and TCSP personnel to negotiate deferred debarment agreements in exchange for serving as cooperating witnesses against criminals who use the front men and TCSP personnel to hide illicit proceeds of criminal activity. These incentives are missing from the current regulatory regime because the current regime does not make the submission of false beneficial owner information illegal and does not establish a system of debarment and criminal penalties for false or misleading information. By criminalizing the submission of false beneficial ownership information and establishing a system of debarment and criminal penalties for false information, APUNCAC would create a risk of punishment for front men and TCSP personnel that is currently missing. The establishment of a credible risk is a necessary step toward the establishment of incentives for front men and TCSP personnel to cooperate with investigators, reveal the true identities of beneficial owners, permit investigators to trace illicit proceeds of crime to the criminals who commit the crimes, and permit investigators to secure convictions against those criminals. In the absence of those incentives, the

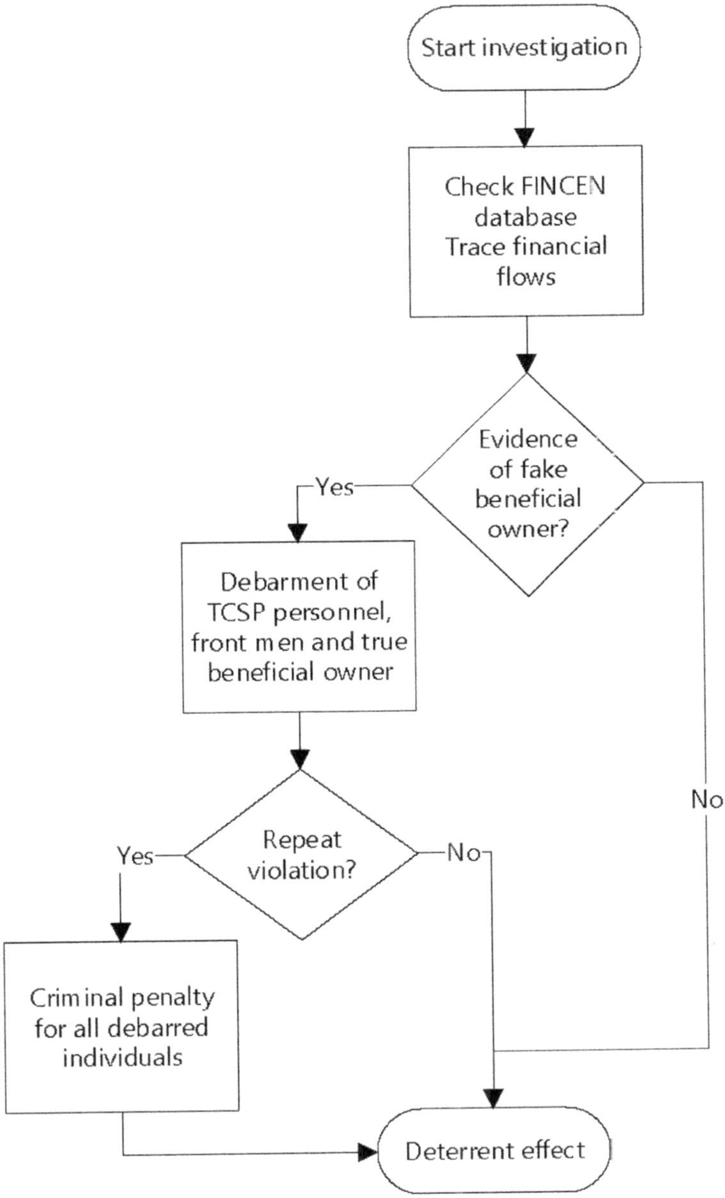

Figure 9.1 False Beneficial Owner Information Is Penalized. *Source*: Figure created by author.

cooperation of front men and TCSP personnel will remain elusive, the links between criminals and the illicit proceeds of their crimes will remain elusive, and investigators will continue to struggle to bring criminals to justice.

APUNCAC would simplify the task of prosecuting financial crimes. Whereas it may be difficult for an investigator to prove money laundering of illicit funds, it may be relatively simple to prove that a corrupt party is directing the actions of a front man who poses as the beneficial owner of those funds. An investigator would merely need to obtain e-mail, text messages, or recordings of phone conversations demonstrating a pattern of communications from the corrupt party directing the front man to send or receive funds.[19] This would be sufficient under APUNCAC to convict a front man of posing as a beneficial owner. This type of conviction is not possible under the current regulatory regime. The current regulatory regime does not criminalize the act of posing as a beneficial owner.[20]

APUNCAC requires parties to the protocol to cooperate, and to seek the cooperation of states with extradition agreements with States Parties, to arrest, extradite, and prosecute violators, regardless of where the offense was committed.[21] In essence, offenders would face a real possibility of incarceration. This feature distinguishes APUNCAC from all other proposals to address corruption and impunity.

Extraterritorial Reach

Perhaps the greatest advantage of APUNCAC is that it allows States Parties to take control of the crime of money laundering even when it occurs offshore in distant jurisdictions such as the BVI, the Cayman Islands, and Panama, where money launderers currently operate with minimal restraints. This extraterritorial reach distinguishes APUNCAC from all other proposed solutions to the problem of corruption and impunity. Unlike a global registry of companies, which would require the cooperation of jurisdictions including the BVI, the Cayman Islands, and Panama, a state such as Kenya that ratifies APUNCAC would gain the capacity to punish money launderers and those who assist money launderers even if they reside in the BVI, the Cayman Islands, or Panama.

This would be accomplished because all parties to APUNCAC would, with few exceptions, be parties to the existing UNTOC, which criminalizes "the concealment or disguise of the true nature, source, location, disposition, movement or ownership of or rights with respect to property, knowing that such property is the proceeds of crime" as well as "participation in, association with or conspiracy to commit, attempts to commit and aiding, abetting, facilitating" such concealment.[22] UNTOC makes these offenses "an extraditable offence in any extradition treaty existing between States Parties."[23]

Furthermore, "States Parties undertake to include such offences as extraditable offences in every extradition treaty to be concluded between them."[24] UNTOC requires States Parties to implement requirements for customer identification and record-keeping to deter and detect money laundering:

> Each State Party: (a) Shall institute a comprehensive domestic regulatory and supervisory regime for banks and non-bank financial institutions and, where appropriate, other bodies particularly susceptible to money-laundering, within its competence, in order to deter and detect all forms of money-laundering, which regime shall emphasize requirements for customer identification, record-keeping and the reporting of suspicious transactions.[25]

These provisions apply to nationals and residents of all States Parties. They apply to bank clerks in the BVI, the Cayman Islands, or Panama who aid, abet, and facilitate the concealment of the true ownership of illicit funds, because Panama, UK, and its overseas territories are parties to UNTOC. A bank clerk who is required to perform, but chooses to willfully, intentionally, and knowingly ignore basic steps designed to identify customers and promote transparency in the ownership, disposition, and movement of property and permit verification of the legitimacy of such property could be found guilty under UNTOC of aiding, abetting, and facilitating the concealment of the true nature, source, and ownership of that property.

Under APUNCAC, customers who deposit currency in amounts exceeding $3,000, or deposit checks or money orders or receive wire transfers in high-risk jurisdictions such as the BVI, the Cayman Islands, or Panama in amounts exceeding $3,000, or transmit international wire transfers in amounts exceeding $3,000, are required to certify the beneficial owners of the sending and receiving accounts and the source of the funds.[26] Bank clerks, including clerks in the BVI, the Cayman Islands, or Panama, who fail to record this information in the FINCEN database, are subject to debarment. Repeat violators are subject to arrest, extradition, and criminal penalties.[27]

The procedure whereby an initial offense would be punished by debarment would ensure that the offending bank clerk was made fully aware of the recordation requirements. After debarment, it would be difficult for an offender to assert that he or she had no knowledge of the recordation requirements. Any subsequent offense would almost certainly be a conscious, deliberate, willful, intentional action, with full knowledge that repeat offenses are criminal violations under UNTOC and criminal violations under APUNCAC.

Compelling Cooperation

The combined provisions of UNTOC and APUNCAC would simplify a prosecutor's task of obtaining a conviction under UNTOC or APUNCAC.

Any bank clerk in any jurisdiction, including the BVI, the Cayman Islands, or Panama, who deliberately, willfully, and intentionally chose to ignore the recordation procedure that is required by APUNCAC and is designed to promote transparency in the ownership, disposition, and movement of property and permit verification of the legitimacy of such property, could potentially be found guilty of the crime of aiding, abetting, and facilitating the concealment of the true nature, source, and ownership of that property.

The extent to which bank clerks would be threatened with imprisonment would depend on the collective response of countries across the world to APUNCAC. If key countries accept and adopt the recordation requirements, it would become increasingly difficult for other countries to ignore the requirements, increasingly difficult for bank clerks in other countries to ignore the requirements, and increasingly likely that bank clerks worldwide would be compelled to cooperate with the requirements.

Since bank clerks would need to know how to respond, APUNCAC would force each jurisdiction to make a formal determination and develop a formal policy stating whether bank clerks within the relevant jurisdiction are required by domestic authorities to observe the FINCEN recordation requirements. In jurisdictions that adopted the requirements, failure to observe the recordation requirements would trigger domestic sanctions. The outcome for bank clerks in other jurisdictions would be less clear. If many jurisdictions adopt the requirements, failure to observe the recordation requirements might present substantial risks to any bank clerk who chose to ignore the requirements, even if the clerk resided in a jurisdiction that chose not to adopt the requirements. Travel to jurisdictions that support extradition would entail the risk of arrest and imprisonment. However, if only a few minor jurisdictions adopt the requirements, and if the overall risk of extradition is low, failure to observe the recordation requirements by clerks in other jurisdictions might pose few risks.

Once a bank clerk traveled to a jurisdiction that supported extradition, a requesting state could submit a request for extradition to the requested state. If the recordation requirements are legal requirements in both jurisdictions, failure to observe the requirements would be a crime in both jurisdictions. If both jurisdictions are parties to UNTOC, then the bank clerk could be extradited for the crime of aiding, abetting, and facilitating the concealment of the true nature, source, and ownership of property.[28]

The beneficial owner identification and recordation provisions of APUNCAC are *precisely* "requirements for customer identification [and] record-keeping" with the *exact* intention of deterring and detecting money laundering.[29] The beneficial owner identification and recordation provisions would plug gaps in existing customer identification requirements by requiring each banking customer to identify the beneficial owner of funds that are deposited in currency, deposited in any form in a high-risk jurisdiction, or transmitted internationally by wire from the territory of a State Party.[30] APUNCAC serves to translate the existing legal commitment of UNTOC parties to identify banking customers for the purpose of revealing the true "ownership of or rights with respect to property" into specific procedures for identifying beneficial owners, for that exact purpose.[31] APUNCAC seeks to achieve UNTOC's goal of establishing the identities of true owners by specifying that banking customers must certify the identities of true beneficial owners under penalty of perjury.[32] An argument that non-State Party nationals (perhaps bank clerks in the BVI, Cayman Islands, or Panama) would not be legally obligated to observe APUNCAC's beneficial owner identification requirement is inconsistent with and contradicts the existing legally binding commitment of UNTOC parties to identify the true identities of banking customers. This argument denies the legally binding commitments that have already been made to require customer identification and record-keeping for the purpose of deterring and detecting money laundering.

A bank clerk in a high-risk jurisdiction who repeatedly completed international wire transfers from the territory of a State Party in an amount exceeding $3,000 without obtaining beneficial ownership information or documentation of the source of the funds would be criminally liable and subject to arrest and extradition under APUNCAC and under UNTOC for aiding, abetting, and facilitating the concealment of the true nature and source of the funds (figure 9.2).[33] A front man who repeatedly submitted false or misleading information regarding beneficial ownership or the source of funds transmitted via bank wire would be criminally liable and subject to arrest and extradition under APUNCAC and under UNTOC for aiding, abetting, and facilitating the concealment of the true nature and source of the funds (figure 9.2).[34]

An Example

To illustrate, consider the following hypothetical scenario. Kenya becomes a party to APUNCAC. The governments of all 196 countries in the world are notified of APUNCAC and the provisions requiring bank clerks to record beneficial ownership information with regard to currency, check, and money order deposits and wire transfers involving Kenyan nationals, entities, or funds. Each government notifies its domestic bank and nonbank financial institutions. However, a bank clerk in the BVI fails to observe the recordation requirement and is debarred. The debarment process includes official notification of debarment and recitation of the recordation requirement. The same bank clerk subsequently handles a $10 million bank wire involving a Kenyan government minister to a BVI corporate account but again fails to observe the recordation requirement. Kenya files a request with BVI for arrest and

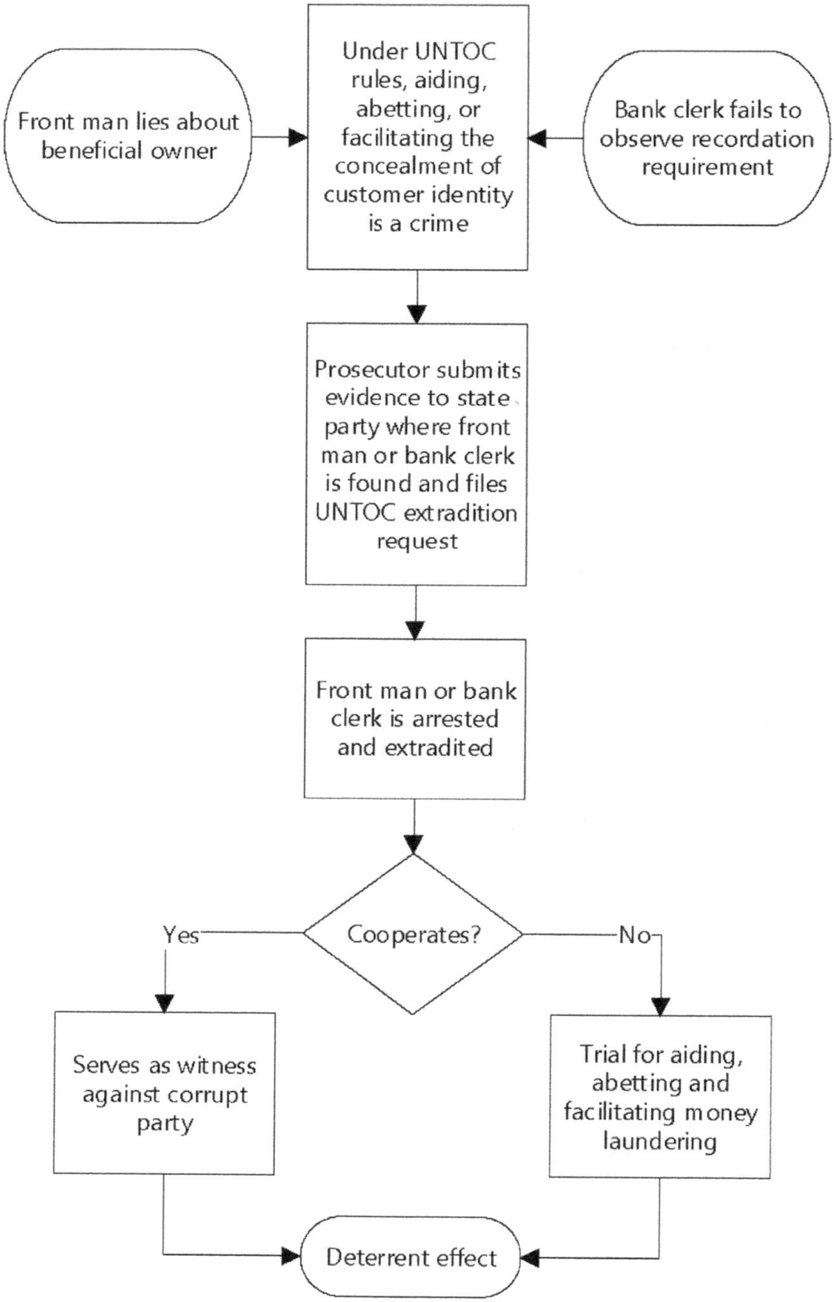

Figure 9.2 APUNCAC Applies UNTOC Extradition Provisions to Exert Extraterritorial Reach. *Source*: Figure created by author.

extradition under the terms of UNTOC for aiding and abetting concealment of the identity of the person who owns the $10 million.

At this point, BVI authorities must decide whether to comply with the request. The decision would hinge on whether, in the view of BVI authorities, the bank clerk's failure to observe the recordation requirement was proper or improper. If BVI authorities determine that the failure was improper and served to aid and abet the concealment of the identity of the person who owns the $10 million, then extradition would presumably be approved. However, if BVI authorities determine that the failure was not improper, it is unlikely that extradition would be approved.

If BVI authorities approve extradition, a precedent would be set. Consistent application of the law dictates that similar cases be treated in the same way, implying that BVI would be forced to make a decision about whether to incorporate the recordation requirement into its domestic regulatory regime and whether to extradite in cases where bank clerks fail to observe the recordation requirement. APUNCAC would, in essence, force jurisdictions around the world to decide whether or not to incorporate the recordation requirement into their domestic regulatory regimes.

Each jurisdiction would make an independent determination about the benefits and costs of incorporating the recordation requirement into its domestic regulatory regime. If the presumed benefits exceed the presumed costs, a jurisdiction would presumably move to incorporate the recordation requirement into its domestic regulatory regime. If the presumed costs exceed the presumed benefits, a jurisdiction would presumably reject the recordation requirement and any request for extradition based on that requirement.

However, the United States, the UK, and the OECD Member States are aggressive leaders in the fight against money laundering because money laundering permits terrorists to hide large amounts of monies that are used to fund terrorism. The recordation requirement would permit investigators to pull back the veil that currently hides the identities of persons who use anonymous corporate vehicles in BVI, the Caymans, and Panama for illicit purposes. The recordation requirement would penetrate the anonymity that currently protects terrorists and criminals by protecting their financial assets. If major OECD Member States begin incorporating the recordation requirement into their domestic regulatory regimes, it would become a de facto world standard for any nation that is serious about fighting money laundering. It would become a litmus test for any nation that claims to fight money laundering.

Panama is a party to UNTOC. If the recordation requirement becomes a de facto world standard, if Panama is judged on the basis of whether it conforms to world standards in the fight against money laundering, and if foreign investment in Panama depends on whether Panama conforms to world standards in the fight against money laundering, Panamanian leaders may feel that it is in their best interests to incorporate the recordation requirement into their domestic regulatory regime and cooperate with extradition requests when bank clerks handle large multimillion dollar bank wires but fail to observe the recordation requirement. If Panamanian leaders choose to reject the recordation requirement and reject extradition requests when bank clerks handle large multimillion dollar bank wires but fail to observe the recordation requirement, they would not be able to say that they are in compliance with world standards regarding regulations to fight money laundering. If Panama is unable to shake its reputation as a jurisdiction where money laundering and criminal activity are rife, foreign investors will be wary of investing in Panama.

Panama might choose to formally adopt the recordation requirement and incorporate the requirement into its domestic regulatory regime, then fail to cooperate with extradition requests. Formal adoption of the requirement would give Panamanian leaders the cover to say that Panama conforms to world standards in the fight against money laundering. However, this tactic would not protect Panamanian nationals who travel abroad.

Panama is a party to UNTOC and is bound by the terms of UNTOC. The act of aiding, abetting, and facilitating the concealment of the identity of persons who acquire illicit funds is a crime under the domestic laws of all UNTOC parties, including Panama. Panama might fail to cooperate with extradition requests, but it would not be in a legal position to protect any of its nationals who travel to another UNTOC party jurisdiction and are arrested for aiding, abetting, and facilitating the concealment of the identity of, for example, a Kenyan government minister who transmits $10 million to a Panamanian bank account.

If a previously debarred Panamanian bank clerk handled the transmission of $10 million from a Kenyan government minister into a Panamanian bank account but failed to observe the recordation requirement and subsequently traveled to a jurisdiction outside of Panama, the clerk would, under APUNCAC, be at risk of arrest and imprisonment for aiding, abetting, and facilitating concealment of the minister's ownership of the $10 million. Significantly, 189 nations are States Parties to UNTOC and are legally bound by the terms of UNTOC, including the terms whereby any State Party can request extradition of a suspect from the jurisdiction of another State Party.[35] The only UN Member States that are not States Parties are Bhutan, the Republic of the Congo, Palau, Papua New Guinea, the Solomon Islands, Somalia, South Sudan, and Tuvalu.[36] This implies that a Panamanian bank clerk who handled the transmission of $10 million from a Kenyan government minister into a Panamanian bank account but failed to observe the recordation requirement and subsequently traveled to a jurisdiction outside of Panama would be at risk of arrest and imprisonment whenever he or she traveled outside of Panama because Kenya could request extradition if the clerk traveled to the territory of any of the 189 nations that are States Parties to UNTOC.

While there may be bank clerks who are content to spend their entire lives within Panama, the risk of traveling to other jurisdictions for business or leisure would be a significant cost of failing to observe the recordation requirement. Many bank clerks would resist employment at a financial institution whose practices and policies are inconsistent with the recordation requirement and place clerks at risk of arrest and imprisonment whenever they travel abroad.

Consequently, APUNCAC would create a powerful mechanism for controlling money laundering in distant offshore locations that is currently absent from all other existing and proposed strategies for controlling corruption and impunity. Ratification and implementation of APUNCAC would fall within the power of potential States Parties. States Parties would not need to wait for distant offshore jurisdictions to implement reforms. States Parties would apply the provisions of APUNCAC requiring documentation of the beneficial owner and source of funds transmitted by bank wire, and would apply UNTOC to extradite individuals who violate this rule in distant offshore locations such as the BVI, the Cayman Islands, or Panama. This suggests why APUNCAC would likely be more effective than the strategy of implementing a global registry of companies, which would require the cooperation of offshore locations such as the BVI, the Cayman Islands, and Panama.

JURISDICTION

The proposal to debar distant offshore banking personnel who fail to observe APUNCAC's recordation requirement raises the issue of jurisdiction, that is, the legal power of a state to exercise governmental authority beyond its territorial borders. What principle would permit a State Party to exercise extraterritorial jurisdiction? It is clear that jurisdiction may be applied to individuals and entities who reside or conduct themselves within state territory.[37] Jurisdiction of a state may also be applied to nationals of the state who travel to territory outside of the state.[38] Significantly, jurisdiction of a state may also extend to extraterritorial conduct by individuals who are not nationals of the state if that conduct has an effect within state territory.[39] The pivotal U.S. case involving the effects principle is *United States v. Aluminum Co. of America*.[40] A Canadian firm participated in a cartel based in Switzerland that restricted imports to the United States. A U.S. federal court held that since the companies in the cartel had affected U.S. commerce by restricting imports to the United States, the Canadian firm's activities were properly within the regulatory purview and legislative jurisdiction of the United States.[41] The court found that extraterritorial application of U.S. law to the Canadian firm was justified because "any state may impose liabilities, even upon persons not within its allegiance, for conduct outside its borders that has consequences within its borders."[42] Subsequently, the *Restatement (Second) of the Foreign Relations Law of the United States* declared:

> A state has jurisdiction to prescribe a rule of law attaching legal consequences to conduct that occurs outside its territory and causes an effect within its territory, if . . . (i) the conduct and its effect are constituent elements of activity to which the rule applies; (ii) the effect within the territory is substantial; (iii) it occurs as a direct and foreseeable result of the conduct outside the territory; and (iv) the rule is not inconsistent with the principles of justice generally recognized by states.[43]

The *Restatement (Third) of the Foreign Relations Law of the United States* reaffirmed the effects principle, declaring that a state has jurisdiction with respect to "conduct outside its territory that has or is intended to have substantial effect within its territory."[44] In 2016, the U.S. Supreme Court reaffirmed the effects principle as a basis for asserting extraterritorial jurisdiction.[45] The court held that the American RICO law applies to both foreign and domestic enterprises with regard to predicate offenses such as money laundering that the U.S. Congress intended to apply to extraterritorial behavior, as long as a RICO enterprise affects commerce directly involving the United States.[46]

According to the effects principle, States Parties to APUNCAC may regulate the conduct of distant offshore banking personnel for the purpose of fighting the effects of money laundering that are experienced within the territory of States Parties. APUNCAC requires banking personnel to record beneficial ownership information in the FINCEN database. A failure to record such information would have the effect of facilitating the crime of money laundering, a crime that has substantial effect within the territory of States Parties to APUNCAC. The effects principle provides the legal basis for APUNCAC's jurisdiction with regard to distant offshore banking personnel.

APUNCAC would debar distant offshore banking personnel who do not comply with the recordation requirements. A precedent for this approach is the U.S. practice of sanctioning foreign nationals who do not reside or conduct business within the territory of the United States but whose conduct has effects within the territory of the United States, for example, individuals whose conduct serves to aid and abet terrorists.[47] APUNCAC seeks to isolate recalcitrant offshore banking personnel by debarring any national of a State Party who conducts financial transactions with the assistance of a debarred person, and by debarring any individual who transmits funds originating from the territory of a State Party with the assistance of a debarred person.[48] Repeat offenses are punishable by criminal penalties.[49] If debarred individuals in high-risk jurisdictions transmit or retransmit funds that originate from the territory of a State Party to a foreign destination, they are subject to criminal penalties.[50] The application of criminal penalties to individuals who cooperate with debarred individuals is analogous to the U.S. practice of enforcing criminal penalties against individuals who violate U.S. sanctions by continuing to do business with persons on the U.S. Treasury Department's Office of Foreign Assets Control (OFAC) list of Specially Designated Nationals and Blocked Persons (SDN list).[51] In both cases, criminal penalties are enforced against individuals who do not cooperate in isolating the sanctioned persons.

One might argue that it would be onerous or impractical for every person wishing to conduct a financial transaction to perform the due diligence necessary to determine if a bank clerk, or any other individual involved in a bank transaction, is on the debarment list. However, the due diligence that is required is no different than the due diligence required to check the SDN list maintained by OFAC. The SDN list is maintained and accessible online.[52] Similarly, APUNCAC proposes that FINCEN would maintain online access to a list of debarred persons and entities.[53]

One might argue that offshore bank clerks might be unaware of a protocol that is signed and ratified in a distant locale. However, the process of negotiating, signing, and ratifying an international UN agreement is normally a lengthy process involving scrutiny by relevant actors worldwide. Implementation of APUNCAC would be preceded by a lengthy period of discussion, negotiation, and communication with domestic banking officials. In states that become parties, the passage of an international agreement would trigger the drafting and passage of domestic legislation that conforms domestic law to the international agreement. Whether or not a particular state becomes a party to APUNCAC, domestic officials would be well aware of the implications and would plan accordingly. Domestic officials would issue guidance to all affected entities. Those entities would then issue guidance to all affected personnel.

It might be argued that offshore bank clerks may, despite this guidance, inadvertently assist a debarred person and be unfairly debarred. However, the due diligence that is required is no different than the due diligence required to check the U.S. sanctions list maintained by OFAC. The penalties for noncompliance are less severe. Furthermore, since the initial penalty for noncompliance with APUNCAC is debarment, and since debarred persons would receive a notice of debarment listing prohibited conduct, debarred persons would necessarily be aware of prohibited conduct prior to engaging in further conduct that would merit criminal penalties.

It might be argued that debarment would violate due process. However, APUNCAC establishes due process procedures. Defendants would be notified of debarment proceedings;[54] receive copies of documentary evidence establishing the basis for debarment;[55] and have rights to submit a rebuttal, sworn affidavits, or any other supporting documentation;[56] request reconsideration of debarment for material errors of fact or law;[57] appeal the decision;[58] or accept a five-year period of debarment in lieu of a request for reconsideration or review.[59] A defendant would also have an opportunity to negotiate a deferred debarment agreement where debarment or a determination of debarment would be suspended in exchange for cooperation as a witness in an ongoing criminal investigation.[60]

CUSTOMER DUE DILIGENCE RULES?

The U.S. Treasury's FinCEN has instituted a customer due diligence rule that requires U.S. banks and other covered financial institutions to verify the beneficial owner of each account.[61] While this rule may seem similar to my proposal, which also requires verification of beneficial ownership, the FinCEN rule would be ineffective in addressing the money laundering that occurs when criminals launder funds through offshore bank secrecy locations. A basic weakness of the FinCEN rule is that it only applies to institutions within the United States—it does not apply to bank secrecy destinations such as the BVI, the Cayman Islands, Guernsey, Hong Kong, Luxembourg, Panama, Singapore, or Switzerland. Therefore, the most egregious offenders are unaffected by the FinCEN rule.

A second weakness of the FinCEN rule is that it only requires that the person who opens an account certify that information provided by that person about beneficial ownership is complete and correct "to the best of" that person's knowledge.[62] That person could be a low-level person whose alibi is that he or she was unaware that the information was incorrect. The FinCEN rule fails to penalize front men who pose as beneficial owners but are not true beneficial owners. The FinCEN rule applies to the person who signs the certification, not the front men. The person who signs the certification form might be punished for false statements, but the front men bear no risk of punishment. There is no penalty for a banking customer who chooses to misrepresent the true beneficial owner of the bank account, unless investigators prove money laundering.[63] This requires proof that the funds are illicit. The difficulty of proving that funds are illicit makes prosecution of nominee account holders difficult. As a consequence, prosecutions are rare and deterrence is weak.

In contrast, APUNCAC criminalizes the act of substituting a nominee account holder for the true beneficial account holder. This gives investigators leverage over peripheral individuals who serve as nominees. An investigator could obtain the nominee's income and employment records, question the nominee about discrepancies between this information and the amount of his or her financial assets, and negotiate a plea agreement or deferred prosecution agreement if the nominee agrees to serve as a witness against the criminal who is hiding illicit funds with the help of the nominee.

A third weakness of the FinCEN rule is that it only applies to the financial institutions that hold accounts for their customers, rather than the individual personnel within those institutions. If a financial institution violated the FinCEN rule, then it might be sanctioned by the U.S. Treasury Department. However, it is unlikely that civil penalties would ever be applied to individuals within that institution unless the violations involved multimillion dollar money laundering transactions and egregious violations of the AML provisions of the Bank Secrecy Act (BSA).[64]

In contrast, APUNCAC criminalizes each instance where a nominee owner poses as the true beneficial owner. Each nominee owner is subject to criminal penalties including debarment followed by fines and imprisonment for repeat violations. This makes it easier to prosecute and obtain the cooperation of nominee owners to serve as witnesses against criminals seeking to hide their control over accounts associated with the nominee owners. In contrast, there is little reason to think that the U.S. Treasury's FinCEN rule would deter criminals who could easily subvert the rule by substituting a trusted confidant who would pose as the beneficial owner.

A GLOBAL REGISTRY?

A second alternative strategy involves the creation of a global registry of companies that would improve transparency in the ownership of corporate vehicles that are currently used by criminals to hide illicit proceeds.[65] While this suggestion is popular, there are major flaws. First, a registry would only be effective to the extent that criminals maintain their funds in jurisdictions that are parties to the registry.[66] Second, a registry would only be effective to the extent that criminals deposit funds into accounts owned by companies that were registered.[67] Third, a registry would only be effective to the extent that criminals use their own names as beneficial owners. However, criminals who are seeking to evade prosecution are unlikely to cooperate in the ways that would be necessary for a global registry to be effective. A World Bank report devoted to the topic of company registries, TCSPs, and money laundering described numerous issues that would make a global registry impractical or ineffective.[68]

- Registries rarely record the name of the beneficial owner.[69] The task of discovering the identity of the beneficial owner in a complicated corporate structure is demanding and requires adequate understanding and knowledge of corporate law.[70] Registry personnel who lack this expertise could not be expected to verify beneficial ownership information.
- The capacity of a registry to collect accurate, complete information would require legal authority to impose sanctions in cases where the registry is supplied with inaccurate or incomplete information.[71] However, jurisdiction to impose criminal sanctions over the person supplying the information is unlikely in cases where such person resides in a foreign jurisdiction.
- A significant obstacle to the usefulness of a registry is the existence of nominee arrangements, whereby individuals who are listed in director or shareholder positions are in fact agents acting on behalf of an unnamed principal who is the true beneficial owner.[72]
- The operations of legitimate businesses typically generate streams of funds that continuously flow into and out of corporate bank accounts. Criminals may, however, obtain access to corporate bank accounts, then commingle flows of illicit funds with legitimate funds for the purpose of laundering the illicit funds.[73] The success of a money laundering investigation depends on knowledge of the sources and destinations of the assets held by a corporate vehicle, as opposed to the mere fact that the assets are held within a given vehicle.[74] A registry would not address this issue.

In sum, registries are not a panacea that would pierce the veil of secrecy that shrouds illicit funds. Proposals to implement a global registry of companies do not anticipate the lengthy list of reasons why a global registry is impractical and unlikely to achieve the objective of permitting investigators to trace flows of illicit funds to their beneficial owners. In contrast, APUNCAC addresses all of these issues (table 9.1).

APUNCAC would create a centralized, searchable, online FINCEN database where beneficial ownership information would be obtained prior to, and as a condition of, the transmission of each bank wire, and would be verified through passport identification and checkbox affirmation by the beneficial party, under criminal penalty for false or misleading information.[75] This regime, in combination with the threat of extradition and enforcement via UNTOC, would ensure that the information is current, verified, accurate, and complete, and would provide investigators with all of the information needed to follow the trail of illicit funds from their source to their final beneficial owners, regardless of the complexity, opacity, and jurisdictional location of the corporate structures involved.

Table 9.1 Comparison of APUNCAC with Global Registry

	APUNCAC	*Registry*
Controlled by States Parties, not bank secrecy havens	Yes	No
Extraterritorial reach	Yes	No
Follows the money	Yes	No
Single online, searchable database	Yes	No
Requires registration of true beneficial owner	Yes	No
Criminal penalties for noncompliance and submission of fake information	Yes	No
Penetrates complex, nested shell corporations	Yes	No
UN-funded, independent inspectors	Yes	No

Source: Created by author.

A CASE EXAMPLE

APUNCAC would impose obligations to report beneficial ownership information on certain financial service professionals who send international wire transfers exceeding $3,000, or receive currency payments in amounts exceeding $3,000, or receive checks, money orders, or wire transfers in certain high-risk jurisdictions in amounts exceeding $3,000.[76] A case example illustrates how these provisions would be used to combat money laundering.

Suppose that a Colombian drug cartel desires to launder illicit proceeds from selling illegal drugs such as cocaine, heroin, or methamphetamines. The drug cartel hires "smurfs" who use illicit currency to buy gems from jewelers. The jewelers deposit the currency into their bank accounts. The smurfs then sell their gems to other jewelers, deposit the proceeds into their bank accounts, and wire the funds to bank accounts controlled by the drug cartel. Through this process, illicit funds are converted into apparently legitimate sales proceeds from the sale of gems, with sales receipts as documentary proof.

In the past, this deceit would likely have remained undetected. Under APUNCAC, however, the deceit would become apparent. At the point when the illicit currency is deposited into bank accounts, APUNCAC requires bank clerks to obtain information regarding the source of the currency.[77] The jewelers would be required to present sales invoices and copies of tax returns for each smurf whose transactions in currency exceeded $3,000. However, the amount of currency transactions conducted by a smurf over the course of a 12-month calendar year far exceeds his or her income. A smurf buys large amounts of gems using large amounts of cartel currency, sells the gems, wires the funds to an account controlled by the drug cartel, and pockets a small fee for the work. A FINCEN database that stores the smurf's tax information and information regarding the amount of each currency transaction would allow investigators to quickly identify smurfs because the annual amount of their currency transactions would greatly exceed their stated levels of income. Under APUNCAC, smurfs would be debarred. Repeat offenses would be punished by criminal sanctions. Subsequently, any individual who handled funds involving those debarred individuals would be subject to debarment and repeat violations would be punished by criminal sanctions.

WHY TAX DOCUMENTS?

APUNCAC permits authorized investigators and financial regulators to investigate possible money laundering. This would be accomplished by collecting information that can be easily checked by investigators. A key provision is the requirement that financial service personnel who handle currency deposits in excess of $3,000 obtain information regarding the source of the currency.[78] If the depositor is a business owner who receives currency in the course of business from clients or customers, APUNCAC requires the owner to list each client or customer who contributed currency in excess of $3,000, list the amount of the contribution, attach the corresponding invoice, and attach—or verify that FINCEN currently maintains—a searchable electronic copy of the client's or customer's most recent tax return that includes the taxpayer's name, address, taxpayer identification number, gross income (or gross revenue), taxable income, and certification of correctness.[79]

While the requirement to obtain tax return documents might seem invasive, a retail customer may avoid the requirement by avoiding the use of currency for retail transactions that exceed $3,000 in value. A retail customer who uses a personal check, credit card, debit card, Apple pay, or Samsung pay would not be subject to the tax document requirement. A retail customer who conducts a currency transaction in an amount exceeding $3,000 but desires to shield his or her tax information from the eyes of retail personnel may, once per year, upload a searchable copy of his or her tax return document to the FINCEN database.[80] At the point of a retail transaction, the database would permit retail personnel to verify by computer the existence of the tax document in the FINCEN database, obviating the need to collect the document at the point of the retail transaction.[81]

The collection of tax documents may raise concerns about access to those documents by unauthorized individuals. While sophisticated hacking is always a possibility, the creation of a FINCEN database that collects and maintains tax documents is no different than the creation of databases maintained by national tax authorities such as the U.S. IRS. The IRS has demonstrated that it is possible to maintain the security and privacy of such information. Regarding the transmission of tax documents via the internet,

WhatsApp has demonstrated how such documents may be encrypted, maintaining the security and privacy of their contents during the process of transmission.[82]

The collection of tax documents is necessary because it would assist investigators in detecting money laundering. Many laundering schemes involve the use of "smurfs," that is, individuals who are hired by the money launderer for the purpose of conducting numerous currency transactions where illicit currency is converted to foreign currency or used to purchase goods from legitimate businesses. After converting the currency to foreign currency or selling the goods, the funds are transmitted to bank accounts controlled by the criminals who hired the smurfs. This process serves to convert dirty money into clean money that appears to derive from legitimate foreign currency transactions or the sale of legitimate goods, rather than illicit sources.

The collection of tax documents would permit investigators to compare the amount of each smurf's reported income with the total amount of each smurf's currency transactions throughout the course of a 12-month period. Since each smurf receives only a small fee for each currency transaction, his or her annual income is much smaller than the total volume of currency transactions conducted by the smurf over a 12-month period. The discrepancy would be obvious to any investigator. The FINCEN database would permit the use of software that would filter and identify any individual whose total currency transactions greatly exceed his or her income, permitting investigators to quickly target those individuals for investigation. Under APUNCAC, smurfs would be debarred. Repeat violations would be punished by criminal sanctions. Many smurfs would no longer be willing to assume the risk and would find other occupations. In the absence of large numbers of individuals willing to serve as smurfs, money laundering would become concentrated among a much smaller number of individuals, permitting investigators to focus their resources, attack the remaining criminals, increase the risk of criminal prosecution, and drive yet more criminals out of the business of money laundering. Investigators could work with prosecutors, use the threat of prosecution under APUNCAC to negotiate deferred prosecution agreements with smurfs, and turn smurfs into cooperating witnesses against criminals engaged in money laundering.

The FINCEN database would also permit the use of software that would filter and identify suspicious currency transactions involving shell corporations. The database could be used to calculate the total amount of currency deposited to bank accounts for the benefit of a particular shell corporation. This amount could then be matched to the amount of revenue reported on the corporation's tax return, according to the tax document on file in the FINCEN database, as required by the model protocol. Currency receipts in excess of reported gross revenue would raise a red flag. While red flags could be avoided by artificially inflating the amount of gross revenue and reporting the entire amount to tax authorities, the corporation would then be liable for taxes on the inflated revenue figure. This dynamic would discourage criminals from using falsified tax documents to evade detection. The requirement to supply tax documents, together with the requirement to record currency deposits and information regarding the beneficial owner of the accounts holding the currency deposits, would ensure that investigators had the information necessary to detect money laundering. Under APUNCAC, audits would be required for all accounts where currency deposits exceed $10,000 annually and all accounts in specified high-risk jurisdictions where deposits of any type exceed $10,000 annually.[83] Audits would be conducted by approved independent auditing firms.[84] If an audit finds insufficient documentation with regard to the origin of a significant portion of all audited transactions, the corporation and all directors and officers may be debarred or fined, and the chief executive officer (CEO) may be imprisoned.[85] An individual who subsequently deposited funds originating from the territory of a State Party to a debarred shell corporation's account would be debarred unless the corporation had passed a financial audit by an independent auditor approved by FINCEN.[86] Repeat offenses would be punished by criminal sanctions.[87] Subsequently, any individual who handled funds involving those debarred individuals would be subject to debarment, and repeat violations would be punished by criminal sanctions, unless the debarred individuals had passed a financial audit by an independent auditor approved by FINCEN.[88] These provisions would discourage individuals who are presently willing to serve as directors and officers of shell corporations involved in money laundering and would discourage the use of shell corporations to launder illicit funds.

CONCLUSION

APUNCAC seeks to extend the territorial reach of parties who sign and ratify APUNCAC by imposing reporting requirements on distant offshore banking and financial service personnel. Those personnel might choose to ignore the reporting requirements, but this act would then become an objective factual circumstance that could lead a court to conclude that the personnel knew, or should have known, that they were aiding and abetting the criminal activity of money laundering. This would, under UNTOC, place the personnel at risk of being arrested, extradited, and prosecuted for aiding and abetting money laundering.

The reporting requirement could only be ignored at the peril of offshore banking personnel who presumably have no desire to risk arrest, extradition, and prosecution. Their incentives would change dramatically. Currently, there is almost no risk of arrest, extradition, and prosecution for money laundering because there is no reporting requirement. Consequently, the predicate that would lead a court to conclude that bank personnel had knowledge of the illicit nature of a large currency deposit is missing. The predicate factual circumstances that would lead a court to conclude that bank personnel were guilty of willfully, intentionally, aiding, and abetting money laundering are missing. Under the current lax reporting regime, there is no effective deterrent to bank personnel in distant offshore jurisdictions who quietly aid and abet money laundering by accepting large currency deposits with few questions.

All of this would change with APUNCAC. APUNCAC would discourage the passive participation by large numbers of financial service personnel and owners of legitimate businesses in aiding and abetting criminals who launder illicit funds. APUNCAC's reporting requirements would trigger a cascade of responses from banking personnel, money transmitters, cambic businesses, owners of jewelry businesses, and owners of any business where criminals seek to launder money. These responses would squeeze money laundering into a smaller operational space that would then become easier for law enforcement personnel to attack. Criminals would be forced to resort to the creation of large amounts of fake receipts, tax returns, and other documentation to hide the illicit nature of their funds. This fraudulent activity would be easier to detect and easier to investigate and prosecute than money laundering because such documentation implicates fictitious individuals and entities whose fictitious nature becomes evident once an investigation is initiated.[89]

The fake receipts, tax returns, and other documentation would be entered into the FINCEN database in the form of electronic, searchable pdf files. Investigators who suspect money laundering could simply enter the names of individuals who are closely associated with suspected criminals, conduct searches, and pull up all of the receipts, tax returns, and other documents presented by those individuals as documentation of the sources of funds deposited in currency, deposited in high-risk jurisdictions, or transmitted internationally. Investigators could then check the legitimacy of the documents. If fake tax returns are submitted, the deceit could be easily discovered by checking information stored by national tax authorities. If real tax returns are submitted, investigators could contact the associated taxpayers to verify the alleged currency transactions for which the tax return documents were submitted as proof of the legitimacy of the transactions. Efforts to launder currency by creating a fake paper trail for fake currency transactions would unravel as soon as an investigator contacted and interviewed taxpayers who disclaim knowledge of the alleged currency transactions.

The FINCEN database would also permit the use of software that would filter and identify suspicious currency transactions. If the operator of a jewelry business presents currency for deposit at a bank, states that the source is sales of jewelry, and submits a copy of the business's tax return as required by APUNCAC, investigators would be able to check the FINCEN database for all currency deposits related to the jewelry business, then compare the total amount to the amount of revenue reported on the business's tax return. Currency receipts in excess of reported gross revenue would raise a red flag. These flags would be a strong sign of money laundering and would trigger an investigation for money laundering.

The net result would be a global level of deterrence regarding international activities that currently facilitate money laundering. When it becomes risky for anyone to associate with money launderers, honest bank clerks, attorneys, accountants, and operators of legitimate businesses will steer away from suspicious clients and customers who seek to conduct large currency transactions, have difficulty documenting the sources of their income, and are unable to explain discrepancies between the amounts of their currency transactions and the amounts of revenue reported to authorities on their tax returns. In the absence of the tacit aid and assistance of large numbers of offshore bank clerks, attorneys, accountants, and operators of legitimate businesses, money laundering would become concentrated among a small hard-core group of criminals located in specific jurisdictions, permitting law enforcement personnel to focus their efforts, raise the risks to criminals even further, alter the benefit-cost calculations of criminals who launder money, deter all but the most hard-core, and significantly reduce the frequency and volume of money laundering.

Chapter 10

Six Case Examples

This chapter builds on the chapter 8 and chapter 9 explanations of APUNCAC's AML strategy.[1] Chapters 8 and 9 described how APUNCAC would extend the jurisdiction of parties who sign and ratify the protocol by imposing reporting requirements on distant offshore banking and financial service personnel.[2] The chapters addressed issues regarding international jurisdiction and enforcement of APUNCAC regarding distant offshore personnel.

This chapter begins by describing six case examples that illustrate the range and complexity of money laundering. The chapter describes the APUNCAC strategy for obtaining accurate beneficial ownership information whenever funds are paid, deposited, transferred, or exchanged, then illustrates the application of APUNCAC regarding each of the six case examples. The case examples have been selected to illustrate how APUNCAC would be implemented across a range of contexts where existing AML regulations have failed to control money laundering, and to explain why the APUNCAC reporting requirements are feasible, practical, and sensible.

SIX CASE EXAMPLES

Six case examples illustrate the range and complexity of money laundering: Danske Bank Estonia, the Vancouver Model, Liberty Reserve, the hawala system, online gaming, and Lightning. These examples suggest how and why existing AML laws and regulations have failed to control money laundering.

Danske Bank—Estonia

Danske Bank is the largest financial institution in Denmark. Until early 2016, the Estonian branch of Danske Bank served thousands of customers residing outside Estonia (the "Non-Resident Portfolio"), including customers from the Russian Federation, Azerbaijan, and Ukraine. On December 27, 2013, an employee of the Estonian branch filed an internal whistleblower report titled "Whistleblowing disclosure—knowingly dealing with criminals in Estonia Branch."[3]

Red Flags

A September 2018 report by Bruun and Hjejle, a Danish law firm, concluded that the "vast majority" of a sample of 6,200 Danske Bank customers were suspicious.[4] Over the nine-year period from 2007 through 2015, the transaction value of the flows into and out of the approximately 10,000 customer accounts in the Non-Resident Portfolio was approximately EUR 200 billion.[5] Red flags included customers sharing the same address, e-mail address, or phone number with numerous other customers; customers previously identified as suspicious in various jurisdictions including the BVI, UK, and Cyprus; customers whose publicly reported revenue figures were inconsistent with their Estonian branch payment activity; and customers regularly associated with large transaction flows, with unusual payment chains, and unexplained or unusual payment descriptions or suspicious counterparties.[6] An especially suspicious type of "mirror trade" activity involved customers who bought bonds using rubles and immediately sold identical bonds of the same value for dollars or euros—a red flag for money laundering.

The Bruun and Hjejle report found that red flags were repeatedly missed. In January 2014, Danske Bank's Executive Board was informed of the whistleblower report and Danske's internal audit investigation into the allegations, but was informed that there was no reason to report the matter to regulatory authorities.[7] An April 2014 report by an external auditor engaged by the AML department within Danske Bank "confined itself to general remarks" in response to the question of whether there had been breaches of AML regulations.[8] In May 2014, Danske's legal department asked Danske's AML department to "take on the task of bringing this whistleblower matter to an end."[9] In July 2014, a formal audit by Danske's internal audit department resulted in "no major comments" regarding the quality of the Estonian branch's due diligence procedures and completeness of the documentation collected and filed by the branch.[10]

In June and July 2014, the Estonian Financial Supervisory Authority (FSA) conducted an inspection of the Estonian branch, focusing on the branch's adherence to AML regulations. A September 2014 draft report by the FSA stated that "Danske Bank systematically established business relationships with persons in whose activities it is possible to see the simplest and most common suspicious circumstances."[11] Having read the draft report from the Estonian FSA, a member of Danske's Executive Board concluded in an internal e-mail dated September 18, 2014, that the report documented "a total and fundamental failure in doing what we should do and doing what we claim to do."[12] Despite this damning report, Danske's internal audit department reported, in October, 2014, that all whistleblower allegations had "been investigated," suggesting that no further action was needed.[13] In general, the Estonian branch was critical of the Estonian FSA's observations.[14] In October 2014, Danske's Executive Board concluded that "there was no cause for panic as the findings have been addressed in the ongoing process improvement."[15]

Red flags were raised through public news stories regarding the "Russian Laundromat." The term "Russian Laundromat" was coined in August 2014 by the Organized Crime and Corruption Reporting Project (OCCRP), an NGO that published reports regarding the money laundering scheme.[16] Danske Bank was unaware of early reports, but was informed prior to publication of the March 20, 2017, OCCRP report on the scheme.[17] The information was shared with Danske Bank's CEO and the bank's internal task force.[18] On March 15, 2017, the CEO informed the Chairman of the Board, and on March 16, 2017, the full Board of Directors was informed.[19] According to an internal Danske Bank memo dated March 17, 2017, "[a]uthorities in Moldova are currently investigating allegations that 20 billion USD have been laundered and transferred from Russia into the European financial system through a complex scheme, known as the 'Russian Laundromat' between 2011 and 2014."[20] The memo noted Danske Bank's prominent role, involving 1,567 transactions and a flow of approximately $1.2 billion.[21]

A major red flag was raised in 2010, when Alexander Perepilichny, a Russian whistleblower, handed over documents, subsequently passed to Swiss police, implicating the involvement of senior Russian officials in the fraudulent theft of $230 million from the Russian Treasury.[22] Perepilichny confessed that he helped to launder the stolen $230 million.[23] Hermitage Capital Management reported Danske Bank and employees of Danske Bank's Estonian branch to the police in Estonia and Denmark in connection with the laundering of the $230 million.[24]

The theft of the $230 million occurred when a corrupt tax official, working in the Moscow tax office, received a bribe worth over $30 million to approve a "tax refund" that was paid to two petty criminals on the basis of stolen documents.[25] A portion of the stolen $230 million was funneled through a series of bogus shell companies created and registered by the Australian GT Group to hide the identity of the beneficial owner of the $230 million.[26] The founder of the GT Group, Geoffrey Taylor, advertised that he could serve as director, shareholder, and front man to distract attention from clients.[27] However, it appears that the actions of the GT Group were not illegal.

When the $230 million were transferred to bank accounts held by shell companies, lax banking regulation made it possible for banks to accept the money without ascertaining the source of the funds. When questioned, the banks responded that they took the issue of money laundering seriously and sought to report suspicious activity.[28] The money was apparently paid into bank accounts for companies that subsequently ceased operations or companies that insisted that the payments were legitimate.[29] However, an investigation raised suspicion that money laundering had occurred. In one instance, a sheepskin firm received $1.2 million from Estonian firms that were known to be major transit companies for money laundering and had no connection to the sheepskin industry.[30]

Between April and August 2017, Danske Bank's internal task force investigation identified a second money laundering scheme, involving mirror trading of bonds labeled by Danske staff as the "solution" or the "bond loop."[31] A customer paid rubles to an intermediary, who then bought Russian government bonds that were transferred to Danske's account at Citibank in Moscow.[32] The intermediary then sold the bonds to Danske, who in turn immediately credited the intermediary's account.[33] The intermediary then paid the customer's supplier.[34] An internal memo circulated to the Executive Committee of Danske Bank Estonia on October 15, 2013, presented the bond loop as "a solution for ten customers in our Non-resident Intermediaries segment using bonds as a faster, cheaper and more reliable way for their end-clients to transfer money overseas than making an international payment through a domestic Russian bank."[35] While there may be customers who have legitimate reasons for conducting this type of transaction, an earlier draft had added: "and therefore potentially this solution could be used for money-laundering," but this language had been deleted from the final version at the initiative of a branch manager.[36]

On August 31, 2017, Danske Bank's AML department informed the Board of Directors of the imminent publication of a new set of news stories regarding a third money laundering scheme, named the "Azerbaijani Laundromat" by the media.[37] This scheme was the subject of global media attention in September 2017. The scheme was, like the "Russian Laundromat," uncovered through a joint investigation by OCCRP and *Berlingske*, a Danish newspaper, of leaked bank records.[38] The scheme was active in the period from 2012 through 2014.[39] Allegedly, $2.9 billion were laundered by four shell companies that were customers of Danske Bank's Estonian branch and registered in the UK.[40]

A Failure of Banking Law

It is clear that problems were reported to Danske Bank's Board of Directors and the Audit Committee, and it is equally clear that such reporting was accompanied by assurances that problems were being dealt with and mitigation was ongoing.[41] The severity of the situation and the risks facing the bank were not fully understood. However, mere failure to comprehend risk is not a crime. The 2018 Bruun and Hjejle report concluded that no legal obligations were breached by Danske's Board of Directors, the Chairman of the Board, the Audit Committee, or Danske's CEO.[42] On May 3, 2018, the Danish FSA issued a statement that it had not found sufficient basis, with regard to existing fitness and propriety regulations, to launch cases against members of Danske's management.[43] In sum, money laundering had occurred, but the crimes were not the result of prosecutable crimes by Danske Bank management or staff. There was no legal basis to prosecute Danske Bank officials.

This conclusion is significant. The fact that money laundering can occur on a grand scale in the absence of any violation of law by a bank official implies a gross failure of international banking laws. The Danske Bank money laundering case illustrates the existence of loopholes that permit criminals to conduct criminal transactions on a massive scale, undetected for years. The only reason that the Danske Bank case was uncovered was that a whistleblower stepped forward.

The nature of the problem is described by the 2018 Bruun and Hjejle report. Customers in the Non-Resident Portfolio received incoming payments. Outgoing payments from these customers were transmitted to recipients outside the Non-Resident Portfolio. A small number of customers were nonregulated entities acting as intermediaries providing cross-border payment solutions, including bond mirror trades, to unknown end-clients in the Russian Federation, Azerbaijan, and Ukraine.[44] However, while numerous customers engaged in suspicious transactions, the fact that a customer or a transaction is deemed suspicious does not in itself demonstrate criminal activity on the part of the customer or any other party.[45] Proof of money laundering requires proof that funds transferred are proceeds of a crime. However, ascertaining whether this is the case typically requires more information than is possessed by a financial institution such as Danske Bank.[46] Existing banking law and regulations are not crafted in a way that compels customers to submit the type of information needed to trace illicit proceeds to their source.

To forestall money laundering and terrorist financing, financial institutions are obligated by law and regulation to establish adequate and appropriate policies and procedures regarding customer due diligence, reporting, record-keeping, internal control, risk assessment, risk management, compliance management, and communication.[47] EU Directive 2005/60 ("Third AML Directive") was implemented into Estonian law on January 28, 2008, in the form of the Money Laundering and Terrorist Financing Prevention Act.[48] Pursuant to this regulation, financial institutions were required to perform customer due diligence, for example, when establishing a business relationship with a customer or when there was a suspicion of money laundering or terrorist financing. The customer due diligence measures included an obligation to establish a customer's identity (and, where applicable, the beneficial owner) and to obtain information on the purpose and intended nature of the business relationship.[49] The customer due diligence obligation is also referred to as KYC. Financial institutions had an obligation to conduct enhanced customer due diligence in situations which by their nature presented a higher risk of money laundering or terrorist financing.

Another important part of the regulation consisted of reporting obligations in cases where a financial institution knew of, suspected, or had reasonable grounds to suspect a customer was engaging in money laundering (or terrorist financing).[50] Advisory guidelines issued by the Estonian Financial Intelligence Unit (FIU) stated that SARs should be submitted with regard to "cash payments to a client's account which will be used for purchasing securities or derivatives," a "single unusually large [national or cross-border] payment not conforming to normal turnover and/or not sufficiently justified," and "large payments (EEK 200,000 [EUR 15,000 according to the 2011 version]) and/or smaller periodic payments with the clients of the banks located in the territories with higher money laundering risks."[51]

Existing AML regulations, however, do not address a significant blind spot. When processing payments for its customers, the Estonian branch of Danske Bank was not privy to information regarding the ultimate source of funds or the ultimate recipient of funds. The Danske Bank customer accounts were simply way stations in a chain of opaque transactions. Existing banking laws required the Estonian branch to collect information regarding the external sender, Estonian branch customer, and external recipient, but permitted staff to accept bland assurances regarding the ultimate source of funds or ultimate recipient of funds. This loophole in international banking law and regulation permits money laundering to occur even when bank staff adhere to existing laws and regulations.

The chain of payments flowing through the Estonian branch of Danske Bank is illustrated in figure 10.1. The Estonian branch only had visibility regarding the parties within the dotted line box in figure 10.1—the branch had little or no visibility regarding the ultimate source of funds that were received by a customer of Danske Bank Estonia, or the ultimate recipient of funds that were transmitted by a customer of Danske Bank Estonia. Regarding a payment made to a customer of the Estonian branch from an external sender, the Estonian branch would, in connection with the payment, obtain information about the external sender (as well as the Estonian branch's customer). This could include the name and country of the sender's bank, information regarding the sender, the value of the payment, and a payment description. Regarding a payment made from a customer of the

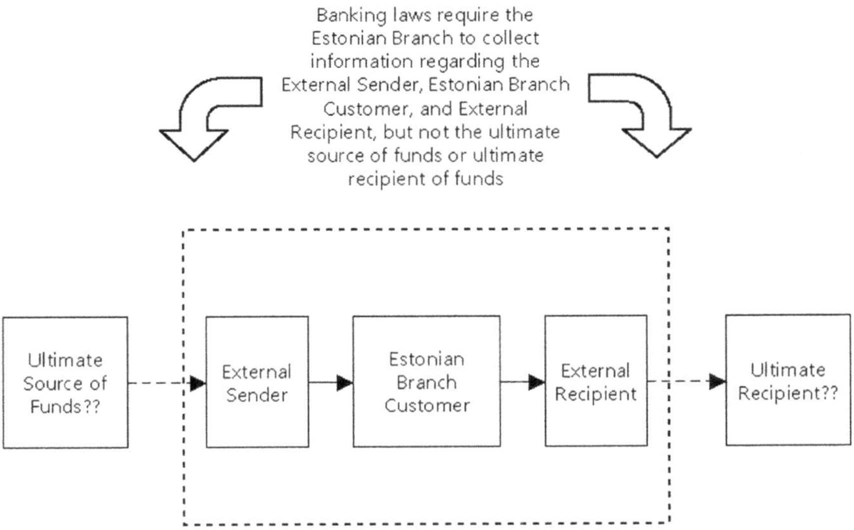

Figure 10.1 Flow of Payments through Estonian Branch of Danske Bank. *Source*: Figure created by author.

Estonian branch to an external recipient, the Estonian branch would, in connection with the payment, obtain information about the external recipient (as well as the Estonian branch's customer). This could include the name and country of the recipient's bank, information regarding the recipient, the value of the payment, and a payment description. This information was limited to the entities in the payment chain within the dotted line box in figure 10.1.

When criminals launder money, they do so by disguising, from bank staff, the identity of the true beneficial owners controlling the transactions. The staff of the Estonian branch only had access to information about the entity that was the immediate source of funds deposited at Danske Bank Estonia or the entity that was the immediate recipient of funds transmitted from Danske Bank Estonia. To cover their tracks, criminals employ accounts at opaque intermediaries or opaque offshore shell companies as the immediate source or destination accounts. Willing front men are employed to hide the identities of the true beneficial owners controlling the accounts. These opaque intermediaries, offshore shell companies, and front men were used by invisible criminals to control the funds that were channeled into, and out of, the Danske Bank Estonia accounts. Existing law does not prohibit the use of opaque accounts that hide the identity of true beneficial owners. The problem, therefore, is that existing banking laws do not compel customers to supply accurate information regarding the identities of the true beneficial owners who actually control financial transactions. Consequently, this information was unavailable to Danske Bank Estonia staff. Danske Bank Estonia staff lacked the legal tools required to extract accurate beneficial owner information and penetrate the veil of secrecy hiding the true beneficial owners controlling the transactions.

Estonian branch staff did not have sufficient information to determine whether the ultimate sender was a criminal, whether the ultimate recipient was a criminal, whether the ultimate sender was the same person as the ultimate recipient, whether the source of the funds was illicit, or whether money laundering or other crimes had occurred. The bank staff would not have had that information even if the staff had been scrupulous in adhering to AML laws and regulations. If existing laws and regulations contain loopholes that permit criminals to launder money on a massive scale, there is a need for new laws and regulations that close those loopholes.

The Vancouver Model

In February 2019, CTV News, a Canadian news channel, broadcast an explosive documentary investigative report regarding money laundering at British Columbia gambling casinos.[52] The report focused on revelations by Ross Alderson, a whistleblower and former head of AML for the British Columbia Lottery Corporation (BCLC), which oversees private casinos in the Canadian province of British Columbia. In 2011, as a newly assigned investigator at River Rock Casino in Richmond, Alderson was astonished to observe customers carrying heavy bags full of cash—hundreds of thousands of dollars—that were accepted without question by the casino's cage cashiers. Video from the casino's surveillance cameras captured one customer after another arriving with large bags that were dumped in plain view of the cameras. The cash, primarily from mainland Chinese customers, was bundled with rubber bands, the same way that cash is delivered by drug dealers, instead of banks. No questions were asked regarding the source of the cash. Alderson was told that "it was their culture to use cash" and was told that it would be offensive to question the source of the cash.[53] Alderson suspected that the source was organized crime—loan sharking to mainland Chinese gamblers.[54] "None" of the customers could identify a legitimate banking institution as the source of the cash.[55] "A lot of these individuals were quite open that they weren't sure who they got their money from."[56] "They were being paid in cash when they got there and they would pay it back as a business transaction either in Canada or in China."[57] Alderson observed customers who repeatedly converted large sums of cash, day after day, at the casino's cage. Alderson reported the activity to senior management but was told that it was not his job to investigate money laundering. Despite the obvious problems observed by Alderson, a review of AML measures in British Columbia casinos conducted by Robert Kroeker, chief compliance officer at BCLC, found that "the Province has a robust anti-money laundering regime in place."[58]

According to Alderson, customers could place orders for large amounts of cash that were delivered on the casino property, play a hand of baccarat in special rooms reserved for "high rollers," then cash out. Cash buy-ins over $10,000 were reported on suspicious transaction reports that were filed with British Columbia's Gaming and Enforcement Branch. However, the reports were never investigated, even though the suspicious cash buy-ins reached $20 million in July 2015. The task force of Royal Canadian Mounted Police (RCMP) and local forces that was supposed to investigate casinos had been shut down in 2009.[59] The integrated gaming unit funded by the province, and the RCMP Proceeds of Crime unit, were abolished in 2013.[60] Demands by opposition lawmakers to revive the casino policing unit were rebuffed with the assertion that sophisticated money laundering controls were already in place, making money laundering impossible. However, the money laundering was taking place

> right outside the front door of the casino, not in the casino, and the issue was that everyone was willfully blind to where the money was coming from—these stacks of $20 and $50 bills that were coming into the casinos.[61]

A two-year RCMP investigation, which became the largest money laundering investigation in Canadian history, offers details regarding the money laundering operation. The offices of Silver International served as a secret, illegal bank that supplied gamblers at British Columbia casinos with bags of cash involving millions of dollars.[62] Surveillance video taken from Silver International's own security cameras documented large deliveries of cash to Silver International that filled the bank's safes. Excess cash was stored in large bags or simply piled in stacks on the office floor. The RCMP observed Paul Jin, a central figure in the operation, entering and departing the offices of Silver International with airline-style luggage and boxes, near the River Rock Casino in Richmond. Police surveillance indicated that Jin transported the bags and handed them to couriers, who then handed the bags to men who walked into the River Rock Casino and produced large sums of buy-in cash.

The investigation revealed that Silver International was linked to multinational drug trafficking, including a high-level drug trafficker and importer who supplied multi-kilogram drug traffickers in the Vancouver area with cocaine.[63] Couriers were tracked to Silver International, where millions of dollars of drug proceeds were deposited at the illegal bank. The bank's financial ledgers documented annual flows of $220 million: drug money in, laundered money out, with an overall impact estimated at $1.2 billion per year.[64]

The RCMP investigation revealed details of the operation. Money from drug dealers was deposited at Silver International. The money would be loaned to Chinese gamblers, local gamblers, or money exchangers, who would repay their debts to one of 600 Silver International bank accounts located in China. The money would then be transferred to drug suppliers of fentanyl in China and cocaine in Peru and Mexico. The drugs would be shipped to Canadian drug dealers to continue the entire cycle. This scheme was labeled the "Vancouver Model."[65]

Peter Germain, former RCMP deputy commissioner and AML expert, was commissioned to conduct an independent review.[66] He concluded that British Columbia casinos were used to conduct large-scale, transnational money laundering, involving not only gamblers but housewives and students, and were used to launder money for offshore entities, including the Mexican Sinaloa drug cartel and Middle Eastern organized crime syndicates: "Vancouver became . . . a laundromat for money, for organized crime domestically and internationally."[67] "For many years, certain mainland casinos unwittingly served as laundromats for the proceeds of organized crime."[68] According to Germain, regulators and BCLC ignored warning signs, in part because $1 billion of gaming revenue was flowing into the provincial treasury each year.[69] There was a reluctance to take any action that might threaten an enormous revenue stream that supported a major portion of budgetary expenditures. Germain recommended tighter regulation and enforcement.[70]

However, the Vancouver case example suggests the need for an entirely new type of law. Robert Kroeker, chief compliance officer at BCLC, noted "The 'Vancouver model' of money laundering does not involve money being laundered *through* the casinos, in any traditional sense. Rather, the model involves money being laundered through financial institutions and unregulated banking channels, away from gaming facilities."[71] "The real issue" is "the risk that proceeds of crime, already laundered through other sectors including the financial sector and legitimate gamblers with substantiated wealth, were being gambled at casinos."[72] According to Kroeker, BCLC regularly "[probed] the source of funds in the case of suspicious transactions irrespective of dollar value . . . based on a risk assessment of the customer and the transaction."[73] However, both legitimate and suspicious gamblers transported large sums of cash in bags. Large sums of cash were not a clear indication of money laundering. Casino cashiers were not able to make a determination about whether a given customer was using illicit funds to buy in at the casino's cage.

It is unlikely that the current regulatory scheme can be fine-tuned in a way that would make existing laws effective. In a trenchant statement submitted to the Commission of Inquiry into Money Laundering in British Columbia, BCLC distinguished between its legal obligations to report suspicious transactions, and the responsibility of regulators and police to enforce AML laws:

> There is a crucial distinction between two important, but separate roles in countering potential money laundering in the gaming industry: (1) responsibility for identifying and reporting specified transactions to the federal government's financial intelligence unit, the Financial Transactions and Reports Analysis Centre of Canada ("FINTRAC"), and for identifying and reporting certain conduct to GPEB;[74] and (2) responsibility for the enforcement of anti-money laundering ("AML") laws. BCLC emphasises that it is BCLC's responsibility to identify and report; it is the responsibility of regulators and the police to enforce. This distinction is central in understanding BCLC's efforts to prevent money laundering in its casinos. While BCLC collaborates with and supports regulators and police, they are ultimately the ones with the authority to detect, investigate, and seek charges against anyone suspected to be involved in money laundering and other criminal activities.[75]

Enforcement, however, can only be effective if laws are constructed in a way that establishes a bright line distinguishing legal and illegal activity. If both legitimate and suspicious gamblers transport large sums of cash in bags, if large sums of cash are not clear indicators of money laundering, if casino cashiers are not in a position to make a determination about whether a given customer is using illicit funds to buy in at a casino's cage, if casinos do not possess the information needed to determine whether buy-in funds are controlled by criminals, and if there is not an effective legal mechanism to force beneficial owners to identify themselves, it should not be surprising that investigators struggle, enforcement is weak, and massive money laundering continues to occur. Instead, the Vancouver case example suggests that there is a need for a new type of law that would be more effective than existing laws that simply require submission of suspicious transaction reports.

Liberty Reserve

Liberty Reserve was a Costa Rica-based centralized virtual currency service that was alleged to have been used to launder more than $6 billion in criminal proceeds during its seven-year history. The scheme was exposed in a federal indictment.[76] To use Liberty Reserve's virtual currency, commonly referred to as "LR," a user was required to open an account through the Liberty Reserve website. The user was required to provide his name, e-mail address, and date of birth. However, unlike traditional banks or legitimate payment processors, Liberty Reserve did not require users to validate their identity by providing official identification documents or a credit card. Accounts could therefore be easily opened using fictitious or anonymous identities. Prosecutors cited blatantly criminal monikers used by Liberty Reserve clients, including "Russia Hackers" and "Hacker Account."[77] An undercover agent was able to register accounts under the name "Joe Bogus" and describe the purpose of the account as "for cocaine," without being questioned.[78] The weak verification system made Liberty Reserve the premier bank for cybercriminals. Believing themselves to be protected by this anonymity, Liberty Reserve users engaged in criminal transactions with impunity.

Once a user established an account with Liberty Reserve, the user could then conduct transactions with other Liberty Reserve users. The user could receive transfers of LR from other users' accounts and could transfer LR from his own account to other users, including any "merchants" that accepted LR as payment. For a "privacy fee" of 75 cents per transaction, a user could hide his own Liberty Reserve account number when transferring funds, effectively making the transfer completely untraceable, even within Liberty Reserve's already opaque system.[79]

To add an additional layer of anonymity, Liberty Reserve did not permit users to fund their accounts by transferring money to Liberty Reserve directly, such as by issuing a credit card payment or wire transfer to Liberty Reserve. Nor could Liberty Reserve users withdraw funds from their accounts directly, such as through an ATM withdrawal. Instead, Liberty Reserve users were required to make any deposits or withdrawals using third-party "exchangers," enabling Liberty Reserve to avoid collecting any information about its users through banking transactions or other activity that would leave a centralized paper trail.

Liberty Reserve's "exchangers" were third-party entities that maintained direct financial relationships with Liberty Reserve, buying and selling LR in bulk from Liberty Reserve in exchange for fiat currency. To fund a Liberty Reserve account, a user was required to transmit fiat currency (e.g., through a money remitter) to an exchanger. Upon receiving the user's payment, the exchanger credited the user's Liberty Reserve account with a corresponding amount of LR by transferring LR from the exchanger's Liberty Reserve account to the user's account. Similarly, if a Liberty Reserve user wished to withdraw funds from his account, the user was required to transfer LR from his Liberty Reserve account to an exchanger's Liberty Reserve account. The exchanger would then arrange to pay the user a corresponding amount of fiat currency. The Liberty Reserve website recommended several "pre-approved" exchangers who tended to be unlicensed money transmitting businesses operating without significant governmental oversight or regulation, concentrated in Malaysia, Russia, Nigeria, and Vietnam.[80]

Liberty Reserve's system was designed so that criminals could conduct financial transactions hidden by multiple layers of anonymity and thereby avoid detection and apprehension by law enforcement officials. Liberty Reserve was in fact used extensively for illegal purposes, functioning as the bank of choice for criminals who, protected by this anonymity, engaged in criminal transactions with impunity. Liberty Reserve facilitated criminal transactions by offering a "shopping cart interface" that "merchant" websites could use to accept LR currency as a form of payment.[81] The "merchants" who accepted LR were overwhelmingly criminal in nature. They included, for example, traffickers of stolen credit card data and personal information, peddlers of various types of online Ponzi and get-rich-quick schemes, computer hackers for hire, unregulated gambling businesses, and underground drug-dealing websites.[82] In addition to being used to process payments for illegal goods and services online, Liberty Reserve was also used by cybercriminals to launder criminal proceeds and transfer funds among criminal associates. Liberty Reserve was used by credit card theft and computer hacking rings operating in countries around the world, including Vietnam, Nigeria, Hong Kong, China, and the United States, to distribute proceeds of these conspiracies among the members involved.[83] In an online chat that was captured by law enforcement between Vladimir Kats and Ahmed Yassine Abdelghani, Kats explicitly described Liberty Reserve's activities as "illegal" and noted that "everyone in USA" such as "DOJ" (the USDOJ) knows "LR is [a] money laundering operation that hackers use."[84]

Hawala

Hawala is a popular informal system that accomplishes long-distance transfer of money without the movement of physical currency or telegraph or computer network wire transfers between banks. Hawala relies instead on the performance and honor of an enormous worldwide network of money brokers known as hawaladars. Most hawaladars are small businessmen who provide hawala services as a sideline operation.

The hawala system bypasses the formal banking system. A customer gives a local hawala broker a sum of money. The broker contacts a distant hawala broker who agrees to pay the sum to the intended recipient. To receive the sum, the recipient must provide a password that is communicated by the sender to the recipient. Each hawala broker maintains an accounting ledger to keep track of the amounts received from, and owed to, other brokers. These debts are settled through any form of payment that is acceptable among the hawaladars. Hawala brokers profit from customer commissions and favorable international settlements that are unencumbered by the conventional banking system's hefty foreign exchange transaction fees.

The unique feature of the system is that no promissory instruments are exchanged between the hawala brokers; the transaction takes place entirely on the honor system. As the system does not depend on the legal enforceability of claims, it can operate even in the absence of a legal and juridical environment. Trust and extensive use of connections are the components that distinguish it from other remittance systems. Hawaladar networks are often based on membership in the same family, village, clan, or ethnic group, and cheating is punished by ex-communication, "loss of honor," and resulting economic hardship.

Hawala is attractive to customers because it provides fast and convenient transfer of funds, typically at a far lower commission than the fees charged by banks. Its advantages are most pronounced when the receiving country applies unprofitable exchange rate regulations or when the receiving country banking and legal system permits this type of informal transaction (e.g., Afghanistan, Yemen, Somalia). In some parts of the world hawala is the most practical option, even for legitimate fund transfers. However, the hawala system can be used for money laundering because it operates outside the traditional banking system's regulations and legal requirements for collecting and verifying customer identity information.

Online Gaming

Online video gaming is especially vulnerable to money laundering because of a lack of AML regulations governing the sector. Regulation is lacking regarding customer identification, due diligence, monitoring, and the submission of SARs. Certain games, such as *Second Life*, attracted money laundering because the game's virtual currency, known as "Linden Dollars," is convertible with fiat currency.[85] This attracted regulatory attention. FinCEN now identifies administrators and exchangers of convertible virtual currencies as "money services businesses" (MSBs) subject to BSA regulation.[86] After FATF members began recognizing Linden Dollars and other convertible in-game currencies as virtual currencies subject to regulation, criminals switched their focus to online games such as *Fortnite*.[87] These games do not use officially convertible virtual currency. However, players of these games can buy and sell nonconvertible game currency and virtual game assets on secondary black markets. The nonconvertible currency and game assets have acquired the characteristics of virtual currency that can be used for money laundering, without attracting the attention of regulators.

Fortnite's digital in-game currency, called "V-Bucks," may be used to buy in-game weapons, skins, and accessories that enhance the attributes of a player's in-game character. V-Bucks may be purchased via credit card or PayPal. Criminals may use illicit proceeds or stolen credit card details to purchase V-Bucks or accessories from the official *Fortnite* store, then sell the account holding the V-Bucks and accessories at a discounted rate on secondary markets such as E-Bay and G2G.com, receiving clean money in return.[88] Payments are processed through PayPal or bitcoin. Buyers receive the log-in and password information used to create the *Fortnite* account, giving the purchaser access to the V-Bucks and accessories held by the account.

Steam is an online gaming platform with characteristics that facilitate money laundering. A user may walk into a participating retail store and use an in-store kiosk device to purchase a Steam gift card or wallet code. Steam gift cards and wallet codes are akin to gift certificates that may be redeemed on Steam for the purchase of online games, software, wallet credit, or tradable in-game items of value. These items may include, for instance, artifacts that vest a player's character with additional powers (such as swords, armor, and magic potions) or "currency" that can be used to purchase the artifacts.

Steam gift cards and wallet codes may be purchased at retail stores across the world in a variety of denominations. In North America, participating stores include Walgreens, Best Buy, GameStop, 7 Eleven Canada, and Walmart Canada. In Latin America, stores include Gamers Stores, Game Planet, Rixty, and GameFan. In Asia, stores include 7-Eleven Hong Kong, 7-Eleven Malaysia, 7-Eleven Philippines, and 7-Eleven Thailand. In Eastern Europe, participating outlets include Pay&Go, iNovine, and EasyPay terminals. Participating retail outlets are available in the Middle East, Western Europe, South Africa, Australia, and New Zealand.

A player may use the Steam online trading platform to electronically gift items to another player in exchange for money that is sent via PayPal. In other instances, in-game items are traded unofficially on online marketplaces. While this type of activity may breach user agreements, several websites such as PlayerAuctions, G2G.com, or iGVault continue to list in-game items for sale.[89]

The system of tradable gift items, however, creates a virtual currency system that may be used by criminals for money laundering. Illicit cash, or stolen credit card details, may be used to purchase tradable in-game items of value. Those items may then be electronically gifted to another player in exchange for money that is sent via PayPal. This process converts illicit money into seemingly legitimate funds obtained from the sale of tradable in-game items of value. Using this system, criminals in one country can send virtual money to associates in another country, bypassing record-keeping and reporting requirements that normally apply to money transmitters, thereby serving to obscure the source of funds that may be illicit.

Kromtech, a software development company, reported that a cybercriminal group had automated the use of stolen card details to create a large number of Apple IDs, bought in-game items in mobile games such as *Clash of Clans* or *Marvel Contest of Champions*, and resold them on third-party websites for fiat currency.[90] The sheer volume of sales of in-game items of value may mask the magnitude of money laundering that may be occurring. For example, sales of electronic "loot boxes," which are collections of randomly selected in-game items, generated 25 percent of the global gaming industry's revenue of $117 billion.[91]

A report published by the Royal United Services Institute's (RUSI) Centre for Financial Crime and Security Studies described additional schemes.[92] A drug trafficker may deposit cash with a poorly regulated overseas bank. Instead of wiring funds to an accomplice's UK bank account, the trafficker could, in an effort to evade banking laws that require banks to report details of wire transfers, choose to secretly transmit the funds using online gaming currency. The trafficker might purchase online game currency, then hand it over to the accomplice's in-game character, who could then resell the game currency for fiat money. Alternatively, instead of transferring specific in-game items, she could hand over the log-in details from her entire game account.

The RUSI report concluded: "If a computer game allows players to transfer in-game items to each other, and these in-game items can be exchanged into fiat currency, the gaming company's position is similar to that of a virtual currency exchange."[93] This type of unregulated virtual currency exchange is vulnerable to money laundering in jurisdictions where there are no legal obligations to collect or report information regarding the identity of users who buy or sell virtual assets. If transactions are completed without a record of user identities, it would be impossible to trace specific transactions to specific individuals. Any strategy to control money laundering must, therefore, control this type of transaction.

In October 2018, the FATF recognized the threat of online gaming and the use of virtual assets for money laundering by recommending that members regulate and license or register virtual asset service providers (VASPs), including exchanges and wallet providers, and require VASPs to implement AML/CFT controls.[94] FATF defines a virtual asset as "a digital representation of value that can be digitally traded, or transferred, and can be used for payment or investment purposes."[95] This definition encompasses in-game items of value as well as virtual currencies, underlining the need to regulate transactions that may fall outside conventional AML regulations—transactions that may otherwise be employed for the purpose of laundering illicit funds. As noted by the RUSI report: "a virtual item can be used as a substitute for value and thus be exploited for money laundering regardless of whether it is traded officially or unofficially."[96]

Lightning

Lightning is a new-generation cryptocurrency technology that may become the dominant method of bitcoin payments because it offers cheaper and faster payments.[97] Lightning makes bitcoin transactions truly anonymous and untraceable.[98] The technology effectively defeats existing AML regulations. Addressing this threat will require a new strategy, involving new banking laws and regulations.

No personal identifiable data is included in bitcoin transactions. However, bitcoin transactions involve the use of public cipher keys that, in principle, can be utilized by blockchain intelligence tools such as *Chainalysis*, *CipherTrace*, *Elliptic*, *Crystal*, and *Qlue* to identify operators of public keys, which allows users of these tools to identify the source and destination of bitcoins.[99] This can include the identification of exchanges, services, merchants, and illicit entities that send or receive funds.

Lightning effectively defeats these tools by moving most transactions off the main network.[100] Suppose, for example, that Alex wishes to send his friend, Britney, 1 bitcoin. Suppose that Alex does not have a payment channel established with Britney, but both Britney and Alex have individual, separate, previously established, open payment channels with a mobile app such as Abra that permits clients to purchase stock using bitcoin.[101] If Abra has established a Lightning node, Alex can send 1 bitcoin to Abra, whose Lightning node then routes the payment to Britney. Like the hawala system, Abra's Lightning node would accept the funds from Alex and note that Britney is owed 1 bitcoin. Abra's Lightning node would then send Britney 1 bitcoin. This means that a user can pay for an item using the Lightning network without needing to open a direct channel to the recipient of the funds. The public cipher information would document that Alex sent 1 bitcoin to Abra. The public cipher information would document that Abra sent 1 bitcoin to Britney.

Suppose, however, that the Lightning network path between Alex and Britney involves multiple Lightning nodes instead of a single node. Transmission of funds from Alex to Britney would involve multiple hawala-like debits and credits. Each node would only have information about the address of the preceding node and the address of the following node—not the sender (Alex) and recipient (Britney). It would be impossible for investigators, using available information, to demonstrate that Alex sent 1 bitcoin to Britney. The transaction between Alex and Britney might involve illicit funds, but this would be hidden because the funds would travel a circuitous path involving multiple intermediary nodes that routinely handle a high volume of legitimate hawala-like fund transfers without collecting and reporting beneficial owner information. It would be impossible for investigators to link Alex's payment to Britney. In essence, the origin and ultimate destination of a fund transfer would be untraceable.

Any individual with internet access can obtain access to the Lightning network, either by purchasing a Lightning node, or by downloading a Lightning wallet. Neither requires user identification. Users do not need to be verified to create a channel with another node.

Existing AML regulations are ineffective in addressing money laundering over the Lightning network. While FinCEN might seek to designate Lightning node operators as money transmitters that are obligated to submit SARs to FinCEN, the identification of suspicious activity would be nearly impossible without reliable information about the true identity of the ultimate sender and receiver involved in each transaction. In the absence of regulations requiring the transmission of this information to FinCEN, and in the absence of an effective scheme for enforcing adherence to this regulation and deterring the submission of false information, any requirement to submit SARs would be ineffective.

APUNCAC

The schemes described above represent six strategies used by criminals to introduce illicit funds into the financial system. Any strategy to control money laundering must control these paths. APUNCAC implements a strategy that is designed to control these paths.

At the heart of APUNCAC are reporting requirements. The true beneficial owner controlling the funds involved in a transaction is required to certify that he or she is, in fact, the true beneficial owner. When funds are paid, deposited, transferred, or exchanged, the beneficial owner must either be present and must certify beneficial ownership in person, or must be contacted and must certify, under penalty of perjury, that he or she is the true beneficial owner. If the funds are paid from one person to another, the receiving person must also certify that he or she is the true beneficial owner controlling the funds that are received. The beneficial recipient may be a customer who is physically present when the transaction is conducted. However, in many cases, the true beneficial recipient will not be the customer who is physically present when the transaction is conducted. The in-store customer may merely serve as an agent for the true beneficial recipient.

The use of digital technology would permit the APUNCAC certification process to be performed quickly. APUNCAC specifies that certification shall be obtained using digital signatures and digital certificates, which are equivalent to digital passports that identify the "holder" of the passport. The technology permits certification to be performed on a smartphone, tablet, or computer. An electronic request would be sent to the beneficial owner or a certified agent of the beneficial owner. The beneficial owner (or his agent) would send an electronic reply using a digital signature and digital certificate that would serve to certify the identity of the beneficial owner. The technology uses RSA public key encryption to ensure that no individual can pose as the person asserting beneficial ownership.[102]

The beneficial owner would be required to respond to the digital request prior to the consummation of the financial transaction. If the beneficial owner is a business owner who cannot be physically present, the beneficial owner might choose to designate, as the beneficial owner's agent, a customer who presents currency for payment, deposit, transfer, or exchange. If the beneficial owner is a business owner who cannot be physically present but must conduct a large volume of time-sensitive financial transactions, he or she could designate multiple dedicated agents who would be authorized to certify the beneficial owner's identity, either in person or remotely, using digital technology. Digital signatures and digital certificates certifying beneficial ownership may be electronically embedded into electronic transactions conducted by entities involved in high-volume transactions, permitting the type of high-volume certification that would be necessary.[103] APUNCAC specifies that certification of beneficial ownership by an agent of the beneficial owner entails the same legal consequences for the beneficial owner if he were to certify his identity in person.

To review, APUNCAC creates a new requirement. The beneficial owner of funds must certify, under penalty of perjury, that he is in fact the true beneficial owner whenever the funds are paid, deposited, exchanged, or transmitted. This requirement applies to a transaction (over $3,000) in currency or involving a bank draft, anywhere in the world, by a national of a State Party.[104] In addition, the requirement applies to a transaction (over $3,000) in currency or involving a bank draft, negotiable instrument, wire transfer, or money order, in high-risk jurisdictions, by a national of a State Party.[105] In addition, the requirement applies to a transaction (over $3,000) in currency or involving a bank draft, negotiable instrument, wire transfer, or money order, with the assistance of a person who provides remittance services or receives cash deposits or cash payments and is under the jurisdiction of a State Party.[106] In addition, the requirement applies when a series of transactions involving any amount, in any form, are structured in a way that seeks to avoid the reporting requirements.[107] The use of smurfs to conduct a series of small currency transactions in an effort to avoid the reporting requirements would be illegal under APUNCAC.

In addition, it is illegal under APUNCAC to act in a manner that seeks to evade or assists in evading the provisions of APUNCAC through "any stratagem or deceptive practice that (a) seeks to obscure, or obscures from an educated person, the true identities of beneficial owners linked to financial transactions as described" by APUNCAC, or the source of such funds described by APUNCAC, or (b) seeks to launder funds obtained through criminal activities or tax evasion.[108]

Chapters 8 and 9 described and explained two strategies to enforce this regime and discourage noncompliance.[109] The chapters addressed numerous issues regarding jurisdiction and enforcement. In brief, APUNCAC would greatly increase the risk that smurfs, front men, bank clerks, accountants, attorneys, and others who currently aid and abet money laundering would, under APUNCAC, be debarred, arrested, fined, or imprisoned. The risk would depend on the number and international significance of States Parties that choose to adopt APUNCAC. If a majority of OECD Member States choose to adopt APUNCAC, the risk would be substantial.

Figure 10.2 diagrams the APUNCAC scheme. The APUNCAC reporting requirement inserts the certification requirement into each covered transaction at the point of the transaction. No covered transaction would be consummated unless the true beneficial owners of the transaction funds are identified and recorded in the FINCEN database,[110] or front men choose to pose as true beneficial owners, flout the law, and risk the consequences of flouting the law. Many individuals who are currently willing to participate in money laundering schemes only because the risks are minimal would, upon adoption of APUNCAC, have to think twice about whether it is worth the risk of falsifying information and being arrested and imprisoned for repeated violations of APUNCAC.

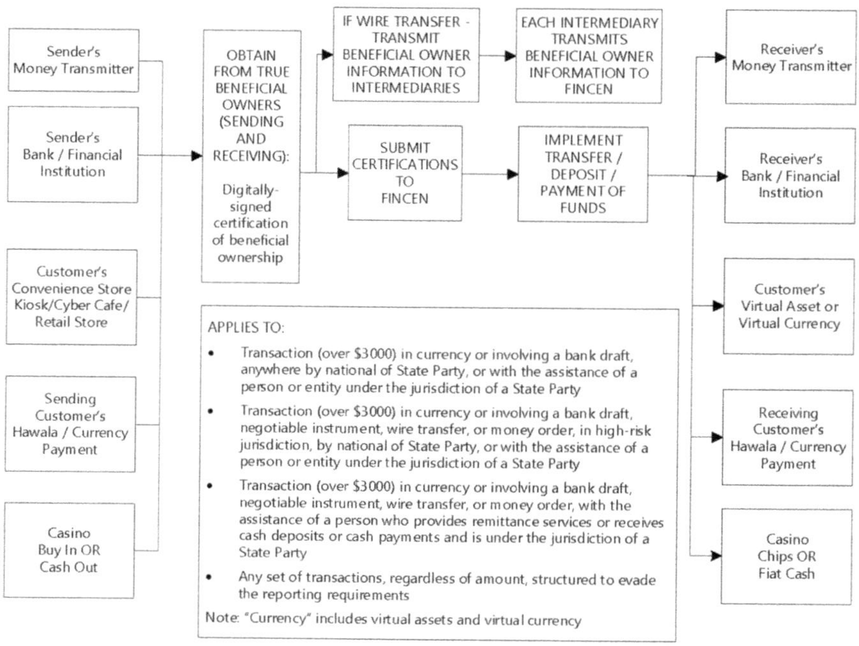

Figure 10.2 APUNCAC Scheme. *Source*: Figure created by author.

The rationale for the reporting requirement is that effective investigation and prosecution of corruption and money laundering depends on the capacity of prosecutors to obtain the cooperation of front men, money transmitters, financial institution personnel, and retail clerks who would otherwise aid, abet, and facilitate money laundering by accepting large currency payments with few questions. The APUNCAC requirements create a risk of punishment for any front man who participates in a scheme to hide the true beneficial owner when funds are paid, deposited, exchanged, or transmitted internationally. APUNCAC creates a risk of punishment for any person who assists with a covered financial transaction but fails to obtain and submit the required beneficial owner certifications to FINCEN. This risk of punishment is a necessary element of any effective strategy to control corruption and money laundering. A failure to institute this risk of punishment ensures that prosecutors have little leverage to obtain the cooperation of front men, money transmitters, financial institution personnel, and retail clerks who either actively or passively aid, abet, and facilitate money laundering. No other anticorruption strategy incorporates the APUNCAC reporting strategy. No other anticorruption strategy criminalizes failure to obtain and submit beneficial owner information, for the vast array of transactions covered by APUNCAC, to a centralized, online database that is readily searchable by financial crime investigators. The creation of this type of database would expose the identity of criminals seeking to hide illicit gains through complicated transactions involving opaque offshore entities and bank secrecy havens. This type of exposure is necessary to end corruption and impunity. It can only be implemented through a binding international treaty that creates a real risk of arrest and extradition whenever a guilty party travels to a State Party jurisdiction, or a jurisdiction that maintains an extradition agreement with a State Party.

In contrast, the existing regulatory regime fails to implement anything similar to the APUNCAC reporting requirement (figure 10.3). In the United States, depository financial institutions are required to verify customer identity when a customer opens a bank account, but the customer is not required to provide certification, under penalty of perjury, regarding the identity of the actual beneficial owner of the account—the customer is only required to sign a statement that the information that is provided is complete and correct "to the best of" the customer's knowledge.[111] This loophole permits criminals to hide their identities by employing other individuals to open and operate bank accounts that are, in fact, controlled by the criminals. A bank customer who opens an account at the direction of a criminal might choose to assert that he or she (i.e., the customer) was unaware that the account was actually controlled by another person (i.e., the criminal). The existing regulatory regime does not discourage or prevent this type of deception. The existing system depends on an assertion by the bank customer about the identity of

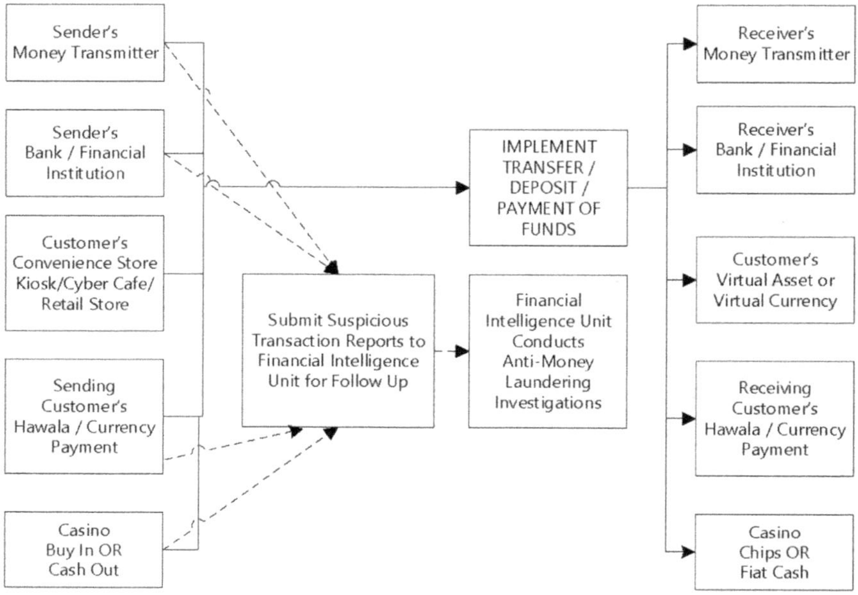

Figure 10.3 Existing Regulatory Scheme. *Source*: Figure created by author.

the beneficial owner that may or may not be true. However, since the bank customer may have been misinformed about the identity of the true beneficial owner, it would not be appropriate to prosecute the bank customer in cases where he or she was indeed misinformed.

The existing regulatory regime does not require the actual beneficial owner—who might not be present when the bank account is opened—to assert ownership through a digitally signed certification and does not require the bank clerks who receive deposits to obtain and submit a certification of beneficial ownership to a centralized database. This loophole makes it difficult for prosecutors to prove that a bank customer violated banking laws by posing as a beneficial owner or providing false information about the identity of the true beneficial owner. In contrast, the APUNCAC reporting requirement installs a tripwire that cannot be avoided by individuals involved in money laundering. Posing as a beneficial owner and submitting a false certification of beneficial ownership is illegal under APUNCAC.

A person who agrees to serve as a front man might choose to violate APUNCAC by digitally signing a certification of beneficial ownership. But this deception can be easily detected by investigators simply by obtaining e-mail or text messages from the beneficial owner to the front man, directing the front man to conduct financial transactions. This type of evidence is a clear indication that the front man is not the true beneficial owner who controls the funds and would be sufficient under APUNCAC to convict a front man of serving as a front man, in violation of APUNCAC. This type of conviction is not possible under the existing regulatory regime because the existing regime does not obtain a certification, under penalty of perjury, from the purported beneficial owner, that he or she is in fact the true beneficial owner. Instead, the existing regime only obtains a statement from the bank customer—instead of the beneficial owner—regarding the name of the beneficial owner. This seemingly minor difference prevents prosecutors from convicting bank customers who make false statements because a bank customer can always assert that the information he or she supplied regarding the name of the beneficial owner was true "to the best of" his or her knowledge.

APUNCAC closes this loophole. By requiring certification from the actual beneficial owner, instead of a dubious statement from the bank customer, a front man who poses as the beneficial owner is forced to digitally sign a certification of beneficial ownership, under penalty of perjury, that is demonstrably false. It would no longer be possible for criminals to employ individuals to open bank accounts, give false information regarding the beneficial ownership of those accounts and—when questioned—assert that this information was true "to the best of" their knowledge.

Under APUNCAC, a front man must certify a statement that is demonstrably false, thereby risking debarment, fines, and imprisonment. This risk is not present in the existing regulatory system. The creation of this risk is a necessary step in controlling money laundering and the crime associated with money laundering. Prosecutors who are unable to threaten front men have little leverage to obtain their cooperation. In the absence of their cooperation, the identities of the criminals that control illicit funds will remain elusive, the capacity of prosecutors to obtain indictments will remain weak, and criminals will continue to engage in acts of violence, corruption, terrorism, and impunity, facilitated by unimpeded money laundering.

APPLICATION

How would APUNCAC work? For illustrative purposes, it is useful to examine exactly how APUNCAC would apply in each of the six case examples described in the first section of this chapter. The basic principle is that the APUNCAC reporting requirement would be inserted at the point when a covered entity receives, transfers, or pays funds that are the subject of a covered transaction, that is, a financial transaction that is covered by APUNCAC. The reporting requirement seeks to make it virtually impossible for a covered transaction to be consummated unless (a) the identity of the true beneficial owner of the funds that are transmitted is obtained and submitted to FINCEN, or (b) the person who poses as the beneficial owner, in violation of APUNCAC, chooses to assume the risk of debarment, fines, and imprisonment.

Danske Bank Estonia

The APUNCAC reporting requirement would, in the case of Danske Bank Estonia, have required bank clerks to obtain, and submit to FINCEN, certification of beneficial ownership of (a) funds deposited at, or transmitted to, Danske Bank Estonia, or (b) funds withdrawn or transmitted from Danske Bank Estonia, in an amount exceeding $3,000.[112] If the beneficial owner is a customer who is physically present, certification would be demanded from the customer. Otherwise, a bank clerk would be required to contact the beneficial owner to obtain a digitally signed certification that the purported beneficial owner is indeed the true beneficial owner.

The sender would have to provide a digitally signed certification that he is the beneficial owner of the source funds. The recipient would have to provide a digitally signed certification that she is the beneficial owner of the funds received from the sender. The certifications would state that the funds do not involve the laundering of funds obtained illegally or through criminal activities and would acknowledge that criminal penalties apply if false or misleading information is provided.

There are two possibilities. Either the person purporting to be the beneficial owner is in fact the beneficial owner, or the person purporting to be the beneficial owner is a front man posing as the beneficial owner, in violation of APUNCAC, who chooses to assume the risk of debarment, fines, and imprisonment. A bank clerk who failed to obtain and submit the required certification would risk debarment, fines, and imprisonment. A front man who posed as a beneficial owner but is not in fact the true beneficial owner would risk debarment, fines, and imprisonment. The APUNCAC regime would encourage compliance and discourage the participation of front men who would have to think twice about whether the risks were worth the rewards of posing as a front man.

The Vancouver Model

The APUNCAC reporting requirement would, in the case of the River Rock Casino, have required cage cashiers to obtain, and submit to FINCEN, certification of beneficial ownership of (a) funds used to buy in at the casino's cage window, or (b) chips used to cash out at the casino's cage window, in an amount exceeding $3,000.[113] If the beneficial owner is a customer who is physically present, certification would be demanded from the customer.

Otherwise, a cage cashier would be required to contact the beneficial owner to obtain a digitally signed certification that the purported beneficial owner is indeed the true beneficial owner.

There are two possibilities. Either the person purporting to be the beneficial owner is in fact the beneficial owner, or the person purporting to be the beneficial owner is a front man posing as the beneficial owner, in violation of APUNCAC, who chooses to assume the risk of debarment, fines, and imprisonment. A cage cashier who failed to obtain and submit the required certification would risk debarment, fines, and imprisonment. A front man who posed as a beneficial owner but is not in fact the true beneficial owner would risk debarment, fines, and imprisonment. The APUNCAC regime would encourage compliance and discourage the participation of front men who would have to think twice about whether the risks were worth the rewards of posing as a front man.

APUNCAC addresses the possibility that a criminal may attempt to obscure the origin of illicit funds by secretly transferring bags of casino chips between front men. Recall that it is illegal under APUNCAC to act in a manner that seeks to evade or assists in evading the beneficial owner reporting provisions of APUNCAC through "any stratagem or deceptive practice."[114] An attempt to subvert the APUNCAC reporting requirements by transferring bags of casino chips between front men would constitute a "stratagem or deceptive practice" that obscures, from an educated person, the true identities of the beneficial owners that were involved in transferring money via the transfer of casino chips.

Liberty Reserve

The APUNCAC reporting requirement would, in the case of Liberty Reserve, have required the third-party "exchangers"—that is, money remitters—to obtain, and submit to FINCEN, certification of beneficial ownership of (a) fiat funds deposited with the remitters and exchanged for LR currency, or (b) LR currency exchanged for fiat funds, in an amount exceeding $3,000.[115] The APUNCAC reporting requirement applies to exchanges in currency; therefore, the exchange of fiat funds for LR currency, or the exchange of LR currency for fiat funds, would have to be reported to FINCEN.[116] If the beneficial owner is a customer who is physically present, certification would be demanded from the customer. Otherwise, a remitter would be required to contact the beneficial owner to obtain a digitally signed certification that the purported beneficial owner is indeed the true beneficial owner.

The APUNCAC reporting requirement also applies to transfers in currency; therefore, the transfer of LR from one person to another would have to be reported to FINCEN.[117] The sender would have to provide a digitally signed certification that he is the beneficial owner of the LR source funds. The recipient would have to provide a digitally signed certification that she is the beneficial owner of the LR funds received from the sender. The certifications would state that the funds do not involve the laundering of funds obtained illegally or through criminal activities and would acknowledge that criminal penalties apply if false or misleading information is provided.

There are two possibilities. Either the person purporting to be the beneficial owner is in fact the beneficial owner, or the person purporting to be the beneficial owner is a front man posing as the beneficial owner, in violation of APUNCAC, who chooses to assume the risk of debarment, fines, and imprisonment. A remitter who failed to obtain and submit the required certifications would risk debarment, fines, and imprisonment. A front man who posed as a beneficial owner but is not in fact the true beneficial owner would risk debarment, fines, and imprisonment. The APUNCAC regime would encourage compliance and discourage the participation of front men who would have to think twice about whether the risks were worth the rewards of posing as a front man.

Hawala

Regarding hawala-based transactions, the APUNCAC reporting requirement would require each hawaladar to obtain, and submit to FINCEN, certification of beneficial ownership of funds paid to, or paid out by, a hawaladar, in an amount exceeding $3,000.[118] If the beneficial owner is a customer who is physically present, certification would be demanded from the customer. Otherwise, a hawaladar would be required to contact the beneficial owner to obtain a digitally signed certification that the purported beneficial owner is indeed the true beneficial owner.

The APUNCAC reporting requirement also applies to transfers in currency; therefore, the transfer of currency from one hawala client to an end client would have to be reported to FINCEN.[119] The sender would have to provide a digitally signed certification that he is the beneficial owner of the source funds. The recipient would have to provide a digitally signed certification that she is the beneficial owner of the funds received from the sender. The certifications would state that the funds do not involve the laundering of funds obtained illegally or through criminal activities and would acknowledge that criminal penalties apply if false or misleading information is provided.

A hawaladar who lacks internet access but wishes to offer hawala services would be limited to transaction amounts under $3,000 because the APUNCAC reporting requirement would require the use of a broadband-enabled mobile phone, tablet, or computer to report transactions in excess of $3,000. A hawaladar who wishes to offer hawala services in amounts exceeding $3,000 would require access to the internet. Typically, however, such hawaladars already have internet access, even in developing countries such as Afghanistan or countries in Africa, through a mobile broadband or internet network.[120] It is unclear whether any hawaladars who currently engage in transactions exceeding $3,000 lack internet access and would be forced to curtail their business in response to the implementation of the APUNCAC reporting requirement. In any case, there would be a significant public benefit of implementing the APUNCAC reporting requirement. The requirement would be expected to reduce criminal activity, corruption, and impunity that serves to perpetuate poverty and inequality among the poorest of the poor in developing countries.

APUNCAC addresses the possibility that a criminal might employ front men to transmit illicit funds using mobile payment solutions in combination with hawala, to obscure the origin of illicit funds. The APUNCAC reporting requirement applies to this type of transaction (a) at the point when a customer pays a hawaladar, and (b) at the point when a hawaladar pays the end client, assuming that a hawaladar is within the jurisdiction of a State Party, and assuming a transaction in currency, or involving a bank draft, bearer instrument, negotiable instrument, electronic fund transfer, or money order.[121]

Online Gaming

Regarding transactions related to online gaming, the APUNCAC reporting requirement would require each retail vendor of game codes, keys, and items of value to obtain, and submit to FINCEN, certification of beneficial ownership of (a) funds used to purchase game codes, keys, and items of value, and (b) funds received from the sale of game codes, keys, and items of value, in an amount exceeding $3,000, because game codes, keys, and items of value are defined as virtual assets that are included in the APUNCAC definition of "currency."[122] The APUNCAC reporting requirement applies to any purchase or sale of game codes, keys, and items of value in amounts exceeding $3,000 in value. If the beneficial owner is a customer who is physically present, certification would be demanded from the customer. Otherwise, a vendor would be required to contact the beneficial owner to obtain a digitally signed certification that the purported beneficial owner is indeed the beneficial owner.

The APUNCAC reporting requirement also applies to any transfer or exchange of game codes, keys, and items of value in amounts exceeding $3,000 in value because game codes, keys, and items of value are defined as virtual assets that are included in the APUNCAC definition of "currency."[123] It would no longer be legal to purchase, sell, transfer, or exchange game keys, codes, or items of value anonymously, in an attempt to use the keys, codes, or items of value to launder illicit funds or conduct illicit activity anonymously.

The vast majority of online gaming transactions fall below the $3,000 reporting threshold and would not be subject to the APUNCAC reporting requirement. However, an attempt by criminals to evade the reporting requirement by structuring the transmission of large amounts of illicit funds in the form of smaller transmissions that fall under the $3,000 reporting threshold would violate the APUNCAC prohibition against structuring.[124] The combination of the APUNCAC reporting requirement and the APUNCAC prohibition against structuring would serve to discourage the use of online gaming for the purpose of money laundering, with minimal interference with the legitimate purchase, sale, transfer, or exchange of online game codes, keys, and items of value.

Lightning

The APUNCAC reporting requirement would, in the Lightning network example, require the Abra mobile app to obtain, and submit to FINCEN, Alex's certification that he is the beneficial owner of the source funds that he transmitted to Britney, as well as Britney's certification that she is the beneficial owner of the funds that she received from Alex, with regard to an amount exceeding $3,000.[125] The APUNCAC reporting requirement applies to transfers in currency; therefore, the transfer of bitcoin from Alex to Britney would have to be reported to FINCEN.[126] Alex would have to provide a digitally signed certification that he is the beneficial owner of the bitcoin source funds. Britney would have to provide a digitally signed certification that she is the beneficial owner of the bitcoin funds received from Alex. The certifications would state that the funds do not involve the laundering of funds obtained illegally or through criminal activities and would acknowledge that criminal penalties apply if false or misleading information is provided.

Failure to observe the APUNCAC reporting requirement would be illegal. If a mobile app's Lightning node is not configured to obtain and submit the required certifications, the creator of the app, the owner or licensee, and anyone providing support for the app would risk debarment, fines, and imprisonment for violating the APUNCAC reporting requirement and the prohibition against assistance with any stratagem or deceptive practice that seeks to obscure, or obscures from an educated person, the true identities of beneficial owners linked to financial transactions as described by APUNCAC.[127] If Alex or Britney is a front man who poses as a beneficial owner of bitcoin, in violation of APUNCAC, but is not in fact a true beneficial owner, he or she would risk debarment, fines, and imprisonment. The APUNCAC regime would encourage compliance and discourage the participation of front men who would have to think twice about whether the risks were worth the rewards of posing as a front man.

A DIGITAL TRAIL

These examples illustrate how the APUNCAC reporting requirement would create a digital trail leading investigators to the identities of criminals conducting illicit activity. It would be much more difficult for criminals to hide their identities by recruiting front men to conduct their illicit transactions. If front men choose to pose as beneficial owners, they will assume risks of debarment, fines, and imprisonment that do not currently exist in the existing regulatory regime. The calculus of the benefits and costs of participating in criminal activity would change dramatically. Front men are willing to pose as beneficial owners when the small fees they earn are relatively risk free. Front men who face a genuine risk of a lengthy term in prison may well decide that those small fees are not worth the risk. The pool of individuals willing to serve as front men would shrink, perhaps dramatically, allowing investigators to focus their resources, increase the risks to the remaining criminals, and deter money laundering among all but the most hard-core criminals.

POTENTIAL ISSUES

In situations where medium and large corporations conduct high-volume wire transactions on a regular basis with established suppliers, vendors, customers, and clients, digital technology would permit the entire APUNCAC reporting process to be automated. Wire transactions can be integrated with digital workflow technology to request, obtain, and submit the required certifications to FINCEN. Existing software applications offer automated digital signing solutions suitable for high-volume applications.[128]

Chapters 8 and 9 addressed issues regarding data security.[129] Both FinCEN and the U.S. IRS have demonstrated the capacity to securely store and manage large amounts of sensitive data. Concerns about the possibility of unauthorized use may be addressed through privileged access management that restricts access, associates individual sessions with individual users, and monitors user activity.[130] Access controls may be employed to limit user access at the individual database row level according to user level, compartment authorization, and group authorization.[131] Special approval may be required from independent controllers for instances where an investigator wishes to copy more than a minimal amount of information. To discourage misuse, the activity related to those sessions may be automatically recorded and subjected to random audits, or systematic audits for sessions that are flagged for suspicious activity. Profiles may be created to flag, and report, suspicious patterns of data access.[132] Users may be required to "earn" access to increased levels of access by demonstrating a pattern of appropriate use over time and across a range of case investigations. Responsibility for sensitive database inquiries could be randomly assigned by lottery across a large group of international investigators to assuage concerns regarding industrial espionage. If necessary, each State Party could be permitted to name (for example) a maximum of two other States Parties whose investigators would be excluded when conducting sensitive FINCEN database queries related to nationals of that State Party. For example, if State Party A does not trust investigators from State Party B, State Party A could exclude investigators from State Party B from conducting sensitive FINCEN inquiries into the activities of nationals of State Party A. The FINCEN database controls could then be set to exclude access by excluded investigators, and permit access by the trusted set of investigators, when conducting investigations related to nationals of State Party A. Any State Party wishing to pursue an investigation related to nationals of State Party A would be required to rely on the approved set of investigators to conduct FINCEN database inquiries involving nationals of State Party A. Approved investigators would be obligated by APUNCAC to provide mutual assistance in conducting FINCEN database inquiries upon request. This system would permit sensitive FINCEN database inquiries while assuaging concerns about industrial espionage.

Chapters 8 and 9 addressed issues regarding jurisdiction and enforcement.[133] The chapters explained why the major OECD Member States might be expected to adopt the APUNCAC reporting requirement, and why they might be expected to cooperate in extraditing individuals who are charged with violations of APUNCAC.

The enforcement of APUNCAC would proceed in the same way that any other law is enforced. In many cases, illegal activity is discovered when unusual patterns of activity are detected or a whistleblower reveals the trickery. APUNCAC includes financial incentives to encourage whistleblowing.[134] The submission of reports to a centralized FINCEN database would facilitate computerized analysis for the purpose of detecting unusual patterns of activity. The APUNCAC reporting requirements would create tripwires that cannot be avoided by front men or duplicitous financial institution and retail personnel. Once they violate the law, they become vulnerable to pressure by prosecutors who are then able to secure the type of cooperation agreements needed to obtain incriminating information and convict the criminals who orchestrate the criminal activity.

One might argue that criminals have already proven to be adept at evading laws against money laundering and question the value of the APUNCAC reporting requirement. However, APUNCAC would make illegal certain activities that are currently legal, that is, the activity of posing as a front man, and the activities of financial institution and retail personnel that serve to facilitate anonymous currency transactions. There is a major difference in participating in activities that are legal, for profit, and participating in activities that are illegal, for profit. The former attracts many individuals who, when those same activities are outlawed, and when the consequences of debarment, fines, and imprisonment are attached to those activities, will no longer be willing to engage in those activities at the risk of their livelihood and personal freedom.

PRIVACY CONCERNS

The APUNCAC reporting rule is designed to permit financial crime investigators to trace the entire path of complex financial transactions that might otherwise be employed by criminals to foil investigators, hide illicit funds, and perpetuate criminal activity. Privacy advocates may argue, however, that the rule is invasive and erodes privacy. It might be argued that the APUNCAC reporting rule is antithetical to a basic right in a free society to conduct transactions without oppressive governmental interference, data collection, and monitoring.

This view is inconsistent with the growing recognition by regulatory authorities of the need to strip away the anonymity that protects criminals and perpetuates criminal activity. Money laundering is a major problem that is not adequately addressed by existing measures. There is a need for new measures that directly address the need to follow the path of illicit funds. In the absence of this information, criminal investigators will continue to struggle in their efforts to bring criminals to justice.

With respect to the type of beneficial owner reporting requirement that is at the heart of APUNCAC, regulators have already decided that the public interest in controlling money laundering outweighs privacy concerns. FATF recommendations state that information regarding beneficial ownership should be collected and recorded for the purpose of detecting and deterring money laundering.[135]

In June 2019, FATF strengthened the recommendations by incorporating a requirement that VASPs—that is, entities that exchange virtual assets such as cryptocurrency for fiat currencies or other forms of virtual assets, or transfer virtual assets from one person to another—implement the "travel rule."[136] The purpose of the rule is to fight money laundering. The rule requires VASPs to collect and record the identities of the sender and recipient of cryptocurrency when a transaction is conducted in cryptocurrency. The rule seeks to ensure that financial crime investigators have sufficient information to trace the path of illicit funds that are transmitted through a series of cryptocurrency transactions. The rule was opposed by users who valued the anonymity offered by cryptocurrency. However, the rule signaled that policymakers valued the need to control money laundering over privacy concerns.

The travel rule refers to section 7(b) in the Interpretive Note to Recommendation 15 in the FATF guidelines.[137] The rule requires "originating VASPs" to "obtain and hold required and accurate originator information and required beneficiary information" and submit the information to "the beneficiary VASP."[138] The rule requires "beneficiary VASPs" to "obtain and hold required originator information and required and accurate beneficiary information on virtual asset transfers, and make it available on request to appropriate authorities."[139] For example, a VASP that originates a bitcoin transaction must obtain accurate customer identity information from the originator of the transaction and must transmit the information to the beneficiary VASP. In turn, the beneficiary VASP must obtain and hold the required originator information as well as required and accurate information regarding the beneficiary. The aim is to ensure that this information is available to financial crime investigators so that investigators have information regarding the source and destination of funds that are transmitted via bitcoin and other cryptocurrencies.

Therefore, FATF already regulates collection of the type of customer identity information that privacy advocates are concerned about. The APUNCAC reporting requirement extends the collection of information to the identities of the actual beneficial owners that control financial transactions, consistent with the FATF statement that information regarding beneficial ownership should be collected and recorded for the purpose of detecting and deterring money laundering.[140]

A travel rule solution is currently available.[141] The product enables VASPs to comply with the FATF travel rule by using digital technology to collect and exchange the identities of the sender and receiver involved in a virtual asset transaction. The solution demonstrates the technological feasibility of collecting and securely transmitting high volumes of the type of customer identity information envisioned by the APUNCAC reporting requirement.

A KEY DISTINCTION

The APUNCAC reporting requirement differs from the FATF travel rule and would arguably be more effective for the purpose of fighting money laundering. While the FATF rule requires the collection of "beneficiary information," the beneficiary of a virtual asset transaction is defined by FATF as the person who receives the virtual assets. The "beneficiary" may or may not be the actual *beneficial owner* who controls the recipient. This loophole opens the door to money laundering.

The FATF rule only requires that a VASP collect information regarding the sender and receiver of virtual assets. These individuals may, however, be front men who pose as beneficial owners and hide the identities of the true beneficial owners controlling the transaction. The FATF requirement does little to deter money laundering by beneficial owners who hide behind front men. In contrast, APUNCAC requires submission of information regarding the identities of the true beneficial owners controlling the transaction.

Furthermore, APUNCAC requires the beneficial sender of a fund transmittal to self-certify, with a digitally signed certification, that he is the beneficial owner of the source funds; and requires the beneficial recipient of a fund transmittal to self-certify, with a digitally signed certification, that she is the beneficial owner of the received funds. The FATF rule omits this requirement and, instead, "requires" each relevant VASP to collect "accurate" information regarding the originator and recipient of a fund transmittal.

In the absence of the APUNCAC rule that requires the beneficial sender to self-certify, with a digitally signed certification, that he is the beneficial owner of the source funds; and requires the beneficial recipient to self-certify, with a digitally signed certification, that she is the beneficial owner of the received funds, it is difficult for a financial crime investigator to pressure front men to provide information regarding the true beneficial owners controlling a fund transmittal. The absence of the APUNCAC rule means that no crime is committed when front men are named as the sender and recipient of virtual assets. When front men have nothing to fear from prosecutors, it is impossible for a prosecutor to threaten the front men with prosecution for serving as front men and difficult to extract useful information regarding the true beneficial owners hiding behind the front men.

CONCLUSION

The contrast between the FATF travel rule and the APUNCAC reporting rule illustrates the gap between existing AML regulations and the type of beneficial owner reporting requirement that is needed. The FATF recommendations endorse the need to collect beneficial owner information but fail to require the beneficial sender to self-certify, with a digitally signed certification, that he is the beneficial owner of the source funds; and fail to require the beneficial recipient to self-certify, with a digitally signed certification, that she is the beneficial owner of the received funds.

The logic of the APUNCAC reporting requirement is simple. The principle of regulating and attaching legal consequences to behavior that is harmful to society underlies nearly every existing law and regulation. Every effective law or regulation attaches legal consequences to harmful behavior.

It is harmful to society when financial institution personnel, casino employees, VASPs, hawaladars, online gaming platforms, Lightning networks, and retail personnel are permitted to accept and transfer funds that may be illicit, without obtaining digitally signed certifications from beneficial senders and recipients certifying, under penalty of perjury, that they are the true beneficial owners of the funds that are transmitted from senders to recipients. The resulting anonymity enables criminals to move illicit funds in a way that cannot be traced by criminal investigators.

The anonymity that currently characterizes illicit financial transactions is the core problem that must be addressed through changes in law and regulation. The APUNCAC reporting requirement is a simple, direct, necessary rule that would strip away that anonymity. The reporting requirement can only be effective if major nation-states band together to implement the requirement by treaty. There is no substitute for coordinated international action in the form of a new international law that implements the APUNCAC reporting requirement and attaches legal consequences to each failure to comply and each effort to thwart criminal investigators by serving as a front man who hides the identity of the true beneficial owners controlling a financial transaction. That type of behavior is clearly harmful to the international community. It must be controlled through the implementation of the type of vigorous international law and regulation that is described by APUNCAC.

Chapter 11

Treble Damages

The treble damages provision of RICO has been described as "the litigation equivalent of a thermonuclear device."[1] This provision allows private litigants to institute a RICO action and recover three times the amount of their damages. APUNCAC retains this provision. Significantly, APUNCAC inserts four bases for instituting a RICO action that are not included in the original RICO language:[2]

1. It is unlawful for any person or entity to handle, receive, hold, transfer, or convey assets that the accused knew, or should have known, were obtained through a pattern of corruption, misappropriation of assets, or any other form of racketeering activity.
2. It is unlawful for any person or entity to provide banking, accounting, legal, financial, or consulting services to an individual or entity that the accused knew, or should have known, was involved in a pattern of corruption, misappropriation of assets, or any other form of racketeering activity.
3. It is unlawful for any person or entity to initiate, facilitate, or benefit from a pattern of corruption, misappropriation of assets, or any other form of racketeering activity, if the accused knew or should have known of the corruption, the asset misappropriation, or other form of racketeering activity.
4. It is unlawful for any person or entity to directly or indirectly extend, guarantee, or receive a loan, if the accused knew, or should have known, that the proceeds would likely be misappropriated.

The key phrase is "knew or should have known." APUNCAC defines the standard for ascertaining whether an accused person "knew or should have known":

> The standard for ascertaining whether an accused person "knew or should have known" is that a reasonable person would infer from the available objective circumstances that the accused "knew or should have known."[3]

A plaintiff would have the burden of establishing that a reasonable person would infer from the available objective circumstances that the accused "knew or should have known." A court would decide whether the plaintiff had met that burden.

EXAMPLES

APUNCAC would permit a private litigant to pursue treble damages regarding a bank clerk in the Cayman Islands who handled, received, held, transferred, or conveyed assets that the bank clerk knew, or should have known, were obtained through a pattern of corruption, misappropriation of assets, or any other form of racketeering activity. For example, suppose that Kenya ratifies APUNCAC and is therefore a party to APUNCAC. Suppose that the Cayman Islands bank clerk handles receipt of a $10 million transfer by a Kenyan minister to a bank account in the Cayman Islands. However, the bank clerk fails to record beneficial ownership, as required by APUNCAC, in the FINCEN database. APUNCAC would permit an NGO such as IJM to file a class action lawsuit on behalf of Kenyan citizens asserting that the $10 million was obtained through corruption, the Kenyan minister defrauded Kenyan citizens, and the bank clerk aided and abetted money laundering by failing to record the beneficial ownership information as required by APUNCAC. APUNCAC would permit the plaintiffs to seek $30 million in damages. If a court found that the bank clerk's comparative responsibility was 10 percent (because the act of failing to record beneficial ownership information served to aid and abet laundering of illicit funds), the court might allocate 10 percent of the responsibility for damages to the bank clerk. This prospect would have a powerful deterrent effect on any bank clerk who contemplates deliberate, willful violations of APUNCAC's recordation requirement.

APUNCAC's provisions would permit a private litigant to pursue treble damages regarding a nominee director of a shell company who opened a bank account in the Cayman Islands to receive assets that the nominee director knew, or should have known, were obtained through a pattern of corruption, misappropriation of assets, or any other form of racketeering activity. For example, suppose that Kenya ratifies APUNCAC and is therefore a party to APUNCAC. Suppose that a nominee director in the Cayman Islands opens a bank account. The nominee director transfers $10 million from a Kenyan minister to the bank account. The nominee director supplies his name, instead of the name of the minister, as beneficial owner, in violation of APUNCAC. APUNCAC would permit an NGO such as IJM to file a class action lawsuit on behalf of Kenyan citizens asserting that the $10 million was obtained through corruption, the Kenyan minister defrauded Kenyan citizens, and the nominee director aided and abetted money laundering by supplying false beneficial owner information, in violation of APUNCAC. APUNCAC would permit the plaintiffs to seek $30 million in damages. If a court found that the nominee director's comparative responsibility was 10 percent (because the act of supplying false beneficial owner information served to aid and abet laundering of illicit funds), the court might allocate 10 percent of the responsibility for damages to the nominee director. This prospect would have a powerful deterrent effect on any nominee director who contemplates deliberate, willful violations of APUNCAC's beneficial ownership reporting requirement.

APUNCAC's language would permit a private litigant to pursue treble damages regarding an attorney who opened a bank account in the Cayman Islands to receive assets that the attorney knew, or should have known, were obtained through a pattern of corruption, misappropriation of assets, or any other form of racketeering activity. For example, suppose that Kenya ratifies APUNCAC and is therefore a party to APUNCAC. Suppose that an attorney in the Cayman Islands opens a bank account. The attorney transfers $10 million from a Kenyan minister to the bank account. The attorney supplies his name, instead of the name of the minister, as beneficial owner, in violation of APUNCAC. APUNCAC would permit an NGO such as IJM to file a class action lawsuit on behalf of Kenyan citizens asserting that the $10 million was obtained through corruption, the Kenyan minister defrauded Kenyan citizens, and the attorney aided and abetted money laundering by supplying false beneficial owner information, in violation of APUNCAC. APUNCAC would permit the plaintiffs to seek $30 million in damages. If a court found that the attorney's comparative responsibility was 10 percent (because the act of supplying false beneficial owner information served to aid and abet laundering of illicit funds), the court might allocate 10 percent of the responsibility for damages to the attorney. This prospect would have a powerful deterrent effect on any attorney who contemplates deliberate, willful violations of APUNCAC's beneficial ownership reporting requirement.

APUNCAC would permit a private litigant to pursue treble damages regarding a bank that extended a loan to a developing country if bank personnel knew, or should have known, that the proceeds would likely be misappropriated. For example, suppose that Armenia ratifies APUNCAC and is therefore a party to APUNCAC. Suppose that the World Bank extends a $30 million loan to Armenia to replace water pipes but, according to a government commission, the funds are misappropriated through a scheme involving corrupt government officials. The World Bank investigates but finds no proof of misappropriation in official documents. The World Bank declares the project was "satisfactory," despite evidence that water pipes continue to rupture and drinking water remains contaminated. Despite the evidence of misappropriation, the World Bank extends a second loan of $20 million. A French company assumes responsibility for repairing the water pipes, but inhabitants report that the repair work is sloppy. Despite the expenditure of $50 million, a water supply expert appointed by Armenia's parliament reports that the water supply remains polluted, and inhabitants continue to suffer waterborne diseases. The director of Armenia's Regional Studies Center charges that the project was a failure, Armenian citizens were defrauded, and corrupt Armenian government officials were responsible. However, the World Bank continues to extend loans to Armenia that are involved in corruption scandals. The World Bank extends a loan to promote transparency and efficacy in the judicial system, but the public tendering process to select a contractor succumbs to fraud. The World Bank extends a second loan to pay for new hospital equipment, but the equipment that is delivered is worn-out. Despite the evidence of misappropriation, the World Bank's rules specify that the loans must be repaid by the beneficiary nation. Instead of establishing monitoring and accountability procedures to prevent misappropriation, World Bank staff based in the capital at the time of the project are simply transferred elsewhere in Central Asia.[4]

APUNCAC would permit an NGO such as IJM to file a class action lawsuit on behalf of Armenian citizens asserting that the $50 million was misappropriated, the Armenian government defrauded Armenian citizens, and the World Bank aided and abetted the corruption by continuing to extend loans that the World Bank should have known would likely be misappropriated. APUNCAC would permit the plaintiffs to seek $150 million in damages. If a court found that the World Bank's comparative responsibility was 10 percent (because the bank continued to extend loans that it should have known would likely be misappropriated), the court might allocate 10 percent of the responsibility for damages to the World Bank. This prospect would create a powerful incentive for the World Bank to implement the type of rigorous project monitoring and accountability that is necessary to check misappropriation.

In sum, APUNCAC provisions would permit an international human rights organization, in the role of a private litigant, to file a class action lawsuit on behalf of a group of citizens who are injured as a consequence of a pattern of corruption, misappropriation of assets, or any other form of racketeering activity, and recover treble damages.

ADVANTAGES

What would be the advantage? First, it may be the case that domestic criminal justice systems in many jurisdictions are dysfunctional, and prosecutors and judges are corrupt. APUNCAC would permit an NGO such as IJM to step forward and seek redress on behalf of, for example, Kenyan citizens. To seek redress, IJM might choose a venue, perhaps a British, French, or U.S. court, that is perceived to be competent. Numerous individuals have been successfully targeted through British, French, and U.S. courts.[5]

Second, NGO staff may have a stronger level of commitment and engagement regarding anticorruption than domestic prosecutors and judges.

Third, NGOs may have the resources to hire attorneys whose capacity and level of legal expertise exceeds the level of expertise possessed by domestic prosecutors regarding anticorruption laws. Attorneys employed by NGOs may be especially knowledgeable and competent regarding the use of discovery procedures to obtain documentary evidence and the use of the court system to impose liens, freeze assets, and prevent corrupt parties from absconding with illicit proceeds. This expertise may be especially significant regarding courts in the UK, United States, or France, if actions are initiated in those courts.

Fourth, the prospect of ruinous civil actions might have a powerful deterrent effect on corrupt parties. They would no longer be able to rely on corrupt control of domestic prosecutors and court systems. The threat of treble damages, pursued by highly competent attorneys under the auspices of highly motivated NGO staff, would introduce a threat to corrupt parties that does not currently exist.

Fifth, civil actions could be implemented that would punish bank clerks, nominee directors, attorneys, and any other party who currently profits by quietly aiding and abetting money laundering, permitting corrupt parties to hide illicit funds, thwarting prosecution, and facilitating criminal activity.

Sixth, the standard of proof for a civil action is typically lower than the standard required in a criminal action. Therefore, it may be easier to obtain a judgment in a civil action.

These advantages strengthen the deterrent effect of APUNCAC.

A "PATTERN"

Article 60 of APUNCAC stipulates that "It is unlawful for any person employed by, or associated with, any enterprise to conduct or participate, directly or indirectly, in such enterprise through a pattern of racketeering activity or the collection of an unlawful debt." The "racketeering activity" must consist of two or more federal criminal offenses, known as "predicate acts," committed within a 10-year period.

Since the language is borrowed from the American RICO Act, one might be tempted to draw upon interpretations of the Act by American courts. However, American courts have interpreted the phrase "pattern of racketeering activity" in a way that significantly narrows the application of the Act and does so in a way that is inconsistent with a plain reading of the language of the Act. The Act defines a "pattern of racketeering activity" as follows:

> "pattern of racketeering activity" requires at least two acts of racketeering activity, one of which occurred after the effective date of this chapter and the last of which occurred within ten years (excluding any period of imprisonment) after the commission of a prior act of racketeering activity.[6]

This definition specifies that a "pattern" may be established through two predicate acts of "racketeering" activity. The definition does not specify a minimum period between these predicate acts. Nor does the definition specify a minimum number of victims or a minimum number of racketeering schemes. In contrast with this plain reading of the language, American courts have effectively imposed additional conditions that are not written into this definition. These conditions serve to narrow the definition in a way that narrows the scope of the Act.

An American prosecutor who alleges a "pattern" of racketeering activity must establish two elements: *continuity* plus *relationship* between predicate acts. "Closed-ended" continuity may be established through a series of related predicates extending over a substantial period. American courts consider three principal factors: (1) the number and duration of the alleged predicate acts, (2) the number of alleged victims, and (3) the number of alleged schemes.[7] American federal courts held: (a) predicate acts extending over a period of six months, in the absence of a threat of future criminal conduct, is "too short a period of time . . . in order to qualify as a pattern of racketeering activity"; (b) three predicate acts allegedly committed over a 15-month period of time are insufficient to establish continuity; (c) one victim or one "set" of victims allegedly injured as the result of a single fraudulent scheme is insufficient to establish continuity; (d) a single racketeering scheme is insufficient to establish continuity.[8]

"Open-ended" continuity may be established by demonstrating that predicate acts involve a threat of continued racketeering activity. American courts consider both the nature of the predicate acts and the nature of the alleged enterprise. If the alleged enterprise is a long-term association that exists primarily for criminal purposes, the threat of repetition is presumed.[9] This prong of the continuity analysis includes activity traditionally labeled as "organized crime."[10] Where the alleged enterprise is not a criminal organization, but conducts a legitimate business, open-ended continuity may be established by demonstrating that alleged predicate acts threaten continued criminal activity or are the way that an enterprise regularly conducts its business.[11] Courts are cautious about basing a RICO claim on predicate acts of mail and wire fraud unless they are related to ongoing unlawful activities whose scope and persistence pose a special threat to social well-being.

Regarding APUNCAC, however, it should be noted that American case law regarding "closed-ended" continuity inserts conditions that are inconsistent with the stated definition of a pattern of racketeering activity. APUNCAC borrows the American definition of a "pattern of racketeering activity":

> "Pattern of racketeering activity" requires at least two acts of racketeering activity, one of which occurred after the effective date of this Protocol and the last of which occurred within ten years (excluding any period of imprisonment) after the commission of a prior act of racketeering activity.[12]

This definition specifies that a "pattern" may be established through two predicate acts of "racketeering" activity. The definition does not specify a minimum period between these predicate acts. Nor does the definition specify a minimum number of victims or a minimum number of racketeering schemes. *Regarding APUNCAC, parties to APUNCAC should not insert conditions that are not stated in the plain language of APUNCAC*. The reason is simple. The insertion of additional conditions would narrow the application of APUNCAC in a way that would potentially exclude its application regarding the types of criminal behavior described as examples in this chapter. For example, the receipt by a Cayman Islands bank clerk of a $10 million transfer by a Kenyan minister to a bank account in the Cayman Islands may involve two predicate acts of racketeering activity that occur within a relatively short period of time. The number of victims of this crime is unclear, but since APUNCAC's language is not conditioned on the number of victims, a prosecutor should not have the burden of establishing the number of victims. It should be sufficient to establish that public funds were misused and, therefore, the people of Kenya were victims of this crime. Nor should a prosecutor have the burden of establishing that more than one criminal scheme was utilized. It should be sufficient to establish that one criminal scheme was used.

Instead of imposing conditions that are not written into APUNCAC, the desire to narrow the application of RICO to crimes whose scope and persistence pose a special threat to social well-being is best implemented through existing prosecutorial policies that prioritize major crimes and patterns of unlawful activity whose scope and persistence pose a special threat to social well-being. A prosecutor should weigh the scope and persistence of alleged crimes and formulate a judgment about the degree to which they pose a special threat to social well-being, without imposing artificially restrictive conditions that would potentially exclude the application of APUNCAC to the types of crimes described as examples in this chapter. APUNCAC is intended to apply, and is written to apply, to those examples. APUNCAC's purpose is to end the type of impunity and corruption that currently permits government ministers and other public officials to profit from their positions of trust and perpetuate the type of crime, corruption, and mismanagement of public resources that promotes and facilitates poverty and violations of basic human rights.

Chapter 12

Treaty Management

Chapter 12, "Treaty Management," focuses on the problem of ensuring that APUNCAC is implemented as intended. Article 8 of APUNCAC creates dedicated anticorruption courts, with special procedures designed to ensure an independent, untainted process for selecting, retaining, and ensuring the accountability of competent judges to serve those courts. Article 11 empowers the United Nations Commission on Crime Prevention and Criminal Justice to appoint entities to monitor domestic compliance with the terms of APUNCAC. Article 10 makes obstruction of justice an offense that may be investigated by a UN inspector. Article 14 provides a mechanism where a UN inspector may, when obstruction of justice has occurred or when cooperation is inadequate, file a request for censure. Article 15 provides a mechanism where the World Bank and IMF would reduce aid and credits in response to the magnitude and frequency of acts of noncooperation with UN inspectors. Article 16 makes the Commission on Crime Prevention and Criminal Justice the final arbiter of disputes regarding the actions of the Commission, ICAC, the Anti-Money Laundering Debarment Office, FINCEN, and each State Party Conflicts of Interest Board and Fair Political Practices Commission. Article 70 establishes a system where the institutional bodies established by APUNCAC may promulgate rules, regulations, and procedures to implement APUNCAC, adapt APUNCAC as needed, and resolve conflicts.

DEDICATED COURTS

Article 8 creates dedicated anticorruption courts, with special procedures designed to ensure an independent, untainted process for selecting, retaining, and ensuring the accountability of competent judges to serve those courts.

> Nominations of individuals to serve on national judicial councils pursuant to paragraph five, and nominations of judges and prosecutors to serve dedicated courts pursuant to paragraph one, shall be submitted to the Commission on Crime Prevention and Criminal Justice. The Commission may, upon a majority vote, veto the nomination of any individual to serve on a national judicial council, veto the nomination of any judge or prosecutor to serve a dedicated court, or request the censure or removal of any individual serving a national judicial council or any judge or prosecutor serving a dedicated court whose performance is alleged to be substandard.[1]

Article 8 creates a mechanism whereby the Commission on Crime Prevention and Criminal Justice would ensure accountability and discipline corrupt prosecutors and judges:

> Failure of a dedicated anticorruption court or prosecutor to observe the highest standards of judicial or prosecutorial conduct shall warrant disciplinary action by the Commission on Crime Prevention and Criminal Justice. Such action may include a letter of reprimand, redirection of funding to higher performing courts or prosecutors, or a recommendation to a national judicial council to suspend, demote, or remove a judge or prosecutor whose conduct contributes to unnecessary delays or falls below the highest standards of judicial or prosecutorial conduct.[2]

COMPLIANCE

APUNCAC includes provisions designed to promote compliance. Article 11 empowers the United Nations Commission on Crime Prevention and Criminal Justice to appoint entities to monitor domestic compliance with the terms of APUNCAC:

> The Commission on Crime Prevention and Criminal Justice shall appoint one or more entities to monitor domestic compliance with the terms of this protocol, with special reference but not limited to Article 9 regarding Cooperation, Article 10 regarding Obstruction of Justice, Article 12 regarding the privileges and immunities of inspectors, staff and surrogates, and Article 13 regarding Protection.[3]
>
> Monitors pursuant to paragraph one of this Article may include national or international human rights institutions or any other entities deemed by the Commission on Crime Prevention and Criminal Justice to be duly qualified for the purpose of monitoring domestic compliance with APUNCAC.[4]

> The Commission on Crime Prevention and Criminal Justice shall ensure that designated monitors have regular and adequate funding to perform the responsibilities described in this Article, shall conduct periodic reviews to evaluate the performance of designated monitors, and may redirect funding based upon these evaluations.[5]

Article 11 specifies that designated monitors "shall not seek nor act on instructions from any source."[6] Article 11 specifies that States Parties would provide access to all reports and information requested by designated monitors for the purpose of formulating an opinion regarding domestic compliance with the terms of APUNCAC, including materials deemed relevant by UN inspectors.[7] Failure to comply with this requirement constitutes a failure of cooperation and obstruction of justice.[8] APUNCAC establishes standing of designated monitors to bring suit in domestic courts to compel the production of reports and information.[9] Monitors are required to publish regular reports regarding domestic compliance with the terms of APUNCAC.[10] The reports would be published online by Transparency International.[11] Article 11 makes the reports admissible as evidence in administrative or judicial proceedings of the State Party

> in which their use proves necessary, in the same way and under the same conditions as administrative reports drawn up by national administrative inspectors . . . subject to the same evaluation rules as those applicable to administrative reports drawn up by national administrative inspectors, [and] "shall be of identical value to such reports."[12]

OBSTRUCTION OF JUSTICE

Article 10 makes obstruction of justice an offense that may be investigated by a UN inspector. Significantly, a UN inspector may seek a judicial opinion from a judge in the state where the investigation is conducted regarding any alleged act involving obstruction of justice.[13] The UN inspector may recommend charges or disciplinary actions to the appropriate prosecuting authorities or disciplinary bodies.[14] UN inspectors would file reports that would be published online by Transparency International.[15] The report would be submitted to the appropriate prosecutorial, disciplinary, or oversight bodies.[16] Prosecution, disciplinary actions, and oversight would follow the relevant statutory, regulatory, disciplinary, or oversight agency procedures, practices, and consequences entailed when an individual is accused of obstruction of justice in the state where the investigation is conducted.[17]

If a UN inspector subsequently determines that prosecution, discipline, or oversight of an individual accused of obstruction of justice has been perverted, the inspector would prepare and submit a report to the appropriate prosecuting authorities, disciplinary bodies, parliamentary institutions, or other institutions exercising oversight.[18] The inspector would submit a report to be published online by Transparency International.[19] UN inspectors would certify the accuracy and integrity of the information presented in their reports.[20]

Article 10 inserts five bases for asserting obstruction of justice: (1) "Any attempt to arrest or interfere with UN inspectors, staff, witnesses, victims or individuals who assist with ICAC investigations, contrary to the wishes of UN inspectors";[21] (2) "Any attempt to delay or thwart the effort of a UN inspector or surrogate to obtain or execute a warrant for arrest, in excess of the discretionary authority of the judge who receives the request for a warrant";[22] (3) "Any attempt to delay or thwart the execution of a lawful warrant for arrest presented by a UN inspector or surrogate, contrary to the wishes of the inspector or surrogate";[23] (4) "Any attempt to delay or thwart the lawful prosecution, trial, disciplinary hearing or oversight hearing of an individual accused of corruption or obstruction of justice, in excess of the discretionary authority of the prosecutor, judge, disciplinary body or oversight agency exercising jurisdiction over the relevant case";[24] and (5) "A prosecution, trial, disciplinary hearing or oversight hearing regarding an individual accused of corruption or obstruction of justice under this Protocol that is substantially irregular, violates accepted prosecutorial, judicial, disciplinary or oversight norms and practices, and perverts the course of justice."[25]

ENFORCEMENT

Article 14 provides a mechanism where a UN inspector may, when obstruction of justice has occurred or when cooperation is inadequate, file a request for censure:

> In cases where an inspector believes that obstruction of justice has occurred, or adequate and timely cooperation, assistance or protection have not been provided by the requisite police, law enforcement, judicial, anti-corruption or government units, the inspector may file a request for censure by the Commission on Crime Prevention and Criminal Justice. The Commission shall review the request and may subpoena evidence and/or interview witnesses. The Commission shall make a determination, by a majority vote, to approve or disapprove the motion for censure no later than 21 days after receiving a request for censure.[26]

Article 15 directs the World Bank and IMF to develop and implement a system of reducing aid and credits in response to the magnitude and frequency of acts of noncooperation with UN inspectors and their surrogates.[27] This provision would become effective if the World Bank and IMF sign APUNCAC.

Article 16 makes the Commission on Crime Prevention and Criminal Justice the final arbiter of disputes regarding the actions of the Commission, ICAC, the Anti-Money Laundering Debarment Office, FINCEN, and each State Party Conflicts of Interest Board and Fair Political Practices Commission.[28]

The provisions of Articles 8, 10, 11, 14, 15, and 16 would ensure that failure to cooperate and obstruction of justice would be investigated, would become public knowledge, would be censured, and would result in reductions in international aid and credits. Individuals who are responsible would be exposed. Corrupt prosecutors and judges would be exposed. Dedicated anticorruption courts would expedite the efficient prosecution of corrupt individuals. Chapter 3 drew upon the experience of the CICIG to explain how and why public exposure of corrupt individuals, prosecutors, and judges would be expected to cause their resignation or removal from office. While the provisions of APUNCAC could not ensure that every corrupt prosecutor, judge, or public official is removed from office, they would support and reinforce the efforts of honest, competent prosecutors, judges, and anticorruption investigators to expose corruption, force corrupt officials to resign, and tilt the balance in favor of honest, competent prosecutors and investigators. CICIG, until the end of its mandate, had been surprisingly successful. The persistent application of APUNCAC's provisions may be expected to have the same salutary effect.

ARTICLE 70

Article 70 inserts a legal mechanism to adapt APUNCAC as needed and resolve conflicts. Article 70 establishes a system where the institutional bodies established by APUNCAC may promulgate rules, regulations, and procedures to implement APUNCAC. Article 70 also establishes a system of ALJs to adjudicate disputes about those rules, regulations, and procedures.

Article 70 draws upon the American Administrative Procedure Act (APA),[29] the South Carolina Administrative Procedure Act,[30] the Rules of Procedure for the South Carolina Administrative Law Court,[31] U.S. Equal Employment Opportunity Commission Complaint Processing Procedures,[32] U.S. CFR section 1614.109(d) regarding discovery,[33] the U.S. OPM rule regarding the Qualification Standard for ALJ Positions,[34] U.S. Code sections

5372 and 5303 regarding the compensation of ALJs,[35] and recommendations by the Administrative Conference of the United States (ACUS) regarding the federal administrative judiciary.[36] ACUS is an independent federal agency charged with convening expert representatives from the public and private sectors to recommend improvements to administrative process and procedure.

To improve the independence of the administrative judiciary, ACUS recommended conversion of administrative judge (AJ) positions to ALJ positions. The APA spells out protections designed to shield ALJs from improper agency influence—protections that are not available regarding AJs. The APA requires the separation of certain functions to protect ALJs from improper influence by agency investigators and prosecutors. ALJs are selected through a special process overseen by the federal OPM. Their pay is set by statute and OPM regulations. Any attempt by an agency to discipline or remove an ALJ requires a formal hearing at the Merit Systems Protection Board. ALJs are also exempt from the performance appraisal requirements applicable to almost all other federal employees under the Civil Service Reform Act.

The APA is complicated because the language seeks to accommodate a complicated federal system of adjudication that combines the employment of ALJs with the employment of AJs. The South Carolina Administrative Procedure Act dispenses with AJs and, instead, offers a simpler, more streamlined model of adjudication that relies entirely on ALJs operating through the South Carolina Administrative Law Court. Article 70 adopts South Carolina's approach of relying entirely on ALJs operating through an administrative law court. Article 70 incorporates language drawn from the Rules of Procedure for the South Carolina Administrative Law Court. These rules simplify and streamline court procedures to facilitate and promote efficiency while maintaining and elaborating APA protections to ensure that adjudication is fair and impartial.

Unlike either the APA or the South Carolina Administrative Procedure Act, Article 70 inserts an optional expedited procedure that may be elected by either party to a dispute. The expedited procedure then becomes mandatory. The expedited procedure sets deadlines for the submission of briefs, reply briefs, a proposed decision by the presiding ALJ, objections if any to the proposed decision, and a final decision and order that is not subject to review. The parties may mutually agree to substitute deadlines in lieu of the deadlines specified in Article 70. The ALJ may pose written questions served on both parties, and may receive written responses, served on both parties. The expedited procedure is designed to expedite decisions in cases where a party believes that the facts are well established and a decision may be reached by applying the law to the facts of the case. Article 70 specifies that in matters involving the assessment of civil penalties, the imposition of sanctions, or the enforcement of administrative orders, the agency shall have the burden of proof.[37]

Article 70 inserts provisions designed to promote the accountability of ALJs:

> The Commission on Crime Prevention and Criminal Justice shall conduct an annual review of the performance of each administrative law judge and shall issue a letter of reprimand, suspension, or an order to retire for a decision or pattern of decisions by such judge that is arbitrary, capricious, manifestly contrary to properly articulated and disseminated rules, procedures, precedents, or policies, is not based on a consideration of relevant factors, or involves a clear error of judgment or a failure to articulate a legally sound conclusion.[38]

Article 70 also includes provisions designed to ensure the independence of the judiciary:

> No administrative law judge shall be disciplined or removed except through a formal hearing before a three-judge panel of administrative law judges drawn by rotation from the pool of such judges ranked in the top quintile by OPM and appointed by the Commission on Crime Prevention and Criminal Justice.[39]

Article 70 seeks to balance the need for an efficient mechanism to resolve disputes with the need to ensure fair and impartial adjudication. It does so by incorporating provisions designed to expedite decision-making together with provisions designed to promote fairness and impartiality.

Chapter 13

Complementarity

The Rome Statute establishing the ICC includes complicated provisions intended to avoid situations where the ICC usurps genuine proceedings conducted by domestic criminal justice systems. These provisions are based on the principle of "complementarity," meaning that the ICC is intended to complement, rather than replace, existing domestic systems. The provisions seek to ensure that the independent prosecutor only proceeds when a State Party's domestic system is *unable* to prosecute an accused person, manifestly takes *no action*, is *unwilling*, or the proceedings are *not genuine*. If this condition is fulfilled and prosecution is in the interest of justice, then a case is *admissible*, meaning that the independent prosecutor may proceed with an investigation and prosecution. However, the evaluation of this condition is fraught with difficulty. Evaluation of the degree to which a domestic criminal justice system is truly unable to prosecute, determination of whether in fact no action has been taken, and assessment of a state's willingness to prosecute or the degree to which proceedings are genuine is a complicated undertaking involving multiple points where knowledgeable observers may disagree.

COMPLEX ISSUES

Jo Stigen, who represented Norway's Ministry of Justice on the United Nations Preparatory Committee on the Establishment of an ICC and at the United Nations Conference of Plenipotentiaries on the Establishment of an ICC, authored a 533-page volume explicating the issues surrounding complementarity. The length of the text indicates that the issues are not simple. For example, Article 17(2) of the Rome Statute lists three factors relevant to the determination of a state's "willingness" to prosecute.[1] Regarding the first factor, Article 17(2) states:

> In order to determine unwillingness in a particular case, the Court shall consider, having regard to the principles of due process recognized by international law, whether . . . [t]he proceedings were or are being undertaken or the national decision was made for the purpose of shielding the person concerned from criminal responsibility for crimes within the jurisdiction of the Court referred to in article 5.[2]

Stigen writes that "[This] Factor . . . reflects the core of the 'unwillingness' criterion . . . [but] demonstrating a purpose of shielding will be . . . challenging. . . . Indeed, it may turn out to be just as difficult as proving a perpetrator's *mens rea*."[3] "Unlike a physical thing or a conduct, the purpose behind a conduct cannot be observed."[4] Stigen continues:

> A subtle way of shielding the perpetrator is to assign the case to inexperienced investigators, prosecutors and/or judges. This strategy might be difficult to reveal, as the participants in the judicial process might be acting in good faith but still be bound to fail due to their inexperience.[5]

However, Stigen notes that "the fact that the investigators merely are doing a sloppy job will not, for instance, indicate unwillingness."[6] To assess whether a case is admissible, the independent prosecutor and the pretrial chamber of the ICC are forced to judge not only whether sloppiness is due to inexperience *but whether that was the intended result of a state's deliberate strategy to shield a perpetrator*. This is only one of numerous thorny judgments that are shouldered by the independent prosecutor when addressing the issue of admissibility. The issues arise because the ICC was created as a court that complements, but does not replace, domestic courts. In sum, there is tremendous potential for confusion and disagreement regarding the conditions under which a case is admissible before the independent prosecutor of the ICC.

APUNCAC STRATEGY

APUNCAC dispenses with these issues because it establishes a clear division of labor. Under APUNCAC, a UN inspector may only investigate a case. Upon completion of an investigation, the case is handed over to an appropriate prosecuting authority. There is no duplication of prosecutorial or judicial functions. The model anticorruption protocol obligates each State Party to create a system of dedicated anticorruption courts that are operated domestically. Under APUNCAC, the UN is responsible for funding the courts.

APUNCAC requires States Parties to establish national judicial councils for the purpose of selecting, evaluating, and maintaining discipline among judges who are appointed to serve the dedicated anticorruption courts. APUNCAC gives the UN Commission on Crime Prevention and Criminal Justice the responsibility to vet, and the power to veto, the selection of individuals who serve on national judicial councils, as well as the selection of prosecutors and judges who serve dedicated anticorruption courts, thereby ensuring the competence and integrity of the councils and the competence and integrity of the prosecutors and judges who are appointed to serve dedicated anticorruption courts.

Under APUNCAC, a UN inspector may begin an investigation immediately upon receiving a request to open an investigation. In contrast, the independent prosecutor of the ICC is hamstrung by the lengthy, time-consuming task of assessing admissibility, involving difficult judgments and issues that require a lengthy period of evaluation. Valuable time may be lost, permitting suspects to destroy evidence, witnesses to disappear, and the investigative trail to grow cold. In contrast, a UN inspector can move swiftly to obtain court orders for wiretaps and other necessary investigative steps without alerting criminal targets that an investigation has begun.

The creation of a single international anticorruption court modeled on the ICC would be inadequate to handle the hundreds—perhaps thousands—of cases that could be expected each year among UN Member States. To handle the volume of cases involving corruption, it is necessary to create a system of dedicated anticorruption courts operated by every State Party. Such courts would necessarily be aligned with local norms, tailored to domestic laws, and more efficient than a single court that cannot be aligned or tailored to local norms and laws.

OBSTRUCTION OF JUSTICE

APUNCAC maintains discipline among prosecutors and judges by defining the crime of obstruction of justice. APUNCAC explicitly states that actions by prosecutors and judges that are substantially irregular and fall outside the norms of prosecutorial and judicial behavior may be investigated as acts constituting obstruction of justice. Since opinions may differ about acts that rise to the level of obstruction of justice, APUNCAC includes a provision whereby a UN inspector may seek an opinion from a domestic court. An opinion that obstruction of justice has occurred would necessarily reflect domestic norms regarding acts that fall outside acceptable behavior. That opinion would not be rendered lightly because it would necessarily be rendered by a court that could, in principle, find itself under investigation for similar acts. APUNCAC makes that opinion admissible evidence in any case that is handed over to domestic prosecutors. It would be powerful evidence. Once published online by Transparency International, it would shame the culpable party and would be difficult to ignore by a national judicial council vested with the responsibility of evaluating the performance of the judiciary and maintaining the integrity and discipline of the judiciary. These provisions obligate prosecutors and judges to adhere to accepted norms of prosecutorial and judicial behavior, enforcing discipline, promoting competence, and rewarding diligent, ethical, prosecutors and judges. APUNCAC serves, in this way, to strengthen domestic criminal justice systems. In contrast, the ICC intervenes when a state is unable or unwilling to genuinely prosecute, but it does not enforce discipline or otherwise promote the competence of domestic criminal justice systems.

A concern is that a domestic anticorruption court may be corrupted in the same way that other domestic courts may be corrupted. Chapter 12 outlined provisions of APUNCAC designed to deter such corruption, involving procedures to vet the selection of competent prosecutors and judges and enforce accountability. Article 10 defines the crime of obstruction of justice in a way that targets corruption in the judiciary and among prosecutors:

> A prosecution, trial, disciplinary hearing or oversight hearing regarding an individual accused of corruption or obstruction of justice under this Protocol that is substantially irregular, violates accepted prosecutorial, judicial, disciplinary or oversight norms and practices, and perverts the course of justice shall constitute obstruction of justice.[7]

UN inspectors employed by the UN, paid by the UN, and insulated from undue influence from domestic authorities are specifically authorized and empowered to conduct investigations into charges of obstruction of justice, with special priority given to prosecutors, judges, and other elements of the judicial system. During an investigation, a UN inspector may seek a judicial opinion from a judge in the state where the investigation is conducted regarding any alleged act involving obstruction of justice.[8] This opinion would constitute an independent judgment, reflecting local judicial norms, about whether the behavior in question constitutes obstruction of justice.

APUNCAC includes provisions designed to ensure that appropriate authorities act upon the information regarding obstruction of justice.

> Upon the conclusion of each investigation, the supervising UN Inspector shall file a report to be published online by Transparency International.[9]

> The report shall include witness statements, a statement of evidence, judicial opinions (if available), rebuttal statements (if available), and a description of the

relevant statutory, disciplinary agency or oversight institution procedures and consequences entailed when an individual is accused of obstruction of justice in the state where the investigation is conducted.[10]

This provision is designed to ensure that a corrupt prosecutor cannot hide evidence of obstruction of justice. It is analogous to the unsealing of a criminal indictment in a U.S. District Court by a U.S. attorney.[11] The provision is designed to expose corrupt individuals in the court of public opinion and to prod relevant disciplinary and oversight institutions to act. While it might be argued that publication by Transparency International of charges of corruption would be inflammatory, the alternative is the status quo, that is, a continuation of the rampant corruption, impunity, and indifference that characterizes certain judicial systems and is described in chapter 1. To avoid the continuation of corruption and impunity, APUNCAC increases public exposure.

This is especially important in cases where prosecutors or judges are involved in obstruction of justice. Provisions of domestic laws designed to insulate prosecutors and judicial officials from undue influence create barriers to the removal of corrupt prosecutors and judges. Corrupt officials use these barriers to fend off institutions that might exert discipline. This creates a need to promote transparency.

Transparency supports and reinforces APUNCAC's disciplinary mechanisms by promoting engagement and oversight by bodies designed by APUNCAC to be insulated from corrupt domestic influences: the UN Commission on Crime Prevention and Criminal Justice and national judicial councils composed of individuals vetted by the Commission on Crime Prevention and Criminal Justice. Transparency exposes corrupt actors within the justice system to the court of public opinion and pressure to behave ethically and responsibly.

CONCLUSION

One might argue that APUNCAC's success depends on the selection of experienced, competent UN inspectors to write balanced, reasoned reports supported by adequate evidence. However, the U.S. justice system also relies upon the selection of experienced, competent U.S. attorneys to write balanced, reasoned indictments supported by adequate evidence. The U.S. justice system offers a model suggesting that it is feasible for experienced, competent UN inspectors to write balanced, reasoned indictments supported by adequate evidence. In either case, a persistent failure to write balanced, reasoned indictments supported by adequate evidence is likely to end an investigator's career. UN inspectors would operate under intense scrutiny by the media, the public, and the accused. This scrutiny would reward competence and punish incompetence in the same way that U.S. attorneys are rewarded for competence and punished for incompetence.

UN inspectors are required by APUNCAC to submit their reports to the appropriate prosecutorial, disciplinary, or oversight bodies:

> The report shall be submitted to the appropriate prosecutorial, disciplinary, or oversight bodies. Prosecution, disciplinary actions and oversight shall follow the relevant statutory, regulatory, disciplinary or oversight agency procedures, practices and consequences entailed when an individual is accused of obstruction of justice in the state where the investigation is conducted but those procedures and practices shall not be abused in a way that would pervert the course of justice. If a UN Inspector subsequently determines that prosecution, discipline or oversight of an individual accused of obstruction of justice has been perverted, the Inspector shall prepare and submit a report to the appropriate prosecuting authorities, disciplinary bodies, parliamentary institutions or other institutions exercising oversight. The Inspector shall submit the report to be published online by Transparency International.[12]

This provision ensures that the appropriate prosecutorial, disciplinary, or oversight bodies would act on reports by UN inspectors regarding obstruction of justice, or risk investigation and public exposure for corruption and obstruction of justice. This provision ensures that corrupt prosecutors and judges would no longer be able to hide their corrupt acts from public view. UN inspectors would name corrupt individuals. Details of their corruption and obstruction of justice would become public knowledge. The experience of CICIG suggests that public exposure would force the resignation or removal of corrupt prosecutors and judges who previously enjoyed impunity.

Chapter 1 described the consequences of rampant corruption in domestic justice systems. When justice fails, the poor suffer. Violations of human rights occur. Corruption and impunity endure.

APUNCAC establishes mechanisms designed to fight corruption and impunity in the institutions that normally fight corruption and impunity. Exposure and punishment of corrupt individuals serve to reinforce and multiply the efforts of honest, competent members of the justice system. Over time, as the proportion of corrupt individuals is reduced, their influence is reduced. The resources of anticorruption investigators and prosecutors can be targeted toward the remaining criminals, increasing the probability of exposure, raising the costs of crime, reducing the benefits, and drastically altering calculations of the benefits and costs of crime. This formula has worked in Hong Kong, Singapore, and Georgia, and there is no reason why it should not also work in any other jurisdiction.

Chapter 14

Why Would Leaders and States Agree?

Chapter 14, "Why Would Leaders and States Agree?", explains that it is not unusual for political leaders to experience strong pressure to sign and implement agreements to fight corruption. Leaders—even those who may be corrupt—may feel compelled, for political reasons, to sign and implement international anticorruption agreements. This explanation is framed within an analysis of Judge Mark Wolf's proposed IACC because the IACC proposal highlights the issue and raises two additional issues. One issue is that the IACC presupposes the existence of criminal investigators armed with powerful investigative tools. This chapter suggests that this issue may be addressed by combining the APUNCAC and IACC proposals. A second issue is that Wolf proposes to compel submission to the jurisdiction of the IACC through coercive measures that have been criticized as unworkable and possibly counterproductive. This chapter suggests that this concern may be addressed by dropping the coercive elements of Wolf's proposal and, instead, relying upon APUNCAC's positive features to incentivize potential States Parties to sign and ratify the combined proposal.

In brief, APUNCAC offers benefits, in the form of innovative provisions that would require beneficial owners to reveal their identities with regard to international transfers to bank secrecy havens. APUNCAC installs a system to collect and centralize accurate beneficial owner information whenever funds are transmitted internationally or to known bank secrecy havens in amounts exceeding $3,000.[1] This would strip away the anonymity that permits criminals, including terrorists, to escape with the proceeds of their crimes. These provisions provide positive incentives that may induce potential States Parties to be bound by APUNCAC. The provisions would be attractive to the United States, the UK, and OECD Member States because their efforts to fight terrorism have been stymied by the ability of terrorists to manipulate the international financial system, hide their funds, and continue to commit terrorist acts. Other states may wish to ratify APUNCAC in order to avoid being seen as pariah states that operate outside the rule of law, and to maintain international concessions regarding aid, trade, and debt relief.

APUNCAC also contains provisions that would permit UN anticorruption inspectors to pursue acts involving abuse of power and obstruction of justice. APUNCAC defines obstruction of justice, creates a procedure where a UN inspector may request an opinion from a domestic judge regarding an allegation involving obstruction of justice, and creates procedures that would ensure transparency regarding allegations involving abuse of power and obstruction of justice. APUNCAC establishes procedures to hand cases to dedicated domestic anticorruption courts.

APUNCAC includes provisions to ensure that the convention would be implemented as intended, States Parties would cooperate, and failure to cooperate would be censured by the UN, sanctioned through penalties imposed by the World Bank and IMF, and exposed through online publication of reports by Transparency International. A failure to cooperate would be investigated by UN inspectors as an obstruction of justice. APUNCAC establishes procedures to vet the selection of prosecutors and judges and mechanisms to ensure the accountability of judges serving dedicated anticorruption courts.

The creation of dedicated domestic anticorruption courts is different from Judge Mark Wolf's proposal to create a single IACC. However, both proposals are ambitious. Both seek to address the problem of corruption and impunity through the implementation of new courts. Both are based on the rationale that endemic corruption can only be addressed by establishing independent investigators, prosecutors, and courts. Both proposals raise thorny questions about why political leaders who themselves may be involved in corruption would ever support or sign the necessary agreements or legislation. Both proposals raise questions about how evidence would be collected, assembled, and presented to an anticorruption court. Both proposals raise questions about the incentives for potential States Parties to ratify the proposed conventions.

The purpose of this chapter is to address these questions. While APUNCAC is designed to be a freestanding proposal, it could be combined with Judge Wolf's proposal for an IACC. I address certain questions by proposing to combine the separate APUNCAC and IACC proposals into a single proposal. The IACC could serve as a supreme court for cases of grand corruption, modeled after the ICC. The APUNCAC courts could serve as first-level courts. UN inspectors would prepare cases for these courts. This chapter explains the rationale for this proposal.

The first section of this chapter describes Judge Wolf's proposal to establish an IACC and notes that momentum is building toward the establishment of an IACC. The second section describes three major criticisms of the IACC, including the concern that leaders who may themselves be corrupt would not voluntarily agree to sign and implement any anticorruption agreement, including APUNCAC, that threatens their control. The third section responds to those criticisms. The focus is an explanation, drawing upon historical examples, suggesting that political leaders tend to experience pressure to sign all types of anticorruption agreements, including the type of international agreement that would be needed to establish the IACC or APUNCAC. The fourth section explains the rationale for combining IACC + APUNCAC. The last section concludes.

IACC

The idea for an IACC was first put forward by Judge Mark L. Wolf at the 2012 St. Petersburg International Legal Forum and subsequently presented at the 2014 World Forum on Governance.[2] Wolf subsequently described his proposal in an article published in the journal *Daedalus*. Wolf justified the proposal by reiterating the need for a credible deterrent to actors who might otherwise choose to engage in acts of corruption:

> It is a fundamental premise of criminal law that the prospect of punishment will deter crime. Research has validated this premise, including with regard to violations of human rights. The absence of risk of punishment, particularly imprisonment, contributes greatly to the pervasiveness and persistence of grand corruption.[3]

Wolf argued that grand corruption and impunity flourish in nations where political leaders control prosecutors and judges, neutering deterrence:

> Many countries do not hold corrupt leaders accountable because those very leaders control every element of the administration of justice. Kleptocrats enjoy impunity because they are able to prevent the honest, effective investigation and prosecution of their colleagues, their friends, their families, and themselves.[4]

Wolf argued that the U.S. system of independent courts and prosecutors offers a promising model:

> The United States provides a model for a new international approach to creating the crucial, credible threat that corrupt leaders will be punished for their crimes. . . . Federal prosecutors are capable of trying complex cases successfully before impartial judges and juries. As a result, public officials convicted

of corruption regularly receive serious sentences, which have the potential to deter others and to create a political climate in which candidates dedicated to governing honestly are elected.[5]

Wolf concluded:

> [A]n IACC is needed for the extraterritorial prosecution and punishment of corrupt leaders of countries that are unwilling or unable to enforce their own laws against powerful offenders. The international consequences of grand corruption justify the creation of an IACC, separate from but similar to the International Criminal Court (ICC).[6] ...[T]he fact that grand corruption continues to flourish demonstrates that the current means alone are inadequate and something new is needed.[7]

Wolf offered preliminary ideas about how the IACC would work:

> [T]he IACC should employ elite prosecutors from around the world with the experience and expertise necessary to develop and present complex cases effectively. In addition, the Court should be led by able and impartial international judges. Importantly, like the ICC, the IACC should operate on the principle of complementarity. National courts would have primary jurisdiction over crimes by corrupt leaders in their countries. The IACC could only exercise jurisdiction if a nation proved unwilling or unable to make good-faith efforts to investigate, prosecute, and punish its leaders and their accomplices for corruption. The IACC would therefore be a court of last resort, to be relied upon only in cases in which national enforcement of existing domestic criminal laws against a country's leaders is not possible.[8]

Wolf's proposed IACC has gained international support. In November 2018, the UN adopted a resolution calling for the convening of a Special Session of the General Assembly "on challenges and measures to prevent and combat corruption and strengthen international cooperation." As noted by Integrity Initiatives International:

> In January 2019, Colombia became the first country to call on the United Nations specifically to create the IACC and make it a key focus of the 2021 Special Session. In May 2019, Peru joined Colombia in backing the IACC, as President of Colombia Iván Duque Márquez and President of Peru Martín Vizcarra signed a Joint Presidential Declaration calling for further study and action to establish an IACC. On June 12, 2019, Colombian Foreign Minister Carlos Holmes Trujillo delivered opening remarks, including a call for support

of the IACC, to the United Nations Office on Drugs and Crime Expert Group Meeting in Oslo, Norway. As a result, recommendation 46 of the Expert Group meeting calls for further study of the IACC. In December 2019, II participated in the Conference of States Parties to the United Nations Convention Against Corruption in Abu Dhabi, United Arab Emirates by advocating for the inclusion of the IACC on the agenda for the 2021 Special Session of the United Nations. Most recently, Congresswoman Jackie Speier (D-California) and Congressman James McGovern (D-Massachusetts) introduced a House Resolution calling on the Congress of the United States to support efforts to establish an IACC.[9]

CRITICISM

While momentum is building in support of the IACC, Harvard law professors Matthew Stephenson and Alex Whiting have questioned the viability of the IACC through articles published as blog posts.[10]

Criticism 1

Stephenson wrote:

> [A]n IACC would require that sovereign states consent to giving an international court the authority to determine whether each state's legal system is adequate to hold accountable senior leaders who engage in acts of grand corruption, and if the international court decides that it isn't, that court would be empowered to arrest, try, convict, and imprison the state's leaders. There's essentially zero chance that states ruled by corrupt elites—or, for that matter, states sensitive to sovereignty concerns—will ever sign onto this. And without that consent, the whole proposal is stillborn. The IACC is thus an example of what my colleague Adrian Vermeule would call a "self-defeating proposal," in which the diagnosis of the problem to be solved (here, the unwillingness of political leaders to surrender their impunity), if accurate, means the proposed solution (here, asking them to consent to a surrender of their impunity) cannot possibly work.[11]

Stephenson argues that political leaders in states characterized by high-level corruption cannot be induced to sign agreements permitting an IACC because they would not voluntarily surrender control. Likewise, Schaefer et al. argue that it is unlikely that a government populated with corrupt individuals would willingly submit to the authority of the IACC.[12]

Criticism 2

Alex Whiting wrote:

> Judge Wolf imagines that IACC prosecutors would function like federal prosecutors in the U.S., able to spring into action, armed with powerful investigative tools to mount effective prosecutions when local authorities fail to act. However, the analogy is false and misleading. As Judge Wolf notes, "Federal investigators are authorized to conduct undercover operations and secretly record conversations, and are adept at unraveling complicated financial transactions." In addition to these tools, federal prosecutors can subpoena records, compel witnesses to testify to the grand jury, get search warrants, and strike deals with cooperating witnesses. But prosecutors and investigators at the ICC, the model for the IACC, have few of these tools. By design, ICC prosecutors are almost entirely reliant on state cooperation to conduct their investigations. If they want to obtain documents or conduct any investigative actions requiring coercive legal measures—such as wiretaps or search warrants—they must make a request to state authorities.[13]

While Wolf stated that "[t]he IACC should employ elite prosecutors from around the world with the experience and expertise necessary to develop and present complex cases effectively,"[14] Whiting's point is that the establishment of prosecutors would be useless unless prosecutors were armed with strong investigative powers, the ability to compel witnesses, and the ability to compel the cooperation of domestic authorities. Schaefer et al. make the same point.[15]

Criticism 3

Matthew Stephenson wrote:

> [To secure the participation of recalcitrant nations, advocates of the IACC] propose extreme coercive measures—like kicking states that don't join the court out of the WTO, denying them foreign aid, expelling them from UNCAC, etc.—that are unworkable and counterproductive. They're unworkable because (A) most of the kinds of coercive pressure envisioned require the agreement of several of the very states that would likely resist the IACC, and (B) because the states where IACC is most needed—kleptocracies—would likely reject the court even at great cost. These coercive proposals are counterproductive because (A) trade and aid sanctions, if imposed, would probably worsen the corruption problem, given that poverty and international isolation are significant drivers of corruption, (B) the threat of such sanctions would likely increase the citizenry's sympathy for the corrupt leaders, and (C) the threat of sanctions—almost certainly targeted at weak developing countries—would send the message that anticorruption is a kind of Western/Northern neo-imperialism (thus undermining two generations' worth of progress in refuting this old canard).[16]

Stephenson argues that stripping recalcitrant states of membership in world organizations, expelling them from UNCAC,[17] and denying foreign aid would be unworkable, counterproductive, and send the message that the IACC is a neo-imperialist instrument that targets weak developing nations. Darling makes a similar point.[18]

RESPONSES

Stephenson's first criticism—that high-level corruption is incompatible with the voluntary adoption of strong measures to fight corruption—is the most challenging of the three criticisms. Stephenson's concern is that leaders who may themselves be corrupt would not voluntarily agree to sign and implement any anticorruption agreement, including APUNCAC, that threatens their control.

In brief, I argue that Criticism #1 is inconsistent with the historical record. The record offers numerous examples demonstrating that the existence of high-level corruption does not preclude the adoption of strong measures to fight crime and corruption. These examples include the United States, which experienced high levels of corruption in the late nineteenth and early twentieth centuries, numerous nations characterized by high-level corruption that are parties to the Rome Statute establishing the independent prosecutor and ICC, plus Romania, Guatemala, Honduras, and Ukraine.

Criticism 1

Stephenson argues that political leaders in states characterized by high-level corruption would not be willing to sign agreements permitting an IACC because they would not voluntarily surrender control. There is, however, a flaw in this logic. According to Stephenson's logic, no state that has experienced endemic corruption would ever ratify aggressive measures to fight corruption. However, history says otherwise. Government corruption was endemic in sixteenth- and seventeenth-century England, in Europe in the eighteenth century, and in America during the late nineteenth and early twentieth centuries.[19] Public pressure for reform ultimately forced political leaders to sign legislation adopting checks and balances against corruption.[20] This included the establishment of strong, independent, protected anticorruption prosecutors. The fact that effective checks and balances currently exist in Western countries indicates that public pressure was ultimately effective in installing powerful measures to fight corruption, despite the existence of endemic corruption. How, according to Stephenson's logic, could England,

Europe, and America have transitioned from a state of endemic corruption to clean government if political leaders were unwilling to relinquish control?

Lessons from America, Romania, the UK, Rome, Guatemala, Honduras, and Ukraine suggest that political decision-makers are influenced by internal domestic pressure, external international pressure, political expediency in the face of domestic and international pressure, and in some cases by the hubris that they can support—but will not be affected by—the installation of strong, independent courts and prosecutors.

Lessons from America

In late nineteenth- and early twentieth-century America, for example, public pressure for reform arose in response to the general deterioration of law and order and the rise of crime, mob violence, and pervasive corruption that reached the highest levels of government.[21] In response to demand for reform, state legislatures abolished private prosecution of crime and granted public prosecutors sole authority to institute prosecution.[22] Prosecutors acquired monopoly control over prosecution.[23] In an effort to isolate prosecutors from political influence, state legislatures altered the process of selecting prosecutors. One state after another implemented legislation requiring popular election, rather than appointment, of prosecutors.[24] By 1945, all but two states had shifted to the elective system of selecting judges and prosecutors.[25] Advocates of popular election sought to isolate prosecutors from the influence of political leaders who previously controlled the prosecutorial appointment process and expected loyalty in return.

These reforms intersected with reforms at the federal level. In 1870, the USDOJ was established.[26] In 1910, Congress passed the Mann Act, extending federal jurisdiction in the area of crime control.[27] In 1919, the Criminal Division of USDOJ was established.[28] U.S. attorneys began investigating criminal complaints under the supervision and authority of the Attorney General.

It soon became clear, however, that corruption extended to the highest levels of government. By the spring of 1924, former president Warren G. Harding, Secretary of the Treasury Andrew Mellon, Attorney General Harry Daugherty, Bureau of Investigation Director William Burns, and numerous congressmen had been implicated in the Teapot Dome bribery and corruption scandal.[29] Former vice president Calvin Coolidge asked for resignations.[30] A National Crime Commission was created.[31] The commission called for new measures to fight crime and corruption. In January 1934, President Franklin Roosevelt identified organized crime as a major threat to the nation's security.[32] Attorney General Homer Cummings described the wave of crime as "a war that threatens the safety of our country—a war with the organized forces of crime."[33] Public criticism intensified. The President of the New York Bar Association traced the failure to weak local investigation and political corruption.[34] Pressure for reform intensified, driven by outrage over political corruption and the view that government officials were inept, corrupt, and controlled by gangsters.[35] A probe into parole and probation practices uncovered extensive corruption.[36] The Federal Bar essentially acknowledged that local justice systems were corrupt and could not perform their basic crime control functions.[37]

Public support grew for the creation of an elite force of federal investigators to fight racketeering and organized crime.[38] State governors, sensitive to public reaction and knowing that failure to act could be used against them as a campaign issue, chose to support the expansion of federal jurisdiction and control.[39] In response, the U. S. Congress passed nine legislative bills to expand federal jurisdiction and control organized crime.[40] Federal prosecutors were empowered to take charge of specific cases at their discretion.[41] Officials vowed that federal agents would pursue corruption and criminal activity regardless of position, power, or status.[42]

The reforms shaped the Federal Bureau of Investigation and the system of independent state and federal prosecutors that is now widely acknowledged as the world standard for integrity, competence, and effectiveness. U.S. attorneys quickly established a reputation for relentless investigation of crime and corruption. Federal agents compiled an impressive record of arrests leading to convictions.[43]

Reforms were implemented despite opposition from senior government officials, and in the face of high levels of corruption and organized crime. Attorney General William D. Mitchell argued vehemently against the federal expansion of criminal law enforcement.[44] Judges, prosecutors, and police officials from all levels of government argued against federal expansion.[45]

Reforms were implemented despite the presence of corrupt actors in key positions. Senator Royal Copeland, the powerful chairman of the Senate Rules Committee, was responsible for chairing congressional hearings regarding racketeering. A beneficiary of the Tammany Hall patronage machine, he displayed little interest in exploring allegations that Tammany Hall was linked to organized crime and a major cause of corruption.[46] The committee accomplished little in the way of substantive investigation and submitted no final report.[47] The committee hearings primarily served to burnish Copeland's crime-fighting image.[48]

Despite this type of interference by corrupt actors, public pressure for reform meant that the vast majority of elected officials, including state legislators, U.S. representatives and senators, governors, and the president, benefited from their public advocacy and support for reform. The reforms placed control of prosecution in the hands of dedicated public prosecutors and U.S.

attorneys, shifted the system of selecting public prosecutors to an elective system, established the Criminal Division of the USDOJ, created an elite force of federal investigators to fight racketeering and organized crime, expanded federal jurisdiction to control organized crime, and empowered federal prosecutors to take charge of specific cases at their discretion. The reforms were the consequence of public pressure for reform and calculations by elected officials that the reputational benefits of supporting the reforms outweighed the risk that the reforms could be turned against them. The reforms shaped the American system of independent state and federal prosecutors that is now widely acknowledged as the world standard for integrity, competence, effectiveness, and relentless investigation of crime and corruption.

The shift to the elective system transformed the role of the American prosecutor.[49] As an elected official endowed with discretionary power by the constitution or by state statutes, the prosecutor's decisions are virtually unreviewable.[50] The prosecutor has absolute discretion in deciding which laws to enforce and which laws to ignore.[51] The change from appointed to elected status meant that prosecutors were directly answerable to the people, not beholden to those who had appointed them, and free to pursue investigations and prosecutions at the highest levels of government.[52]

The laws mandating these changes were passed during an era of endemic corruption by legislatures widely viewed as riddled with corrupt individuals. Political leaders supported and signed legislation, regardless of their probity and personal ethics, out of political expediency, or when compelled by veto-proof majorities. They calculated that the political benefits outweighed the possibility that the new laws might be turned against them. This dynamic explains how strong anticrime legislation was signed into law despite the existence of corrupt actors in positions of power.

Lessons from Romania and the UK

A case study of Romania suggests an alternative explanation—that political leaders frequently miscalculate the possibility that new laws might be turned against them.[53] Between 2000 and 2004, Romania adopted a series of anticorruption reforms. In 2012, the prime minister who led the reforms—Adrian Nastase—was sentenced to jail for corruption.[54] The case analysis concluded that the existence of widespread corruption can breed complacency among decision-makers. Decision-makers adopt anticorruption policies because they want to signal their integrity and gain reputational benefits but miscalculate the consequences. They incorrectly assume they will be able to control implementation and avoid becoming ensnared by the laws they helped to install. Leaked transcripts showed the ruling Social Democratic Party leaders discussing how they could control and manipulate the judiciary, media, and civil society.[55] The evidence suggests that they did not really expect the anticorruption policies they had installed to be enforced.[56] The Social Democratic Party, according to civil society measures, had by far the most "tainted"—that is, corrupt—electoral candidates.[57] The civil society assessments were based on asset and income disclosures required by the 2003 anticorruption law.[58] The prime minister and leader of the Social Democratic Party, who ensured the adoption of the 2003 law, was Adrian Nastase. He had defended the law in parliament as sending "a very clear signal to the political class, the Romanian society, and our external partners" that the government intended to start a massive anticorruption effort.[59] He ensured the passage of the anticorruption reforms because he desired the reputational benefits, but miscalculated the consequences.

Once the reforms were installed, they were difficult to remove. Every attempt at weakening the laws provoked not only international rebukes but also domestic public and political outrage.[60] The public viewed opposition to the laws as evidence of corrupt intent.[61] This made opposition to the policies politically costly, which made the policies difficult to reverse and increased pressure for more stringent enforcement.[62] In sum, decision-makers in high-corruption countries adopt anticorruption policies because they seek to signal their honesty and integrity, and assume they will be able to control the implementation of the policies.[63]

A study of anticorruption legislation in the UK found the same dynamic: "Few politicians can ignore or resist the political credibility that can be gained" by supporting reform.[64] Once installed, the reforms were difficult to remove:

> Any backing down would disappoint and raise suspicions as to why and, almost inevitably, what there is to hide, and could create a dangerous narrative about betrayal of people, principle or "radical" intent. A government's or leader's trust and faithfulness would be eroded, and with it their capacity to make powerful moral arguments, especially if linked to the "betrayal" of a particular promise. This symbolic betrayal could then have real political consequences.[65]

Rejection "would be likely to become a recurrent trope and line of attack for opponents, as well as a policy 'gift' to other political parties," leading to a loss of trust and erosion of legitimacy.[66]

Lessons from Rome, Guatemala, Honduras, and Ukraine

One cannot argue that the conditions for establishing strong, independent, protected prosecutors only existed in England, Europe, and America, or only in the distant past. Consider the past two decades. The Rome Statute established an independent ICC and an independent prosecutor with the capacity to initiate cases *proprio motu*.[67] The Rome Statute was signed by 123 nations, including many nations characterized by endemic corruption, meaning that 123 nations are States Parties to an international convention that requires the surrender of domestic sovereignty with regard to the types of crimes covered by the Rome Statute. In these nations, no domestic political leader is immune to prosecution by the independent prosecutor or the ICC. The ICC has been effective in conducting successful investigations, indicting alleged criminals for committing mass atrocities, executing arrest warrants with the assistance of domestic authorities, and bringing suspects to trial.[68] The ICC's success demonstrates that it is not a paper tiger, and adoption and ratification are not empty gestures by politicians to placate the international community. The ICC is bringing criminals to justice in cases covering Uganda, the Democratic Republic of the Congo, Darfur/Sudan, and the Central African Republic.[69] The evidence suggests that international investigators can be effective and can obtain the cooperation and assistance of domestic authorities in executing arrest warrants, even in nations characterized by high corruption and weak rule of law.

In Guatemala, the CICIG was created through an international agreement with the UN.[70] The agreement stated that "CICIG shall enjoy complete functional independence in discharging its mandate."[71] Carlos Castresana, CICIG's first head, was a respected Spanish career prosecutor who had no Guatemalan connections. Castresana recruited other Spanish-speaking prosecutors and investigators to staff CICIG, individuals who could pass a rigorous integrity check and were also strangers to Guatemala. CICIG enjoyed tremendous success over its 12-year mandate, securing the conviction of dozens of senior military and political leaders and forcing a sitting president and vice president to resign over corruption charges.[72]

Remarkably, CICIG's initial two-year mandate was renewed in April 2009, in January 2011, in April 2015, and again in April 2016.[73] What explains the fact that CICIG's mandate was repeatedly renewed by one president after another when some proved to be deeply corrupt and had every reason to fear a CICIG investigation into their corrupt dealings? A report by the Center for Latin American and Latino Studies (CLALS) found the same pattern of presidential hubris and miscalculation that characterized Romania's Adrian Nastase. One president after another renewed CICIG's mandate only to suffer the consequences of CICIG's aggressive anticorruption investigations:

> Why did president after president keep acquiescing to the international presence and efforts to help combat corruption when some proved to be deeply corrupt? What sort of hubris or blind optimism exists for decision-makers to create

> (and renew) a mechanism whose mandate is to uncover their own criminal behavior?[74]

The answer was domestic and international pressure:

> These choices cannot be explained without acknowledging the pressures to approve such mechanisms from both domestic and international actors.[75]

Apparently, this pressure can be decisive. This offers a reason to think that domestic and international actors might also apply the same type of pressure to force the adoption of CICIG-like investigative bodies such as the type of body that would be established by APUNCAC, even when corrupt actors control the Office of the President in potential States Parties to APUNCAC.

The experience of CICIG in Guatemala suggests what could be accomplished in potential States Parties to APUNCAC through a CICIG-like treaty arrangement that operates through domestic laws and courts:

> The International Commission Against Impunity in Guatemala (CICIG) represents an innovative effort to curb criminal threats to democratic rule and to strengthen state capacity that diverged from the dominant mode of technical assistance. Working through treaty-based international authority, this "hybrid" U.N.-backed mission combined international and national capacities working through Guatemalan laws and courts. The Commission successfully investigated and helped prosecute multiple high-ranking Guatemalan officials, ex-military officers and business elites. Those investigations precipitated anti-corruption protests that ousted the sitting president and vice president in the "Guatemalan Spring" of 2015. CICIG investigations led to 1,540 indictments in 120 cases involving over 70 illicit networks. The mission showed Guatemalans that the rule of law can be applied even to the most powerful, had far-reaching political impact, and contributed to the effectiveness of the Attorney-General's office.[76]

Honduras implemented a version of CICIG that assigned supervisory, evaluative and, by delegation of the attorney general, investigative and prosecutorial roles to independent international prosecutors experienced with high-level corruption cases.[77] Ukraine implemented a system where a council of non-Ukrainian international experts review and vet individuals nominated for Ukraine's anticorruption court.[78] Ukrainian president Petro Poroshenko, a corrupt Ukrainian oligarch, signed the law establishing the High Anti-Corruption Court on June 26, 2018.[79]

These examples indicate that it is feasible to obtain agreements permitting independent international inspectors, dedicated domestic anticorruption courts, and independent vetting of judges selected for those courts—even in nations where corruption thrives and even in cases where corrupt individuals control the president's office. The examples from Guatemala, Honduras, and Ukraine, as well as the example of the Rome Statute establishing an independent international court and an independent prosecutor with the capacity to initiate cases *proprio motu*, demonstrate that it is feasible to secure agreements where domestic control is relinquished to international investigators and prosecutors.

APUNCAC combines these ideas. APUNCAC seeks to implement aggressive measures to fight corruption and impunity, including UN inspectors who would conduct independent investigations into allegations of corruption and hand cases to dedicated domestic anticorruption courts. Similar to CICIG, APUNCAC involves a treaty arrangement that operates through domestic laws and courts. Similar to CICIG, APUNCAC would create a body of experienced investigators endowed with strong investigative powers. Similar to Guatemala and Honduras, APUNCAC would involve the assumption of investigative roles by international investigators experienced with high-level cases of corruption. Similar to Ukraine, APUNCAC would establish dedicated domestic anticorruption courts and implement a system of reviewing and vetting individuals nominated to serve those courts. Similar to the Rome Statute, the CICIG Agreement, the agreement establishing the Honduran MACCIH, the law establishing Ukraine's anticorruption court, the 2003 Romanian anticorruption laws, and every strong measure establishing independent prosecutors endowed with strong powers to investigate corruption in England, Europe, and America over the past 150 years, APUNCAC would rely on domestic and/or international pressure to force the hand of political leaders who might otherwise oppose APUNCAC. Numerous studies have investigated APUNCAC's provisions.[80]

Criticism 2

Whiting notes that Wolf's proposal for an IACC assumes the existence of independent investigators endowed with strong investigative powers. The idea of combining the IACC with APUNCAC would address this gap by creating a body of UN-funded and supported inspectors with powers similar to the powers of CICIG's UN-funded and supported inspectors. CICIG successfully employed the type of investigative tools that Whiting believes are necessary for effective investigation and prosecution. CICIG employed wiretaps to link Guatemalan attorney general Conrad Reyes to a criminal conspiracy designed to undermine CICIG.[81] CICIG employed wiretaps and seized documents to prove that President Otto Pérez Molina and Vice President Roxana Baldetti were the leaders of the criminal La Linea state corruption scheme.[82] CICIG was extraordinarily effective in Guatemala, achieving numerous high-profile successes, including the arrest and imprisonment of President Otto Pérez Molina and Vice President Roxana Baldetti.[83] The creation of an independent body of UN inspectors with the same powers as CICIG investigators would address a major criticism of the IACC—that it does not include independent investigators endowed with strong investigative powers.

In addition, APUNCAC creates incentives and procedures for private parties to fight corruption. APUNCAC would permit private parties to file civil actions to recover damages related to corruption. APUNCAC incorporates the provisions of the FCA.[84] APUNCAC also incorporates a version of the RICO Act, including the treble damages provision.[85] This provision would allow private litigants to commence a civil action and recover three times the amount of their damages. While few nations have implemented broad RICO-style laws designed to attack racketeering, the endemic corruption that is the target of APUNCAC and the IACC often involves the type of systematic, organized crime that spawned RICO and was effectively fought using RICO. RICO-style laws are arguably needed to fight endemic corruption. The paucity of laws designed to fight endemic corruption indicates that new laws are needed.

Criticism 3

The proposal to combine IACC + APUNCAC means that Judge Wolf's coercive measures designed to compel participation could be dropped. The benefits of ratifying IACC + APUNCAC would be substantial and could be emphasized to incentivize ratification. APUNCAC contains innovative, aggressive measures to fight money laundering and terrorist financing that would plug a major gap in the international sanction regime against terrorist financing. This would be highly attractive to the United States, the UK, the OECD Member States, and reform-oriented elements in each potential State Party.

Innovative APUNCAC provisions would permit investigators to trace international flows of funds into and out of bank secrecy havens such as the BVI, the Cayman Islands, and Panama and would permit investigators to follow and prosecute funding of terrorism, transnational criminal organizations, and criminal activities of corporations and executives that currently go unpunished.[86] These provisions would be attractive to the United States and its allies because their efforts to halt terrorist financing have been stymied by the ability of terrorists to hide their funds in offshore havens. In addition, the United States and its allies are likely to be supportive of the proposed treaty as a means of addressing government corruption in developing nations that promotes resentment, extremism, and terrorism.

The APUNCAC provisions would be attractive to reform-oriented elements in every potential State Party where corrupt elites utilize the international banking system to move illicit funds offshore and hide the funds in anonymous offshore accounts.

If the United States, the UK, and the OECD Member States become parties to APUNCAC, many (but not all) African, Asian, and Latin American nations could be expected to follow. They would not wish to be seen as pariah states that refuse to adopt international conventions to fight corruption. The same type of pressure was effective in securing widespread adoption of the UNCAC, the Rome Statute, and the UNTOC. This type of pressure has been cited as a reason that Uganda, for example, adopted the Rome Statute.[87] Uganda viewed ratification as a signal to the international community that it would fulfill its commitments to the World Bank, IMF, and international financial institutions and justify continued concessions regarding aid, trade, and debt relief.[88]

APUNCAC + IACC

In principle, passage of IACC + APUNCAC could be obtained through the same type of coordinated campaign waged by the Coalition for the International Criminal Court that led to the Rome Statute establishing the ICC. While Alex Whiting disagrees,[89] arguing that the Rome Statute was a special case enabled by a golden moment that is unlikely to be repeated, this dissent ignores the previously recited historical record. In England, Europe, and America, as well as Guatemala, Honduras, Ukraine, and the 123 nations that are parties to the Rome Statute, the record indicates that it is possible to obtain agreements or the passage of laws establishing strong independent prosecutors, and to do so in spite of endemic corruption that reaches the highest levels of government. Public pressure can, and has, forced the hand of political leaders, regardless of their personal preferences and ethics. They signed agreements or laws in response to domestic and/or international pressure, out of political expediency, or when legislation was passed with veto-proof majorities.

The difficulties encountered by the ICC in conducting investigations and arresting accused individuals raise concern that the IACC would encounter similar problems. The proposal to combine IACC + APUNCAC addresses that concern by creating a body of UN inspectors modeled on CICIG, with all of the powers of CICIG's investigators, but without the time-limited mandate that eventually ended CICIG. CICIG's 12-year record of achievement demonstrates the viability of that model of UN-supported investigators operating through domestic laws and courts, even in a state characterized by mafia-like control of major government departments.

An advantage of combining IACC + APUNCAC is that the combination may serve to address the major criticisms levied by Stephenson and Whiting regarding the proposal for a single supranational international court, that is, IACC alone. APUNCAC would implement dedicated domestic anticorruption courts, with strong measures to protect the integrity of those courts. It would be difficult for a critic to assert that those courts violate domestic sovereignty, lack legitimacy, or are a one-size-fits-all solution. APUNCAC courts would be tailored to local culture and conditions and implemented and operated locally. Jurisdictions based on the British civil law legal system would implement APUNCAC courts aligned with the civil law system. Jurisdictions based on the common law legal system would implement APUNCAC courts aligned with the common law system.

When combined with APUNCAC, the IACC could serve as a hammer and could be reserved for cases where corrupt elites undermine the APUNCAC courts and cause them to be unable or unwilling to prosecute egregious cases of corruption. It would presumably be in the best interests of domestic elites wishing to avoid referrals to the IACC to accept the APUNCAC courts and avoid the type of obvious interference that would prompt referrals to the IACC.

The proposal to combine IACC + APUNCAC would defuse the argument that the IACC represents an unacceptable intrusion on domestic sovereignty. Only cases where the APUNCAC courts are compromised would result in referrals to the IACC. Presumably, the vast majority of cases would be handled by the domestic APUNCAC courts and would never reach the IACC.

The proposal to combine IACC + APUNCAC defuses the key arguments against the IACC. It shifts the burden of adjudication to the domestic court system. It reinforces and supports the domestic court system. It distributes the task of adjudication across a large number of domestic courts. It builds capacity to handle a large number of cases. It avoids overloading the IACC with a large number of cases. It avoids a one-size-fits-all approach by implementing a system of domestically operated APUNCAC courts tailored to local conditions.

By addressing the key arguments against the IACC, the proposal to combine IACC + APUNCAC may enable broad public support in nations that would require public support in order to secure ratification. Public support for ratification would be critical in overcoming entrenched elites who benefit from the continuation of corruption. Events in Tunisia, Libya, and Egypt indicate the significance of public sentiment in overcoming powerful authoritarian leaders who engage in corruption. The same events indicate that powerful leaders are not immune to pressure for reform. Leaders know that they cannot blatantly defy public opinion for long periods of time and expect to remain in power. Regardless of their true feelings, it would be difficult to refuse support if a compelling reform is posed as a public litmus test of their willingness to fight corruption.

CONCLUSION

Matthew Stephenson's and Alex Whiting's critiques of Judge Wolf's IACC raise important issues. The first issue is the apparent contradiction of asking heads of state who may themselves be corrupt to sign an agreement that would give an IACC the power to try and convict any citizen of a State Party to the agreement, including the heads of state. Why would a corrupt head of state ever agree to subject himself (or herself) to the jurisdiction of this type of anticorruption court?

The historical record reviewed above suggests that the answer involves a mixture of political expedience and hubris. When domestic and international actors frame the issue as a litmus test, that is, a test of whether a head of state truly supports strong anticorruption measures, it can be politically costly for a head of state to reject those measures. The historical record repeatedly demonstrates that heads of state choose to publicly sign and support anticorruption measures, regardless of their probity and personal ethics. They appear undeterred by the many instances where heads of state have been ensnared by the anticorruption measures they helped to install. Their hubris is the belief that they are above the law and will not be caught by the law. This hubris is reinforced by the blatant impunity that persists in one state after another. This hubris can infect any head of state. These individuals act as if they are above the law. They believe that they are above the law. They advocate tough laws. They sign tough laws. The act of signing tough laws is an act of bravado. It signals to the world that this person is a strong leader, a person who knows right from wrong, and a champion of safety and security.

There are enormous political benefits. Public safety and security are perennial issues. Political corruption is a perennial issue. Voters prefer the candidate who appears to be tough on crime. Voters hunger for candidates who campaign on a promise that they will "drain the swamp" of government corruption.

The significance of the historical record reviewed above is that it challenges the assertion that states characterized by high-level corruption cannot be induced to adopt strong measures to fight corruption. Falsification of this type of assertion involves the presentation of counterexamples that disprove the assertion. The historical record reviewed above involves counterexamples from America, Romania, the UK, Rome, Guatemala, Honduras, and Ukraine;

involves all 123 nations that signed and ratified the Rome Statute; and involves all states that previously experienced endemic corruption, including England, European states, and America, but now exhibit strong prosecutors and independent courts. These nations represent a majority of the 193 UN Member States, include the OECD Member States, and include nations such as Romania, Guatemala, Honduras, and Ukraine, where high-level corruption appears to be endemic. The number of nations (123) that implemented the Rome Statute establishing an independent prosecutor and the independent ICC—including nations characterized by endemic corruption—strongly suggests that it is feasible to establish independent prosecutors and independent courts across a range of jurisdictions, in nations characterized by high levels of corruption, and despite the existence of corrupt actors who seek to thwart the implementation of strong measures, independent prosecutors, and independent courts. CICIG was effective in addressing corruption at the highest levels of government despite mafia-like control of the Office of the President, the Office of the Vice President, and key government departments. This challenges the notion that endemic corruption would prevent the implementation of strong measures to fight corruption.

Stephenson's assertion that states characterized by high-level corruption cannot be induced to adopt strong measures to fight corruption is contradicted by the historical record in one state after another. Strong prosecutors and independent courts were installed despite endemic corruption, in the presence of endemic corruption, and in the presence of corrupt actors who sought to forestall strong measures to fight corruption.

The issue is not whether it is possible to establish strong prosecutors and independent courts in states characterized by endemic corruption, but how the international community can accelerate the process. The historical record suggests that a sufficient condition is strong international and domestic pressure for reform. Pressure may be exerted by public outrage regarding corruption; transparency regarding acts of corruption; media exposure of corruption; a public litmus test in the form of an international convention or a domestic legislative bill; desire to maintain concessions regarding aid, trade, or debt relief; political expediency; or calculations that the political cost of failure to support strong measures outweighs any concern that strong measures might ultimately be used against the leaders who sign and support those measures.

When political leaders sign strong measures, they calculate that the immediate political benefits outweigh what may seem to be the remote possibility that those reforms could lead to investigations and convictions of the same leaders. "Hubris" is an appropriate characterization of this phenomenon. However, neither APUNCAC nor Wolf's proposal for an IACC rely on the existence of hubris. It is sufficient to say that all political leaders calculate the political benefits of supporting strong measures against the possibility that those leaders might be ensnared by those measures. Political leaders are realists. Their actions are calculated to maximize their current and future political careers. When they sign strong measures to fight corruption, they calculate that the political benefits exceed the potential cost, in terms of the possibility that the measures could be used against them.

The significance of the APUNCAC and IACC proposals is that they create public litmus tests that cannot be easily ignored by political leaders, regardless of their personal ethics, probity, and preferences. A political leader might prefer to engage in conduct that is unfettered by strong prosecutors and independent courts, but when a public litmus test demands a public answer, and when the answer determines the outcome of a public referendum regarding the career of that political leader, that leader may calculate that his or her political future is best served by signing agreements and publicly supporting the installation of strong prosecutors and independent courts.

Alex Whiting raises a second issue. He correctly notes that Judge Wolf's IACC assumes the existence of a body of independent investigators armed with strong investigative powers. In the absence of this body of investigators, the IACC would have no means of collecting evidence and preparing cases.

APUNCAC would, on the other hand, create a body of experienced, independent investigators supported by the UN, endow the investigators with strong investigative powers, endow the investigators with all of the tools available to domestic prosecutors, and enable the investigators to hand cases to dedicated anticorruption courts staffed by prosecutors and judges vetted by the UN Commission on Crime Prevention and Criminal Justice. APUNCAC would install a mechanism to ensure the accountability of prosecutors and judges serving the dedicated anticorruption courts.

The creation of independent investigators endowed with strong investigative powers and the capacity to refer corrupt elements of domestic judicial and law enforcement systems to robust anticorruption courts would serve to punish corrupt individuals, restore the capacity of competent individuals to advance through the ranks of government and, over time, restore the type of clean, efficient government that promotes and facilitates the efforts of independent investigators and courts. UN inspectors may initially be hindered to the extent that domestic law enforcement is corrupt and ineffective, but inspectors would, over time, root out corrupt individuals, restore clean government, and reap the benefits of clean government. This process would take time, but the formula has been effective in all jurisdictions previously characterized by high levels of corruption, including America, the UK, Europe, Hong Kong, and Singapore.

It would make sense to combine IACC + APUNCAC into a single unified proposal. APUNCAC would create independent investigators endowed with strong investigative powers and the capacity to refer cases to dedicated domestic anticorruption courts, with strong measures to protect the integrity of those courts. Primary reliance on this type of protected, domestic court would reduce the concern that the IACC is an international court that violates domestic sovereignty and is a one-size-fits-all solution. The role of the IACC would, instead, be reserved for cases where corrupt elites undermine the APUNCAC courts and cause them to be unable or unwilling to prosecute egregious cases of corruption.

The proposal to combine IACC + APUNCAC means that Judge Wolf's coercive measures designed to compel participation could be dropped. APUNCAC contains innovative, aggressive measures to fight money laundering and terrorist financing that would plug a major gap in the international sanction regime against terrorist financing. The provisions would be highly attractive to the United States, the UK, the OECD Member States, and reform-oriented elements in each potential State Party. The substantial benefits of ratifying IACC + APUNCAC could be emphasized to incentivize ratification.

While American leaders have previously displayed reluctance to sign any type of international agreement that could subject them to investigation and prosecution, rejection of an international convention that would fight corruption and implement aggressive measures to fight money laundering and terrorist financing would be contrary to American interests, inconsistent with stated goals, and difficult to explain to American citizens. In any case, the Rome Statute was rejected by the United States but adopted by 123 other UN Member States. The United States might choose the same route regarding IACC + APUNCAC, but the other 186 parties to UNCAC may decide that aggressive measures are needed to fight corruption.

The combination of IACC + APUNCAC would eliminate the coercive aspects of Judge Wolf's proposal for an IACC, add attractive benefits, and address major concerns. It would make sense to combine the two proposals and push them forward as a package.

Conclusion

This book has argued that previous failure to adequately address poverty, underdevelopment, and basic human rights may be addressed through implementation of a powerful international institution designed to restore accountability in dysfunctional domestic criminal justice systems. By addressing a significant constraint on development, this strategy offers a promising approach that could be adopted by the international community.

This book suggests that the Rome Statute and the bilateral treaty establishing Guatemala's CICIG are strong precedents for the type of international treaty that I have proposed—a treaty that would establish the same type of powerful investigative capacity that is effective in all modern democracies in fighting corruption, addressing impunity, and ensuring effective domestic public justice systems. This offers a promising solution for seemingly insoluble problems—corruption, poverty, underdevelopment, and human rights. What is needed is an accurate understanding of the availability of an option that has not previously been considered, and the will to pursue it.

A barrier to the proposed treaty is the canard that one-size-fits-all strategies seldom work. Critics argue that tailored, homegrown solutions are needed. They argue that international treaties are blunt instruments, and the devil is in the details. However, no matter what strategy is pursued regarding corruption, poverty, underdevelopment, and human rights, there is widespread agreement that unchecked corruption and impunity undermine those strategies. Corruption and impunity undermine everything. The first order of business must be to identify the source of unchecked corruption and impunity and craft an institution that targets the source.

This book has identified the source as corruption, by powerful domestic elites, of the governmental institutions that normally fight corruption and impunity—the police, judiciary, and law enforcement system. Logically, there is a need to implement a solution that restores the capacity of those institutions. The proposed treaty would accomplish this by ensuring that no corrupt police officer, judge, prosecutor, or anticorruption official could commit corrupt acts without fear of investigation and exposure by skilled, independent investigators. The rationale for APUNCAC involves recognition that the international community must establish this deterrent wherever corrupt forces overwhelm domestic capacity to fight corruption.

The canard that APUNCAC violates domestic sovereignty overlooks the fact that international treaties are, by definition, voluntary agreements. In states where citizens believe that the costs of the proposed treaty outweigh potential benefits, they will reject it. If citizens believe that the proposed treaty would interfere with well-functioning domestic justice and governance structures, they will reject it. If citizens believe that the proposed treaty is a one-size-fits-all strategy that will not work, and believe instead that tailored, homegrown solutions are better, they will reject it. No one can force a treaty on citizens who do not want it.

While the proposed treaty may seem utopian, it is useful to recall that until its signature by 111 nations in 1998, the Rome Statute establishing the ICC was also a utopian idea. The ICC is now a firmly established reality. It poses a clear threat to any individual who contemplates genocide, war crimes, or crimes against humanity. The process that led to the establishment of the Rome Statute offers a model for pursuing the proposed anticorruption treaty. A coalition of 2,500 NGOs built support for the Statute in each of the 111 nations that signed the treaty in Rome.

A potential concern is that APUNCAC involves 200 pages of detailed provisions. It is more detailed than any previous international convention. The detailed provisions may exacerbate the difficulty of obtaining agreement among UN Member States. Ultimately, the issue is whether APUNCAC's language is feasible, practical, and sensible.

Much of this book has been devoted to this topic. The detailed provisions, and the analysis offered in this book, seek to demonstrate that it is indeed feasible, practical, and sensible to implement APUNCAC. Much of the language draws upon existing model laws and regulations. APUNCAC offers a model for the implementing legislation that would be necessary upon ratification of the convention. The detailed language explains precisely what would be required by each actor. This level of detail arguably paves the way for acceptance and ratification, to the extent that it dispels uncertainty and lack of clarity that might otherwise contribute to dissension.

All international conventions require significant effort to iron out disagreements. But the effort that is required should not distract attention from the need for aggressive action by the international community. Every reader of this book has an opportunity to make a difference by organizing his or her colleagues, friends, and acquaintances into a small coalition seeking to educate others about APUNCAC and build support for the protocol across the coalition for the ICC. Interested readers may contact the coalition at communications@coalitionfortheicc.org. The founder of the coalition is William R. Pace, executive director of the World Federalist Movement-Institute for Global Policy and cofounder of the International Coalition for the Responsibility to Protect. He has been engaged in international justice, rule of law, and human rights for the past 30 years. He previously served as the secretary-general of the Hague Appeal for Peace and the director of the Center for the Development of International Law. Pace has authored numerous articles and reports on international justice, international affairs, UN issues, multilateral treaty processes, and civil society participation in international decision-making.

The responsibility to protect the most vulnerable people in the world begins with those who possess the luxuries of advanced education, knowledge about what works, and physical and financial security. This book seeks to place knowledge about a promising approach into your hands so that you may act. Begin the process by speaking to one person. Write one letter. Share your thoughts and ideas. Be proactive, have faith that your actions matter, and join the effort to restore the rule of law, human rights, and justice wherever corruption and impunity prevail.

List of Acronyms

ACUS	Administrative Conference of the United States
AFI	Federal Investigation Agency (Mexico)
AJ	Administrative Judge
AJR	Acemoglu, Johnson, and Robinson
ALJ	Administrative Law Judge
AML	Anti-Money Laundering
APA	Administrative Procedure Act
APC	All Peoples Congress
APRM	African Peer Review Mechanism
APUNCAC	Anticorruption Protocol to the United Nations Convention against Corruption
ATM	Automated Teller Machine
AU	African Union
AUCPCC	African Union Convention on Preventing and Combating Corruption
BCLC	British Columbia Lottery Corporation
BEPS	Base Erosion and Profit-Shifting
BSA	Bank Secrecy Act
BVI	British Virgin Islands
CEO	Chief Executive Officer
CFR	Code of Federal Regulations (United States)
CICIG	Commission against Impunity in Guatemala
CLALS	Center for Latin American and Latino Studies
CPI	Corruption Perceptions Index
CSO	Civil Society Organization
DEA	Drug Enforcement Agency (United States)
DFS	Federal Security Directorate (Mexico)

DG	Director General
DPP	Directorate of Public Prosecutions (Uganda)
EFCC	Economic and Financial Crimes Commission (Nigeria)
EU	European Union
FATCA	Foreign Account Tax Compliance Act
FATF	Financial Action Task Force
FBI	Federal Bureau of Investigation (United States)
FCA	False Claims Act
FFI	Foreign Financial Institution
FinCEN	U.S. Treasury Department Financial Crimes Enforcement Network
FINCEN	Financial Crimes Enforcement Network established by APUNCAC
FIU	Financial Intelligence Unit
FSA	Financial Supervisory Authority
FSRB	FATF-Style Regional Body
G7	Group of 7
G8	Group of 8
GDP	Gross Domestic Product
HIV	Human Immunodeficiency Virus
IACC	International Anti-Corruption Court
ICAC	International Commission Against Corruption
ICC	International Criminal Court
ICCPR	International Covenant on Civil and Political Rights
ICPC	Independent Corrupt Practices Commission (Nigeria)
ICRC	International Committee of the Red Cross
IGG	Office of Inspector General of Government (Uganda)
III	Integrity Initiatives International
IJM	International Justice Mission
IMF	International Monetary Fund
INTERPOL	International Criminal Police Organization
IRS	Internal Revenue Service (United States)
KYC	Know Your Customer
LR	Liberty Reserve Virtual Currency
MCC	Millennium Challenge Corporation
MACCIH	Mission to Support the Fight against Corruption and Impunity in Honduras
MSB	Money Services Business
NAS	Native Authority Scheme
NDMC	National Diamond Mining Company
NGO	Nongovernmental Organization
NJC	National Judicial Council (Nigeria)

OCCRP	Organized Crime and Corruption Reporting Project
OECD	Organisation for Economic Co-operation and Development
OFAC	Office of Foreign Assets Control
OPM	Office of Personnel Management
PCA	Prevention of Corruption Act
PCB	Prevention of Corruption Bureau (Tanzania)
PCCB	Prevention and Combating of Corruption Bureau (Tanzania)
PCI	Permanent Commission of Inquiry (Tanzania)
PGR	Office of the Attorney General of Mexico
PJF	Federal Judicial Police (Mexico)
PRI	Institutional Revolutionary Party
RCMP	Royal Canadian Mounted Police
RICO	Racketeer Influenced and Corrupt Organizations Act
RSA	Rivest–Shamir–Adleman
RUSI	Royal United Services Institute
SAR	Suspicious Activity Report
SD	Standard Deviation
SDN	Specially Designated Nationals and Blocked Persons
SDNY	Southern District of New York
SDR	Special Drawing Rights
SIEDO	Office for Special Investigations on Organized Crime
SLPP	Sierra Leone People's Party
SLST	Sierra Leone Selection Trust
TCSP	Trust or Company Service Provider
UK	United Kingdom
UN	United Nations
UNCAC	United Nations Convention against Corruption
UNTOC	United Nations Convention against Transnational Organized Crime
UNTS	United Nations Treaty Series
U.S.	United States
USA	United States of America
USD	United States Dollar
USDOJ	United States Department of Justice
VASP	Virtual Asset Service Provider
WTO	World Trade Organization

Notes

INTRODUCTION

1. Gary A. Haugen and Victor Boutros, *The Locust Effect: Why the End of Poverty Requires the End of Violence* (New York: Oxford University Press, 2014), 156.
2. Anticorruption Protocol to the United Nations Convention against Corruption [hereinafter APUNCAC], art. 10, para. 7, http://tinyurl.com/y6bkpott.
3. APUNCAC, art. 10, para. 1.
4. APUNCAC, art. 10, para. 1.
5. APUNCAC, art. 10, para. 1.

CHAPTER 1

1. Haugen and Boutros, *The Locust Effect: Why the End of Poverty Requires the End of Violence*, xi.
2. Ibid., xvi.
3. Ibid., xiii.
4. Ibid.
5. Ibid.
6. Ibid., xiv.
7. Ibid.
8. Ibid.
9. Ibid., 43.
10. Ibid.
11. Deepa Narayan et al., *Voices of the Poor: Crying Out for Change* (New York: Oxford University Press, 2000); Deepa Narayan et al., *Voices of the Poor: Can Anyone Hear Us?* (New York: Oxford University Press, 2000).

12. Haugen and Boutros, *The Locust Effect: Why the End of Poverty Requires the End of Violence*, 74.

13. Ibid., 75.

14. Ibid., 81.

15. Ibid., 82.

16. Ibid.

17. Ibid., 83.

18. Ibid., 87.

19. Open Society Foundations, "Criminal Force: Torture, Abuse, and Extrajudicial Killings by the Nigeria Police Force," 2010, https://www.refworld.org/docid/4cbc44742.html; ibid.

20. Open Society Foundations, "The Socioeconomic Impact of Pretrial Detention: A Global Campaign for Pretrial Justice Report," February, 2010, https://www.justiceinitiative.org/publications/socioeconomic-impact-pretrial-detention.

21. Alfred de Zayas, "Human Rights and Indefinite Detention," *International Review of the Red Cross* 87, no. 857 (2005).

22. Haugen and Boutros, *The Locust Effect: Why the End of Poverty Requires the End of Violence*, 92–93.

23. Open Society Foundations, *Pretrial Detention and Torture: Why Pretrial Detainees Face the Greatest Risk* (New York: Open Society Initiative, 2011), 30.

24. Haugen and Boutros, *The Locust Effect: Why the End of Poverty Requires the End of Violence*, 94.

25. de Zayas, "Human Rights and Indefinite Detention."

26. Open Society Foundations, "Pretrial Detention and Torture: Why Pretrial Detainees Face the Greatest Risk," 17.

27. United Nations, "Interim Report of the Special Rapporteur on Torture and Other Cruel, Inhuman or Degrading Treatment or Punishment," United Nations, 2009, accessed July 18, 2017, http://antitorture.org/wp-content/uploads/2012/07/V-Thematic-Report-Conditions-of-Detention-Children-in-Detention.pdf.

28. Haugen and Boutros, *The Locust Effect: Why the End of Poverty Requires the End of Violence*, 87.

29. Ibid., 83.

30. Ibid., 94–95.

31. Charles Kenny, *Getting Better: Why Global Development Is Succeeding—And How We Can Improve the World Even More* (New York: Basic Books, 2011), 170.

32. Haugen and Boutros, *The Locust Effect: Why the End of Poverty Requires the End of Violence*, 135.

33. Ibid.

34. Ibid.

35. Ibid., 145.

36. Ibid.

37. Ibid.

38. Ibid., 147.

39. Universal Declaration of Human Rights, G.A. Res. 217A, U.N. GAOR, 3rd Sess., 183rd plen. mtg., U.N. Doc. A/810 (December 10, 1948).

40. Ibid., art. 8.

41. International Covenant on Civil and Political Rights, G.A. Res. 2200A, U.N. GAOR, 21st Sess., 1496th plen. mtg. (December 16, 1966).

42. Haugen and Boutros, *The Locust Effect: Why the End of Poverty Requires the End of Violence* (New York: Oxford University Press, 2014), 168–9.

43. Ibid., 169.

44. Ibid.

45. Ibid., 170.

46. Ibid.

47. Ibid.

48. Ibid., 181.

49. Ibid., 180.

50. Ibid., 196.

51. Samuel Walker and Charles Katz, *The Police in America: An Introduction* (New York: McGraw-Hill, 2007), 40.

52. Haugen and Boutros, *The Locust Effect: Why the End of Poverty Requires the End of Violence* (New York: Oxford University Press, 2014), 221

53. The Group of Seven (G7) is an international intergovernmental economic organization consisting of seven major developed countries: Canada, France, Germany, Italy, Japan, UK, and the United States, which are among the largest and most advanced economies in the world.

54. Haugen and Boutros, *The Locust Effect: Why the End of Poverty Requires the End of Violence*, 238.

55. Ibid., 238–9.

56. Walker and Katz, *The Police in America: An Introduction*, 135.

57. Haugen and Boutros, *The Locust Effect: Why the End of Poverty Requires the End of Violence*, 243.

58. Ibid., 244.

59. Ibid.

60. Ibid., 250.

61. Ibid.

62. Ibid., 262.

63. Transparency International, "Corruption Perceptions Index 2003," 2003, accessed July 19, 2017, https://www.transparency.org/research/cpi/cpi_2003/0/#results.

64. Haugen and Boutros, *The Locust Effect: Why the End of Poverty Requires the End of Violence*, 263.

65. World Bank, *Fighting Corruption in Public Services: Chronicling Georgia's Reforms* (Washington, DC: The World Bank, 2012), 1.

66. Ibid., 21.

67. Ibid., 7.

68. Ibid., 21.

69. Haugen and Boutros, *The Locust Effect: Why the End of Poverty Requires the End of Violence*, 265.

70. Ibid., 266.

CHAPTER 2

1. Paolo Mauro, "Corruption and Growth," *The Quarterly Journal of Economics* 110, no. 3 (1995); Fabio Méndez and Facundo Sepúlveda, "Corruption, Growth and Political Regimes: Cross Country Evidence," *European Journal of Political Economy* 22, no. 1 (2006); Pierre-Guillaume Méon and Khalid Sekkat, "Does Corruption Grease or Sand the Wheels of Growth?" *Public Choice* 122, no. 1–2 (2005); Pak Hung Mo, "Corruption and Economic Growth," *Journal of Comparative Economics* 29, no. 1 (2001); Lorenzo Pelligrini and Reyer Gerlagh, "Corruption's Effect on Growth and Its Transmission Channels," *KYKLOS* 57, no. 3 (2004); Kwabena Gyimah-Brepong, "Corruption, Economic Growth, and Income Inequality in Africa," *Economics of Governance* 3, no. 3 (2002); Mushfiq us Swaleheen and Dean Stansel, "Economic Freedom, Corruption, and Growth," *Cato Journal* 27, no. 3 (2007).

2. The United Nations Conference on Trade and Development Secretariat, *The Least Developed Countries 2000 Report: Aid, Private Capital Flows and External Debt: The Challenge of Financing Development in the LDCs* (New York: United Nations, 2000), 102.

3. Ibid.

4. Mahmood Mamdani, *Citizen and Subject: Contemporary Africa and the Legacy of Late Colonialism* (Princeton, NJ: Princeton University Press, 1996); G.B.N. Ayittey, *Africa Unchained: The Blueprint for Africa's Future* (New York: Palgrave Macmillan, 2005); John M. Mbaku, "Bureaucratic and Political Corruption in Africa," in *Corruption and the Crisis of Institutional Reforms in Africa: African Studies Vol 47*, ed. John M. Mbaku (Lewiston, NY: Edwin Mellon Press, 1998); John M. Mbaku, "Corruption and the Crisis of Institutional Reforms in Africa," in *Corruption and the Crisis of Institutional Reforms in Africa: African Studies Vol 47*, ed. John M. Mbaku (Lewiston, NY: Edwin Mellon Press, 1998); Mbaku, "Bureaucratic Corruption in Africa"; George B.N. Ayittey, "The African Development Conundrum," in *Making Poor Nations Rich: Entrepreneurship and the Process of Economic Development*, ed. Benjamin Powell (Stanford, CA: Stanford University Press, 2008).

5. Mbaku, "Corruption and the Crisis of Institutional Reforms in Africa"; Ayittey, *Africa Unchained*; Mamdani, *Citizen and Subject: Contemporary Africa and the Legacy of Late Colonialism.*

6. Ayittey, *Africa Unchained.*

7. Mamdani, *Citizen and Subject: Contemporary Africa and the Legacy of Late Colonialism.*

8. Mbaku, "Corruption and the Crisis of Institutional Reforms in Africa"; Mbaku, "Bureaucratic and Political Corruption in Africa"; Ayittey, *Africa Unchained.*

9. Ayittey, *Africa Unchained*; Mbaku, "Bureaucratic Corruption in Africa."

10. Ayittey, "The African Development Conundrum."

11. Ayittey, *Africa Unchained*, 48.

12. Mbaku, "Bureaucratic and Political Corruption in Africa"; Ayittey, "The African Development Conundrum."

13. Ayittey, "The African Development Conundrum."

14. Mbaku, "Bureaucratic and Political Corruption in Africa"; Ayittey, "The African Development Conundrum."

15. Ayittey, *Africa Unchained.*

16. Ayittey, "The African Development Conundrum."

17. Mbaku, "Corruption and the Crisis of Institutional Reforms in Africa."

18. Kempe R. Hope Sr., *From Crisis to Renewal: Development Policy and Management in Africa* (Leiden, Netherlands: Brill, 2002), 102.

19. Ibid., 109.

20. Ibid., 127.

21. Jean-Pierre Olivier de Sardan, "A Moral Economy of Corruption in Africa," *Journal of Modern African Studies* 37, no. 1 (1999): 28.

22. Hope Sr., *From Crisis to Renewal*, 100.

23. Nicolas van de Walle, *African Economies and the Politics of Permanent Crisis, 1979–1999* (Cambridge: Cambridge University Press, 2001).

24. Hope Sr., *From Crisis to Renewal*, 12.

25. R. J. Barro, "Democracy and the Rule of Law," in *Governing for Prosperity*, ed. Bruce Bueno de Mesquita and Hilton L. Root (New Haven, CT: Yale University Press, 2000), 230.

26. van de Walle, *African Economies and the Politics of Permanent Crisis.*

27. Shahrzad Sedigh and Augustine Ruzindana, "The Fight against Corruption in Uganda," in *Curbing Corruption: Toward a Model for Building National Integrity*, ed. Rick Stapenhurst and Sahr J. Kpundeh (Washington, DC: The World Bank, 1999).

28. Ibid.

29. Ibid.

30. Shahrzad Sedigh and Alex Muganda, "The Fight against Corruption in Tanzania," in *Curbing Corruption: Toward a Model for Building National Integrity*, ed. Rick Stapenhurst and Sahr J. Kpundeh (Washington, DC: The World Bank, 1999); Transparency International, "Corruption Perceptions Index—Tanzania," 2020, https://www.transparency.org/en/countries/tanzania.

31. Sedigh and Muganda, "The Fight against Corruption in Tanzania."

32. AfriMAP, *Effectiveness of Anti-Corruption Agencies in East Africa: Kenya, Tanzania and Uganda* (New York: African Minds, 2015), 49.

33. Anti-Corruption Authorities, "Tanzania," 2020, https://www.acauthorities.org/country/tz.

34. AfriMAP, *Effectiveness of Anti-Corruption Agencies in East Africa: Kenya, Tanzania and Uganda*, 49.

35. Ibid.

36. Bertrand de Speville, *Hong Kong: Policy Initiatives against Corruption* (Paris: Development Centre of the OECD, 1997), 12.

37. Melanie Manion, *Corruption by Design: Building Clean Government in Mainland China and Hong Kong* (Cambridge, MA: Harvard University Press, 2004).

38. Beatrice Weder and Aymo Brunetti, "Another Tale of Two Cities: A Note on Institutions in Hong Kong and Singapore," *Journal of Institutional and Theoretical Economics-Zeitschrift Fur Die Gesamte Staatswissenschaft* 156, no. 2 (2000).

39. Nicolaas Groenewold and Sam Hak Kan Tang, "Killing the Goose That Lays the Golden Egg: Institutional Change and Economic Growth in Hong Kong," *Economic Inquiry* 45, no. 4 (2007).

40. Weder and Brunetti, "Another Tale of Two Cities: A Note on Institutions in Hong Kong and Singapore."

41. Bertrand E.D. de Speville, "The Experience of Hong Kong, China, in Combating Corruption," in *Curbing Corruption: Toward a Model for Building National Integrity*, ed. Rick Stapenhurst and Sahr J. Kpundeh (Washington, DC: The World Bank, 1999).

42. Effective July 18, 2016, Acting Chief of Operations Rebecca Li was removed from her position. Li was in the middle of an investigation into Hong Kong's top official, Chief Executive Leung Chun-ying, who was accused in 2014 of possessing over $6 million in undeclared assets from an Australian firm. Li's removal triggered a revolt by commission staff who believed that the action was politically motivated and undermined the commission's independence. This episode underlines the need to insulate anticorruption investigators, including Hong Kong's Independent Commission Against Corruption, from manipulation. See Rishi Iyengar, "Hong Kong's Anti-Graft Agency Is in Turmoil, Prompting Fears for the City's Transparency," *Time*, July 14, 2016, https://time.com/4405736/hong-kong-icac-corruption-china-transparency/; Niall Fraser, "First Woman to Lead ICAC's Operations Department Is Replaced in Major Shake-up at Hong Kong's Anti-Corruption Body," *South China Morning Post*, July 8, 2016, https://www.scmp.com/news/hong-kong/law-crime/article/1986862/first-woman-lead-icacs-operations-department-replaced-major.

43. Ladipo Adamolekun, "Transferability of Governance Institutions: The Ombudsman and the Independent Commission against Corruption," in *Innovations in Governance and Public Administration: Replicating What Works*, ed. Adriana Alberti and Vilhelm Klareskov (New York: United Nations, 2006).

44. Ibid.

45. Oona A. Hathaway, "Between Power and Principle: An Integrated Theory of International Law," *The University of Chicago Law Review* 72, no. 2 (2005).

46. Kempe R. Hope Sr., "Toward Good Governance and Sustainable Development: The African Peer Review Mechanism," *Governance: An International Journal of Policy, Administration, and Institutions* 18, no. 2 (2005).

47. NEPAD Secretariat, *Declaration on Democracy, Political, Economic and Corporate Governance* (Midrand, South Africa: NEPAD Secretariat, 2003).

48. Ibid., 3–4.

49. Hope Sr., "Toward Good Governance and Sustainable Development."

50. Curt Tarnoff, "Millennium Challenge Corporation," *CRS Report* (Washington, DC: Congressional Research Service, 2017).

51. Rick Stapenhurst and Sahr J. Kpundeh, eds., *Curbing Corruption: Toward a Model for Building National Integrity* (Washington, DC: The World Bank, 1999).

52. Frederico S. Finan, "Political Patronage, Corruption, and Local Development" (Doctoral dissertation, University of California, 2006). The natural experiment involved a study in which mayors were assigned to the treatment (the anticorruption program) in a nonrandom manner.

53. Yunjong Wang and Deok Ryong Yoon, *Mechanisms of Regional Surveillance in East Asia and Its Prospects* (Tokyo: Institute for International Monetary Affairs-Kobe Research Project, 2002).

54. C. Randall Henning, "Peer Review" (paper presented at the Meeting of the Commission on Capital Flows to Africa, Washington, DC, February 21, 2003).

55. Henry J. Lethbridge, *Hard Graft in Hong Kong: Scandal, Corruption, the ICAC* (New York: Oxford University Press, 1985), 110; Jack Cater, *Annual Report by the Commissioner of the Independent Commission against Corruption* (Hong Kong: Independent Commission Against Corruption, 1975), 2.

56. APUNCAC, http://tinyurl.com/y6bkpott.

57. United Nations Convention against Corruption, *opened for signature* October 31, 2003, 2349 U.N.T.S. 41 (entered into force December 14, 2005) [hereinafter UNCAC], 166.

58. Paulina Vega Gonzalez and Carla Ferstman, *Ending Threats and Reprisals against Victims of Torture and Related International Crimes: A Call to Action* (London: Redress, 2009), 37–38.

59. See de Speville, "The Experience of Hong Kong, China, in Combating Corruption"; Manion, *Corruption by Design*; T.A. Leak, "The Experience of Singapore in Combating Corruption," in *Curbing Corruption: Toward a Model for Building National Integrity*, ed. R. Stapenhurst and S.J. Kpundeh (Washington, DC: The World Bank, 1999); Weder and Brunetti, "Another Tale of Two Cities: A Note on Institutions in Hong Kong and Singapore"; Lethbridge, *Hard Graft in Hong Kong: Scandal, Corruption, the ICAC*, 126.

60. Lincoln Steffens, *The Shame of the Cities* (Mineola, NY: Dover, 2004); Ari Hoogenboom, "Did Gilded Age Scandals Bring Reform?" in *Before Watergate: Problems of Corruption in American Society*, ed. Abraham S. Eisenstadt, Ari Hoogenboom, and Hans L. Trefousse, *Brooklyn College Studies on Society in Change* (Brooklyn, NY: Brooklyn College Press, 1979); Morton Keller, "Corruption in America: Continuity and Change," in *Before Watergate: Problems of Corruption in American Society*, ed. Abraham S. Eisenstadt, Ari Hoogenboom, and Hans L. Trefousse, *Brooklyn College Studies on Society in Change* (Brooklyn, NY: Brooklyn College Press, 1979); Nathan Miller, *Stealing from America: A History of Corruption from Jamestown to Reagan*, 2nd ed. (Saint Paul, MN: Paragon House, 1992); Linda Levy Peck, "The British Case: Corruption and Political Development in the Early Modern State," in *Before Watergate: Problems of Corruption in American Society*, ed. Abraham S. Eisenstadt, Ari Hoogenboom, and Hans L. Trefousse, *Brooklyn College Studies on Society in Change* (Brooklyn, NY: Brooklyn College Press, 1979).

61. Hoogenboom, "Did Gilded Age Scandals Bring Reform?"; Peck, "The British Case."

62. Michael J. Struett, *The Politics of Constructing the International Criminal Court* (New York: Palgrave Macmillan, 2008).

63. Ibid.

64. Ibid.

CHAPTER 3

1. United Nations Convention Against Corruption, *opened for signature* October 31, 2003, 2349 UNTS 41 (entered into force December 14, 2005) [hereinafter UNCAC].

2. United Nations Office on Drugs and Crime, "United Nations Convention against Corruption: Signature and Ratification Status as of February 6, 2020," accessed July 16, 2020, https://www.unodc.org/unodc/en/corruption/ratification-status.html.

3. Rome Statute of the International Criminal Court, *opened for signature* July 17, 1998, 2187 UNTS 90 (entered into force July 1, 2002) [hereinafter Rome Statute].

4. See Letitia Lawson, "The Politics of Anti-Corruption Reform in Africa," *Journal of Modern African Studies* 47, no. 1 (2009): 83–84.

5. See ibid., 85.

6. Ibid.

7. Ibid., 91.

8. Ibid.

9. Ibid., 90.

10. Ibid., 91.

11. Ibid., 87.

12. Ibid., 88.

13. "Fayose, Ibori Sent to Prison," *All Africa*, December 18, 2007, http://www.allafrica.com/stories/200712180033.html. Ibori was subsequently sentenced to 13 years in prison. BBC, "Former Nigeria Governor James Ibori Jailed for 13 Years," April 17, 2012, http://www.bbc.com/news/world-africa-17739388.

14. Abdullahi Yahaya Bello, "EFCC/ICPC/CCB: One Merger, Many Questions," *All Africa*, December 22, 2007, http://allafrica.com/stories/200712220006.html; Kingsley Omonobi and Emmanuel Ulayi, "EFCC: Okiro Confirms Ribadu's Exit," *All Africa*, December 27, 2007, http://allafrica.com/stories/200712280320.html.

15. Misbahu Bashir, "Nigeria: Ribadu Demoted—with 139 Others—Doubts over His NIPSS Course," *AllAfrica*, August 6, 2008, http://www.allafrica.com/stories/200808060176.html.

16. Human Rights Watch, "Nigeria: Firing of Anti-Corruption Chief Would Boost Abusive Politicians," January 1, 2008, http://hrw.org/english/docs/2008/01/01/nigeri17671_txt.htm.

17. See Agreement between the United Nations and the State of Guatemala on the Establishment of an International Commission against Impunity in Guatemala ("CICIG"), December 12, 2006, 2472 UNTS 47 [hereinafter CICIG]; Patrick Gavigan, "Organized Crime, Illicit Power Structures and Guatemala's Threatened Peace Process," *International Peacekeeping* 16, no. 1 (2009); CICIG, "Background," March 5, 2018, https://www.cicig.org/cicig/antecedentes/.

18. See CICIG, "Background."

19. Gavigan, "Organized Crime, Illicit Power Structures and Guatemala's Threatened Peace Process," 70.

20. Ibid.

21. Ibid.

22. Human Rights Watch, "Guatemala," January 2011, http://www.hrw.org/sites/default/files/related_material/guatemala_0.pdf; ibid.

23. See Andrew Hudson and Alexandra W. Taylor, "The International Commission against Impunity in Guatemala: A New Model for International Criminal Justice Mechanisms," *Journal of International Criminal Justice* 8, no. 1 (2010).

24. Ibid., 56.

25. Ibid., 57.

26. See Matthew Kennis, "The Creation of the International Commission against Impunity in Guatemala: Miscalculation by a 'Corporate Mafia State'?," Originally published in *Peace and Conflict Monitor*, June 29, 2012, accessed November 16, 2020, https://www.ideasforpeace.org/content/the-creation-of-the-international-commission-against-impunity-in-guatemala-miscalculation-by-a-corporate-mafia-state/.

27. See generally "CICIG Mandate and Agreement," March 5, 2018, https://www.cicig.org/cicig/mandato-y-acuerdo-cicig/. (Describing the main objectives of CICIG's mandate).

28. Ibid.

29. See CICIG, 50–51.

30. Ibid., 53.

31. Ibid., 54–55.

32. See ibid., 52–53.

33. See generally ibid., 50–56 (lacking specificity on potential penalties for failure to cooperate with the CICIG).

34. See Hudson and Taylor, 66–67. Rios Montt was found guilty and sentenced to 80 years in prison for genocide and crimes against humanity. Emi McLean, "Guatemala's Constitutional Court Overturns Rios Montt Conviction and Sends Trial Back to April 19," *International Justice Monitor*, May 21, 2013, http://www.ijmonitor.org/2013/05/constitutional-court-overturns-rios-montt-conviction-and-sends-trial-back-to-april-19/. The Constitutional Court overturned the decision, sending the trial back to the lower courts. Ibid. Portillo was "acquitted despite damning evidence against him" but later extradited to the United States "to face charges of money laundering, fraud, and embezzlement of public funds." James Bargent, "Last Rites for Guatemala's Anti-Impunity Crusaders CICIG?," *Insight Crime*, September 6, 2013, http://www.insightcrime.org/news-analysis/last-rites-for-guatemalas-anti-impunity-warriors. An initial two-year mandate was established by the agreement between the UN and the Government of Guatemala and was renewed in April 2009, January 2011, April 2015, and again in April 2016. After the commission opened an investigation into President Jimmy Morales, his brother, and son, he declined to renew CICIG's mandate, effectively ending the commission in September 2019 after 12 years of operation and over 400 convictions, and despite public opinion polls demonstrating that over 70 percent of Guatemalans support CICIG. See United Nations, "CICIG: International Commission against Impunity in Guatemala," accessed November 6, 2020, https://dppa.un.org/en/mission/cicig.

35. Hudson and Taylor, 65.

36. See Francisco Goldman, "From President to Prison: Otto Pérez Molina and a Day for Hope in Guatemala," *The New Yorker*, September 4, 2015.

37. Sandra Cuffe, "Thousands of Guatemalans Protest in Support of Anti-Corruption Commission," *Los Angeles Times*, January 14, 2019, https://www.latimes.com/world/la-fg-guatemala-protests-20190114-story.html; Goldman, "From President to Prison: Otto Pérez Molina and a Day for Hope in Guatemala"; Eddy Coronado, "Otto Pérez Molina Will Remain in Prison for the La Línea Case, Court Decides," November 28, 2019, https://www.prensalibre.com/guatemala/justicia/otto-perez-molina-pide-salir-de-prision-por-el-caso-la-linea/.

38. Sonia D. Perez, "Former Guatemala Vice President Sentenced in Corruption Case," AP, October 9, 2018, https://www.apnews.com/feda24dafebc44cc9e6a0330e5fcfc9a; BBC, "Guatemala Ex-VP Roxana Baldetti Jailed in 'Magic Water' Scandal," October 10, 2018, https://www.bbc.com/news/world-latin-america-45806524.

39. See ibid., 69.

40. Ibid.

41. Ibid.

42. See *Witness Protection: A Necessary Tool in Justice Administration*, CICIG (September 27, 2011), http://www.cicig.org/index.php?page=0046-20110927E.

43. Hudson and Taylor, 64.

44. Jeff Abbott, "Guatemala's CICIG: UN-Backed Anti-Corruption Body Shuts Its Doors," Al Jazeera, September 3, 2019, https://www.aljazeera.com/news/2019/09/guatemala-cicig-backed-anti-corruption-body-shuts-doors-190903132411201.html; Sandra Cuffe, "Guatemala's Anti-Corruption CICIG Body to Shut Down: What to Know," Al Jazeera, September 1, 2019, https://www.aljazeera.com/news/2019/08/guatemala-anti-corruption-cicig-body-shut-190830225625800.html.

45. See Stuart S. Yeh, "Why UN Inspections? The Accountability Gap in Sub-Saharan Africa," *International Public Policy Review* 7, no. 2 (2013): 19.

46. See Lawson, 88.

47. UN investigators would be more likely than domestic investigators to act vigorously. While Ribadu could have filed a complaint with Nigeria's PCC or the ICPC, it is unlikely that these agencies would have requested charges against the Attorney General because all prosecutions are handled by the Attorney General. See ibid., 81. In contrast, an independent UN investigation and report that referred charges to Nigeria's public prosecutor would force the prosecutor to either prosecute or risk public outrage over a clear failure to prosecute an egregious case of corruption and risk being forced to resign in the same way that the CICIG forced the resignations of public prosecutors in Guatemala for corruption or obstruction of justice, including Attorney General Juan Luis Florido, Senior Prosecutor Álvaro Matus, and Administrative Crimes Prosecutor Patricia Lainfiesta. See, for example, Hudson and Taylor, 69–70. The proposed international treaty contains provisions to ensure that the tactics employed by Aondoakaa could not be used in the future without risking prosecution for obstruction of justice. The proposed treaty defines the crime of obstruction of justice, defines a procedure whereby UN inspectors may request an opinion from a domestic court, and defines a process whereby reports of obstruction would be published online by Transparency

International in a way that would publicly identify individuals accused of obstructing justice and would expose these individuals to the court of public opinion.

48. See Hudson and Taylor, 69.

49. See Stuart S. Yeh, "Ending Corruption in Africa through United Nations Inspections," *International Affairs* 87, no. 3 (2011): 639; Stuart S. Yeh, "Is an International Treaty Needed to Fight Corruption and the Narco-Insurgency in Mexico?," *International Criminal Justice Review* 22, no. 3 (2012): 235, 242; Yeh, "Why UN Inspections? The Accountability Gap in Sub-Saharan Africa," 7; Stuart S. Yeh, "Why UN Inspections? Corruption, Accountability, and the Rule of Law," *South Carolina Journal of International Law and Business* 11, no. 2 (2015).

50. See Hudson and Taylor, 56–57.

51. See Lawson, 91.

52. See United Nations Office on Drugs and Crime, "United Nations Convention against Corruption Signature and Ratification Status as of February 6, 2020."

53. See Kolawole Olaniyan, *Introductory Note to African Union (AU): Convention on Combating and Preventing Corruption*, 43 I.L.M., 1 (2004). See also African Union Convention on Preventing and Combating Corruption, August 5, 2006, 43 I.L.M., 5 [hereinafter AUCPCC].

54. See CICIG, 55–57; AUCPCC, 5–6.

55. I am not suggesting that there are not differences between Nigeria and Guatemala. However, there is a striking similarity among all states where the rule of law is weak: they are characterized by high rates of violent deaths, glaring impunity, corruption, the inability of the state to handle crime, public outrage, and demands for reform. See Hudson and Taylor, 69; Chinedum Odenyi, "The Domestic Implementation of International Treaties in Nigeria," Nigerian Coalition for the International Criminal Court, July 23, 2014, http://ncicc.org.ng/2017/05/24/the-domestic-implementation-of-international-treaties-in-nigeria-by-chinedum-odenyi/. It is not unreasonable to think that independent investigators who offer a real hope for action would be welcomed in any state where these conditions exist.

56. See Rome Statute, 115–26.

57. Ibid.

58. See Rome Statute, 91.

59. See Rome Statute, 92.

60. See Odenyi, "The Domestic Implementation of International Treaties in Nigeria."

61. See Yeh, "Is an International Treaty Needed to Fight Corruption and the Narco-Insurgency in Mexico?," 246.

62. The States Parties to the Rome Statute, Int'l Criminal Court, https://asp.icc-cpi.int/en_menus/asp/states%20parties/Pages/the%20states%20parties%20to%20the%20rome%20statute.aspx (last visited October 10, 2019).

63. See United Nations, "United Nations Treaty Collection Treaty Reference Guide" (New York: United Nations, 1999).

64. See Stephen Brown and Chandra Lekha Sriram, "The Big Fish Won't Fry Themselves: Criminal Accountability for Post-Election Violence in Kenya," *African Affairs* 111, no. 443 (2012): 245.

65. Ibid., 257.

66. In 2007, Nigerian president Umaru Yar'Adua invited British police experts to "reinvent" Nigeria's police force. See Abegunde Babalola, "Power of Police to Prosecute Criminal Cases: Nigeria and International Perspectives," *European Journal of Business and Social Sciences* 2, no. 11 (2014): 138. Nigeria's inspector general of police, Mike Okiro, endorsed this invitation and expressed strong support: "The British police need to repackage, retrain and give the Nigerian policemen what it takes to combat crime in the modern world." Ibid., 138 (citations omitted).

67. See Yeh, "Why UN Inspections? The Accountability Gap in Sub-Saharan Africa," 4.

68. See ibid.

69. These countries include Afghanistan, Albania, Angola, Bangladesh, Benin, Bolivia, Burkina Faso, Burundi, Cameroon, Central African Republic, Chad, Colombia, Congo, Côte d'Ivoire, Democratic Republic of the Congo, Egypt, El Salvador, Eritrea, Gabon, Gambia, Ghana, Guatemala, Guinea, Guinea-Bissau, Guyana, Haiti, Honduras, Kenya, Lesotho, Liberia, Malawi, Mali, Mexico, Mozambique, Niger, Nigeria, Panama, Pakistan, Paraguay, Senegal, Sierra Leone, Sudan, Suriname, Syrian Arab Republic, Tajikistan, Timor-Leste, Uganda, Tanzania, Yemen, and Zambia. Transparency International, "Corruption Perceptions Index 2016," January 25, 2017, https://www.transparency.org/news/feature/corruption_perceptions_index_2016#table. See "The States Parties to the Rome Statute," Int'l Criminal Court.

70. Rome Statute, 103.

71. Beth A. Simmons and Allison Danner, "Credible Commitments and the International Criminal Court," *International Organization* 64, no. 2 (2010): 252. "[T]he least accountable governments—the least democratic, with the weakest reputations for respecting the rule of law, the least politically constrained—with a recent past of civil violence were at the highest 'risk' of ratifying the Rome Statute."

72. United Nations Office on Drugs and Crime, "United Nations Convention against Corruption Signature and Ratification Status as of February 6, 2020," https://www.unodc.org/unodc/en/corruption/ratification-status.html (last visited August 23, 2020).

73. African Union, "List of Countries Which Have Signed, Ratified/Acceded to the African Union Convention on Preventing and Combatting Corruption," June 7, 2020, https://docs.google.com/viewerng/viewer?url=http://www.auanticorruption.org/uploads/AFRICAN_UNION_CONVENTION_ON_PREVENTING_AND_COMBATING_CORRUPTION_UPDATED.pdf.

74. See Simmons and Danner, 239.

75. See Stuart S. Yeh, "Building a Global Institution to Fight Corruption and Address the Roots of Insurgency," *International Public Policy Review* 8, no. 1 (2014): 20.

76. The provisions of the proposed treaty are described in the author's previous publications. See Yeh, "Ending Corruption in Africa through United Nations Inspections," 640; Yeh, "Is an International Treaty Needed to Fight Corruption and the Narco-Insurgency in Mexico?," 245.

77. For more information regarding the role of national human rights institutions in monitoring compliance with international treaties, see generally Chris Sidoti, "National Human Rights Institutions and the International Human Rights System," in *Human Rights, State Compliance, and Social Change*, ed. Ryan Goodman and Thomas Pegram (New York: Cambridge University Press, 2012); and Richard Carver, "National Human Rights Institutions in Central and Eastern Europe," in *Human Rights, State Compliance, and Social Change*, ed. Ryan Goodman and Thomas Pegram (New York: Cambridge University Press, 2012).

78. Simmons and Danner, 247–48.

79. Ibid., 253.

80. See ibid., 227.

81. Senator Iroegbu, "Nigeria: EFCC Secures 603 Convictions in Three Years," *All Africa*, May 29, 2018, https://allafrica.com/stories/201805290530.html.

82. "EFCC Records 1,000 Convictions in 10 Years—Lamorde," *Premium Times*, December 9, 2013, http://www.premiumtimesng.com/news/151190-efcc-records-1000-convictions-10-years-lamorde.html. See Lawson, 91.

83. Sahara Reporters, "Breaking: Court Jails Jolly Nyame, Ex-Taraba Governor, for 14 Years over N1.64bn Fraud," May 30, 2018, http://saharareporters.com/2018/05/30/breaking-court-jails-jolly-nyame-ex-taraba-governor-14-years-over-n164bn-fraud.

84. Vanguard, "Nwobike, SAN, Sent to Jail for Perverting Course of Justice," April 30, 2018, https://www.vanguardngr.com/2018/04/nwobike-san-sent-jail-perverting-course-justice/.

85. "Situations Under Investigation," Int'l Crim. Ct., http://www.icc-cpi.int/en_menus/icc/situations%20and%20cases/Pages/situations%20and%20cases.aspx (last visited November 16, 2017).

86. *Prosecutor v. Thomas Lubanga Dyilo*, Case No. ICC-01/04-01/06, Crimes, ¶ 19 (March 14, 2012), http://www.icc-cpi.int/iccdocs/PIDS/publications/LubangaENG.pdf.

87. International Criminal Court, "Katanga Case: The Prosecutor v. Germain Katanga," accessed November 16, 2017, https://www.icc-cpi.int/drc/katanga.

88. International Criminal Court, "Ntaganda Case: The Prosecutor v. Bosco Ntaganda," accessed August 4, 2019, https://www.icc-cpi.int/drc/ntaganda.

89. International Criminal Court, "Al Bashir Case: The Prosecutor v. Omar Hassan Ahmad Al Bashir," accessed November 20, 2017, https://www.icc-cpi.int/darfur/albashir.

90. Tamerra Griffin, "Sudanese President Omar Al-Bashir Has Been Arrested," April 11, 2019, https://www.buzzfeednews.com/article/tamerragriffin/sudan-president-omar-al-bashir-removed-military.

91. Sudarsan Raghavan, "Former Sudanese Ruler Omar Hassan Al-Bashir Is Convicted of Corruption, Money Laundering," *Washington Post*, December 14, 2019, https://www.washingtonpost.com/world/africa/former-sudanese-ruler-omar-al-bashir-convicted-of-corruption-money-laundering/2019/12/14/90ddc7ee-1e71-11ea-9ddd-3e0321c180e7_story.html.

92. BBC, "Omar al-Bashir: Sudan Agrees Ex-President Must Face ICC," February 11, 2020, https://www.bbc.com/news/world-africa-51462613.

93. Criminal Code Act (1990) Cap. (4), § 126 (Nigeria), available at http://www.nigeria-law.org/Criminal%20Code%20Act-PartIII-IV.htm#Chapter.

94. UNCAC, 155.

95. Government of Nigeria, "Nigeria Police Code of Conduct," Government of Nigeria, accessed November 20, 2017, http://eie.ng/wp-content/uploads/2014/02/NIGERIAPOLICECODEOFCONDUCT.pdf.

96. Ibid.

97. While certain judges might be corrupt and might refuse to issue an arrest warrant, UN inspectors could consult local staff, such as EFCC staff, who are knowledgeable about local judges, have successfully obtained arrest warrants from competent judges, and can readily identify competent judges.

98. Ibid.

99. UNCAC, 155.

100. Hudson and Taylor, 69.

101. Sahara Reporters, "Nigeria's National Judicial Council Forces 2 Judges into Compulsory Retirement, Reprimands 3 Others," February 27, 2014, http://saharareporters.com/2014/02/27/nigerias-national-judicial-council-forces-2-judges-compulsory-retirement-reprimands-3. See Mohammed Shosanya and John Chuks Azu, "Lawyers Call for Prosecution of Corrupt Judges," *Daily Trust*, March 4, 2014, https://tinyurl.com/y5q63x44.

102. Constitution of the Federal Republic of Nigeria (1999), Third Schedule, Part I, § 20(a)–(j), available at http://www.nigeria-law.org/ConstitutionOfTheFederalRepublicOfNigeria.htm#FederalExecutiveBodies.

103. National Judicial Council of Nigeria, "Profile of NJC." http://www.njcgov.org/aboutus/aboutusprofile.

104. Ibid.

105. R. E. Badejogbin and M. E. Onoriode, "Judicial Accountability and Discipline in Nigeria: Imperatives for the New Democratic Order." https://tinyurl.com/yy9nkcye. "Any aggrieved person may lodge a complaint against any judge either to the chairperson (who is the Chief Justice of Nigeria) or Secretary of the Council." Ibid. The Chief Justice issues a query and copy of the complaint to the subject of the complaint. Ibid. The subject "must respond within two weeks." Ibid. "The Council then sits to determine whether there is a prima facie case against the" subject. Ibid. "[I]f no prima facie case is established, the complaint is thrown out, otherwise a panel is [arranged] to hear the matter." Ibid. Subjects "are free to [obtain] legal representation." Ibid. The panel's decision "is presented to the Council for confirmation." Ibid. "If the [subject] is found guilty, the Council may" write a letter of admonishment, recommend compulsory retirement, "or recommend dismissal to the President or [State] Governor" of Nigeria. Ibid. "[T]he Council may indefinitely suspend the [subject] without salary" "pending the response of the President or Governor." Ibid.

106. Sahara Reporters, "Nigeria's National Judicial Council"; Shosanya and Azu, "Lawyers Call for Prosecution of Corrupt Judges."

107. Sahara Reporters, "Nigeria's National Judicial Council"; Shosanya and Azu, "Lawyers Call for Prosecution of Corrupt Judges."

108. Sahara Reporters, "Nigeria's National Judicial Council"; Shosanya and Azu, "Lawyers Call for Prosecution of Corrupt Judges."

109. See Sahara Reporters, "Nigeria's National Judicial Council."

110. Ibid.; Shosanya and Azu, "Lawyers Call for Prosecution of Corrupt Judges."

111. Sahara Reporters, "Nigeria's National Judicial Council"; Shosanya and Azu, "Lawyers Call for Prosecution of Corrupt Judges."

112. Shosanya and Azu, "Lawyers Call for Prosecution of Corrupt Judges."

113. Ibid.

114. Ibid.

115. Ibid.

116. See generally ibid. (showing results from investigations and referral to a disciplinary body).

117. Internet World Stats, "Internet Penetration in Africa: 2020—Q1—March," March 21, 2020, http://www.internetworldstats.com/stats1.htm.

118. Bruce Mutsvairo, Simon Columbus, and Iris Leijendekker, "Reconnoitering the Role of (Citizen) Journalism Ethics in the Emerging Networked Public Sphere," *African Journalism Studies* 35, no. 3 (2014): 4.

119. Mary Omogor Ifukor, "Channels of Information Acquisition and Dissemination among Rural Dwellers," *International Journal of Library and Information Science* 5, no. 10 (2013): 307.

120. Hudson and Taylor, 69–70.

121. Shosanya and Azu, "Lawyers Call for Prosecution of Corrupt Judges."

122. See de Speville, "The Experience of Hong Kong, China, in Combating Corruption," 51–58; Manion, *Corruption by Design*, 27–83; Leak, "The Experience of Singapore in Combating Corruption," 59; Weder and Brunetti, "Another Tale of Two Cities: A Note on Institutions in Hong Kong and Singapore," 314.

123. See ICAC, "Brief History"; de Speville, 51.

124. See de Speville, 53.

125. Ibid., 52.

126. See ibid., 56.

127. See Human Rights Watch, "Nigeria: Firing of Anti-Corruption Chief Would Boost Abusive Politicians."

128. Yeh, "Ending Corruption in Africa through United Nations Inspections."

129. Yeh, "Why UN Inspections? The Accountability Gap in Sub-Saharan Africa."

130. Yeh, "Is an International Treaty Needed to Fight Corruption and the Narco-Insurgency in Mexico?"

131. Yeh, "Anti-Corruption Inspections: A Missing Element of the IMF/World Bank Agenda?"

CHAPTER 4

1. U.S. Department of State, "International Narcotics Control Strategy Report: Volume 1—Drug and Chemical Control" (Washington, DC: Bureau for International Narcotics and Law Enforcement Affairs, 2017), 215.

2. U.S. Joint Forces Command, *The 2008 Joint Operating Environment: Challenges and Implications for the Future Joint Force* (Suffolk, VA: U.S. Joint Forces Command, 2008), 36.

3. U.S. Department of Justice, "2017 National Drug Threat Assessment," Report No. DEA-DCT-DIR-040-17 (Washington, DC: Drug Enforcement Administration, 2017), vi.

4. CBS News, "100,000 Dead, 30,000 Missing: Mexico's War on Drugs Turns 10," December 11, 2016, http://www.cbsnews.com/news/100000-dead-30000-missing-mexico-war-on-drugs-turns-10/.

5. Kate Linthicum, "More and More People Are Being Murdered in Mexico—and Once More Drug Cartels Are to Blame," *Los Angeles Times*, March 3, 2017, http://www.latimes.com/world/mexico-americas/la-fg-mexico-murders-20170301-story.html; AP, "Mexico Homicide Rate Edges up in 2019; Rate of Rise Slows," January 21, 2020, https://apnews.com/86acd349ffd6713f9d485ce9ab169a06#:~:text=MEXICO%20CITY%20(AP)%20%E2%80%94%20The,the%20toughest%20challenges%20he%20faces.

6. Hal Brands, "Mexico's Narco-Insurgency and U.S. Counterdrug Policy" (Carlisle, PA: U.S. Army War College, Strategic Studies Institute, 2009).

7. Ibid.

8. Stanley Pimentel, "The Nexus of Organized Crime and Politics in Mexico," *Trends in Organized Crime* 4, no. 3 (1999); Ioan Grillo, *El Narco: Inside Mexico's Criminal Insurgency* (New York: Bloomsbury, 2011); Anabel Hernandez, *Narcoland: The Mexican Drug Lords and Their Godfathers*, trans. Iain Bruce and Lorna Scott Fox (New York: Verso, 2013); Ricardo Ravelo, *Los Capos, Las Narco-Rutas De Mexico* (Barcelona: Grijalbo, 2007); Sylvia Longmire, *Cartel: The Coming Invasion of Mexico's Drug Wars* (Hampshire, UK: Palgrave Macmillan, 2011); George W. Grayson, *Mexico: Narco-Violence and a Failed State?* (Piscataway, NJ: Transaction Publishers, 2009).

9. Pimentel, "The Nexus of Organized Crime and Politics in Mexico"; Ed Vulliamy, *Amexica: War Along the Borderline* (New York: Farrar, Straus and Giroux, 2010); Ravelo, *Los Capos, Las Narco-Rutas De Mexico*; Longmire, *Cartel: The Coming Invasion of Mexico's Drug Wars*; Grayson, *Mexico: Narco-Violence and a Failed State?*

10. Pimentel, "The Nexus of Organized Crime and Politics in Mexico"; Terence E. Poppa, *Drug Lord* (El Paso, TX: Cinco Puntos, 2010); Ravelo, *Los Capos, Las Narco-Rutas De Mexico*; Longmire, *Cartel: The Coming Invasion of Mexico's Drug Wars*; Grayson, *Mexico: Narco-Violence and a Failed State?*

11. See Hernandez, *Narcoland: The Mexican Drug Lords and Their Godfathers*; U.S. Department of Justice, "2015 National Drug Threat Assessment Summary," Report No. DEA-DCT-DIR-008-16 (Washington, DC: Drug Enforcement Administration, 2015), 1. Map 1 depicts areas of dominant Mexican cartel influence.

12. CNN, "Mexico Suspects Ex-Drug Czar Took Huge Bribes from Traffickers," November 21, 2008, http://edition.cnn.com/2008/WORLD/americas/11/21/mexico.arrest/index.html; Ken Ellingwood, "Mexico Traffickers Bribed Former Anti-Drug Chief, Officials Say," November 22, 2008, http://www.latimes.com/news/nationworld

/world/latinamerica/la-fg-bribe22-2008nov22,0,5384359.story; *Latin American Herald Tribune*, "Former Interpol Mexico Director Faces Money Laundering Charges," accessed November 21, 2017, http://www.laht.com/article.asp?ArticleId=357830&CategoryId=14091.

13. PBS, "Family Tree: General Jesus Gutierrez Rebollo," accessed August 26, 2020, https://www.pbs.org/wgbh/pages/frontline/shows/mexico/family/genrebollo.html.

14. "Heads of Mexico Interpol to Face Trial for Drug Cartel Ties," *Latin American Herald Tribune*, November 21, 2017, http://www.laht.com/article.asp?CategoryId=14091&ArticleId=325709; William Booth, "Mexico's Police Liaison for Interpol Arrested in Drug Probe," *The Washington Post*, November 19, 2008, http://www.washingtonpost.com/wp-dyn/content/article/2008/11/18/AR2008111804214.html; Associate Press, "In Drug Inquiry, Mexico Arrests Another Top Police Official," November 18, 2008, http://www.nytimes.com/2008/11/19/world/americas/19mexico.html.

15. Jason Meisner, "Top Mexican Cop Leaked Sensitive Info to Drug Cartels, Prosecutors Charge," *Chicago Tribune*, April 5, 2017, http://www.chicagotribune.com/news/local/breaking/ct-mexican-police-cartel-corruption-charges-20170405-story.html.

16. U.S. Department of Justice, "Former Mexican Federal Police Commander Arrested for Drug-Trafficking Conspiracy: Ivan Reyes Arzate Allegedly Received Hundreds of Thousands of Dollars in Bribes from Mexican Drug Cartels," January 24, 2020, https://www.justice.gov/usao-edny/pr/former-mexican-federal-police-commander-arrested-drug-trafficking-conspiracy.

17. Alan Feuer, "El Chapo Trial Shows That Mexico's Corruption Is Even Worse Than You Think," *The New York Times*, December 28, 2018, https://www.nytimes.com/2018/12/28/nyregion/el-chapo-trial-mexico-corruption.html?module=inline.

18. Ibid.

19. "Heads of Mexico Interpol to Face Trial for Drug Cartel Ties"; Gustavo Castillo Garcia, "Arraigan Por 40 Días a Rodolfo De La Guardia, Ex Director De La AFI," *La Jornada*, accessed November 21, 2017, http://www.jornada.unam.mx/2008/11/08/index.php?section=politica&article=013n2pol; Associate Press, "In Drug Inquiry, Mexico Arrests Another Top Police Official"; *Latin American Herald Tribune*, "Former Interpol Mexico Director Faces Money Laundering Charges."

20. Kristina Davis, "Mexican Attorney General Arrested on New York Drug Trafficking Charges Is Part-Time Chula Vista Resident," *The San Diego Union Tribune*, April 7, 2017, http://www.sandiegouniontribune.com/news/courts/sd-me-mexicanag-hearing-20170407-story.html.

21. Patrick J. McDonnell, "Former Governor of Mexico's Veracruz State Extradited from Guatemala to Face Corruption Charges," *Los Angeles Times*, July 17, 2017, http://www.latimes.com/world/mexico-americas/la-fg-mexico-duarte-20170717-story.html.

22. La Prensa, "El Policía De Los 'Narcos,'" December 17, 2008, https://www.prensa.com/impresa/mundo/policia-narcos_0_2454504620.html.

23. Ricardo Ravelo and Kristin Bricker, "Up to the Highest Level: Narco Infiltration in Felipe Calderon's Government: The Agencies in Charge of Mexico's Drug War Have High-Ranking Officials Who Protect the Cartels," *Proceso*, November 12, 2008, https://tinyurl.com/yy8awnv7.

24. BBC, "Joaquín 'El Chapo' Guzmán's Trial: From Shocking to Bizarre," February 4, 2019, https://www.bbc.com/news/world-us-canada-46282173.

25. Ibid.

26. Ibid.

27. José de Córdoba and Juan Montes, "Fugitive Mexican Ex-Governor Tomás Yarrington Had State Security While on the Run; Documents Show He Was Assigned Police Bodyguards While Eluding Arrest Warrants Last Year," *The Wall Street Journal*, April 15, 2017, https://www.wsj.com/articles/fugitive-mexican-ex-governor-tomas-yarrington-had-state-security-while-on-the-run-1492264404.

28. Ibid.

29. Reuters, "Crime-Torn Mexican 'FBI' Investigates 1,500 Agents," December, 2005, http://www.banderasnews.com/0512/nr-mexfbi.htm.

30. Poppa, *Drug Lord*.

31. See Alasdair Baverstock, "Mexican Forces Raid Police Precinct, Find 20 Officers Had Drug Trafficking Ties," May 26, 2017, http://www.foxnews.com/world/2017/05/26/mexican-forces-raid-police-precinct-find-20-officers-had-drug-trafficking-ties.html.

32. "Mexico: Cartels Pay Corrupt Cops $100 Million a Month," *Latin American Herald Tribune*, November 21, 2017, http://laht.com/article.asp?CategoryId=14091&ArticleId=362206.

33. International Crisis Group, "Veracruz: Fixing Mexico's State of Terror," Report No. 61 (Brussels, Belgium: International Crisis Group, 2017), 15.

34. Ibid., 16.

35. Carlos Marin, "Testimony Obtained by the Department of Justice: Raul Salinas Lozano, His Children Carlos, Raul and Adriana, the Ruiz Brothers and Colosio All Linked to Major Drug Lords," *Proceso*, February 16, 1997, http://www.pbs.org/wgbh/pages/frontline/shows/mexico/news/proceso.html.

36. Ibid.

37. Julia Preston, "Raul Salinas Guilty in Killing and Is Sentenced to 50 Years," *The New York Times*, January 22, 1999, http://www.nytimes.com/1999/01/22/world/raul-salinas-guilty-in-killing-and-is-sentenced-to-50-years.html?ref=mario-ruizmassieu; Marcus Patrick Capetillo, "Drug Trafficking in Mexico: Causes and Consequences of the Militarization of Mexico" (Honors thesis, Baylor University, 2012).

38. PBS, "Murder, Money and Mexico," April 8, 1997, http://www.pbs.org/wgbh/pages/frontline/shows/mexico/etc/script.html.

39. Ibid.

40. Preston, "Raul Salinas Guilty in Killing and Is Sentenced to 50 Years."

41. Tim Golden, "In Breakthrough, Mexican Official Testifies in Texas," *The New York Times*, July 15, 1998, http://www.nytimes.com/1998/07/15/world/in-breakthrough-mexican-official-testifies-in-texas.html?ref=marioruizmassieu.

42. Marin, "Testimony Obtained by the Department of Justice: Raul Salinas Lozano, His Children Carlos, Raul and Adriana, the Ruiz Brothers and Colosio All Linked to Major Drug Lords."

43. Pimentel, "The Nexus of Organized Crime and Politics in Mexico," 16; Ravelo, *Los Capos, Las Narco-Rutas De Mexico*. The PGR is the Office of Mexico's Federal Attorney General. The PJF was the federal judicial police force of Mexico. To address corruption, the PJF was replaced in 2002 by the AFI. In 2009, the AFI was dissolved and replaced by the Federal Ministerial Police.

44. Pimentel, "The Nexus of Organized Crime and Politics in Mexico," 17; Ravelo, *Los Capos, Las Narco-Rutas De Mexico*.

45. Pimentel, "The Nexus of Organized Crime and Politics in Mexico," 17; Ravelo, *Los Capos, Las Narco-Rutas De Mexico*.

46. Pimentel, "The Nexus of Organized Crime and Politics in Mexico," 18.

47. Peter A. Lupsha, "Drug Lords and Narco-Corruption: The Players Change but the Game Continues," *Crime, Law and Social Change* 16, no. 1 (1991): 53.

48. Aljazeera, "US Charges Former Mexican Minister with Drug Trafficking: Ex-Defence Chief Salvador Cienfuegos, Who Was Arrested in Los Angeles, Used His Power to Protect a Drug Cartel, According to a US Indictment," October 16, 2020, https://www.aljazeera.com/news/2020/10/16/us-charges-former-mexican-minister-with-drug-trafficking; Aljazeera, "Mexico Denies Deal to Nab Cartel Leader in Return for Cienfuegos: Salvador Cienfuegos Was Accused of Conspiring with a Cartel to Smuggle Drugs While Serving as Defence Secretary," November 23, 2020, https://www.aljazeera.com/news/2020/11/23/mexico-denies-deal-to-nab-cartel-leader-in-return-for-cienfuegos.

49. Aljazeera, "US Charges Former Mexican Minister with Drug Trafficking: Ex-Defence Chief Salvador Cienfuegos, Who Was Arrested in Los Angeles, Used His Power to Protect a Drug Cartel, According to a US Indictment."

50. Ibid.

51. Aljazeera, "Mexico Denies Deal to Nab Cartel Leader in Return for Cienfuegos: Salvador Cienfuegos Was Accused of Conspiring with a Cartel to Smuggle Drugs While Serving as Defence Secretary."

52. Aljazeera, "US to Drop Drug Charges against Mexico's Former Defence Chief: Charges against Salvador Cienfuegos to Be Dropped So He Can Be Investigated in Mexico, Says US Attorney General," November 18, 2020, https://www.aljazeera.com/news/2020/11/18/us-drops-drug-charges-against-mexicos-former-defense-chief.

53. Ibid.

54. Ibid.

55. Mary Beth Sheridan, "Mexico Declines to Prosecute Ex-Defense Minister Cienfuegos on Drug Charges," *The Washington Post*, January 14, 2021, https://www.washingtonpost.com/world/mexico-drops-charges-salvador-cienfuegos/2021/01/14/4cfc0954-56e3-11eb-a817-e5e7f8a406d6_story.html.

56. Yolanda Figueroa, *El Capo Del Golfo* (Mexico D.F.: Editorial Grijalbo, 1997), 137; Ravelo, *Los Capos, Las Narco-Rutas De Mexico*; Grillo, *El Narco: Inside Mexico's Criminal Insurgency*.

57. Pimentel, "The Nexus of Organized Crime and Politics in Mexico," 20; Ravelo, *Los Capos, Las Narco-Rutas De Mexico*.

58. Pimentel, "The Nexus of Organized Crime and Politics in Mexico," 20.

59. Ibid.

60. Ibid., 21; Ravelo, *Los Capos, Las Narco-Rutas De Mexico*. Beginning in 1986, the U.S. Congress required the U.S. president to annually certify, subject to congressional review, that drug producing or drug transit countries had cooperated fully with the United States in drug control efforts. Certification avoids a series of aid and trade sanctions. While Mexico has been fully certified each year, Congress closely monitored these certification decisions and, in some years, submitted resolutions of disapproval.

61. Pimentel, "The Nexus of Organized Crime and Politics in Mexico," 21; Ravelo, *Los Capos, Las Narco-Rutas De Mexico*.

62. Pimentel, "The Nexus of Organized Crime and Politics in Mexico," 21; Ravelo, *Los Capos, Las Narco-Rutas De Mexico*.

63. Pimentel, "The Nexus of Organized Crime and Politics in Mexico," 21; Ravelo, *Los Capos, Las Narco-Rutas De Mexico*; Grillo, *El Narco: Inside Mexico's Criminal Insurgency*.

64. Pimentel, "The Nexus of Organized Crime and Politics in Mexico," 23; Hernandez, *Narcoland: The Mexican Drug Lords and Their Godfathers*.

65. J. Jesus Blancornelas, *Una Vez, Nada Mas* (Mexico D.F.: Editorial Oceano, 1997), 143. As translated and quoted in Pimentel, 23; Grillo, *El Narco: Inside Mexico's Criminal Insurgency*; Ravelo, *Los Capos, Las Narco-Rutas De Mexico*; Hernandez, *Narcoland: The Mexican Drug Lords and Their Godfathers*.

66. Pimentel, "The Nexus of Organized Crime and Politics in Mexico," 23; Grillo, *El Narco: Inside Mexico's Criminal Insurgency*; Ravelo, *Los Capos, Las Narco-Rutas De Mexico*; Hernandez, *Narcoland: The Mexican Drug Lords and Their Godfathers*.

67. See "Federal PGR Arrests 209—of Its Own," *Mexico News Daily*, December 21, 2015, http://mexiconewsdaily.com/news/federal-pgr-arrests-209-of-its-own/.

68. See Charles R. Morris, "Corruption, Drug Trafficking, and Violence in Mexico," *The Brown Journal of World Affairs* 18, no. 2 (2012); Nubia Nieto, "Political Corruption and Narcotrafficking in Mexico," *Transcience* 3, no. 2 (2012); Hernandez, *Narcoland: The Mexican Drug Lords and Their Godfathers*.

69. Azam Ahmed and J. Jesus Esquivel, "Presidential Ally Is Arrested, and Mexico Corruption Investigation Deepens," *The New York Times*, December 20, 2017, https://www.nytimes.com/2017/12/20/world/americas/mexico-corruption-pri.html.

70. Azam Ahmed, "Mexico's Government Is Blocking Its Own Anti-Corruption Drive, Commissioners Say," *The New York Times*, December 2, 2017, https://www.nytimes.com/2017/12/02/world/americas/mexico-corruption-commission.html.

71. See Elisabeth Malkin, "Corruption at a Level of Audacity 'Never Seen in Mexico,'" *The New York Times*, April 19, 2017, https://www.nytimes.com/2017/04/19/world/americas/in-mexico-mounting-misdeeds-but-governors-escape-justice.html.

72. Daniel Lizárraga et al., *La Casa Blanca De Peña Nieto* (Mexico City, Mexico: Grijalbo, 2017); Joshua Partlow, "Luxurious Presidential House Draws Mexican Press Scrutiny," *The Washington Post*, November 9, 2014, https://www.washingtonpost.com/world/luxurious-presidential-house-draws-mexican-press-scrutiny/2014/11/09/33bba1ee-65fd-11e4-ab86-46000e1d0035_story.html?utm_term=.87fc9b0cf75d.

73. Tom Phillips and David Agren, "Mexico Rocked by Claims of Corruption against Three Former Presidents: Leaked Deposition by Recently Extradited Former Head of State Oil Company Pemex Alleges Staggering Scale of High-Level Corruption," *The Guardian*, August 20, 2020, https://www.theguardian.com/world/2020/aug/20/mexico-corruption-former-presidents-emilio-lozoya.

74. BBC, "Joaquín 'El Chapo' Guzmán's Trial: From Shocking to Bizarre"; Alan Feuer, "Former Mexican President Peña Nieto Took $100 Million Bribe, Witness at El Chapo Trial Says," *The New York Times*, January 15, 2019, https://www.nytimes.com/2019/01/15/nyregion/el-chapo-trial.html.

75. Feuer, "El Chapo Trial Shows That Mexico's Corruption Is Even Worse Than You Think."

76. Vulliamy, *Amexica: War Along the Borderline*, 253.

77. Ibid.; Grillo, *El Narco: Inside Mexico's Criminal Insurgency*; Ravelo, *Los Capos, Las Narco-Rutas De Mexico*.

78. Vulliamy, *Amexica: War Along the Borderline*.

79. Ibid.

80. Ibid.

81. Ibid.

82. Molly Molloy and Charles Bowden, eds., *El Sicario: The Autobiography of a Mexican Assassin* (New York: Nation Books, 2011).

83. Ibid., 74–75.

84. Chris Arsenault, "US-Trained Cartel Terrorises Mexico," November 3, 2010, http://www.aljazeera.com/indepth/features/2010/10/201010192124406C9775.html.

85. Molloy and Bowden, *El Sicario*, 75.

86. Ibid., 79.

87. Ibid.

88. Ibid.

89. Ibid.

90. Ibid.

91. Ibid., 91–95, 104.

92. Alfredo Corchado and Ricardo Sandoval, "Inquiry Indicates Police, Drug Ties: Disturbing Reports Say Women Were Tortured and Slain as Celebration," *Dallas Morning News*, February 28, 2004, http://www.latinamericanstudies.org/drugs/inquiry.htm.

93. International Crisis Group, "Veracruz: Fixing Mexico's State of Terror," 17.

94. Molloy and Bowden, *El Sicario*.

95. Rory Carroll, "Mexico's Drugs War: In the City of Death," *The Guardian*, September 16, 2010, http://www.guardian.co.uk/world/2010/sep/16/mexico-drugs-war-massacre-in-torreon.

96. Molloy and Bowden, *El Sicario*.

97. See Hudson and Taylor, "The International Commission against Impunity in Guatemala: A New Model for International Criminal Justice Mechanisms."

98. Ibid., 56.

99. See Kennis, "The Creation of the International Commission against Impunity in Guatemala: Miscalculation by a 'Corporate Mafia State'?".

100. See CICIG, 50–51.

101. Ibid., 53.

102. Ibid., 54–55.

103. See ibid., 52–53.

104. Grillo, *El Narco: Inside Mexico's Criminal Insurgency*.

105. Ibid., 287.

106. APUNCAC, http://tinyurl.com/y6bkpott.

107. de Speville, "Hong Kong: Policy Initiatives against Corruption," 12.

108. Weder and Brunetti, "Another Tale of Two Cities: A Note on Institutions in Hong Kong and Singapore"; Manion, *Corruption by Design*, 2.

109. *Situations under Investigation*, INT'L CRIM. CT., http://www.icc-cpi.int/en_menus/icc/situations%20and%20cases/Pages/situations%20and%20cases.aspx (last visited July 15, 2020).

110. Enrique Peña Nieto, "Mexico's Next Chapter," *The New York Times*, 2012, accessed August 8, 2012, http://travel.nytimes.com/2012/07/03/opinion/mexicos-next-chapter.html.

CHAPTER 5

1. Frank Ledwidge, "Justice and Counter-Insurgency in Afghanistan: A Missing Link," *The RUSI Journal* 154, no. 1 (2009): 6, 9.

2. Mujib Mashal, "C.I.A.'s Afghan Forces Leave a Trail of Abuse and Anger," *The New York Times*, December 31, 2018, 2018, https://www.nytimes.com/2018/12/31/world/asia/cia-afghanistan-strike-force.html.

3. Ibid.

4. Ibid.

5. Ibid.

6. Ted R. Gurr, *Why Men Rebel: Fortieth Anniversary Edition* (Boulder, CO: Paradigm, 2011).

7. David Kilcullen, *Counterinsurgency* (New York: Oxford University Press, 2010).

8. Ibid., 10.

9. The term "theory" is used to describe Kilcullen's hypotheses regarding the use of military intervention to suppress insurgency. As described by Kilcullen, counterinsurgency theory hypothesizes that insurgency is suppressed when military intervention is applied in conjunction with the introduction of local security forces, protective measures, governance reforms, and reforms that promote economic and political development.

10. Kilcullen, *Counterinsurgency*, 12.

11. BBC, "Afghanistan: Obama Orders Withdrawal of 33,000 Troops," June 23, 2011, http://www.bbc.co.uk/news/world-us-canada-13851930; Andy Bloxham, "Former Head of Army: Taliban Will Be Part of Afghanistan's Future," *The Telegraph*, June 23, 2011, http://www.telegraph.co.uk/news/worldnews/asia/afghanistan/8594075/Former-head-of-Army-Taliban-will-be-part-of-Afghanistans-future.html; Jim Sciutto, Mary Bruce, and Devin Dwyer, "Obama Orders Start to US Troop Withdrawal from Afghanistan," *ABC News*, June 22, 2011, http://abcnews.go.com/Politics/president-obama-orders-start-us-troop-withdrawal-afghanistan/story?id=13908291. On December 28, 2014, NATO formally ended combat operations in Afghanistan and transferred full security responsibility to the Afghan government. However, NATO maintained a force of 13,000 troops, including 9,800 Americans, in an advisory and counterterrorism role through 2015 and into 2016. In response to the Doha Agreement, signed in February 2020 by the U.S. government and the Taliban, U.S. forces were reduced from 13,000 to 8,600 troops by July 2020, followed by a reduction to 2,500 troops in January 2021. After a brief surge to 7,000 troops in August 2021, American forces were completely withdrawn by August 30, 2021.

12. Ray Rivera, "In an Afghan Village, Living in Fear of Both Sides," *The New York Times*, April 24, 2011, I9.

13. Ibid.

14. Rod Nordland and Alissa J. Rubin, "Taliban Captives Dispute U.S. View on State of War," *The New York Times*, February 2, 2012.

15. Kilcullen, *Counterinsurgency*, 53.

16. This is not to say that corruption is the only factor that promotes insurgency. The Afghan insurgency also has its roots in resentment regarding the presence of occupying forces. However, I am suggesting that corruption is a prime factor and that it can and should be addressed. It should be noted that the insurgency existed prior to the insertion of American military forces into Afghanistan in 2001, so it cannot be the case that the American presence caused the insurgency. While Afghans resisted the Soviet occupation, those forces were withdrawn in 1989. There was an extended period after the withdrawal of Soviet forces and before the introduction of American forces when the insurgency bloomed. The explanation for this must go beyond the presence of anger regarding foreign occupying forces. In another context, Wickham-Crowley has documented how peasant resentment of oppressive government officials translates into support provided by peasants to insurgents. See Timothy P. Wickham-Crowley, *Guerrillas and Revolutions in Latin America* (Princeton, NJ: Princeton University Press, 1993).

17. Gurr, *Why Men Rebel: Fortieth Anniversary Edition.*

18. In November 2017, the Special Inspector General for Afghanistan Reconstruction testified before the U.S. Congress that "we have no strategy for fighting corruption" in Afghanistan.

19. Kilcullen, *Counterinsurgency*, 54.

20. Ahmed Rashid, "How Obama Lost Karzai," *Foreign Policy*, March/April 2011.

21. Krisanne Campos and Candace Rondeaux, "Interview with Ambassador Douglas Lute, NATO Permanent Rep, Former Director of Iraq/Afghanistan, NSC 2007–2014," Office of the Special Inspector General for Afghanistan Reconstruction (SIGAR), February 20, 2015, https://www.washingtonpost.com/graphics/2019/investigations/afghanistan-papers/documents-database/documents/lute_doug_ll_01_d5_02202015.pdf?v=25.

22. Ahmed Rashid, *Descent into Chaos: The U.S. And the Disaster in Pakistan, Afghanistan, and Central Asia* (New York: Penguin, 2009), 204.

23. Craig Whitlock, "At War with the Truth: The Afghanistan Papers: A Secret History of the War," *The Washington Post*, December 9, 2019, https://www.washingtonpost.com/graphics/2019/investigations/afghanistan-papers/afghanistan-war-confidential-documents/.

24. Transparency International, "Corruption Perceptions Index 2010" (Berlin: Transparency International, 2010).

25. Scott Shane, Mark Mazzetti, and Dexter Filkins, "Cables Depict Afghan Graft, Starting at the Top," *The New York Times*, December 2, 2010, http://www.nytimes.com/2010/12/03/world/asia/03wikileaks-corruption.html?_r=1&scp=1&sq=Afghan+corruption&st=nyt.

26. Dexter Filkins, "The American Awakening," *The New Republic*, March 11, 2010, 24.

27. Dexter Filkins, "Inside Corrupt-Istan," *The New York Times*, September 5, 2010.

28. C.J. Chivers et al., "The Afghan Struggle: A Secret Archive," *The New York Times*, July 26, 2010, A10; Alissa J. Rubin, "Taliban Exploit Openings in Neglected Province," *The New York Times*, July 30, 2010.

29. Rashid, *Descent into Chaos*.

30. Ibid.

31. Ibid.

32. Ibid.

33. Daniel L. Byman, "The Changing Nature of State Sponsorship of Terrorism," Analysis Paper No. 16 (Washington, DC: Brookings Institution, The Saban Center for Middle East Policy, 2008), 7.

34. Carlotta Gall, "Taliban Show Strain as Afghan Fighting Nears," *The New York Times*, April 1, 2011.

35. Ibid.

36. Ibid.

37. Ibid.

38. Ibid.

39. Peter Oborne, "How to Beat Terrorism: Over the Past Three Years, the Country Has Seen an Extraordinary Reduction in Violence," *The Spectator*, December 31, 2016.

40. Ibid.

41. Ibid.

42. Ibid.

43. Ibid.

44. Ibid.
45. Ibid.
46. Ibid.
47. Ibid.
48. However, see Jeffrey A. Dressler, "The Haqqani Network: From Pakistan to Afghanistan," Afghanistan Report No. 6 (Washington, DC: Institute for the Study of War, 2010). Dressler suggests that Pakistan remained a safe haven for the Haqqani network.
49. Amira Jadoon and Sara Mahmood, "Fixing the Cracks in the Pakistani Taliban's Foundation: TTP's Leadership Returns to the Mehsud Tribe," *CTC Sentinel* 11, no. 11 (2018): 21.
50. Ibid., 21–22.
51. "Fatalities in Terrorist Violence in Pakistan 2000–2018," https://commons.wikimedia.org/wiki/File:Fatalities_in_Terrorist_Violence_in_Pakistan.png; South Asia Terrorism Portal, "Fatalities in Terrorist Violence in Pakistan 2000–2019," June 23, 2019, https://www.satp.org/satporgtp/countries/pakistan/database/casualties.htm.
52. Significantly, a natural experiment tested the effect of an anticorruption program in Brazil and found that a one SD increase in mayoral corruption, disclosed through random audits of municipal expenditures and posted on the internet, reduced the likelihood that an incumbent mayor would be re-elected by 25 percent. See Finan, "Political Patronage, Corruption, and Local Development." Reports by UN inspectors regarding corrupt practices might be expected to have a similar influence on elections in Pakistan.

CHAPTER 6

1. Numerous theories have been advanced to explain the puzzling failure of development in sub-Saharan Africa, where annual growth of GDP per capita averaged negative 1.0 percent from 1975 through 1999. See United Nations Development Program, "Human Development Report" (New York: United Nations, 2001). I selected theories for analysis based on the prominence of the theorists, typically signaled by the publication of books articulating their views, suggesting that they have achieved a level of prominence that may influence policymakers. For example, Moyo is included because her book has achieved prominence among policymakers and represents a view that may influence policy. See Dambisa Moyo, *Dead Aid: Why Aid Is Not Working and How There Is Another Way for Africa* (London: Penguin Books, 2009). However, it is not feasible to address every theory of underdevelopment here. The neoliberal theories underlying IMF and World Bank policies are addressed in chapter 7 and theories such as dependency theory have been adequately addressed elsewhere. See H. W. Singer, "The Distribution of Gains between Investing and Borrowing Countries," *The American Economic Review* 40, no. 2 (1950).
2. R. J. Barro, "Determinants of Economic Growth in a Panel of Countries," *Annals of Economics and Finance* 4, no. 2 (2003).
3. Barro, "Democracy and the Rule of Law," 230.

4. Barro, "Determinants of Economic Growth in a Panel of Countries," 239.

5. Ibid.

6. Ibid. Barro entered a measure of corruption simultaneously with the measure of the rule of law and found that corruption had a positive but insignificant effect on economic growth. However, it is likely that the null result is due to collinearity between corruption and the rule of law measures, which would arise if these indicators measure the same underlying construct, that is, if the poor rule of law in Africa is due to corruption. In the presence of collinearity, it would be necessary to enter the corruption measure *instead of* (rather than simultaneously with) the rule of law measure in order to obtain an unbiased estimate of the effect of corruption on economic growth.

7. Robert A. Lawson, "Economic Freedom and Property Rights: The Institutional Environment of Productive Entrepreneurship," in *Making Poor Nations Rich: Entrepreneurship and the Process of Economic Development*, ed. Benjamin Powell (Stanford, CA: Stanford University Press, 2008).

8. Mancur Olson Jr., "Big Bills Left on the Sidewalk: Why Some Nations Are Rich, and Others Poor," in *Making Poor Nations Rich: Entrepreneurship and the Process of Economic Development*, ed. Benjamin Powell (Stanford, CA: Stanford University Press, 2008), 29.

9. Martin Meredith, *The State of Africa: A History of Fifty Years of Independence* (London: The Free Press, 2005).

10. Mbaku, "Corruption and the Crisis of Institutional Reforms in Africa."

11. E.A. Brett, "Theorising Crisis and Reform: Institutional Theories and Social Change in Uganda" (Sussex, England: Institute for Development Studies, Sussex University, 1993).

12. Jacqueline Coolidge and Susan Rose-Ackerman, "High-Level Rent-Seeking and Corruption in African Regimes: Theory and Cases," Policy Research Working Paper No. 1780 (Washington DC: World Bank, 1997).

13. Ibid.

14. Larry Diamond, "Nigeria's Perennial Struggle against Corruption: Prospects for the Third Republic," *Corruption and Reform* 7, no. 3 (1993); Jeffrey Herbst, "Is Nigeria a Viable State?," *The Washington Quarterly*, Spring, 1996.

15. Patrick Chabal and Jean-Pascal Deloz, *Africa Works: Disorder as Political Instrument* (Oxford: James Currey, 1999).

16. Frederick Cooper, *Africa since 1940: The Past of the Present* (Cambridge, UK: Cambridge University Press, 2002).

17. Bryan Riley and Terry Miller, "2017 Index of Economic Freedom: Trade and Prosperity at Risk," Report No. 3168 (Washington, DC: The Heritage Foundation, 2016).

18. Mauro, "Corruption and Growth"; Méndez and Sepúlveda, "Corruption, Growth and Political Regimes: Cross Country Evidence"; Méon and Sekkat, "Does Corruption Grease or Sand the Wheels of Growth?"; Mo, "Corruption and Economic Growth"; Pelligrini and Gerlagh, "Corruption's Effect on Growth and Its Transmission Channels"; Gyimah-Brepong, "Corruption, Economic Growth, and Income Inequality in Africa"; us Swaleheen and Stansel, "Economic Freedom, Corruption, and Growth."

19. Gyimah-Brepong, "Corruption, Economic Growth, and Income Inequality in Africa."

20. Ibid., 199.

21. Peter Baker and Rachel Donadio, "Obama Wins More Food Aid but Presses African Nations on Corruption," *The New York Times*, July 11, 2009, A4.

22. Petter Langseth, Rick Stapenhurst, and Jeremy Pope, "National Integrity Systems," in *Curbing Corruption: Toward a Model for Building National Integrity*, ed. Rick Stapenhurst and Sahr J. Kpundeh (Washington, DC: The World Bank, 1999); Economic Commission for Africa, "Combating Corruption, Improving Governance in Africa: Regional Anti-Corruption Programme for Africa (2011–2016)" (Addis Ababa, Ethiopia: Economic Commission for Africa, 2011). The Regional Anti-Corruption Programme for Africa is an initiative that offers technical advice and advocates for changes in domestic laws to fight corruption but does not involve the creation of a body of anticorruption inspectors.

23. World Bank, *World Development Report 1997: The State in a Changing World* (New York: Oxford University Press, 1997), 8.

24. World Bank, "Anticorruption," https://tinyurl.com/yynbyckc.

25. *The New York Times*, "Zambia: A Reversal on Anticorruption Efforts," August 27, 2009, A10.

26. APUNCAC, http://tinyurl.com/y6bkpott.

27. Jared Diamond, *Guns, Germs, and Steel: The Fates of Human Societies* (New York: W.W. Norton, 2005).

28. D. Rodrik, *One Economics, Many Recipes: Globalization, Institutions, and Economic Growth* (Princeton, NJ: Princeton University Press, 2007).

29. Stapenhurst and Kpundeh, *Curbing Corruption.*

30. Moyo, *Dead Aid*, 47.

31. Ibid., 49.

32. Ibid.

33. Ibid.

34. Ibid., 143.

35. Ibid.

36. Ibid., 87.

37. Ibid.

38. Ibid.

39. Ibid., 113.

40. Ibid.

41. Ibid., 124.

42. Ibid., 125.

43. Ibid., 146.

44. David Warsh, "The Man Who Succeeded Gerschenkron," April 24, 2005, http://www.economicprincipals.com/issues/2005.04.24/145.html.

45. Daron Acemoglu, Simon Johnson, and James A. Robinson, "Institutions as a Fundamental Cause of Long-Run Growth," in *Handbook of Economic Growth*, ed. Philippe Aghion and Steven N. Durlauf (Amsterdam: Elsevier, 2005), 438.

46. Ibid.

47. Ibid., 395–96.

48. R.H. Bates, *Markets and States in Tropical Africa* (Berkeley, CA: University of California Press, 1981), 95.

49. Acemoglu, Johnson, and Robinson, "Institutions as a Fundamental Cause of Long-Run Growth," 457.

50. Ibid., 464.

51. William Reno, *Corruption and State Politics in Sierra Leone* (Cambridge, UK: Cambridge University Press, 1995); William Reno, *Warlord Politics and African States* (Boulder, CO: Lynne Rienner Publishers, 1998).

52. Rodrik, *One Economics, Many Recipes*, 5.

53. Ibid.

54. Ibid., 31.

55. Ibid.

56. Ibid., 55.

57. Ibid.

58. William Easterly, *The White Man's Burden: Why the West's Efforts to Aid the Rest Have Done So Much Ill and So Little Good* (London: Penguin Press, 2006), 15.

59. Ibid., 17.

60. Ibid.

61. Ibid.

62. Ibid., 379.

63. J. Sachs, *The End of Poverty: Economic Possibilities for Our Time* (New York, NY: Penguin, 2006), 56–57.

64. Easterly, *The White Man's Burden*; Sachs, *The End of Poverty.*

65. Easterly, *The White Man's Burden.*

66. Ibid.

67. Ibid., 39.

68. Ibid., 41.

69. Aart Kraay and Claudio Raddatz, "Poverty Traps, Aid, and Growth," Policy Research Working Paper No. 3631 (Washington, DC: World Bank, 2005).

70. Easterly, *The White Man's Burden*, 43.

71. Ibid.

72. Paul Collier, *The Bottom Billion: Why the Poorest Countries Are Failing and What Can Be Done About It* (Oxford: Oxford University Press, 2007).

73. Ibid.

74. Ibid., 37.

75. Ibid., 42.

76. Ibid.

77. Ibid.

78. Ibid.

79. Meredith, *The State of Africa.*

80. Ibid.

81. Ibid.

82. Collier, *The Bottom Billion*, 64.

83. Ibid., 182.

84. Moyo, *Dead Aid.*
85. Acemoglu, Johnson, and Robinson, "Institutions as a Fundamental Cause of Long-Run Growth."
86. Rodrik, *One Economics, Many Recipes.*
87. Easterly, *The White Man's Burden.*
88. Collier, *The Bottom Billion.*
89. Sachs, *The End of Poverty*; Easterly, *The White Man's Burden.*
90. Ayittey, *Africa Unchained.*
91. Ibid.
92. Ibid.
93. Moyo, *Dead Aid.*
94. Acemoglu, Johnson, and Robinson, "Institutions as a Fundamental Cause of Long-Run Growth."
95. Rodrik, *One Economics, Many Recipes.*
96. Easterly, *The White Man's Burden*; Collier, *The Bottom Billion.*
97. Sachs, *The End of Poverty*; Easterly, *The White Man's Burden.*
98. Stapenhurst and Kpundeh, *Curbing Corruption.*
99. Finan, "Political Patronage, Corruption, and Local Development."

CHAPTER 7

1. The United Nations Conference on Trade and Development Secretariat, "The Least Developed Countries 2000 Report: Aid, Private Capital Flows and External Debt: The Challenge of Financing Development in the LDCs."
2. World Bank, *World Development Report 1997: The State in a Changing World*, 23.
3. Martin Wolf, *Why Globalization Works* (New Haven, CT: Yale University Press, 2005), xiii.
4. Ayittey, *Africa Unchained*; Mbaku, "Bureaucratic and Political Corruption in Africa"; Mbaku, "Corruption and the Crisis of Institutional Reforms in Africa"; Mbaku, "Bureaucratic Corruption in Africa."
5. World Bank, "Anticorruption in Transition: A Contribution to the Policy Debate" (Washington, DC: The World Bank, 2000), 27.
6. George T. Abed and Hamid R. Davoodi, "Corruption, Structural Reforms, and Economic Performance in the Transition Economies" (Washington, DC: The International Monetary Fund, 2000), 4.
7. World Bank, *World Development Report 1997: The State in a Changing World*, 8.
8. World Bank, "Anticorruption."
9. World Bank, "Anticorruption in Transition: A Contribution to the Policy Debate," 48.
10. George T. Abed and Sanjeev Gupta, "The Economics of Corruption: An Overview," The International Monetary Fund, September 23, 2002, http://www.imf.org/external/pubs/nft/2002/govern/#chp1.

11. Abed and Davoodi, "Corruption, Structural Reforms, and Economic Performance in the Transition Economies," 7–8.

12. Mauro, "Corruption and Growth"; Méndez and Sepúlveda, "Corruption, Growth and Political Regimes: Cross Country Evidence"; Méon and Sekkat, "Does Corruption Grease or Sand the Wheels of Growth?"; Mo, "Corruption and Economic Growth"; Pelligrini and Gerlagh, "Corruption's Effect on Growth and Its Transmission Channels"; Gyimah-Brepong, "Corruption, Economic Growth, and Income Inequality in Africa"; us Swaleheen and Stansel, "Economic Freedom, Corruption, and Growth."

13. Christine Lagarde, "Addressing Corruption—Openly," United Kingdom Prime Minister's Office, May 12, 2016, https://www.gov.uk/government/publications/against-corruption-a-collection-of-essays/against-corruption-a-collection-of-essays#christine-lagarde-addressing-corruption--openly. Lagarde cites Svensson (2005) to support her statement, but Svensson's brief essay omits a substantive review of the empirical literature and instead "updated Mauro's calculations." See Jakob Svensson, "Eight Questions About Corruption," *Journal of Economic Perspectives* 19, no. 3 (2005): 38.

14. Lagarde, "Addressing Corruption—Openly."

15. The United Nations Conference on Trade and Development Secretariat, "The Least Developed Countries 2000 Report: Aid, Private Capital Flows and External Debt: The Challenge of Financing Development in the LDCs," 102.

16. Reno, *Corruption and State Politics in Sierra Leone.*

17. Mbaku, "Corruption and the Crisis of Institutional Reforms in Africa"; Ayittey, *Africa Unchained*; Mamdani, *Citizen and Subject: Contemporary Africa and the Legacy of Late Colonialism.*

18. Ayittey, *Africa Unchained.*

19. Mamdani, *Citizen and Subject: Contemporary Africa and the Legacy of Late Colonialism*, 54.

20. Ibid.

21. Ibid.

22. Ibid.

23. Ibid.

24. Ibid.

25. Mbaku, "Corruption and the Crisis of Institutional Reforms in Africa"; Mbaku, "Bureaucratic Corruption in Africa."

26. Mbaku, "Corruption and the Crisis of Institutional Reforms in Africa."

27. Ibid.; Mbaku, "Bureaucratic and Political Corruption in Africa"; Ayittey, *Africa Unchained.*

28. Hope Sr., *From Crisis to Renewal*, 12.

29. Barro, "Democracy and the Rule of Law," 230.

30. van de Walle, *African Economies and the Politics of Permanent Crisis.*

31. See Reno, *Corruption and State Politics in Sierra Leone*; Reno, *Warlord Politics and African States.*

32. See, for example, Meredith, *The State of Africa.*

33. Ayittey, *Africa Unchained.*

34. Reno, *Corruption and State Politics in Sierra Leone*.
35. Ibid.
36. Ibid.
37. Ibid.
38. Ibid.
39. Ibid.
40. Ibid.
41. Ibid.
42. Ibid.
43. Ibid.
44. Ibid.
45. Ibid.
46. Ibid.
47. Ibid.
48. Ibid.
49. Ibid.
50. Ibid.
51. Ibid.
52. Ibid.
53. Ibid.
54. Ibid.
55. Ibid.
56. Ibid.
57. Ibid.
58. Ibid.
59. Ibid.
60. Ibid.
61. Ibid.
62. Ibid.
63. Ibid.
64. Ibid.
65. Ibid.
66. Ibid.
67. Ibid.
68. Ibid.
69. Ibid.
70. Ibid.
71. Ibid.
72. Ibid.
73. Ibid.
74. Ibid.
75. Ibid.
76. Ibid.
77. Ibid.
78. Ibid.

79. Reno, *Warlord Politics and African States.*

80. Ibid.

81. Ibid.

82. Reno, *Corruption and State Politics in Sierra Leone.*

83. Ibid.

84. Reno, *Warlord Politics and African States*; Nicolas van de Walle, "The Politics of Non-Reform in Cameroon," in *Hemmed In: Responses to Africa's Economic Decline*, ed. Thomas Callaghy and John Ravenhill (New York: Columbia University Press, 1993).

85. Reno, *Warlord Politics and African States.*

86. Ibid.

87. Ibid.

88. Ibid.

89. Ibid.

90. Ibid.

91. Ibid.

92. Ibid.

93. Ibid.

94. Ibid.

95. Ibid.

96. Ibid.

97. But see Collier, *The Bottom Billion*. Collier advocates international charters that would create codes of conduct, increase transparency regarding revenues from natural resource extraction, promote free elections and a free mass media, promote transparency in budgeting, outlaw government expropriation of private assets, and require international banks to report the deposit of large sums of money. However, none of these tactics would create a powerful, independent check against corruption, free from manipulation by corrupt leaders.

98. See Manion, *Corruption by Design*; de Speville, "The Experience of Hong Kong, China, in Combating Corruption"; Leak, "The Experience of Singapore in Combating Corruption."

99. See Collier, *The Bottom Billion*; Easterly, *The White Man's Burden*; Rodrik, *One Economics, Many Recipes*; Sachs, *The End of Poverty*.

CHAPTER 8

1. Racketeer Influenced and Corrupt Organizations Act, Pub. L. No. 91-452, s.901(a), 84 Stat. 922-3 (1970) (codified at 18 U.S.C. ss.1961–1968 (2018)).

2. Racketeer Influenced and Corrupt Organizations Act, Pub. L. No. 91-452, s.901(a), 84 Stat. 922-3 (1970) (codified at 18 U.S.C. ss.1961–1968 (2018)).

3. Fla. Stat. s.895 (2018).

4. APUNCAC art. 60, 61, 62, http://tinyurl.com/y6bkpott.

5. APUNCAC art. 62, para. 6.

6. APUNCAC art. 62, para. 6.

7. APUNCAC art. 62, paras. 2, 13.

8. Center for Governmental Studies, *Public Campaign Financing in California: A Model Law for 21st Century Reform* (Los Angeles, CA: Center for Governmental Studies, 2011).

9. NYC Charter ss.2600–2607 (2010); NYC Admin. Code s.12-110 (2016).

10. Transparency International, *Integrity Pacts in Public Procurement: An Implementation Guide* (Berlin: Transparency International, 2013), Annex 1.

11. False Claims Act 31 U.S.C. ss.3729–3733 (2012 Supp. 4).

12. APUNCAC art. 49, para. 6.

13. APUNCAC art. 48, para. 1.

14. APUNCAC art. 19, para. 6.

15. APUNCAC art. 47, para. 1.

16. OECD, *OECD Transfer Pricing Guidelines for Multinational Enterprises and Tax Administrations 2017* (Paris: OECD, 2017).

17. APUNCAC art. 50, para. 2.

18. APUNCAC art. 50, para. 3.

19. APUNCAC art. 50, para. 4.

20. APUNCAC permits a defendant to appeal a FINCEN debarment decision before an ALJ. See APUNCAC art. 18, para. 9. APUNCAC spells out due process procedures, including a procedure for appealing a decision by a first-level ALJ in a proceeding presided by a second-level ALJ. See APUNCAC art. 71, para. 15(b).

APUNCAC also offers an optional expedited procedure for reviewing debarment decisions that may be elected by either party (FINCEN or the defendant), see APUNCAC art. 71, para. 14(o). If the expedited procedure is elected by either party, it becomes mandatory, see art. 71 para. 14(o). Under this procedure, each party would submit briefs, followed by reply briefs, to the presiding ALJ, who would draft a proposed decision. Each party would have an opportunity to raise objections to the proposed decision. The ALJ would then issue a final decision not subject to review. It may be expected that neither party would elect the expedited procedure unless the facts are easily established and the law is clear. For example, FINCEN might be expected to elect the expedited procedure if a bank clerk was required to collect and report beneficial ownership information but failed to do so. A defendant might be expected to elect the expedited procedure if the Chief Debarment Officer failed to follow the procedures required by APUNCAC. APUNCAC would permit the ALJ to pose written questions, served on both parties, and receive responses, served on both parties. The burden of proof would be on the Chief Debarment Officer to demonstrate that required procedures were followed. If the Chief Debarment Officer could not demonstrate, to the satisfaction of the ALJ, that required procedures were followed, then the ALJ would be compelled to reject FINCEN's request to debar the defendant.

A model and precedent for the expedited procedure is the use of mandatory binding arbitration in international disputes. Mandatory binding arbitration is viewed as a relatively smooth, speedy, cost-efficient way to resolve disputes. Arbitration provisions have been incorporated into 2,946 bilateral investment treaties and 358 treaties with investment provisions, such as the North American Free Trade Agreement. See United Nations Conference on Trade and Development, *World Investment Report*

2016 (Geneva: United Nations, 2016), p. 101. Arbitration has become the primary means for settling international commercial and investment disputes. Typically, the parties to an arbitration choose a single arbitrator. The arbitrator is required to remain independent and impartial. Typically, either party may elect arbitration—mutual agreement is not necessary. The United Nations Commission on International Trade Law (UNCITRAL) Model Law on International Commercial Arbitration states: "A court . . . shall, if a party so requests . . . refer the parties to arbitration." See UNCITRAL Model Law on International Commercial Arbitration art. 8(1). This is analogous to APUNCAC's provision that permits either party in a dispute to elect an expedited review procedure. Under the UNCITRAL Model Law, and under APUNCAC, either party may elect a procedure that expedites the decision process and results in a binding decision.

The binding nature of arbitration means that there is no possibility to appeal the resulting decision to a superior tribunal or national court. This offers a model and precedent for the binding nature of the expedited review process that is incorporated into APUNCAC.

While a potential concern is that an ALJ may not be competent, APUNCAC includes provisions that would promote the selection of competent individuals to serve as ALJs. APUNCAC requires that judges be selected based on qualifying experience and an examination, administered by the Office of Personnel Management (OPM), to evaluate the competencies/knowledge, skills, and abilities essential to performing the work of an ALJ. See APUNCAC art. 71 para. 13(d)–(e).

APUNCAC also includes provisions that would promote decisions that adhere to the law. The Commission on Crime Prevention and Criminal Justice would be required to conduct an annual review of the performance of each ALJ and would issue a letter of reprimand, suspension, or an order to retire for a decision or pattern of decisions by a judge that is arbitrary, capricious, manifestly contrary to properly articulated and disseminated rules, procedures, precedents, or policies, not based on a consideration of relevant factors, or involves a clear error of judgment or a failure to articulate a legally sound conclusion. See APUNCAC art. 71 para. 13(i). This provision would apply pressure on ALJs to avoid decisions that are arbitrary, capricious, manifestly contrary to properly articulated and disseminated rules, procedures, precedents, or policies, not based on a consideration of relevant factors, or involve a clear error of judgment or a failure to articulate a legally sound conclusion.

APUNCAC includes provisions that would preserve the independence of ALJs. No ALJ would be disciplined or removed except through a formal hearing before a three-judge panel of ALJs drawn by rotation from the pool of such judges ranked in the top quintile by OPM and appointed by the Commission on Crime Prevention and Criminal Justice. See APUNCAC art. 71 para. 13(i).

21. See David M. Summers, "Third Party Beneficiaries and the Restatement (Second) of Contracts," *Cornell Law Review* 67, no. 4 (1982); James T. Gathii, "Incorporating the Third Party Beneficiary Principle in Natural Resource Contracts," *Georgia Journal of International and Comparative Law* 43, no. 1 (2014); Neil Andrews, "Strangers to Justice No Longer: The Reversal of the Privity Rule under

the Contracts (Rights of Third Parties) Act 1999," *Cambridge Law Journal* 60, no. 2 (2001).

22. APUNCAC, art. 19, para. 4(e)(ii).

23. APUNCAC does not attempt to enforce a top-down beneficial owner reporting requirement on, for example, all SWIFT or Fedwire transactions because that type of requirement would have been vociferously opposed by powerful banking lobbyists. That type of requirement is impractical because it would have required the agreement of all banks that use SWIFT and Fedwire, including banks not within the jurisdiction of APUNCAC States Parties. Banks are sensitive to the concerns of their customers. Only customers who oppose greater transparency would make their voices heard. Customers who have nothing to hide have no reason to lobby for beneficial owner reporting requirements. For this reason, the weight of customer opinion would oppose greater transparency. Opposition from customers who oppose greater transparency would translate into opposition from the banking lobby that would torpedo APUNCAC. Furthermore, a rule governing SWIFT and Fedwire transactions would only apply to transactions and institutions that use SWIFT and Fedwire. It would not cover the many other types of financial transactions. In contrast, APUNCAC solves these problems by securing the agreement of voluntary States Parties who would then extend the beneficial owner reporting requirement to any entity and beneficial owner who receives funds transferred from an entity governed by APUNCAC.

24. Contracts (Rights of Third Parties) Act 1999, c. 31 § 1(1); Restatement (Second) of Contracts § 302(1) (1981); The Law of Contract, the General Regime of Obligations, and Proof of Obligations (John Cartwright, Bénédicte Fauvarque-Cosson, and Simon Whittaker, trans., 2016) art. 1205, 1206, 1208, 1209 [hereinafter The Law of Contract].

25. The Law of Contract art. 1205, 1206, 1209.

26. Convention on the Law Applicable to Contractual Obligations [1980] OJ L266/1 (opened for signature June 19, 1980, entered into force April 1, 1991); Regulation 593/2008 on the law applicable to contractual obligations [2008] OJ L177/6 [hereinafter Rome I] (opened for signature June 17, 2008, entered into force July 24, 2008) art. 3 para. 1 ("A contract shall be governed by the law chosen by the parties").

27. Clare Stanley, "Submission to the Jurisdiction," Wilberforce Chambers, September, 2016, https://www.wilberforce.co.uk/wp-content/uploads/2016/06/Submission-to-the-Jurisdiction-Clare-Stanley-QC.pdf.

28. *Astro Exito Navegacion SA v. WT Hsu (The Messiniaki Tolmi)* [1984] 1 Lloyd's Rep. 266 at 270; (1984) 128 S.J. 265 CA (Civ Div).

29. *M/S Bremen v. Zapata Off-Shore Co* 407 US 1, 92 S.Ct 1907, 1916, 32 L.Ed.2d 513 (1972).

30. *M/S Bremen* 407 US 1 at 7 (1972).

31. *M/S Bremen* 407 US 1 at 10, 15 (1972).

32. *M/S Bremen* 407 US 1 at 12 (1972).

33. *Forschner Group Inc v. B-LINE AG* 943 F.Supp. 287, 292 n.8 (SDNY 1996).

34. *Koninklijke Philips Electronics v. Digital Works Inc* 358 F.Supp.2d 328 at 332, 333, 334 (SDNY 2005).

35. *Koninklijke Philips Electronics* 358 F.Supp.2d 328 at 333 (SDNY 2005).

36. *Ultracashmere House, Ltd v. Madison's of Columbus Inc* 534 F.Supp. 542 at 545 (SDNY 1982).

37. *Greene's Ready Mixed Concrete Co v. Fillmore Pacific Associates Ltd Partnership* 808 F.Supp. 307 at 309, 310, 311 (SDNY 1992).

38. *United States ex rel. Pensacola Constr. Co v. St Paul Fire and Marine Ins. Co* 705 F.Supp. 306 at 314 (WD La. 1989).

39. See Regulation 44/2001 on jurisdiction and the recognition and enforcement of judgments in civil and commercial matters [2000] OJ L12/1.

40. See Regulation 44/2001 art. 23.

41. Regulation 593/2008 on the law applicable to contractual obligations [2008] OJ L177/6 [hereinafter Rome I Regulation] art. 3(1) ("A contract shall be governed by the law chosen by the parties").

42. *Commerzbank Aktiengesellschaft v. Liquimar Tankers Management Inc* [2017] EWHC 161 (Comm); [2017] 1 W.L.R. 3497.

43. Regulation 1215/2012 on jurisdiction and the recognition and enforcement of judgments in civil and commercial matters [2012] OJ L351/1 [hereinafter Brussels Recast].

44. Brussels Recast art. 31(2).

45. *Meeth v. Glacetal Sarl* (C23/78) EU:C:1978:198; [1979] C.M.L.R. 520.

46. See *Gerling Konzern Speziale Kreditversicherung AG v. Amministrazione del Tesoro dello Stato* (201/82) EU:C:1983:217; [1983] E.C.R. 2503; [1984] 3 C.M.L.R. 638; and per Léger AG in *Trasporti Castelletti Spedizioni Internazionali SpA v. Hugo Trumpy SpA* (C-159/97) EU:C:1999:142; [1999] I.L.Pr. 492. See also *Firswood Ltd v. Petra Bank* unreported December 13, 1995 CA (Civ Div); and Hélène Gaudemet-Tallon, *Les Conventions de Bruxelles et de Lugano* (Montchrestien, 1996), para. 141. In *Gerling* [1983] E.C.R. 2503 at 2507, the European Court stated: "What is actually at issue is a contract of insurance entered into by a party in his own name but on behalf of a third party," *Gerling* [1983] E.C.R. 2503 at 2507. "That type of contract . . . implies that the parties wish to confer an entitlement on that third party who none the less stands outside the contract." "The [Court] takes the view that even if the third party insured does not physically sign the clause conferring jurisdiction (if any) which would entitle him to institute proceedings before a given court, he may none the less avail himself thereof," *Gerling* [1983] E.C.R. 2503 at 2508. "The insurer, having clearly signified his consent, may not contest the application of that clause," *Gerling* [1983] E.C.R. 2503 at 2510. "In a contract concluded in favour of a third party, if that third party wishes to take the benefit of the stipulation made in his favour, he himself acquires rights arising under the contract independently of any acceptance, solely on the strength of the stipulation agreed between the parties," *Gerling* [1983] E.C.R. 2503 at 2511. The court held that such jurisdiction clauses, giving a third party the right to institute proceedings before a given court, are also valid for third party "persons whose identity may even be unknown when the contract is signed," *Gerling* [1983] E.C.R. 2503 at 2516. This implies that such jurisdiction clauses would also be valid with regard to a guarantee pursuant to APUNCAC that names "a State Party

plaintiff" as beneficiary and gives the plaintiff the right to choose a competent authority to resolve disputes about the guarantee, *even if the precise identity of the "State Party plaintiff" is unknown when the guarantee is signed.*

47. Model Guarantee para. 2(f)–(g).

48. Convention on Choice of Court Agreements (2005) 44 I.L.M. 1294.

49. Convention on Choice of Court Agreements (2005) 44 I.L.M. 1294 art. 6.

50. Convention on Choice of Court Agreements (2005) 44 I.L.M. 1294 art. 8; see also art. 9.

51. Contracts (Rights of Third Parties) Act 1999 (c.31) s.1(3) ("The third party must be expressly identified in the contract by name, as a member of a class or as answering a particular description").

52. Model Guarantee para. 1(b).

53. Model Guarantee para. 1(b) s.1(5).

54. APUNCAC art. 19 para. 6.

55. Serious Organised Crime and Police Act 2005 ss.76(3)(a), 76(3)(c).

56. Serious Organised Crime and Police Act 2005 ss.76(1), 76(3)(a), 76(7)(b), 79(3), 79(4).

57. Serious Organised Crime and Police Act 2005 s.81(5)(a).

58. Serious Organised Crime and Police Act 2005 s.79(10).

59. 18 USC ss.1956, 1957 (2016).

60. 31 CFR ss.1010.410, 1020.410, 103.36, 103.37 (2017).

61. 31 CFR s.103.23 (2017).

62. 31 CFR ss.103.24, 103.25 (2017).

63. RSA is an encryption algorithm that was publicly described by Ron Rivest, Adi Shamir, and Leonard Adleman in 1978. A user of RSA creates and then publishes the product of two large prime numbers, along with an auxiliary value, as the user's public key. The prime factors must be kept secret. Anyone can use the public key to encrypt a message. If the public key is large enough, only a person with knowledge of the prime factors can feasibly decode the message. The capacity to encrypt messages gives user A the capacity to receive an encrypted request for "passport" information from user B. User A can then send an encrypted message to user B containing the "passport" information. This process assures user B that the passport information is received from user A and not someone posing as user A.

64. 31 CFR s.1020.315 (2017).

65. 31 USC s.5324 (2016).

66. 31 CFR ss.103.18, 103.19, 103.20, 103.21 (2017); 12 CFR s.563.180 (2017).

67. 31 CFR s.1010.330 (2017).

68. 31 CFR ss.103.57, 103.59 (2017).

69. APUNCAC art. 18, para. 6.

70. See Gabriel Zucman, *The Hidden Wealth of Nations: The Scourge of Tax Havens* (Chicago: The University of Chicago Press, 2015), 95–97.

71. Foreign Account Tax Compliance Act 2010 Pub. L. No. 111-147, 124 Stat. 71, 97-117 (2010) (codified at 26 USC ss.1471–1474, s.6038D (2016)).

CHAPTER 9

1. International Consortium of Investigative Journalists, "Global Banks Defy U.S. Crackdowns by Serving Oligarchs, Criminals and Terrorists: The FinCEN Files Show Trillions in Tainted Dollars Flow Freely through Major Banks, Swamping a Broken Enforcement System," September 20, 2020, https://www.icij.org/investigations/fincen-files/global-banks-defy-u-s-crackdowns-by-serving-oligarchs-criminals-and-terrorists/.

2. United Nations Convention against Corruption, *opened for signature* October 31, 2003, 2349 UNTS 41 (entered into force December 14, 2005) [hereinafter UNCAC].

3. United Nations Convention against Transnational Organized Crime, December 12, 2000, 2225 UNTS 277 [hereinafter UNTOC].

4. United Nations Convention against Illicit Traffic in Narcotic Drugs and Psychotropic Substances, *opened for signature* December 20, 1988, 1582 UNTS 95 (entered into force November 11, 1990).

5. International Convention for the Suppression of Financing of Terrorism, *opened for signature* January 10, 2000, 2178 UNTS 197 (entered into force April 10, 2002).

6. APUNCAC, http://tinyurl.com/y6bkpott.

7. The special nature of the BVI, the Cayman Islands, and Panama regarding money laundering and financial crime is indicated by their inclusion on the U.S. State Department's list of jurisdictions "of primary concern." See Bureau for International Narcotics and Law Enforcement Affairs, *International Narcotics Control Strategy Report, Volume 2* (Washington, DC: United States Department of State, 2017).

8. Yeh, "Ending Corruption in Africa through United Nations Inspections"; Stuart S. Yeh, "Anti-Corruption Inspections: A Missing Element of the IMF/World Bank Agenda?" *Journal of African Policy Studies* 18, no. 1 (2012); Yeh, "Is an International Treaty Needed to Fight Corruption and the Narco-Insurgency in Mexico?"; Yeh, "Why UN Inspections? The Accountability Gap in Sub-Saharan Africa"; Yeh, "Building a Global Institution to Fight Corruption and Address the Roots of Insurgency"; Stuart S. Yeh, "Poverty and the Rule of Law in Africa: A Missing International Actor?" *Poverty and Public Policy* 6, no. 4 (2014); Yeh, "Why UN Inspections? Corruption, Accountability, and the Rule of Law"; Stuart S. Yeh, "An International Law Approach to End Money Laundering," *Journal of International Banking Law and Regulation* 35, no. 4 (2020); Stuart S. Yeh, "An International Treaty to Fight Money Laundering," *Journal of International Banking Law and Regulation* 35, no. 5 (2020); Stuart S. Yeh, "Application of a Model International Treaty to Money Laundering," *Journal of International Banking Law and Regulation* 35, no. 11 (2020).

9. Emile van der Does de Willebois et al., *The Puppet Masters: How the Corrupt Use Legal Structures to Hide Stolen Assets and What to Do About It* (Washington, DC: The International Bank for Reconstruction and Development, 2011), 97.

10. See Riggs Bank case study report prepared by Minority Staff of the Permanent Subcommittee on Investigations of the Committee on Governmental Affairs, *Money*

Laundering and Foreign Corruption: Enforcement and Effectiveness of the Patriot Act, 108th Cong., 2nd Sess., July 15, 2004.

11. Ibid.

12. van der Does de Willebois et al., "The Puppet Masters: How the Corrupt Use Legal Structures to Hide Stolen Assets and What to Do About It," 9.

13. Ibid., 58.

14. APUNCAC, art. 21, para. 2, art. 22, para. 1, art. 30.

15. Ibid., art. 21, para. 2, art. 22, para. 1, art. 30.

16. Ibid., art. 39, paras. 2, 7, art. 40, paras. 2–5.

17. Ibid., art. 40, para. 7.

18. Ibid., art. 19, para. 6, art. 40, para. 1.

19. Through a court order, authorities in the United States can obtain e-mail, text messages, and recordings of phone conversations. 18 U.S.C. § 2518. See also Theodoric Meyer, "No Warrant, No Problem: How the Government Can Get Your Digital Data," *ProPublica*, June 27, 2014, https://www.propublica.org/article/no-warrant-no-problem-how-the-government-can-still-get-your-digital-data.

20. van der Does de Willebois et al., "The Puppet Masters: How the Corrupt Use Legal Structures to Hide Stolen Assets and What to Do About It," 60.

21. APUNCAC, art. 19, para. 19.

22. UNTOC, art. 6, para. 1.

23. UNTOC, art. 16, para. 3. Significantly, 189 nations are parties to UNTOC. United Nations, "United Nations Convention against Transnational Organized Crime Signature and Ratification Status as of November 18, 2017," 2017, accessed November 18, 2017, https://treaties.un.org/pages/viewdetails.aspx?src=ind&mtdsg_no=xviii-12&chapter=18&lang=en. The only UN Member States that are not parties are Bhutan, Republic of the Congo, Palau, Papua New Guinea, the Solomon Islands, Somalia, South Sudan, and Tuvalu. This implies that extradition for crimes covered by UNTOC is available to all nations except these eight states.

24. Ibid.

25. Ibid., art. 7, para. 1, 2225 UNTS 278.

26. APUNCAC, art. 21, para. 2, art. 22, para. 1, art. 30. Technically, the model protocol only applies to transactions involving State Party nationals, or funds that originate from the territory of the State Party. However, rather than attempting to distinguish transactions that trigger the reporting requirement from transactions that do not trigger the reporting requirement, a bank clerk could simply report all transactions exceeding $3,000 to FINCEN. There is no penalty for over-reporting. A bank clerk who adopts this approach would avoid the possibility of debarment, fines, and criminal penalties for failing to report a covered transaction.

27. Ibid., art. 19, paras. 17, 19, art. 40, para. 7.

28. United Nations Convention against Transnational Organized Crime, December 12, 2000, art. 16, para. 3, 2225 UNTS 284.

29. United Nations Convention against Transnational Organized Crime, December 12, 2000, art. 7, para. 1, 2225 UNTS 278.

30. APUNCAC, art. 21, para. 2, art. 22, para. 1, art. 30.

31. United Nations Convention against Transnational Organized Crime, December 12, 2000, art. 6, para. 1, 2225 UNTS 277.

32. APUNCAC, art. 21, para. 2, art. 22, para. 1, art. 30.

33. APUNCAC, art. 19, paras. 17, 19, art. 30, art. 40, paras. 3, 7. United Nations Convention against Transnational Organized Crime, December 12, 2000, art. 6, para. 1, art. 16, para. 3, 2225 UNTS 278.

34. APUNCAC, art. 19, paras. 6, 17, 19, art. 40, paras. 1, 7. United Nations Convention against Transnational Organized Crime, December 12, 2000, art. 6, para. 1, art. 16, para. 3, 2225 UNTS 278.

35. United Nations, "United Nations Convention against Transnational Organized Crime Signature and Ratification Status as of November 18, 2017."

36. Ibid.

37. Mark W. Janis, *An Introduction to International Law*, 4th ed. (New York: Aspen, 2003), 318.

38. Ibid., 320.

39. Ibid., 322.

40. 148 F.2d 416, 442–448 (2d Cir. 1945).

41. Ibid.

42. Id. at 443.

43. *Restatement (Second) of the Foreign Relations Law of the United States* §17 (St. Paul, MN: American Law Institute Publishers, 1965).

44. *Restatement (Third) of the Foreign Relations Law of the United States* §402(1)(c) (St. Paul, MN: American Law Institute Publishers, 1987).

45. *RJR Nabisco*, 136 S. Ct. 2090, 2102, 2104, 2105 (2016).

46. Ibid.

47. 74 Fed. Reg. 57593, 57594 (2009).

48. APUNCAC, art. 19, paras. 10, 11, art. 39, para. 1, art. 40, para. 1.

49. Ibid, art. 40, para. 7.

50. Ibid., art. 30, art. 40, paras. 3, 7.

51. U.S. Department of the Treasury, "Specially Designated Nationals and Blocked Persons List (SDN) Human Readable Lists," January 12, 2018, https://www.treasury.gov/resource-center/sanctions/SDN-List/Pages/default.aspx; 31 C.F.R. §§ 595.204, 595.701(a)(2).

52. Ibid.

53. APUNCAC, art. 18, paras. 11, 12, art. 19, para. 2.

54. APUNCAC, art. 18, para. 4.

55. Ibid.

56. Ibid.

57. Ibid., art. 18, para. 7.

58. Ibid, art. 18, para. 9, art. 71, paras. 11, 14.

59. Ibid, art. 18, para. 8.

60. Ibid., art. 18, para. 6.

61. 31 CFR § 1010.230 (2017).

62. 31 CFR § 1010.230 (2017).

63. FinCEN considered and rejected a suggestion that certification be made under penalty of perjury. 81 Fed. Reg. 29398, 29405–29406 (2016).

64. In January 2016, a federal district court held that the BSA permits FinCEN to sue an individual employee for willfully violating the BSA's AML program requirement. *U.S. Dep't of Treasury v. Haider*, Civ. No. 15-1518, 2016 WL 107940 (D. Minn. January 8, 2016). FinCEN levied a $1 million penalty against Thomas Haider, chief compliance officer and senior vice president of Government Affairs at MoneyGram International Inc. ("MoneyGram"). *In re Thomas E. Haider*, FinCEN No. 2014-08 (December 18, 2014) (Assessment of Civil Money Penalty),

https://www.fincen.gov/sites/default/files/enforcement_action/Haider_ Assessment.pdf. Haider was responsible for MoneyGram's compliance with BSA. MoneyGram admitted to "willful" failure to maintain an effective AML program and Haider willfully failed to maintain an effective AML program, serving to aid and abet fraud involving approximately $60 million. The case illustrates that FinCEN, in general, reserves individual penalties for egregious cases involving large sums, proof of money laundering, and senior personnel.

65. See Zucman, *The Hidden Wealth of Nations: The Scourge of Tax Havens*, 95–97.

66. In December 2020, the U.S. Congress passed legislation that would require all U.S. corporations to register the identity of their beneficial owners in a database operated by the U.S. Treasury Department's FinCEN in order to discourage criminals from using shell companies to conceal illicit funds. Robert Armstrong and Kiran Stacey, "US to Shift Burden from Banks in Overhaul of Money Laundering Laws: Companies Will Have to Register Their Beneficial Owners Directly with US Treasury," *Financial Times*, December 8, 2020, https://www.ft.com/content /498493c4-a138-4e5d-b926-a86ae317b8f4; Paul McLeod et al., "Congress Has Passed Sweeping Anti-Money Laundering Legislation—Now It's up to Trump," *BuzzFeed News*, December 11, 2020, https://www.buzzfeednews.com/article/paulmcleod/congress-closes-loop-hole-shell-companies. However, criminals may simply move their funds to a jurisdiction that does not require identification of beneficial ownership. In addition, companies with more than 20 employees and at least $5 million in annual sales, as well as a physical presence in the United States, would be exempt. Ibid. This raises the possibility that criminals could simply buy a legitimate entity meeting these criteria, then launder illicit funds through the corporate accounts.

67. A provision in the U.S. National Defense Authorization Act would require companies formed in the United States to disclose the identity of the true beneficial owner. Anonymous shell companies would no longer be permitted. However, the law exempts trusts and partnerships. Jen Kirby, "The US Is on the Verge of the Biggest Anti-Money-Laundering Update in Years: Congress Included a Provision to Ban Anonymous Shell Companies," *Vox*, December 21, 2020, https://www.vox .com/22188223/congress-anti-money-laundering-anonymous-shell-companies-ban -defense-bill. The law permits hedge funds and private equity funds to invest and distribute funds received from private investors without disclosing the beneficial owners of those funds. The fund adviser will be required to disclose the beneficial owner of the adviser, but not the beneficial owners of the funds deposited with the adviser. Criminals who seek to launder illicit funds could simply switch their accounts to hedge funds and private equity funds.

68. van der Does de Willebois et al., "The Puppet Masters: How the Corrupt Use Legal Structures to Hide Stolen Assets and What to Do About It."
69. Ibid., 98.
70. Ibid., 75.
71. Ibid.
72. Ibid., 72.
73. Ibid., 39.
74. Ibid., 55.
75. APUNCAC, art. 22, para. 1.
76. APUNCAC, art. 21, para. 2, art. 22, para. 1, art. 30.
77. Ibid.
78. Ibid.
79. Ibid.
80. Ibid., art. 19, para. 2.
81. Ibid.
82. WhatsApp, "Whatsapp Encryption Overview White Paper" (2017).
83. APUNCAC, art. 19, para. 4.
84. Ibid.
85. Ibid, art. 39, para. 1, art. 40, para. 1.
86. Ibid., art. 19, para. 10, art. 39, para. 1, art. 40, para. 1.
87. Ibid, art. 40, para. 7.
88. Ibid art. 19, para. 10, art. 39, para. 1, art. 40, paras. 1, 7.
89. If a document names a real person or entity that is uninvolved in the fraud, an investigator can conduct an interview that quickly establishes the fake nature of a purported transaction or business record. If the document names a fictitious person or entity, an investigator can establish the fictitious nature by checking birth, tax, business, or social security records.

CHAPTER 10

1. APUNCAC, http://tinyurl.com/y6bkpott.
2. S.S. Yeh, "An International Law Approach to End Money Laundering" (2020) 35 *J.I.B.L.R.* 148; S.S. Yeh, "An International Treaty to Fight Money Laundering" (2020) 35 *J.I.B.L.R.* 190.
3. Bruun and Hjejle, *Report on the Non-Resident Portfolio at Danske Bank's Estonian Branch* (Copenhagen, Denmark: Bruun and Hjejle, 2018), 50–51.
4. Ibid., 7.
5. Ibid., 6.
6. Ibid., 31.
7. Ibid., 64.
8. Ibid., 55.
9. Ibid., 56.
10. Ibid., 57.
11. Ibid., 60.

12. Ibid., 61.
13. Ibid., 57.
14. Ibid., 61.
15. Ibid., 62.
16. Ibid., 73.
17. Ibid., 74.
18. Ibid.
19. Ibid.
20. Ibid.
21. Ibid.
22. Luke Harding and Shaun Walker, "'Poisoned' Russian Whistleblower Was Fatalistic over Death Threats," *The Guardian*, May 19, 2015, https://www.theguardian.com/uk-news/2015/may/19/poisoned-russian-whistleblower-was-fatalistic-over-death-threats.
23. Matt Doran and Melissa Doyle. Documentary film. *Dirty Money: Russia's Largest Tax Refund Laundered into Foreign Banks* (Sydney, Australia: Sunday Night, 2018).
24. Bruun and Hjejle, "Report on the Non-Resident Portfolio at Danske Bank's Estonian Branch," 33.
25. "Dirty Money: Russia's Largest Tax Refund Laundered into Foreign Banks."
26. Ibid.
27. Ibid.
28. Ibid.
29. Ibid.
30. Ibid.
31. Bruun and Hjejle, "Report on the Non-Resident Portfolio at Danske Bank's Estonian Branch," 75.
32. Richard Milne and Caroline Binham, "Danske Bank Memo Shows How Russians Moved Money," *Financial Times*, October 4, 2018, https://www.ft.com/content/f13ae77a-c7f1-11e8-ba8f-ee390057b8c9.
33. Ibid.
34. Ibid.
35. Bruun and Hjejle, "Report on the Non-Resident Portfolio at Danske Bank's Estonian Branch," 49.
36. Ibid.
37. Ibid., 76.
38. Ibid.
39. Ibid.
40. Ibid.
41. Ibid., 81.
42. Ibid., 82–83, 86.
43. Ibid., 86. In April 2021, Danish prosecutors dropped all charges against former Chief Executive Thomas Borgen, former Chief Financial Officer Henrik Ramlau-Hanse, and former Head of International Banking Lars Morch. Prosecutors did not find sufficient evidence to show gross negligence, as required under Danish law.

44. Ibid., 22.
45. Ibid., 8.
46. Ibid.
47. Ibid., 12.
48. Directive 2005/60/EC on the prevention of the use of the financial system for the purpose of money laundering and terrorist financing [2005] OJ L309/15; Money Laundering and Terrorist Financing Prevention Act [2008] RT I 2008, 3, 21.
49. Bruun and Hjejle, "Report on the Non-Resident Portfolio at Danske Bank's Estonian Branch," 11.
50. Ibid.
51. Ibid., 11–12. EEK, or the Estonian kroon, was the official currency of Estonia during the 1928–1940 and 1992–2011 time periods. After January 2011, the euro became the sole legal tender in Estonia.
52. Kevin Newman. *The Laundromat: Investigation of Money Laundering at B.C. Casinos*. Documentary film. Directed by Allan Myers. Toronto, Canada: CTV News, 2019.
53. Ibid.
54. Ibid.
55. Ibid.
56. Ibid.
57. Ibid.
58. Ibid.
59. Ibid.
60. Ibid.
61. Ibid.
62. Ibid.
63. Ibid.
64. Ibid.
65. Ibid.
66. Peter M. Germain, "Dirty Money: An Independent Review of Money Laundering in Lower Mainland Casinos Conducted for the Attorney General of British Columbia," March 31, 2018, http://assetforfeiturelaw.us/wp-content/uploads/2018/06/German_Gaming_Final_Report.pdf.
67. Myers, "The Laundromat: Investigation of Money Laundering at B.C. Casinos."
68. Ibid.
69. Contrary to Germain, Robert Kroeker stated that BCLC did not depend on gaming revenue and, therefore, dependence on gaming revenue could not have motivated BCLC inaction. Commission of Inquiry into Money Laundering in British Columbia, *Opening Statement of Robert Kroeker*, February 25, 2020, 18, https://cullencommission.ca/files/OpeningStatement-Kroeker.pdf.
70. Myers, "The Laundromat: Investigation of Money Laundering at B.C. Casinos."
71. *Opening Statement of Robert Kroeker*, 5–6.
72. Ibid., 6.

73. Ibid., 16.

74. GPEB refers to the British Columbia Gaming Policy and Enforcement Branch of the Ministry of Public Safety. GPEB was responsible for regulating gaming conducted, managed, and/or operated by the BCLC.

75. Commission of Inquiry into Money Laundering in British Columbia, *Opening Statement of British Columbia Lottery Corporation*, February 24, 2020. 1–2, https://cullencommission.ca/files/OpeningStatement-BCLC.pdf.

76. *United States v. Liberty Reserve S.A.*, SDNY https://www.justice.gov/sites/default/files/usao-sdny/legacy/2015/03/25/Liberty%20Reserve%2C%20et%20al.%20Indictment%20-%20Redacted_0.pdf (accessed April 14, 2020). Details regarding the case are drawn from the federal indictment.

77. *United States v. Liberty Reserve S.A.*, s.19.

78. Marc Santora, William K. Rashbaum, and Nicole Perlroth, "Online Currency Exchange Accused of Laundering $6 Billion," *The New York Times*, May 28, 2013, https://www.nytimes.com/2013/05/29/nyregion/liberty-reserve-operators-accused-of-money-laundering.html.

79. *United States v. Liberty Reserve S.A.*, s.15.

80. *United States v. Liberty Reserve S.A.*, s.18.

81. *United States v. Liberty Reserve S.A.*, s.20.

82. *United States v. Liberty Reserve S.A.*, s.20.

83. *United States v. Liberty Reserve S.A.*, s.21.

84. *United States v. Liberty Reserve S.A.*, s.22.

85. Stefano Siggia, "Online Video Games: Regulatory Overview," *ACAMS Today*, November 20, 2019, https://www.acamstoday.org/online-video-games-regulatory-overview/.

86. FinCEN, "Application of FinCEN's Regulations to Persons Administering, Exchanging, or Using Virtual Currencies," March 18, 2013, https://www.fincen.gov/sites/default/files/shared/FIN-2013-G001.pdf.

87. FATF is an intergovernmental body involving 39 members that set international standards to fight money laundering and financial crime. Over 200 members of FSRBs have committed to implementation of FATF recommendations. FATF, "Who We Are," 2019, https://www.fatf-gafi.org/about/whoweare/.

88. Siggia, "Online Video Games: Regulatory Overview."

89. Anton Moiseienko and Kayla Izenman, "Gaming the System: Money Laundering through Online Games," *RUSI Newsbrief* 39, no. 9 (2019), https://rusi.org/publication/rusi-newsbrief/gaming-system-money-laundering-through-online-games, 1.

90. Ibid., 1–2.

91. Ibid.

92. Ibid., 2.

93. Ibid., 3.

94. FATF, "Outcomes FATF Plenary, 17–19 October 2018," 2018, http://www.fatf-gafi.org/publications/fatfgeneral/documents/outcomes-plenary-october-2018.html. "AML/CFT" refers to anti-money laundering/combating the financing of terrorism regulations promulgated by FATF and FSRBs.

95. FATF, "FATF Glossary," 2019, https://www.fatf-gafi.org/glossary/u-z/.

96. Moiseienko and Izenman, "Gaming the System: Money Laundering through Online Games," 3.

97. Alyssa Hertig, "Grasping Lightning: Mapping the Key Players in Bitcoin's Next Phase," June 11, 2020, https://www.coindesk.com/grasping-lightning-mapping-the-key-players-in-bitcoins-next-phase.

98. Melanie Lefebvre, Yasmine Ibrahim, and Peter Warrack, "The Lightning Network: Deconstructed and Evaluated," *Association of Certified Financial Crime Specialists*, January 8, 2020, https://www.acfcs.org/wp-content/uploads/2020/01/The-Lightning-Network-Deconstructed-and-Evaluated-final.pdf.

99. Ibid.

100. Ibid., 16–18.

101. Esther Kim, "Consumers in over 150 Countries Can Now Buy Stocks with Bitcoin," May 29, 2019, https://bitcoinist.com/bitcoin-buy-stocks-150-countries-abra/. Abra asserts that it is not a custodian of funds and, therefore, is exempt from regulations that apply to fund custodians. Abra asserts that it is not required to collect personal details from clients who deposit bitcoin into the app. Giulio Prisco, "Abra Is Introducing KYC-Less Stock Investing with Cryptocurrencies," February 7, 2019, https://medium.com/chainrift-research/abra-is-introducing-kyc-less-stock-investing-with-cryptocurrencies-c4ff60828121.

102. RSA is a public key cryptosystem widely used for secure data transmission and identity verification. Trusted Certificate Authorities create tamperproof digital certificates that bind each user's identity with each user's unique public key. RSA permits a user to send and receive encrypted messages, and to determine whether the content of the message or the digital signature was altered. With RSA, anyone can request that a user certify beneficial ownership of funds in question and can be assured that the user (instead of a poseur) provided the certification.

103. For example, both GlobalSign and ColumbiaSoft offer automated digital signing solutions suitable for high-volume applications. GlobalSign, "Digital Signatures for Organizations Using Automated Document Generation Software," 2020, https://www.globalsign.com/en/digital-signatures/high-volume-hsm; ColumbiaSoft, "Digital Signature Automation," 2020, https://www.documentlocator.com/solutions/digital-signature-workflow-automation/.

104. APUNCAC, art. 30, para. i.

105. APUNCAC, art. 30, para. ii.

106. APUNCAC, art. 30, para. iii.

107. APUNCAC, art. 32, para. 1.

108. APUNCAC, art. 19, para. 6.

109. S.S. Yeh, "An International Law Approach to End Money Laundering" (2020) 35 *J.I.B.L.R.* 148; S.S. Yeh, "An International Treaty to Fight Money Laundering" (2020) 35 *J.I.B.L.R.* 190.

110. The FINCEN database is a database established by APUNCAC for the purpose of collecting and centralizing beneficial ownership information and making the information accessible to financial crime investigators. FINCEN is the Financial Crime Enforcement Network established by APUNCAC and modeled on the U.S.

Treasury Department's FinCEN FIU. FINCEN is intended to be an international version of FinCEN.

111. 31 CFR § 1010.230 (2017). FinCEN considered and rejected a suggestion that certification be made under penalty of perjury. 81 Fed. Reg. 29398, 29405–29406 (2016).

112. Assuming that Denmark was a State Party to APUNCAC. APUNCAC, art. 22, para. 1, art. 30, para. iii.

113. Assuming that Canada was a State Party to APUNCAC. APUNCAC, art. 30, para. iii.

114. APUNCAC, art. 19, para. 6.

115. Assuming that the beneficial owner was a national of a State Party to APUNCAC. APUNCAC, art. 30, para. i.

116. APUNCAC, art. 30, para. i.

117. APUNCAC, art. 30, para. i.

118. Assuming that the beneficial owner was a national of a State Party to APUNCAC, and assuming a transaction in currency or involving a bank draft or bearer instrument. APUNCAC, art. 30, para. i. Alternatively, assuming that a hawaladar is within the jurisdiction of a State Party, and assuming a transaction in currency, or involving a bank draft, bearer instrument, negotiable instrument, wire transfer, or money order. APUNCAC, art. 30, para. iii.

119. APUNCAC, art. 30, para. i.

120. As of 2019, 93 percent of the world's population lives within reach of a mobile broadband or internet service network. International Telecommunications Union, "Measuring Digital Development: Facts and Figures 2019" (Geneva, Switzerland, 2019), 8. Expansion of mobile broadband is rapidly transforming the hawala and money services industry. In 2017, for example, the World Bank estimated that 73 percent of the Somali population over the age of 16 use mobile money services. Mobile money is the primary access point to financial services in Somalia. Mohamed Elmi and Ojelanki Ngwenyama, "The Role of Mobile Money in Somalia's Remittance System," in *HCI in Business, Government and Organizations*, ed. F.H. Nah and K. Siau (Basel, Switzerland: Springer Nature, 2019), 119. In Africa, nearly 40 percent of the population, including most business owners that offer hawala services, have internet access. Internet World Stats, "Internet Penetration in Africa," March 21, 2020. http://www.Internetworldstats.com/stats1.htm. Hawala is typically offered by travel agencies, transport companies, import/export businesses, gold and jewelry exchanges, and shipping companies that have internet access. See Peter Tinti and Tuesday Reitano, *Migrant, Refugee, Smuggler, Saviour* (London: Hurst and Company, 2018), 69. In Kabul, Afghanistan, approximately 5,000 money traders typically offer hawala money transfers as well as nonfinancial telephone and fax services, regional and trade services, and internet access. International Monetary Fund, *Islamic State of Afghanistan: Rebuilding a Macroeconomic Framework for Reconstruction and Growth* (Washington, DC: International Monetary Fund, 2003), 130.

121. APUNCAC, art. 30, para. iii, art. 70.

122. Assuming that the beneficial owner was a national of a State Party to APUNCAC. APUNCAC, art. 30, para. i.

123. APUNCAC, art. 30, para. i, art. 70.

124. APUNCAC, art. 32.

125. Assuming that Alex or Britney is a national of a State Party to APUNCAC. FinCEN is beginning to recognize the risks associated with cryptocurrency. In December 2020, FinCEN proposed a rule that would require banks and MSBs to file a report of each withdrawal, exchange, or other payment or transfer which involves a transaction in convertible virtual currency or a digital asset with legal tender status with a value of more than $10,000, involving a counterparty whose account is held at a financial institution not regulated by the BSA, or an FFI in a jurisdiction designated by the U.S. Treasury Department as a jurisdiction "of primary money laundering concern." The report must include the name and address of each counterparty. Prior to the conclusion of such transaction, the financial institution must verify and record the name and address of the individual presenting the transaction, and must record the identity, account number, and the social security or taxpayer identification number of "any person or entity on whose behalf such transaction is to be effected." FinCEN, "Notice of Proposed Rulemaking RIN 1506-AB47: Requirements for Certain Transactions Involving Convertible Virtual Currency or Digital Assets," U.S. Department of the Treasury, December 18, 2020, https://public-inspection.federalregister.gov/2020-28437.pdf. While the intent is to close the type of loophole that currently permits cryptocurrency users to store convertible virtual currency in private "wallets," conduct anonymous transactions, and evade anti-money laundering regulations, the proposed rule does not apply to transactions that do not involve a bank or MSB, such as the type of Lightning-based cryptocurrency transaction described here, involving Alex and Britney, nor does the rule address the possibility that a criminal would substitute a trusted confidant to serve as a fake beneficial owner. APUNCAC addresses both issues.

126. APUNCAC, art. 30, para. i.

127. APUNCAC, art. 19, para. 6.

128. For example, both GlobalSign and ColumbiaSoft offer automated digital signing solutions suitable for high-volume applications. GlobalSign, "Digital Signatures for Organizations Using Automated Document Generation Software"; ColumbiaSoft, "Digital Signature Automation."

129. S.S. Yeh, "An International Law Approach to End Money Laundering" (2020) 35 *J.I.B.L.R.* 148; S.S. Yeh, "An International Treaty to Fight Money Laundering" (2020) 35 *J.I.B.L.R.* 190.

130. See Ekran System, "Light-Weight Privileged Access Management (PAM)," 2020, https://www.ekransystem.com/en/product/privileged-access-management.

131. Oracle, "Access Controls and Privileges," 2019, https://docs.oracle.com/en/database/oracle/oracle-database/18/olsag/access-controls-and-privileges.html#GUID-A222EB99-83C4-4BCC-84F6-D20087101E9D.

132. This type of analysis has been successfully employed by credit card companies such as VISA and American Express to flag and respond to suspicious activity. Algorithms to detect suspicious activity utilize information about patterns of previous use to flag instances of suspicious use. Suspicious activity triggers an investigation.

133. S.S. Yeh, "An International Law Approach to End Money Laundering" (2020) 35 *J.I.B.L.R.* 148; S.S. Yeh, "An International Treaty to Fight Money Laundering" (2020) 35 *J.I.B.L.R.* 190.

134. APUNCAC, art. 59, para. 7, art. 62, para. 6.

135. Financial Action Task Force, *Transparency and Beneficial Ownership* (Paris: Financial Action Task Force, 2014).

136. Financial Action Task Force, *Virtual Assets and Virtual Asset Service Providers* (Paris: Financial Action Task Force, 2019).

137. Ibid., 56.

138. Ibid.

139. Ibid.

140. Financial Action Task Force, "Transparency and Beneficial Ownership."

141. See CoolBitX, "Bridge: Enabling VASPs to Collect and Exchange Compliance-Required Transaction Information," 2020, https://www.sygna.io/bridge/; CoolBitX, "Sygna Bridge Report: FATF Recommendation 16 Technical Solution for Virtual Asset Transactions" (Arcadia, CA: CoolBitX, 2020).

CHAPTER 11

1. *Katzman v. Victoria's Secret Catalogue*, 167 F.R.D. 649, 655 (SDNY 1996).

2. APUNCAC, art. 60, paras. 4–7, http://tinyurl.com/y6bkpott.

3. This standard is consistent with the definition codified in the U.S. CFR regarding the term "knows or has reason to know." The definition relies on what "a reasonable person . . . would conclude . . . based on all the facts reasonably available" at the time a financial transaction was approved, or at the time financial services were obtained or delivered. 26 CFR § 53.4965-6(b)(1).

4. The hypothetical scenario outlined in this paragraph is based on an investigation of the World Bank's Yerevan water project. See Laurence Soustras et al., "World Bank: Tales of the Missing Millions," *France 24*, June 27, 2016, http://webdoc.france24.com/world-bank-corruption-development-armenia-kenya-somalia-transparency/.

5. Britain has targeted more than 20 of the world's most corrupt politicians laundering millions of pounds through the City of London. Paul Peachey, "'Britain's FBI' Target More Than 20 of the World's Most Corrupt Politicians Laundering Millions of Pounds through City of London," *Independent*, September 4, 2015, https://www.independent.co.uk/news/uk/crime/britains-fbi-target-more-than-20-of-the-worlds-most-corrupt-politicians-laundering-millions-of-10487589.html. See also the case of Teodorin Nguema Obiang, who was tried in a French court on corruption charges. Adam Withnall, "The Brutal Central African Dictator Whose Playboy Son Faces French Corruption Trial," *Independent*, September 12, 2016, https://www.independent.co.uk/news/world/africa/teodoro-obiang-nguema-mbasogo-equatorial-guinea-french-corruption-trial-a7238501.html. A former government minister in Guinea, Mahmoud Thiam, was tried in a U.S. court on corruption charges. Brendan Pierson, "Ex-Guinea Minister Charged with Laundering Bribes Goes to Trial," *Reuters*,

April 24, 2017, https://www.reuters.com/article/us-usa-guinea-corruption/ex-guinea-minister-charged-with-laundering-bribes-goes-to-trial-idUSKBN17Q2DF. U.S. prosecutors seized $144 million in assets amassed through bribery of Diezani Alison-Madueke, Nigeria's minister for petroleum resources. David J. Lynch, "Nigeria's Former Oil Minister Named in US Bribery Complaint," *Financial Times*, July 14, 2017, https://www.ft.com/content/88a4b26a-68d7-11e7-8526-7b38dcaef614.

6. Racketeer Influenced and Corrupt Organizations Act, Pub. L. 91-452, 84 Stat. 922-3 (1970) (codified at 18 U.S.C. §§ 1961–1968, 1961 (2016)).

7. Karen D. Walker and Michael G. Tanner, "RICO Claims: The Challenge of Alleging the 'Pattern' Element," *The Florida Bar Journal* 76, no. 5 (2002), https://www.hklaw.com/files/Publication/5961c979-3acb-4d63-bd95-2e36b1450c50/Presentation/PublicationAttachment/4387711b-c615-4247-bdd5-6b37b9bccb4c/46193.PDF, 36.

8. Ibid.

9. Ibid.

10. *H.J. Inc. v. Northwestern Bell Tel. Co.*, 492 U.S. 229, 243 (1989).

11. Walker and Tanner, "RICO Claims: The Challenge of Alleging the 'Pattern' Element," 36.

12. APUNCAC, art. 69, para. ssss.

CHAPTER 12

1. APUNCAC, art. 8, para. 6, http://tinyurl.com/y6bkpott.
2. APUNCAC, art. 8, para. 9.
3. APUNCAC, art. 11, para. 1.
4. APUNCAC, art. 11, para. 2.
5. APUNCAC, art. 11, para. 3.
6. APUNCAC, art. 11, para. 4.
7. APUNCAC, art. 11, para. 5.
8. APUNCAC, art. 11, para. 6.
9. APUNCAC, art. 11, para. 7.
10. APUNCAC, art. 11, para. 8.
11. APUNCAC, art. 11, para. 8.
12. APUNCAC, art. 11, para. 9.
13. APUNCAC, art. 10, para. 7.
14. APUNCAC, art. 10, para. 1.
15. APUNCAC, art. 10, para. 1.
16. APUNCAC, art. 10, para. 1.
17. APUNCAC, art. 10, para. 1.
18. APUNCAC, art. 10, para. 1.
19. APUNCAC, art. 10, para. 1.
20. APUNCAC, art. 10, para. 1.
21. APUNCAC, art. 10, para. 2.
22. APUNCAC, art. 10, para. 3.

23. APUNCAC, art. 10, para. 4.
24. APUNCAC, art. 10, para. 5.
25. APUNCAC, art. 10, para. 6.
26. APUNCAC, art. 14.
27. APUNCAC, art. 15.
28. APUNCAC, art. 16.
29. 5 U.S.C. §§ 551–559 (2016).
30. S.C. Code Ann. §§ 1-23-310 to 1-23-400 (2018).
31. South Carolina Administrative Law Court, "Rules of Procedure for the Administrative Law Court," April 27, 2016, accessed December 19, 2018, http://www.scalc.net/pub/pubOfficialrules2011.pdf.
32. U.S. Equal Employment Opportunity Commission, "Federal EEO Complaint Processing Procedures," 2018, accessed December 19, 2018, https://www.eeoc.gov/eeoc/publications/fedprocess.cfm.
33. 29 CFR § 1614.109(d) (2017).
34. Office of Personnel Management, "Qualification Standard for Administrative Law Judge Positions," 2018, accessed December 19, 2018, https://www.opm.gov/policy-data-oversight/classification-qualifications/general-schedule-qualification-standards/specialty-areas/administrative-law-judge-positions/.
35. 5 U.S.C. §§ 5303, 5372 (2016).
36. Administrative Conference of the United States, "Recommendation 92-7: The Federal Administrative Judiciary," 1992, accessed December 19, 2018, https://www.acus.gov/sites/default/files/documents/92-7.pdf.
37. APUNCAC, art. 70, para. 16(e).
38. APUNCAC, art. 70, para. 13(i).
39. APUNCAC, art. 70, para. 13(i).

CHAPTER 13

1. Rome Statute of the International Criminal Court, *opened for signature* July 17, 1998, 2187 UNTS 90 (entered into force July 1, 2002) [hereinafter Rome Statute].
2. Rome Statute, art. 17(2).
3. Jo Stigen, *The Relationship between the International Criminal Court and National Jurisdictions: The Principle of Complementarity*, The Raoul Wallenberg Institute Human Rights Library (Leiden, Netherlands: Martinus Nijhoff Publishers, 2008), 259, 261. *Mens rea* refers to criminal intent. The literal translation from Latin is "guilty mind." A *mens rea* refers to the state of mind statutorily required in order to convict a particular defendant of a particular crime. See, for example, *Staples v. United States*, 511 US 600 (1994). Establishing the *mens rea* of an offender is usually necessary to prove guilt in a criminal trial. The prosecution typically must prove beyond reasonable doubt that the defendant committed the offense with a culpable state of mind. The *mens rea* requirement is premised upon the idea that one must possess a guilty state of mind and be aware of his or her misconduct; however, a defendant need not know that his conduct is illegal to be guilty of a crime. Rather,

the defendant must be conscious of the facts that make his conduct fit the definition of the offense.

4. Ibid., 261.
5. Ibid., 270–71.
6. Ibid., 273.
7. APUNCAC, art. 10, para. 6, http://tinyurl.com/y6bkpott.
8. APUNCAC, art. 10, para. 7.
9. APUNCAC, art. 10, para. 1.
10. APUNCAC, art. 10, para. 1.
11. A difference is that a typical indictment does not include witness statements. However, there is a heightened need for transparency regarding allegations of corruption involving prosecutors and judges.
12. APUNCAC, art. 10, para. 1

CHAPTER 14

1. Anticorruption activists acknowledge the need to fight bribery, illicit financial flows, corruption in the extractives sector, and corruption in public administration, but less attention has been paid to the need to establish a body of UN anticorruption inspectors, dedicated anticorruption courts, and strong measures to enforce the submission of accurate beneficial owner information. See World Bank, "Ending Impunity for Corruption: Global Knowledge for Local Impact" (proceedings of the Third Biennial Meeting of the World Bank Group's International Corruption Hunters Alliance (ICHA), Washington, DC, December 8–10, 2014). Existing efforts focus on establishing registries to register beneficial ownership of companies, but this would not help investigators in cases where criminals obtain control of legitimate companies and illicit flows are intermingled with legitimate funds. APUNCAC focuses, instead, on requirements that would force beneficial owners to reveal their identities regarding international transfers to known bank secrecy havens, defined as jurisdictions on the U.S. State Department's list of jurisdictions "of primary concern." See Bureau for International Narcotics and Law Enforcement Affairs, "International Narcotics Control Strategy Report, Volume 2." The rationale for this focus is that criminals use jurisdictions where regulation is lax to hide illicit funds.
2. Mark L. Wolf, *The Case for an International Anti-Corruption Court* (Washington, DC: Brookings, 2014), 1.
3. Mark L. Wolf, "The World Needs an International Anti-Corruption Court," *Daedalus* 147, no. 3 (2018): 145.
4. Ibid., 147.
5. Ibid.
6. Ibid., 145–46.
7. Ibid., 148.
8. Ibid., 149–50.

9. Integrity Initiatives International, "The International Anti-Corruption Court," 2020, accessed November 25, 2020, http://www.integrityinitiatives.org/international-anticorruption-court.

10. Alex Whiting, "Is an International Anti-Corruption Court a Dream or a Distraction?," October 4, 2018, https://globalanticorruptionblog.com/2018/10/04/guest-post-is-an-international-anti-corruption-court-a-dream-or-a-distraction/; Matthew Stephenson, "Dear International Anticorruption Court Advocates: It's Time to Answer Your Critics," March 1, 2016, accessed November 4, 2020, https://globalanticorruptionblog.com/2016/03/01/dear-international-anticorruption-court-advocates-its-time-to-answer-the-critics/.

11. Stephenson, "Dear International Anticorruption Court Advocates: It's Time to Answer Your Critics."

12. Brett D. Schaefer, Steven Groves, and James M. Roberts, *Why the U.S. Should Oppose the Creation of an International Anti-Corruption Court* (Washington, DC: The Heritage Foundation, 2014), 12.

13. Whiting, "Is an International Anti-Corruption Court a Dream or a Distraction?".

14. Wolf, "The World Needs an International Anti-Corruption Court," 149.

15. Schaefer, Groves, and Roberts, "Why the U.S. Should Oppose the Creation of an International Anti-Corruption Court," 11.

16. Stephenson, "Dear International Anticorruption Court Advocates: It's Time to Answer Your Critics."

17. United Nations Convention against Corruption, *opened for signature* October 31, 2003, 2349 UNTS 41 (entered into force December 14, 2005) [hereinafter UNCAC].

18. Michael R. Darling, "I Can Resist Everything except Temptation: An International Solution to African Resource Corruption," *Texas International Law Journal* 52, no. 3 (2017): 439.

19. Steffens, *The Shame of the Cities*; Hoogenboom, "Did Gilded Age Scandals Bring Reform?"; Keller, "Corruption in America"; Miller, *Stealing from America*; Peck, "The British Case"; Florian Ramseger, "Historical Perspectives on Corruption in Europe," February 26, 2007, accessed November 4, 2020, https://www.u4.no/publications/historical-perspectives-on-corruption-in-europe/.

20. Hoogenboom, "Did Gilded Age Scandals Bring Reform?"; Peck, "The British Case."

21. Yue Ma, "Exploring the Origins of Public Prosecution," *International Criminal Justice Review* 18, no. 2 (2008): 202–203.

22. Ibid., 203.

23. Ibid.; Carolyn B. Ramsey, "The Discretionary Power of 'Public' Prosecutors in Historical Perspective," *American Criminal Law Review* 39 (2002).

24. Ma, "Exploring the Origins of Public Prosecution," 202–3.

25. Ibid., 202.

26. U.S. Department of Justice, "About DOJ," n.d., accessed November 1, 2020, https://www.justice.gov/about#:~:text=150%2C%2016%20Stat.,United%20States%20had%20an%20interest.

27. Mann Act, Pub. L. 61-277, 36 Stat. 825a (1910).

28. U.S. Department of Justice, "History," July 25, 2019, accessed December 23, 2020, https://www.justice.gov/criminal/history.

29. Claire B. Potter, *War on Crime: Bandits, G-Men, and the Politics of Mass Culture* (New Brunswick, NJ: Rutgers University Press, 1998), 10.

30. Ibid.

31. Kenneth O'Reilly, "A New Deal for the FBI: The Roosevelt Administration, Crime Control, and National Security," *The Journal of American History* 69, no. 3 (1982): 641.

32. Ibid.

33. Ibid.

34. John A. Conley, *The New Deal's Response to Crime: The Politics of Law and Order* (Michigan State University, 1971), 34.

35. Ibid., 11, 36.

36. Ibid., 30.

37. Ibid., 31.

38. Ibid., 20, 22–25, 32.

39. Ibid., 31.

40. O'Reilly, "A New Deal for the FBI: The Roosevelt Administration, Crime Control, and National Security," 643; Conley, "The New Deal's Response to Crime: The Politics of Law and Order," 34, 38, 39.

41. O'Reilly, "A New Deal for the FBI: The Roosevelt Administration, Crime Control, and National Security," 643.

42. Conley, "The New Deal's Response to Crime: The Politics of Law and Order," 47.

43. Ibid., 51.

44. Ibid., 48.

45. Ibid., 37.

46. Ibid., 27, 28, 83. Tammany Hall was a New York City political organization that served as the main local political machine of the Democratic Party and played a major role in controlling New York City and New York State politics from the 1790s to the 1960s. It typically controlled Democratic Party nominations and used its patronage resources to build a loyal, well-rewarded core of district and precinct leaders. Tammany Hall infamously served as an engine for graft and political corruption under William M. "Boss" Tweed in the mid-nineteenth century. In 1928, New York governor Al Smith, supported by Tammany Hall, won the Democratic presidential nomination.

47. Ibid., 28.

48. Ibid.

49. Ma, "Exploring the Origins of Public Prosecution," 203.

50. Gwladys Gilliéron, *Public Prosecutors in the United States and Europe: A Comparative Analysis with Special Focus on Switzerland, France, and Germany* (Cham, Switzerland: Springer International Publishing, 2014), 51; Ma, "Exploring the Origins of Public Prosecution," 206–7.

51. Gilliéron, *Public Prosecutors in the United States and Europe: A Comparative Analysis with Special Focus on Switzerland, France, and Germany*, 51; Ma, "Exploring the Origins of Public Prosecution," 206–7.

52. Gilliéron, *Public Prosecutors in the United States and Europe: A Comparative Analysis with Special Focus on Switzerland, France, and Germany*. 51.

53. Sabina Schnell, "Cheap Talk or Incredible Commitment? (Mis)Calculating Transparency and Anti-Corruption," *Governance: An International Journal of Policy, Administration, and Institutions* 31, no. 3 (2018).

54. Liliana Ciobanu, "Romania's Former Prime Minister Sentenced to Prison for Corruption," *CNN*, January 30, 2012, accessed November 4, 2020, https://www.cnn.com/2012/01/30/world/europe/romania-politician-convicted/index.html.

55. Schnell, "Cheap Talk or Incredible Commitment? (Mis)Calculating Transparency and Anti-Corruption," 422.

56. Ibid.

57. Ibid., 421.

58. Ibid., 420–21.

59. Ibid., 422.

60. Ibid., 423.

61. Ibid., 424.

62. Ibid.

63. Ibid., 425.

64. Ben Worthy, *The Politics of Freedom of Information: How and Why Governments Pass Laws That Threaten Their Power* (Manchester, UK: Manchester University Press, 2017), 188.

65. Ibid., 189.

66. Ibid.

67. Rome Statute of the International Criminal Court, *opened for signature* July 17, 1998, 2187 UNTS 90 (entered into force July 1, 2002) [hereinafter Rome Statute].

68. There are numerous examples of successful ICC investigations and prosecutions. See Yeh, "Why UN Inspections? Corruption, Accountability, and the Rule of Law."

69. "Situations Under Investigation," INT'L CRIM. CT., http://www.icc-cpi.int/en_menus/icc/situations%20and%20cases/Pages/situations%20and%20cases.aspx (last visited November 16, 2017).

70. Agreement between the United Nations and the State of Guatemala on the Establishment of an International Commission against Impunity in Guatemala, *opened for signature* December 12, 2006, 2472 UNTS 47 (entered into force September 4, 2007) [hereinafter CICIG Agreement]. After CICIG opened an investigation into President Jimmy Morales, his brother, and son, he declined to renew CICIG's mandate, effectively ending the commission after 12 years of operation and over 400 convictions, and despite public opinion polls demonstrating that over 70 percent of Guatemalans support CICIG. This outcome underlines the importance of establishing a permanent international institution insulated from domestic tampering and dedicated to the investigation of corruption.

71. CICIG Agreement, art. 2 para. 2.

72. Charles T. Call and Jeffrey Hallock, "Too Much Success? The Legacy and Lessons of the International Commission against Impunity in Guatemala," CLALS Working Paper No. 24 (Washington, DC: Center for Latin American and Latino Studies, 2020), 2; ibid.

73. United Nations, "CICIG: International Commission against Impunity in Guatemala."

74. Call and Hallock, "Too Much Success? The Legacy and Lessons of the International Commission against Impunity in Guatemala," 72.

75. Ibid.

76. Charles T. Call and Jeffrey Hallock, "Too Much Success? The Legacy and Lessons of the International Commission against Impunity in Guatemala," March 15, 2020, accessed November 6, 2020, https://papers.ssrn.com/sol3/papers.cfm?abstract_id=3526865.

77. Agreement between the Government of the Republic of Honduras and the General Secretariat of the Organization of American States for the Establishment of the Mission to Support the Fight against Corruption and Impunity in Honduras. Accessed September 9, 2020. http://www.oas.org/documents/eng/press/agreement-MACCIH-jan19-2016.pdf [hereinafter MACCIH]. In four years of operation, MACCIH assisted in the prosecution of 133 individuals, involving 14 cases. On January 17, 2020, the Organization of American States and the Government of Honduras announced that they had failed to reach an agreement to renew the Agreement's original four-year mandate. This underlines the need for the type of permanent investigative body that would be established by APUNCAC.

78. Council of Europe, "Twelve Candidates Have Been Nominated for the Public Council of International Experts for the Creation of an Anti-Corruption Court," September, 2018, accessed November 4, 2020, https://www.coe.int/en/web/corruption/bilateral-activities/ukraine/-/asset_publisher/plqBCeLYiBJQ/content/twelve-candidates-have-been-nominated-for-the-public-council-of-international-experts-for-the-creation-of-an-anti-corruption-court?inheritRedirect=false; Ihor Zabokrytskyy, "Transnational Civil Society Influence on Anti-Corruption Courts: Ukraine's Experience," *Global Jurist* 20, no. 1 (2020).

79. UNIAN, "Poroshenko Signs Law on Establishing High Anti-Corruption Court," June 26, 2018, accessed November 4, 2020, https://www.unian.info/politics/10165775-poroshenko-signs-law-on-establishing-high-anti-corruption-court.html.

80. Stuart S. Yeh, "Corruption and the Rule of Law in Sub-Saharan Africa," *African Journal of Legal Studies* 4, no. 2 (2011); Yeh, "Ending Corruption in Africa through United Nations Inspections"; Yeh, "Anti-Corruption Inspections: A Missing Element of the IMF/World Bank Agenda?"; Yeh, "Is an International Treaty Needed to Fight Corruption and the Narco-Insurgency in Mexico?"; Yeh, "Why UN Inspections? The Accountability Gap in Sub-Saharan Africa"; Yeh, "Building a Global Institution to Fight Corruption and Address the Roots of Insurgency"; Yeh, "Poverty and the Rule of Law in Africa: A Missing International Actor?"; Yeh, "Why UN Inspections? Corruption, Accountability, and the Rule of Law"; Yeh, "An International Law Approach to End Money Laundering"; Yeh, "An International

Treaty to Fight Money Laundering"; Yeh, "Application of a Model International Treaty to Money Laundering"; Stuart S. Yeh, "APUNCAC: An International Convention to Fight Corruption, Money Laundering, and Terrorist Financing," *Law and Development Review* 14, no. 2 (2021).

81. Open Society Foundations, *Against the Odds: CICIG in Guatemala* (Washington, DC: Open Society Foundations, 2016), 53.

82. Ibid., 85.

83. Ibid., 6.

84. Judge Wolf advocates the implementation of an international convention modeled on the FCA that would permit private parties to pursue civil actions. Wolf, "The Case for an International Anti-Corruption Court," 10–11. See also Darling, "I Can Resist Everything except Temptation: An International Solution to African Resource Corruption" (Arguing that an international civil statute modeled on the FCA, permitting private parties to pursue civil actions, could be a powerful tool to fight corruption). *See also* Anita Ramasastry, "Is There a Right to Be Free from Corruption?," *UC Davis Law Review* 49, no. 2 (2015). (Arguing that civil litigation can be a powerful tool to fight corruption).

85. Racketeer Influenced and Corrupt Organizations Act, Pub. L. No. 91-452, s.901(a), 84 Stat. 922-3 (1970) (codified at 18 U.S.C. ss.1961–1968 (2018)).

86. Yeh, "An International Law Approach to End Money Laundering"; Yeh, "An International Treaty to Fight Money Laundering"; Yeh, "Application of a Model International Treaty to Money Laundering."

87. Struett, *The Politics of Constructing the International Criminal Court.*

88. Ibid.

89. Whiting, "Is an International Anti-Corruption Court a Dream or a Distraction?"

Bibliography

Abbott, Jeff. "Guatemala's CICIG: UN-Backed Anti-Corruption Body Shuts Its Doors." *Al Jazeera*. Accessed August 25, 2020. https://www.aljazeera.com/news/2019/09/guatemala-cicig-backed-anti-corruption-body-shuts-doors-190903132411201.html.

Abed, George T., and Hamid R. Davoodi. *Corruption, Structural Reforms, and Economic Performance in the Transition Economies*. Washington, DC: The International Monetary Fund, 2000.

Abed, George T., and Sanjeev Gupta. "The Economics of Corruption: An Overview." *The International Monetary Fund*. Accessed August 25, 2020. http://www.imf.org/external/pubs/nft/2002/govern/#chp1.

Acemoglu, Daron, Simon Johnson, and James A. Robinson. "Institutions as a Fundamental Cause of Long-Run Growth." In *Handbook of Economic Growth*, edited by Philippe Aghion and Steven N. Durlauf, 385–471. Amsterdam: Elsevier, 2005.

Adamolekun, Ladipo. "Transferability of Governance Institutions: The Ombudsman and the Independent Commission against Corruption." In *Innovations in Governance and Public Administration: Replicating What Works*, edited by Adriana Alberti and Vilhelm Klareskov, 61–66. New York: United Nations, 2006.

Administrative Conference of the United States. "Recommendation 92–7: The Federal Administrative Judiciary." Accessed August 25, 2020. https://www.acus.gov/sites/default/files/documents/92-7.pdf.

African Union. "List of Countries Which Have Signed, Ratified/Acceded to the African Union Convention on Preventing and Combatting Corruption." Accessed August 25, 2020. https://au.int/sites/default/files/treaties/36382-sl-AFRICAN%20UNION%20CONVENTION%20ON%20PREVENTING%20AND%20COMBATING%20CORRUPTION.pdf.

African Union Convention on Preventing and Combating Corruption, August 5, 2006, 43 I.L.M., 5.

AfriMAP. *Effectiveness of Anti-Corruption Agencies in East Africa: Kenya, Tanzania and Uganda*. New York: African Minds, 2015.

Agreement between the Government of the Republic of Honduras and the General Secretariat of the Organization of American States for the Establishment of the Mission to Support the Fight against Corruption and Impunity in Honduras [MACCIH]. Accessed September 9, 2020. http://www.oas.org/documents/eng/press/agreement-MACCIH-jan19-2016.pdf.

Agreement between the United Nations and the State of Guatemala on the Establishment of an International Commission against Impunity in Guatemala, Dec. 12, 2006, 2472 UNTS 47.

Ahmed, Azam. "Mexico's Government Is Blocking Its Own Anti-Corruption Drive, Commissioners Say." *The New York Times*, December 2, 2017. Accessed August 25, 2020. https://www.nytimes.com/2017/12/02/world/americas/mexico-corruption-commission.html.

Ahmed, Azam, and J. Jesus Esquivel. "Presidential Ally Is Arrested, and Mexico Corruption Investigation Deepens." *The New York Times*, December 20, 2017. Accessed August 25, 2020. https://www.nytimes.com/2017/12/20/world/americas/mexico-corruption-pri.html.

Aljazeera. "Mexico Denies Deal to Nab Cartel Leader in Return for Cienfuegos: Salvador Cienfuegos was Accused of Conspiring with a Cartel to Smuggle Drugs While Serving as Defence Secretary." November 23, 2020. https://www.aljazeera.com/news/2020/11/23/mexico-denies-deal-to-nab-cartel-leader-in-return-for-cienfuegos.

Aljazeera. "US Charges Former Mexican Minister with Drug Trafficking: Ex-Defence Chief Salvador Cienfuegos, Who Was Arrested in Los Angeles, Used His Power to Protect a Drug Cartel, According to a US Indictment." October 16, 2020. https://www.aljazeera.com/news/2020/10/16/us-charges-former-mexican-minister-with-drug-trafficking.

Aljazeera. "US to Drop Drug Charges against Mexico's Former Defence Chief: Charges against Salvador Cienfuegos to Be Dropped So He Can Be Investigated in Mexico, Says US Attorney General." November 18, 2020. https://www.aljazeera.com/news/2020/11/18/us-drops-drug-charges-against-mexicos-former-defense-chief.

Andrews, Neil. "Strangers to Justice No Longer: The Reversal of the Privity Rule under the Contracts (Rights of Third Parties) Act 1999." *Cambridge Law Journal* 60, no. 2 (2001): 353–381.

Anti-Corruption Authorities. "Tanzania." Accessed August 25, 2020. https://www.acauthorities.org/country/tz.

Anticorruption Protocol to the United Nations Convention against Corruption [APUNCAC]. Accessed November 16, 2020. http://tinyurl.com/y6bkpott.

AP. "Mexico Homicide Rate Edges up in 2019; Rate of Rise Slows." Accessed August 25, 2020. https://apnews.com/86acd349ffd6713f9d485ce9ab169a06#:~:text=MEXICO%20CITY%20(AP)%20%E2%80%94%20The,the%20toughest%20challenges%20he%20faces.

APUNCAC. *see* Anticorruption Protocol to the United Nations Convention against Corruption.

Armstrong, Robert, and Kiran Stacey. "US to Shift Burden from Banks in Overhaul of Money Laundering Laws: Companies Will Have to Register Their Beneficial Owners Directly with US Treasury." *Financial Times*. December 8, 2020. https://www.ft.com/content/498493c4-a138-4e5d-b926-a86ae317b8f4.

Arsenault, Chris. "US-Trained Cartel Terrorises Mexico." Accessed August 25, 2020. http://www.aljazeera.com/indepth/features/2010/10/201010192122440609775.html.

Associated Press. "In Drug Inquiry, Mexico Arrests Another Top Police Official." *The New York Times*, November 18, 2008. http://www.nytimes.com/2008/11/19/world/americas/19mexico.html.

Astro Exito Navegacion SA v. WT Hsu (The Messiniaki Tolmi) [1984] 1 Lloyd's Rep. 266; (1984) 128 S.J. 265 CA (Civ Div).

AUCPCC. *see* African Union Convention on Preventing and Combating Corruption.

Ayittey, G.B.N. *Africa Unchained: The Blueprint for Africa's Future*. New York: Palgrave Macmillan, 2005.

Ayittey, George B.N. "The African Development Conundrum." In *Making Poor Nations Rich: Entrepreneurship and the Process of Economic Development*, edited by Benjamin Powell, 137–188. Stanford, CA: Stanford University Press, 2008.

Babalola, Abegunde. "Power of Police to Prosecute Criminal Cases: Nigeria and International Perspectives." *European Journal of Business and Social Sciences* 2, no. 11 (2014): 127–138.

Badejogbin, R.E., and M.E. Onoriode, "Judicial Accountability and Discipline in Nigeria: Imperatives for the New Democratic Order." Accessed August 26, 2020. https://tinyurl.com/yy9nkcye.

Baker, Peter, and Rachel Donadio. "Obama Wins More Food Aid but Presses African Nations on Corruption." *The New York Times*, July 11, 2009, A4, A6.

Bargent, James. "Last Rites for Guatemala's Anti-Impunity Crusaders CICIG?" *Insight Crime*, September 6, 2013. Accessed August 25, 2020. https://www.insightcrime.org/news/analysis/last-rites-for-guatemalas-anti-impunity-warriors/.

Barro, R.J. "Democracy and the Rule of Law." In *Governing for Prosperity*, edited by Bruce Bueno de Mesquita and Hilton L. Root, 209–231. New Haven, CT: Yale University Press, 2000.

Barro, R.J. "Determinants of Economic Growth in a Panel of Countries." *Annals of Economics and Finance* 4, no. 2 (2003): 231–274.

Bashir, Misbahu. "Nigeria: Ribadu Demoted—With 139 Others—Doubts Over His NIPSS Course." *AllAfrica*, August 6, 2008. http://www.allafrica.com/stories/200808060176.html.

Bates, R.H. *Markets and States in Tropical Africa*. Berkeley: University of California Press, 1981.

Baverstock, Alasdair. "Mexican Forces Raid Police Precinct, Find 20 Officers Had Drug Trafficking Ties." May 26, 2017. http://www.foxnews.com/world/2017/05/26/mexican-forces-raid-police-precinct-find-20-officers-had-drug-trafficking-ties.html.

BBC. "Afghanistan: Obama Orders Withdrawal of 33,000 Troops." June 23, 2011. http://www.bbc.co.uk/news/world-us-canada-13851930.

BBC. "Former Nigeria Governor James Ibori Jailed for 13 Years." April 17, 2012. http://www.bbc.com/news/world-africa-17739388.

BBC. "Guatemala Ex-VP Roxana Baldetti Jailed in 'Magic Water' Scandal." October 18, 2018. https://www.bbc.com/news/world-latin-america-45806524.

BBC. "Joaquín 'El Chapo' Guzmán's Trial: From Shocking to Bizarre." February 4, 2019. https://www.bbc.com/news/world-us-canada-46282173.

BBC. "Omar al-Bashir: Sudan Agrees Ex-President Must Face ICC." February 11, 2020. https://www.bbc.com/news/world-africa-51462613.

Bello, Abdullahi Yahaya. "EFCC/ICPC/CCB: One Merger, Many Questions." *All Africa*, December 22, 2007. https://allafrica.com/stories/200712220006.html.

Blancornelas, J. Jesus. *Una Vez, Nada Mas*. Mexico D.F.: Editorial Oceano, 1997.

Bloxham, Andy. "Former Head of Army: Taliban Will Be Part of Afghanistan's Future." *The Telegraph*, June 23, 2011. https://www.telegraph.co.uk/news/worldnews/asia/afghanistan/8594075/Former-head-of-Army-Taliban-will-be-part-of-Afghanistans-future.html.

Booth, William. "Mexico's Police Liaison for Interpol Arrested in Drug Probe." *The Washington Post*, November 19, 2008. http://www.washingtonpost.com/wp-dyn/content/article/2008/11/18/AR2008111804214.html.

Brands, Hal. "Mexico's Narco-Insurgency and U.S. Counterdrug Policy." Carlisle, PA: U.S. Army War College, Strategic Studies Institute, 2009.

Brett, E.A. "Theorising Crisis and Reform: Institutional Theories and Social Change in Uganda." Sussex, England: Institute for Development Studies, Sussex University, 1993.

Brown, Stephen, and Chandra Lekha Sriram. "The Big Fish Won't Fry Themselves: Criminal Accountability for Post-Election Violence in Kenya." *African Affairs* 111, no. 443 (2012): 244–260.

Brussels Recast *see* Regulation 1215/2012 on Jurisdiction and the Recognition and Enforcement of Judgments in Civil and Commercial Matters.

Bruun and Hjejle. *Report on the Non-Resident Portfolio at Danske Bank's Estonian Branch*. Copenhagen, Denmark: Bruun and Hjejle, 2018.

Bureau for International Narcotics and Law Enforcement Affairs. *International Narcotics Control Strategy Report*, Volume 2. Washington, DC: United States Department of State, 2017.

Byman, Daniel L. "The Changing Nature of State Sponsorship of Terrorism." *Analysis Paper No. 16*. Washington, DC: Brookings Institution, The Saban Center for Middle East Policy, 2008.

Call, Charles T., and Jeffrey Hallock. "Too Much Success? The Legacy and Lessons of the International Commission against Impunity in Guatemala." *CLALS Working Paper No. 24*. Washington, DC: Center for Latin American and Latino Studies, 2020.

Call, Charles T., and Jeffrey Hallock. "Too Much Success? The Legacy and Lessons of the International Commission against Impunity in Guatemala." March 15, 2020. Accessed November 6, 2020. https://papers.ssrn.com/sol3/papers.cfm?abstract_id=3526865.

Campos, Krisanne, and Candace Rondeaux. "Interview with Ambassador Douglas Lute, NATO Permanent Rep, Former Director of Iraq/Afghanistan,

NSC 2007–2014." *Office of the Special Inspector General for Afghanistan Reconstruction (SIGAR)*. Accessed August 25, 2020. https://www.washingtonpost.com/graphics/2019/investigations/afghanistan-papers/documents-database/documents/lute_doug_ll_01_d5_02202015.pdf?v=25.

Capetillo, Marcus Patrick. "Drug Trafficking in Mexico: Causes and Consequences of the Militarization of Mexico." Honors thesis, Baylor University, May, 2012. https://baylor-ir.tdl.org/bitstream/handle/2104/8378/Abstract.pdf?sequence=1.

Carroll, Rory. "Mexico's Drugs War: In the City of Death." *The Guardian*, September 16, 2010. https://www.theguardian.com/world/2010/sep/16/mexico-drugs-war-massacre-in-torreon.

Carver, Richard. "National Human Rights Institutions in Central and Eastern Europe." In *Human Rights, State Compliance, and Social Change*, edited by Ryan Goodman and Thomas Pegram, 181–209. New York: Cambridge University Press, 2012.

Cater, Jack. *Annual Report by the Commissioner of the Independent Commission against Corruption*. Hong Kong: Independent Commission Against Corruption, 1975.

CBS News. "100,000 Dead, 30,000 Missing: Mexico's War on Drugs Turns 10." December 11, 2016. http://www.cbsnews.com/news/100000-dead-30000-missing-mexico-war-on-drugs-turns-10/.

Center for Governmental Studies. *Public Campaign Financing in California: A Model Law for 21st Century Reform*. Los Angeles: Center for Governmental Studies, August, 2011. https://cgs.policyarchive.org/index?section=5&id=96493.

Chabal, Patrick, and Jean-Pascal Deloz. *Africa Works: Disorder as Political Instrument*. Oxford, UK: James Currey, 1999.

Chivers, C.J., Carlotta Gall, Andrew W. Lehren, Mark Mazzetti, Jane Perlez, Eric Schmitt, Jacob Harris, and Alan McLean. "The Afghan Struggle: A Secret Archive." *The New York Times*, July 26, 2010, A1, A8–A12.

CICIG. *see* Agreement between the United Nations and Guatemala on the Establishment of an International Commission against Corruption in Guatemala.

CICIG. "Background." March 5, 2018. https://www.cicig.org/cicig/antecedentes/

CICIG. "Mandate and Agreement." March 5, 2018. https://www.cicig.org/cicig/mandato-y-acuerdo-cicig/.

Ciobanu, Liliana. "Romania's Former Prime Minister Sentenced to Prison for Corruption." *CNN*. January 30, 2012. Accessed November 4, 2020. https://www.cnn.com/2012/01/30/world/europe/romania-politician-convicted/index.html.

CNN. "Mexico Suspects Ex-Drug Czar Took Huge Bribes from Traffickers." November 21, 2008. http://edition.cnn.com/2008/WORLD/americas/11/21/mexico.arrest/index.html.

Collier, Paul. *The Bottom Billion: Why the Poorest Countries Are Failing and What Can Be Done About It*. Oxford, UK: Oxford University Press, 2007.

ColumbiaSoft. "Digital Signature Automation." Accessed August 25, 2020. https://www.documentlocator.com/solutions/digital-signature-workflow-automation/.

Commerzbank Aktiengesellschaft v. Liquimar Tankers Management Inc [2017] EWHC 161 (Comm); [2017] 1 W.L.R. 3497.

Commission of Inquiry into Money Laundering in British Columbia. *Opening Statement of British Columbia Lottery Corporation*, February 24, 2020. https://cullencommission.ca/files/OpeningStatement-BCLC.pdf.

Commission of Inquiry into Money Laundering in British Columbia. *Opening Statement of Robert Kroeker*, February 25, 2020. https://cullencommission.ca/files/OpeningStatement-Kroeker.pdf.

Conley, John A. *The New Deal's Response to Crime: The Politics of Law and Order*. Michigan State University, 1971.

Constitution of the Federal Republic of Nigeria (1999). Accessed August 25, 2020. https://www.ilo.org/wcmsp5/groups/public/---ed_protect/---protrav/---ilo_aids/documents/legaldocument/wcms_127563.pdf.

Contracts (Rights of Third Parties) Act 1999, c. 31. Accessed August 24, 2020. https://www.legislation.gov.uk/ukpga/1999/31/contents.

Convention on the Law Applicable to Contractual Obligations [1980] OJ L266/1, June 19, 1980.

CoolBitX. "Bridge: Enabling VASPs to Collect and Exchange Compliance-Required Transaction Information." Accessed August 25, 2020. https://www.sygna.io/bridge/.

CoolBitX. *Sygna Bridge Report: FATF Recommendation 16 Technical Solution for Virtual Asset Transactions*. Arcadia, CA: CoolBitX, 2020.

Coolidge, Jacqueline, and Susan Rose-Ackerman. "High-Level Rent-Seeking and Corruption in African Regimes: Theory and Cases." *Policy Research Working Paper No. 1780*. Washington DC: World Bank, 1997.

Cooper, Frederick. *Africa since 1940: The Past of the Present*. Cambridge: Cambridge University Press, 2002.

Cooper, Helene. "U.S. Says It Has 11,000 Troops in Afghanistan, More Than Formerly Disclosed." *The New York Times*, August 30, 2017. https://www.nytimes.com/2017/08/30/world/asia/afghanistan-troop-totals.html.

Corchado, Alfredo, and Ricardo Sandoval. "Inquiry Indicates Police, Drug Ties: Disturbing Reports Say Women Were Tortured and Slain as Celebration." *Dallas Morning News*, February 28, 2004. http://www.latinamericanstudies.org/drugs/inquiry.htm.

Coronado, Eddy. "Otto Pérez Molina Will Remain in Prison for the La Línea Case, Court Decides." November 28, 2019. https://www.prensalibre.com/guatemala/justicia/otto-perez-molina-pide-salir-de-prision-por-el-caso-la-linea/.

Council of Europe. "Twelve Candidates Have Been Nominated for the Public Council of International Experts for the Creation of an Anti-Corruption Court." September, 2018. Accessed November 4, 2020. https://www.coe.int/en/web/corruption/bilateral-activities/ukraine/-/asset_publisher/plqBCeLYiBJQ/content/twelve-candidates-have-been-nominated-for-the-public-council-of-international-experts-for-the-creation-of-an-anti-corruption-court?inheritRedirect=false.

Criminal Code Act (1990) Cap. (4), § 126 (Nigeria). Accessed August 25, 2020. https://www.refworld.org/cgi-bin/texis/vtx/rwmain/opendocpdf.pdf?reldoc=y&docid=54f975004.

Cuffe, Sandra. "Guatemala's Anti-Corruption CICIG Body to Shut Down: What to Know." *Al Jazeera*, September 1, 2019. https://www.aljazeera.com/news/2019/08/guatemala-anti-corruption-cicig-body-shut-190830225625800.html.

Cuffe, Sandra. "Thousands of Guatemalans Protest in Support of Anti-Corruption Commission." *Los Angeles Times*, January 14, 2019. https://www.latimes.com/world/la-fg-guatemala-protests-20190114-story.html.

Darling, Michael R. "I Can Resist Everything except Temptation: An International Solution to African Resource Corruption." *Texas International Law Journal* 52, no. 3 (2017): 421–448.

Davis, Kristina. "Mexican Attorney General Arrested on New York Drug Trafficking Charges Is Part-Time Chula Vista Resident." *The San Diego Union Tribune*, April 7, 2017. https://www.sandiegouniontribune.com/news/courts/sd-me-mexicanag-hearing-20170407-story.html.

de Córdoba, José, and Juan Montes. "Fugitive Mexican Ex-Governor Tomás Yarrington Had State Security While on the Run; Documents Show He Was Assigned Police Bodyguards While Eluding Arrest Warrants Last Year." *The Wall Street Journal*, April 15, 2017. https://www.wsj.com/articles/fugitive-mexican-ex-governor-tomas-yarrington-had-state-security-while-on-the-run-1492264404.

de Speville, Bertrand. *Hong Kong: Policy Initiatives against Corruption*. Paris: Development Centre of the OECD, 1997.

de Speville, Bertrand E.D. "The Experience of Hong Kong, China, in Combating Corruption." In *Curbing Corruption: Toward a Model for Building National Integrity*, edited by Rick Stapenhurst and Sahr J. Kpundeh, 51–58. Washington, DC: The World Bank, 1999.

de Zayas, Alfred. "Human Rights and Indefinite Detention." *International Review of the Red Cross* 87, no. 857 (2005): 15–38.

Diamond, Jared. *Guns, Germs, and Steel: The Fates of Human Societies*. New York: W.W. Norton, 2005.

Diamond, Larry. "Nigeria's Perennial Struggle against Corruption: Prospects for the Third Republic." *Corruption and Reform* 7, no. 3 (1993): 215–225.

Directive 2005/60/EC on the Prevention of the Use of the Financial System for the Purpose of Money Laundering and Terrorist Financing [2005] OJ L309/15.

"Dirty Money: Russia's Largest Tax Refund Laundered into Foreign Banks." Documentary Film. Sydney, Australia: Sunday Night, 2018. Accessed August 25, 2020. https://documentaries.io/dirty-money-russias-largest-tax-refund-laundered-into-foreign-banks-sunday-night/.

Dressler, Jeffrey A. "The Haqqani Network: From Pakistan to Afghanistan." *Afghanistan Report No. 6*. Washington, DC: Institute for the Study of War, 2010.

Easterly, William. *The White Man's Burden: Why the West's Efforts to Aid the Rest Have Done So Much Ill and So Little Good*. London: Penguin Press, 2006.

Economic Commission for Africa. *Combating Corruption, Improving Governance in Africa: Regional Anti-Corruption Programme for Africa (2011–2016)*. Addis Ababa, Ethiopia: Economic Commission for Africa, 2011.

"EFCC Records 1,000 Convictions in 10 Years—Lamorde." *Premium Times*, December 9, 2013. https://www.premiumtimesng.com/news/151190-efcc-records-1000-convictions-10-years-lamorde.html.

Ekran System. "Light-Weight Privileged Access Management (PAM)." Accessed August 25, 2020. https://www.ekransystem.com/en/product/privileged-access-management.

Ellingwood, Ken. "Mexico Traffickers Bribed Former Anti-Drug Chief, Officials Say." *Los Angeles Times*, November 22, 2008. https://www.latimes.com/world/mexico-americas/la-fg-bribe22-2008nov22-story.html.

Elmi, Mohamed, and Ojelanki Ngwenyama. "The Role of Mobile Money in Somalia's Remittance System." In *HCI in Business, Government and Organizations*, edited by F.H. Nah and K. Siau, 119–136. Basel, Switzerland: Springer Nature, 2019.

False Claims Act. 31 U.S.C. ss.3729–3733 (2012 Supp.4).

"Fatalities in Terrorist Violence in Pakistan 2000–2018." Accessed August 26, 2020. https://commons.wikimedia.org/wiki/File:Fatalities_in_Terrorist_Violence_in_Pakistan.png.

FATF. "FATF Glossary." Accessed August 25, 2020. https://www.fatf-gafi.org/glossary/u-z/.

FATF. "Outcomes FATF Plenary, 17–19 October 2018." Accessed August 25, 2020. http://www.fatf-gafi.org/publications/fatfgeneral/documents/outcomes-plenary-october-2018.html.

FATF. "Who We Are." Accessed August 25, 2020. https://www.fatf-gafi.org/about/whoweare/.

"Fayose, Ibori Sent to Prison." *All Africa*, December 18, 2007. https://allafrica.com/stories/200712180033.html.

"Federal PGR Arrests 209—Of Its Own." *Mexico News Daily*, December 21, 2015. https://mexiconewsdaily.com/news/federal-pgr-arrests-209-of-its-own/.

Feuer, Alan. "El Chapo Trial Shows That Mexico's Corruption Is Even Worse Than You Think." *The New York Times*, December 28, 2018, A22. https://www.nytimes.com/2018/12/28/nyregion/el-chapo-trial-mexico-corruption.html?module=inline.

Feuer, Alan. "Former Mexican President Peña Nieto Took $100 Million Bribe, Witness at El Chapo Trial Says." *The New York Times*, January 15, 2019, A19. https://www.nytimes.com/2019/01/15/nyregion/el-chapo-trial.html.

Figueroa, Yolanda. *El Capo Del Golfo*. Mexico D.F.: Editorial Grijalbo, 1997.

Filkins, Dexter. "The American Awakening." *The New Republic*, March 11, 2010, 23–28.

Filkins, Dexter. "Inside Corrupt-Istan." *The New York Times*, September 5, 2010, 1, 6.

Finan, Frederico S. "Political Patronage, Corruption, and Local Development." Doctoral dissertation, University of California, 2006.

Financial Action Task Force. *Transparency and Beneficial Ownership*. Paris: Financial Action Task Force, 2014.

Financial Action Task Force. *Virtual Assets and Virtual Asset Service Providers*. Paris: Financial Action Task Force, 2019.

FinCEN. "Application of FinCEN's Regulations to Persons Administering, Exchanging, or Using Virtual Currencies." March 18, 2013. https://www.fincen.gov/sites/default/files/shared/FIN-2013-G001.pdf.

FinCEN. "Notice of Proposed Rulemaking RIN 1506-AB47: Requirements for Certain Transactions Involving Convertible Virtual Currency or Digital Assets." U.S. Department of the Treasury. December 18, 2020. https://public-inspection.federalregister.gov/2020-28437.pdf.

Firswood Ltd v. Petra Bank. Unreported, December 13, 1995 CA (Civ Div).

Fla. Stat. s.895 (2018).

Forschner Group Inc v. B-LINE AG 943 F.Supp. 287 n.8 (SDNY 1996)

Fraser, Niall. "First Woman to Lead ICAC's Operations Department Is Replaced in Major Shake-up at Hong Kong's Anti-Corruption Body." *South China Morning Post*, July 8, 2016. https://www.scmp.com/news/hong-kong/law-crime/article/1986862/first-woman-lead-icacs-operations-department-replaced-major.

Gall, Carlotta. "Taliban Show Strain as Afghan Fighting Nears." *The New York Times*, April 1, 2011, A1, A8.

Garcia, Gustavo Castillo. "Arraigan Por 40 Días a Rodolfo De La Guardia, Ex Director De La Afi." *La Jornada*, November 8, 2008. http://www.jornada.unam.mx/2008/11/08/index.php?section=politica&article=013n2pol.

Gathii, James T. "Incorporating the Third Party Beneficiary Principle in Natural Resource Contracts." *Georgia Journal of International and Comparative Law* 43, no. 1 (2014): 93–139.

Gaudemet-Tallon, Hélène. *Les Conventions de Bruxelles et de Lugano*. Paris: Montchrestien, 1996.

Gavigan, Patrick. "Organized Crime, Illicit Power Structures and Guatemala's Threatened Peace Process." *International Peacekeeping* 16, no. 1 (2009): 62–76.

General Assembly resolution 73/191, *Special session of the General Assembly against Corruption*, A/RES/73/191 (9 January 2019), available from https://undocs.org/en/A/RES/73/191.

Gerling Konzern Speziale Kreditversicherung AG v. Amministrazione del Tesoro dello Stato (201/82) EU:C:1983:217; [1983] E.C.R. 2503; [1984] 3 C.M.L.R. 638.

Germain, Peter M. "Dirty Money: An Independent Review of Money Laundering in Lower Mainland Casinos Conducted for the Attorney General of British Columbia." Accessed August 25, 2020. http://assetforfeiturelaw.us/wp-content/uploads/2018/06/German_Gaming_Final_Report.pdf.

Gilliéron, Gwladys. *Public Prosecutors in the United States and Europe: A Comparative Analysis with Special Focus on Switzerland, France, and Germany*. Cham, Switzerland: Springer International Publishing, 2014.

GlobalSign. "Digital Signatures for Organizations Using Automated Document Generation Software." Accessed August 25, 2020. https://www.globalsign.com/en/digital-signatures/high-volume-hsm.

Golden, Tim. "In Breakthrough, Mexican Official Testifies in Texas." *The New York Times*, July 15, 1998. http://www.nytimes.com/1998/07/15/world/in-breakthrough-mexican-official-testifies-in-texas.html?ref=marioruizmassieu.

Goldman, Francisco "From President to Prison: Otto Pérez Molina and a Day for Hope in Guatemala." *The New Yorker*, September 4, 2015. https://www.newyorker.com/news/news-desk/from-president-to-prison-otto-perez-molina-and-a-day-for-hope-in-guatemala.

Gonzalez, Paulina Vega, and Carla Ferstman. *Ending Threats and Reprisals against Victims of Torture and Related International Crimes: A Call to Action*. London: Redress, 2009.

Government of Nigeria. "Nigeria Police Code of Conduct." *Government of Nigeria*. Accessed August 25, 2020. https://www.premiumtimesng.com/docs_download/NIGERIAPOLICECODEOFCONDUCT.pdf.

Grayson, George W. *Mexico: Narco-Violence and a Failed State?* Piscataway, NJ: Transaction Publishers, 2009.

Greene's Ready Mixed Concrete Co v. Fillmore Pacific Associates Ltd Partnership 808 F.Supp. 307 (SDNY 1992).

Griffin, Tamerra. "Sudanese President Omar Al-Bashir Has Been Arrested." April 11, 2019. https://www.buzzfeednews.com/article/tamerragriffin/sudan-president-omar-al-bashir-removed-military.

Grillo, Ioan. *El Narco: Inside Mexico's Criminal Insurgency*. New York: Bloomsbury, 2011.

Groenewold, Nicolaas, and Sam Hak Kan Tang. "Killing the Goose That Lays the Golden Egg: Institutional Change and Economic Growth in Hong Kong." *Economic Inquiry* 45, no. 4 (Oct 2007): 787–799.

Gurr, Ted R. *Why Men Rebel: Fortieth Anniversary Edition*. Boulder, CO: Paradigm, 2011.

Gyimah-Brepong, Kwabena. "Corruption, Economic Growth, and Income Inequality in Africa." *Economics of Governance* 3, no. 3 (2002): 183–209.

Harding, Luke, and Shaun Walker. "'Poisoned' Russian Whistleblower Was Fatalistic over Death Threats." *The Guardian*, May 19, 2015. https://www.theguardian.com/uk-news/2015/may/19/poisoned-russian-whistleblower-was-fatalistic-over-death-threats.

Hathaway, Oona A. "Between Power and Principle: An Integrated Theory of International Law." *The University of Chicago Law Review* 72, no. 2 (2005): 469–536.

Haugen, Gary A., and Victor Boutros. *The Locust Effect: Why the End of Poverty Requires the End of Violence*. New York: Oxford University Press, 2014.

"Heads of Mexico Interpol to Face Trial for Drug Cartel Ties." *Latin American Herald Tribune*. Accessed August 25, 2020. http://www.laht.com/article.asp?CategoryId=14091&ArticleId=325709.

Henning, C. Randall. "Peer Review." *Paper presented at the Meeting of the Commission on Capital Flows to Africa*, Washington, DC, February 21, 2003.

Herbst, Jeffrey. "Is Nigeria a Viable State?" *The Washington Quarterly*, Spring 1996, 151–172.

Hernandez, Anabel. *Narcoland: The Mexican Drug Lords and Their Godfathers*. Translated by Iain Bruce and Lorna Scott Fox. New York: Verso, 2013.

Hertig, Alyssa. "Grasping Lightning: Mapping the Key Players in Bitcoin's Next Phase." January 17, 2020. https://www.coindesk.com/grasping-lightning-mapping-the-key-players-in-bitcoins-next-phase.

H.J. Inc. v. Northwestern Bell Tel. Co., 492 U.S. 229 (1989).

Hoogenboom, Ari. "Did Gilded Age Scandals Bring Reform?". In *Before Watergate: Problems of Corruption in American Society*, edited by Abraham S. Eisenstadt, Ari Hoogenboom and Hans L. Trefousse. Brooklyn College Studies on Society in Change, 125–142. Brooklyn, NY: Brooklyn College Press, 1979.

Hope Sr., Kempe R. *From Crisis to Renewal: Development Policy and Management in Africa*. Leiden, Netherlands: Brill, 2002.

Hope Sr., Kempe R. "Toward Good Governance and Sustainable Development: The African Peer Review Mechanism." *Governance: An International Journal of Policy, Administration, and Institutions* 18, no. 2 (2005): 283–311.

Hudson, Andrew, and Alexandra W. Taylor. "The International Commission against Impunity in Guatemala: A New Model for International Criminal Justice Mechanisms." *Journal of International Criminal Justice* 8, no. 1 (2010): 53–74.

Human Rights Watch. "Guatemala." January 2011. http://www.hrw.org/sites/default/files/related_material/guatemala_0.pdf.

Human Rights Watch. "Nigeria: Firing of Anti-Corruption Chief Would Boost Abusive Politicians." January 1, 2008. https://www.hrw.org/news/2008/01/01/nigeria-firing-anti-corruption-chief-would-boost-abusive-politicians.

ICAC. "Brief History." Accessed August 25, 2020. http://www.icac.org.hk/en/about/history/index.html.

Ifukor, Mary Omogor. "Channels of Information Acquisition and Dissemination among Rural Dwellers." *International Journal of Library and Information Science* 5, no. 10 (2013): 306–312.

In re Thomas E. Haider, FinCEN No. 2014-08 (Dec. 18, 2014) (Assessment of Civil Money Penalty). Accessed August 25, 2020. https://www.fincen.gov/sites/default/files/enforcement_action/Haider_Assessment.pdf.

Integrity Initiatives International. "The International Anti-Corruption Court." Accessed November 25, 2020. http://www.integrityinitiatives.org/international-anticorruption-court.

International Consortium of Investigative Journalists. "Global Banks Defy U.S. Crackdowns by Serving Oligarchs, Criminals and Terrorists: The FinCEN Files Show Trillions in Tainted Dollars Flow Freely through Major Banks, Swamping a Broken Enforcement System." September 20, 2020. https://www.icij.org/investigations/fincen-files/global-banks-defy-u-s-crackdowns-by-serving-oligarchs-criminals-and-terrorists/.

International Convention for the Suppression of Financing of Terrorism, January 10, 2000, 2178 UNTS 197.

International Covenant on Civil and Political Rights, December 16, 1966, 999 UNTS 171.

International Criminal Court. "Al Bashir Case: The Prosecutor v. Omar Hassan Ahmad Al Bashir." Accessed August 25, 2020. https://www.icc-cpi.int/darfur/albashir.

International Criminal Court. "Katanga Case: The Prosecutor v. Germain Katanga." Accessed August 25, 2020. https://www.icc-cpi.int/drc/katanga.

International Criminal Court. "Ntaganda Case: The Prosecutor v. Bosco Ntaganda." Accessed August 25, 2020. https://www.icc-cpi.int/drc/ntaganda.

International Crisis Group. "Veracruz: Fixing Mexico's State of Terror." *Report No. 61*. Brussels, Belgium: International Crisis Group, 2017.

International Monetary Fund. *Islamic State of Afghanistan: Rebuilding a Macroeconomic Framework for Reconstruction and Growth*. Washington, DC: International Monetary Fund, 2003.

International Telecommunications Union. *Measuring Digital Development: Facts and Figures 2019*. Geneva, Switzerland: International Telecommunications Union, 2019. Accessed August 25, 2020. https://www.itu.int/en/ITU-D/Statistics/Documents/facts/FactsFigures2019.pdf.

Internet World Stats. "Internet Penetration in Africa." March 21, 2020. http://www.internetworldstats.com/stats1.htm.

Iroegbu, Senator. "Nigeria: EFCC Secures 603 Convictions in Three Years." *AllAfrica*, May 29, 2018. https://allafrica.com/stories/201805290530.html.

Iyengar, Rishi. "Hong Kong's Anti-Graft Agency Is in Turmoil, Prompting Fears for the City's Transparency." *Time*, July 14, 2016. https://time.com/4405736/hong-kong-icac-corruption-china-transparency/.

Jadoon, Amira, and Sara Mahmood. "Fixing the Cracks in the Pakistani Taliban's Foundation: TTP's Leadership Returns to the Mehsud Tribe." *CTC Sentinel* 11, no. 11 (2018): 21–25.

Janis, Mark W. *An Introduction to International Law*. 4th ed. New York: Aspen, 2003.

Katzman v. Victoria's Secret Catalogue, 167 F.R.D. 649 (SDNY 1996).

Keller, Morton. "Corruption in America: Continuity and Change." In *Before Watergate: Problems of Corruption in American Society*, edited by Abraham S. Eisenstadt, Ari Hoogenboom and Hans L. Trefousse. Brooklyn College Studies on Society in Change, 7–19. Brooklyn, NY: Brooklyn College Press, 1979.

Kennis, Matthew. "The Creation of the International Commission against Impunity in Guatemala: Miscalculation by a 'Corporate Mafia State'?" Originally published in *Peace and Conflict Monitor*. June 29, 2012. Accessed November 16, 2020. https://www.ideasforpeace.org/content/the-creation-of-the-international-commission-against-impunity-in-guatemala-miscalculation-by-a-corporate-mafia-state/.

Kenny, Charles. *Getting Better: Why Global Development Is Succeeding--And How We Can Improve the World Even More*. New York: Basic Books, 2011.

Kilcullen, David. *Counterinsurgency*. New York: Oxford University Press, 2010.

Kim, Esther. "Consumers in over 150 Countries Can Now Buy Stocks with Bitcoin." May 29, 2019. https://bitcoinist.com/bitcoin-buy-stocks-150-countries-abra/.

Kirby, Jen. "The US Is on the Verge of the Biggest Anti-Money-Laundering Update in Years: Congress Included a Provision to Ban Anonymous Shell Companies." *Vox*. December 21, 2020. https://www.vox.com/22188223/congress-anti-money-laundering-anonymous-shell-companies-ban-defense-bill.

Koninklijke Philips Electronics v. Digital Works Inc 358 F.Supp.2d 328 (SDNY 2005).

Kraay, Aart, and Claudio Raddatz. "Poverty Traps, Aid, and Growth." *Policy Research Working Paper No. 3631*. Washington, DC: World Bank, 2005.

La Prensa. "El Policía De Los 'Narcos'." December 16, 2008. https://www.prensa.com/impresa/mundo/policia-narcos_0_2454504620.html.

Lagarde, Christine. "Addressing Corruption—Openly." *United Kingdom Prime Minister's Office*. Accessed August 25, 2020. https://www.gov.uk/government/publications/against-corruption-a-collection-of-essays/against-corruption-a-collection-of-essays#christine-lagarde-addressing-corruption--openly.

Langseth, Petter, Rick Stapenhurst, and Jeremy Pope. "National Integrity Systems." In *Curbing Corruption: Toward a Model for Building National Integrity*, edited by Rick Stapenhurst and Sahr J. Kpundeh, 127–148. Washington, DC: The World Bank, 1999.

Latin American Herald Tribune. "Former Interpol Mexico Director Faces Money Laundering Charges." Accessed August 25, 2020. http://www.laht.com/article.asp?ArticleId=357830&CategoryId=14091.

Lawson, Letitia. "The Politics of Anti-Corruption Reform in Africa." *Journal of Modern African Studies* 47, no. 1 (2009): 73–100.

Lawson, Robert A. "Economic Freedom and Property Rights: The Institutional Environment of Productive Entrepreneurship." In *Making Poor Nations Rich: Entrepreneurship and the Process of Economic Development*, edited by Benjamin Powell, 112–133. Stanford, CA: Stanford University Press, 2008.

Leak, T.A. "The Experience of Singapore in Combating Corruption." In *Curbing Corruption: Toward a Model for Building National Integrity*, edited by R. Stapenhurst and S.J. Kpundeh, 59–66. Washington, DC: The World Bank, 1999.

Ledwidge, Frank. "Justice and Counter-Insurgency in Afghanistan: A Missing Link." *The RUSI Journal* 154, no. 1 (2009): 6–9.

Lefebvre, Melanie, Yasmine Ibrahim, and Peter Warrack. "The Lightning Network: Deconstructed and Evaluated." *Association of Certified Financial Crime Specialists*. Accessed August 25, 2020. https://www.acfcs.org/wp-content/uploads/2020/01/The-Lightning-Network-Deconstructed-and-Evaluated-final.pdf.

Lethbridge, Henry J. *Hard Graft in Hong Kong: Scandal, Corruption, the ICAC*. New York: Oxford University Press, 1985.

Linthicum, Kate. "More and More People Are Being Murdered in Mexico — And Once More Drug Cartels Are to Blame." *Los Angeles Times*, March 3, 2017. https://www.latimes.com/world/mexico-americas/la-fg-mexico-murders-20170301-story.html.

Lizárraga, Daniel, Rafael Cabrera, Irving Huerta, and Sebastián Barragán. *La Casa Blanca De Peña Nieto*. Mexico City, Mexico: Grijalbo, 2017.

Longmire, Sylvia *Cartel: The Coming Invasion of Mexico's Drug Wars*. Hampshire, UK: Palgrave Macmillan, 2011.

Lupsha, Peter A. "Drug Lords and Narco-Corruption: The Players Change but the Game Continues." *Crime, Law and Social Change* 16, no. 1 (1991): 41–58.

Lynch, David J. "Nigeria's Former Oil Minister Named in US Bribery Complaint." *Financial Times*, July 14, 2017. https://www.ft.com/content/88a4b26a-68d7-11e7-8526-7b38dcaef614.

Ma, Yue. "Exploring the Origins of Public Prosecution." *International Criminal Justice Review* 18, no. 2 (2008): 190–211.

Malkin, Elisabeth. "Corruption at a Level of Audacity 'Never Seen in Mexico'." *The New York Times*, April 19, 2017. https://www.nytimes.com/2017/04/19/world/americas/in-mexico-mounting-misdeeds-but-governors-escape-justice.html.

Mamdani, Mahmood. *Citizen and Subject: Contemporary Africa and the Legacy of Late Colonialism*. Princeton, NJ: Princeton University Press, 1996.

Manion, Melanie. *Corruption by Design: Building Clean Government in Mainland China and Hong Kong*. Cambridge, MA: Harvard University Press, 2004.

Mann Act, Pub.L. 61–277, 36 Stat. 825a (1910).

Marin, Carlos. "Testimony Obtained by the Department of Justice: Raul Salinas Lozano, His Children Carlos, Raul and Adriana, the Ruiz Brothers and Colosio All Linked to Major Drug Lords." *Proceso*, February 16, 1997. http://www.pbs.org/wgbh/pages/frontline/shows/mexico/news/proceso.html.

Mashal, Mujib. "C.I.A.'s Afghan Forces Leave a Trail of Abuse and Anger." *The New York Times*, December 31, 2018, 2018, A1. https://www.nytimes.com/2018/12/31/world/asia/cia-afghanistan-strike-force.html.

Mauro, Paolo. "Corruption and Growth." *The Quarterly Journal of Economics* 110, no. 3 (1995): 681–712.

Mbaku, John M. "Bureaucratic and Political Corruption in Africa." In *Corruption and the Crisis of Institutional Reforms in Africa: African Studies*, Volume 47, edited by John M. Mbaku, 33–83. Lewiston, NY: Edwin Mellon Press, 1998.

Mbaku, John M. "Bureaucratic Corruption in Africa: The Futility of Cleanups." In *Corruption and the Crisis of Institutional Reforms in Africa: African Studies*, Volume 47, edited by John M. Mbaku, 263–287. Lewiston, NY: Edwin Mellon Press, 1998.

Mbaku, John M. "Corruption and the Crisis of Institutional Reforms in Africa." In *Corruption and the Crisis of Institutional Reforms in Africa: African Studies*, Volume 47, edited by John M. Mbaku, 237–262. Lewiston, NY: Edwin Mellon Press, 1998.

McDonnell, Patrick J. "Former Governor of Mexico's Veracruz State Extradited from Guatemala to Face Corruption Charges." *Los Angeles Times*, July 17, 2017. https://www.latimes.com/world/mexico-americas/la-fg-mexico-duarte-20170717-story.html.

McLean, Emi. "Guatemala's Constitutional Court Overturns Rios Montt Conviction and Sends Trial Back to April 19." *International Justice Monitor*, May 21, 2013. https://www.ijmonitor.org/2013/05/constitutional-court-overturns-rios-montt-conviction-and-sends-trial-back-to-april-19/.

McLeod, Paul, Anthony Cormier, Scott Pham, Jason Leopold, Tom Warren, Jeremy Singer-Vine, John Templon, and Richard Holmes. "Congress Has Passed Sweeping Anti-Money Laundering Legislation—Now It's up to Trump." *BuzzFeed*

News. December 11, 2020. https://www.buzzfeednews.com/article/paulmcleod/congress-closes-loop-hole-shell-companies.

Meeth v. Glacetal Sarl (C23/78) EU:C:1978:198; [1979] C.M.L.R. 520.

Meisner, Jason. "Top Mexican Cop Leaked Sensitive Info to Drug Cartels, Prosecutors Charge." *Chicago Tribune*, April 5, 2017. https://www.chicagotribune.com/news/breaking/ct-mexican-police-cartel-corruption-charges-20170405-story.html.

Melanovski, Jason, and Clara Weiss. "Former Ukrainian President Poroshenko Faces Charges over Corruption and 'High Treason'." August 24, 2019. https://www.wsws.org/en/articles/2019/08/24/ukra-a24.html.

Méndez, Fabio, and Facundo Sepúlveda. "Corruption, Growth and Political Regimes: Cross Country Evidence." *European Journal of Political Economy* 22, no. 1 (2006): 82–98.

Méon, Pierre-Guillaume, and Khalid Sekkat. "Does Corruption Grease or Sand the Wheels of Growth?" *Public Choice* 122, no. 1–2 (Jan 2005): 69–97.

Meredith, Martin. *The State of Africa: A History of Fifty Years of Independence*. London: The Free Press, 2005.

"Mexico: Cartels Pay Corrupt Cops $100 Million a Month." *Latin American Herald Tribune*, November 21, 2017. http://laht.com/article.asp?CategoryId=14091&ArticleId=362206.

Meyer, Theodoric. "No Warrant, No Problem: How the Government Can Get Your Digital Data." *ProPublica*, June 27, 2014. https://www.propublica.org/article/no-warrant-no-problem-how-the-government-can-still-get-your-digital-data.

Miller, Nathan. *Stealing from America: A History of Corruption from Jamestown to Reagan*. 2nd ed. Saint Paul, MN: Paragon House, 1992.

Milne, Richard, and Caroline Binham. "Danske Bank Memo Shows How Russians Moved Money." *Financial Times*, October 4, 2018. https://www.ft.com/content/f13ae77a-c7f1-11e8-ba8f-ee390057b8c9.

Minority Staff of the Permanent Subcommittee on Investigations of the Committee on Governmental Affairs. *Money Laundering and Foreign Corruption: Enforcement and Effectiveness of the Patriot Act*, 108th Cong., 2nd Sess., July 15, 2004. Accessed August 25, 2020. https://www.govinfo.gov/content/pkg/CHRG-108shrg95501/html/CHRG-108shrg95501.htm.

Mo, Pak Hung. "Corruption and Economic Growth." *Journal of Comparative Economics* 29, no. 1 (2001): 66–79.

Moiseienko, Anton, and Kayla Izenman. "Gaming the System: Money Laundering through Online Games." *RUSI Newsbrief* 39, no. 9 (2019): 1–5. https://rusi.org/publication/rusi-newsbrief/gaming-system-money-laundering-through-online-games.

Molloy, Molly, and Charles Bowden, eds. *El Sicario: The Autobiography of a Mexican Assassin*. New York: Nation Books, 2011.

Money Laundering and Terrorist Financing Prevention Act [2008] RT I 2008.

Morris, Charles R. "Corruption, Drug Trafficking, and Violence in Mexico." *The Brown Journal of World Affairs* 18, no. 2 (2012): 29–43.

Moyo, Dambisa. *Dead Aid: Why Aid Is Not Working and How There Is Another Way for Africa*. London: Penguin Books, 2009.

M/S Bremen v. Zapata Off-Shore Co 407 US 1, S.Ct 1907, 32 L.Ed.2d 513 (1972).

Mutsvairo, Bruce, Simon Columbus, and Iris Leijendekker. "Reconnoitering the Role of (Citizen) Journalism Ethics in the Emerging Networked Public Sphere." *African Journalism Studies* 35, no. 3 (2014): 4–22.

Myers, Allan. *The Laundromat: Investigation of Money Laundering at B.C. Casinos*. (Documentary film). Toronto, Canada: CTV News, February 9, 2019. https://www.youtube.com/watch?v=ddsGyJ-7Zw0.

Narayan, Deepa, Raj Patel, Kai Schafft, Anne Rademaher, and Sarah Koch-Schulte. *Voices of the Poor: Can Anyone Hear Us?* New York: Oxford University Press, 2000.

Narayan, Deepa, Robert Chambers, Meera K. Shah, and Patti Petesch. *Voices of the Poor: Crying out for Change*. New York: Oxford University Press, 2000.

National Judicial Council of Nigeria. "Profile of NJC." Accessed August 25, 2020. https://njc.gov.ng/profile-of-NJC.

NEPAD Secretariat. *Declaration on Democracy, Political, Economic and Corporate Governance*. Midrand, South Africa: NEPAD Secretariat, 2003.

Nieto, Nubia. "Political Corruption and Narcotrafficking in Mexico." *Transcience* 3, no. 2 (2012): 24–36.

Nordland, Rod, and Alissa J. Rubin. "Taliban Captives Dispute U.S. View on State of War." *The New York Times*, February 2, 2012, A1, A8.

NYC Admin. Code s.12-110 (2016).

NYC Charter ss.2600–2607 (2010).

Oborne, Peter. "How to Beat Terrorism: Over the Past Three Years, the Country Has Seen an Extraordinary Reduction in Violence." *The Spectator*, December 31, 2016. https://www.spectator.co.uk/article/how-to-beat-terrorism.

Odenyi, Chinedum. "The Domestic Implementation of International Treaties in Nigeria: Understanding the Role of the National Assembly in the Implementation of the International Criminal Court Bill." *Nigerian Coalition for the International Criminal Court (NCICC)*. July 23, 2014. http://ncicc.org.ng/2017/05/24/the-domestic-implementation-of-international-treaties-in-nigeria-by-chinedum-odenyi/.

OECD. *OECD Transfer Pricing Guidelines for Multinational Enterprises and Tax Administrations 2017*. Paris: OECD, 2017.

Office of Personnel Management. "Qualification Standard for Administrative Law Judge Positions." Accessed August 25, 2020. https://www.opm.gov/policy-data-oversight/classification-qualifications/general-schedule-qualification-standards/specialty-areas/administrative-law-judge-positions/.

Olaniyan, Kolawole. "Introductory Note to African Union (AU): Convention on Combating and Preventing Corruption," 43 I.L.M., 1 (2004).

Olivier de Sardan, Jean-Pierre. "A Moral Economy of Corruption in Africa." *Journal of Modern African Studies* 37, no. 1 (1999): 25–52.

Olson Jr., Mancur. "Big Bills Left on the Sidewalk: Why Some Nations Are Rich, and Others Poor." In *Making Poor Nations Rich: Entrepreneurship and the Process of Economic Development*, edited by Benjamin Powell, 25–53. Stanford, CA: Stanford University Press, 2008.

Omonobi, Kingsley, and Emmanuel Ulayi. "EFCC: Okiro Confirms Ribadu's Exit." *AllAfrica*, December 27, 2007. https://allafrica.com/stories/200712280320.html.

Open Society Foundations. "Criminal Force: Torture, Abuse, and Extrajudicial Killings by the Nigeria Police Force." May 2010. https://www.refworld.org/docid/4cbc44742.html.

Open Society Foundations. "Pretrial Detention and Torture: Why Pretrial Detainees Face the Greatest Risk." June 2011. https://www.justiceinitiative.org/publications/pretrial-detention-and-torture-why-pretrial-detainees-face-greatest-risk.

Open Society Foundations. "The Socioeconomic Impact of Pretrial Detention: A Global Campaign for Pretrial Justice Report." February 2011. https://www.justiceinitiative.org/publications/socioeconomic-impact-pretrial-detention.

Oracle. "Access Controls and Privileges." Accessed August 26, 2020. https://docs.oracle.com/en/database/oracle/oracle-database/18/olsag/access-controls-and-privileges.html#GUID-A222EB99-83C4-4BCC-84F6-D20087101E9D.

O'Reilly, Kenneth. "A New Deal for the FBI: The Roosevelt Administration, Crime Control, and National Security." *The Journal of American History* 69, no. 3 (1982): 638–658.

Open Society Foundations. *Against the Odds: CICIG in Guatemala*. Washington, DC: Open Society Foundations, 2016.

Partlow, Joshua. "Luxurious Presidential House Draws Mexican Press Scrutiny." *The Washington Post*, November 9, 2014. https://www.washingtonpost.com/world/luxurious-presidential-house-draws-mexican-press-scrutiny/2014/11/09/33bba1ee-65fd-11e4-ab86-46000e1d0035_story.html?utm_term=.87fc9b0cf75d.

PBS. "Family Tree: General Jesus Gutierrez Rebollo." *Frontline*. Accessed August 26, 2020. https://www.pbs.org/wgbh/pages/frontline/shows/mexico/family/genrebollo.html.

PBS. "Murder, Money and Mexico." *Frontline*. Accessed August 26, 2020. http://www.pbs.org/wgbh/pages/frontline/shows/mexico/etc/script.html.

Peachey, Paul. "'Britain's FBI' Target More Than 20 of the World's Most Corrupt Politicians Laundering Millions of Pounds through City of London." *Independent*, September 4, 2015. https://www.independent.co.uk/news/uk/crime/britains-fbi-target-more-than-20-of-the-worlds-most-corrupt-politicians-laundering-millions-of-10487589.html.

Peck, Linda Levy. "The British Case: Corruption and Political Development in the Early Modern State." In *Before Watergate: Problems of Corruption in American Society*, edited by Abraham S. Eisenstadt, Ari Hoogenboom and Hans L. Trefousse. Brooklyn College Studies on Society in Change, 35–49. Brooklyn, NY: Brooklyn College Press, 1979.

Pelligrini, Lorenzo, and Reyer Gerlagh. "Corruption's Effect on Growth and Its Transmission Channels." *KYKLOS* 57, no. 3 (2004): 429–456.

Peña Nieto, Enrique. "Mexico's Next Chapter." *The New York Times*, July 2, 2012. Accessed August 26, 2020. http://travel.nytimes.com/2012/07/03/opinion/mexicos-next-chapter.html.

Perez, Sonia D. "Former Guatemala Vice President Sentenced in Corruption Case." *AP*, October 9, 2018. https://www.apnews.com/feda24dafebc44cc9e6a0330e5fcfc9a.

per Léger AG in *Trasporti Castelletti Spedizioni Internazionali SpA v. Hugo Trumpy SpA* (C-159/97) EU:C:1999:142; [1999] I.L.Pr. 492.

Phillips, Tom, and David Agren. "Mexico Rocked by Claims of Corruption against Three Former Presidents: Leaked Deposition by Recently Extradited Former Head of State Oil Company Pemex Alleges Staggering Scale of High-Level Corruption." *The Guardian*, August 20, 2020. https://www.theguardian.com/world/2020/aug/20/mexico-corruption-former-presidents-emilio-lozoya.

Pierson, Brendan. "Ex-Guinea Minister Charged with Laundering Bribes Goes to Trial." *Reuters*, April 24, 2017. https://www.reuters.com/article/us-usa-guinea-corruption/ex-guinea-minister-charged-with-laundering-bribes-goes-to-trial-idUSKBN17Q2DF.

Pimentel, Stanley. "The Nexus of Organized Crime and Politics in Mexico." *Trends in Organized Crime* 4, no. 3 (1999): 9–28.

Poppa, Terence E. *Drug Lord*. El Paso, TX: Cinco Puntos, 2010.

Potter, Claire B. *War on Crime: Bandits, G-Men, and the Politics of Mass Culture*. New Brunswick, NJ: Rutgers University Press, 1998.

Preston, Julia. "Raul Salinas Guilty in Killing and Is Sentenced to 50 Years." *The New York Times*, January 22, 1999. http://www.nytimes.com/1999/01/22/world/raul-salinas-guilty-in-killing-and-is-sentenced-to-50-years.html?ref=marioruizmassieu.

Prisco, Giulio. "Abra Is Introducing KYC-Less Stock Investing with Cryptocurrencies." February 7, 2019. https://medium.com/chainrift-research/abra-is-introducing-kyc-less-stock-investing-with-cryptocurrencies-c4ff60828121.

Prosecutor v. Thomas Lubanga Dyilo, Case No. ICC-01/04-01/06. Accessed August 26, 2020. https://www.icc-cpi.int/drc/lubanga.

Racketeer Influenced and Corrupt Organizations Act, Pub. L. No. 91-452, s.901(a), 84 Stat. 922-3 (1970) [codified at 18 U.S.C. ss.1961–1968 (2018)].

Raghavan, Sudarsan. "Former Sudanese Ruler Omar Hassan Al-Bashir Is Convicted of Corruption, Money Laundering." *Washington Post*, December 14, 2019. https://www.washingtonpost.com/world/africa/former-sudanese-ruler-omar-al-bashir-convicted-of-corruption-money-laundering/2019/12/14/90ddc7ee-1e71-11ea-9ddd-3e0321c180e7_story.html.

Ramasastry, Anita. "Is There a Right to Be Free from Corruption?" *UC Davis Law Review* 49, no. 2 (2015): 703–739.

Ramseger, Florian. "Historical Perspectives on Corruption in Europe." February 26, 2007. https://www.u4.no/publications/historical-perspectives-on-corruption-in-europe/.

Ramsey, Carolyn B. "The Discretionary Power of 'Public' Prosecutors in Historical Perspective." *American Criminal Law Review* 39 (2002): 1309–1393.

Rashid, Ahmed. *Descent into Chaos: The U.S. And the Disaster in Pakistan, Afghanistan, and Central Asia*. New York: Penguin, 2009.

Rashid, Ahmed. "How Obama Lost Karzai." *Foreign Policy*, March/April, 2011, 71–76.

Ravelo, Ricardo, and Kristin Bricker. "Up to the Highest Level: Narco Infiltration in Felipe Calderon's Government: The Agencies in Charge of Mexico's Drug War Have High-Ranking Officials Who Protect the Cartels." *Proceso*, November 12, 2008. https://tinyurl.com/yy8awnv7.

Ravelo, Ricardo. *Los Capos, Las Narco-Rutas De Mexico*. Barcelona: Grijalbo, 2007.

Regulation 44/2001 on Jurisdiction and the Recognition and Enforcement of Judgments in Civil and Commercial Matters [2000] OJ L12/1.

Regulation 593/2008 on the Law Applicable to Contractual Obligations [2008] OJ L177/6 [Rome I Regulation].

Regulation 1215/2012 on Jurisdiction and the Recognition and Enforcement of Judgments in Civil and Commercial Matters [2012] OJ L351/1 [Brussels Recast].

Reno, William. *Corruption and State Politics in Sierra Leone*. Cambridge, UK: Cambridge University Press, 1995.

Reno, William. *Warlord Politics and African States*. Boulder, CO: Lynne Rienner Publishers, 1998.

Restatement (Second) of Contracts. Reporters: Robert Braucher [to 1971], E. Allan Farnsworth, [from 1971]. St. Paul, MN: American Law Institute Publishers, 1981.

Restatement (Second) of the Foreign Relations Law of the United States. Reporters: Adrian S. Fisher, Covey T. Oliver, Cecil J. Olmstead, I. N. P. Stokes, Joseph M. Sweeney. Revisers: Noyes Leech, Robert E. Stein. St. Paul, MN: American Law Institute Publishers, 1965.

Restatement (Third) of the Foreign Relations Law of the United States. Chief Reporter: Louis Henkin. Associate Reporters: Andreas F. Lowenfeld, Louis B. Sohn, Detlev F. Vagts. St. Paul, MN: American Law Institute Publishers, 1987.

Reuters. "Crime-Torn Mexican 'FBI' Investigates 1,500 Agents." December 2005. http://www.banderasnews.com/0512/nr-mexfbi.htm.

Riley, Bryan, and Terry Miller. "2017 Index of Economic Freedom: Trade and Prosperity at Risk." *Report No. 3168*. Washington, DC: The Heritage Foundation, 2016.

Rivera, Ray. "In an Afghan Village, Living in Fear of Both Sides." *The New York Times*, April 24, 2011, 9.

RJR Nabisco, 136 S. Ct. 2090 (2016), 195 L. Ed. 2d 476.

Rodrik, D. *One Economics, Many Recipes: Globalization, Institutions, and Economic Growth*. Princeton, NJ: Princeton University Press, 2007.

Rome Statute of the International Criminal Court, July 17, 1998, 2187 UNTS 90.

Rubin, Alissa J. "Taliban Exploit Openings in Neglected Province." *The New York Times*, July 30, 2010, A1, A9.

Sachs, J. *The End of Poverty: Economic Possibilities for Our Time*. New York: Penguin, 2006.

Sahara Reporters. "Breaking: Court Jails Jolly Nyame, Ex-Taraba Governor, for 14 Years over N1.64bn Fraud." May 30, 2018. http://saharareporters.com/2018/05/30/breaking-court-jails-jolly-nyame-ex-taraba-governor-14-years-over-n164bn-fraud.

Sahara Reporters. "Nigeria's National Judicial Council Forces 2 Judges into Compulsory Retirement, Reprimands 3 Others." February 27, 2014. http://

saharareporters.com/2014/02/27/nigerias-national-judicial-council-forces-2-judges-compulsory-retirement-reprimands-3.

Santora, Marc, William K. Rashbaum, and Nicole Perlroth. "Online Currency Exchange Accused of Laundering $6 Billion." *The New York Times*, May 28, 2013. https://www.nytimes.com/2013/05/29/nyregion/liberty-reserve-operators-accused-of-money-laundering.html.

Schaefer, Brett D., Steven Groves, and James M. Roberts. *Why the U.S. Should Oppose the Creation of an International Anti-Corruption Court*. Washington, DC: The Heritage Foundation, 2014.

Schnell, Sabina. "Cheap Talk or Incredible Commitment? (Mis)Calculating Transparency and Anti-Corruption." *Governance: An International Journal of Policy, Administration, and Institutions* 31, no. 3 (2018): 415–430.

Sciutto, Jim, Mary Bruce, and Devin Dwyer. "Obama Orders Start to US Troop Withdrawal from Afghanistan." *ABC News*, June 22, 2011. http://abcnews.go.com/Politics/president-obama-orders-start-us-troop-withdrawal-afghanistan/story?id=13908291.

Sedigh, Shahrzad, and Alex Muganda. "The Fight against Corruption in Tanzania." In *Curbing Corruption: Toward a Model for Building National Integrity*, edited by Rick Stapenhurst and Sahr J. Kpundeh, 151–177. Washington, DC: The World Bank, 1999.

Sedigh, Shahrzad, and Augustine Ruzindana. "The Fight against Corruption in Uganda." In *Curbing Corruption: Toward a Model for Building National Integrity*, edited by Rick Stapenhurst and Sahr J. Kpundeh, 179–205. Washington, DC: The World Bank, 1999.

Serious Organised Crime and Police Act 2005, c. 15. Accessed August 24, 2020. https://www.legislation.gov.uk/ukpga/2005/15/contents.

Shane, Scott, Mark Mazzetti, and Dexter Filkins. "Cables Depict Afghan Graft, Starting at the Top." *The New York Times*, December 2, 2010. https://www.nytimes.com/2010/12/03/world/asia/03wikileaks-corruption.html?_r=1&scp=1&sq=Afghan+corruption&st=nyt.

Sheridan, Mary Beth. "Mexico Declines to Prosecute Ex-Defense Minister Cienfuegos on Drug Charges." *The Washington Post*. January 14, 2021. https://www.washingtonpost.com/world/mexico-drops-charges-salvador-cienfuegos/2021/01/14/4cfc0954-56e3-11eb-a817-e5e7f8a406d6_story.html

Shosanya, Mohammed, and John Chuks Azu. "Lawyers Call for Prosecution of Corrupt Judges." *Daily Trust*, March 4, 2014. https://tinyurl.com/y5q63x44.

Sidoti, Chris. "National Human Rights Institutions and the International Human Rights System." In *Human Rights, State Compliance, and Social Change*, edited by Ryan Goodman and Thomas Pegram, 93–123. New York: Cambridge University Press, 2012.

Siggia, Stefano. "Online Video Games: Regulatory Overview." *ACAMS Today*, November 20, 2019. https://www.acamstoday.org/online-video-games-regulatory-overview/.

Silva Ávalos, Héctor , and Seth Robbins. "A Death Foretold: MACCIH Shuts Down in Honduras." *InSight Crime*. January 22, 2020. https://www.insightcrime.org/news/analysis/a-death-foretold-maccih-shuts-down-in-honduras/.

Simmons, Beth A., and Allison Danner. "Credible Commitments and the International Criminal Court." *International Organization* 64, no. 2 (2010): 225–256.

Singer, H. W. "The Distribution of Gains between Investing and Borrowing Countries." *The American Economic Review* 40, no. 2 (1950): 473–485.

"Situations Under Investigation." Int'l Crim. Ct. August 26, 2020. http://www.icc-cpi.int/en_menus/icc/situations%20and%20cases/Pages/situations%20and%20cases.aspx.

Soustras, Laurence, Christine Khachikyan, Edwin Kariuki, and Ruud Elmendoorp. "World Bank: Tales of the Missing Millions." *France 24*. Accessed August 26, 2020. http://webdoc.france24.com/world-bank-corruption-development-armenia-kenya-somalia-transparency/.

South Asia Terrorism Portal. "Fatalities in Terrorist Violence in Pakistan 2000–2019." Accessed August 26, 2020. https://www.satp.org/satporgtp/countries/pakistan/database/casualties.htm.

South Carolina Administrative Law Court. "Rules of Procedure for the Administrative Law Court." Accessed August 26, 2020. http://www.scalc.net/pub/pubOfficial rules2011.pdf.

Stanley, Clare. "Submission to the Jurisdiction." Wilberforce Chambers. Accessed August 26, 2020. https://www.wilberforce.co.uk/wp-content/uploads/2016/06/Submission-to-the-Jurisdiction-Clare-Stanley-QC.pdf.

Stapenhurst, Rick, and Sahr J. Kpundeh, eds. *Curbing Corruption: Toward a Model for Building National Integrity*. Washington, DC: The World Bank, 1999.

Staples v. United States, 511 US 600 (1994).

Steffens, Lincoln. *The Shame of the Cities*. Mineola, NY: Dover, 2004.

Stephenson, Matthew. "Dear International Anticorruption Court Advocates: It's Time to Answer Your Critics." March 1, 2016. Accessed November 4, 2020. https://globalanticorruptionblog.com/2016/03/01/dear-international-anticorruption-court-advocates-its-time-to-answer-the-critics/.

Stigen, Jo. *The Relationship between the International Criminal Court and National Jurisdictions: The Principle of Complementarity*. The Raoul Wallenberg Institute Human Rights Library. Leiden, The Netherlands: Martinus Nijhoff Publishers, 2008.

Struett, Michael J. *The Politics of Constructing the International Criminal Court*. New York: Palgrave Macmillan, 2008.

Summers, David M. "Third Party Beneficiaries and the Restatement (Second) of Contracts." *Cornell Law Review* 67, no. 4 (1982): 880–899.

Svensson, Jakob. "Eight Questions About Corruption." *Journal of Economic Perspectives* 19, no. 3 (2005): 19–42.

Tarnoff, Curt. "Millennium Challenge Corporation." *CRS Report*. Washington, DC: Congressional Research Service, 2017.

The Law of Contract, the General Regime of Obligations, and Proof of Obligations (John Cartwright, Bénédicte Fauvarque-Cosson, and Simon Whittaker, trans.). Accessed August 26, 2020. http://www.textes.justice.gouv.fr/art_pix/THE-LAW-OF-CONTRACT-2-5-16.pdf.

The New York Times. "Zambia: A Reversal on Anticorruption Efforts." August 27, 2009, A10.

"The States Parties to the Rome Statute." Int'l Criminal Court. Accessed August 26, 2020. https://asp.icc-cpi.int/en_menus/asp/states%20parties/Pages/the%20states%20parties%20to%20the%20rome%20statute.aspx.

The United Nations Conference on Trade and Development Secretariat. *The Least Developed Countries 2000 Report: Aid, Private Capital Flows and External Debt: The Challenge of Financing Development in the LDCs*. New York: United Nations, 2000.

Tinti, Peter, and Tuesday Reitano. *Migrant, Refugee, Smuggler, Saviour*. London: Hurst and Company, 2018.

Transparency International. "Corruption Perceptions Index 2003." Accessed August 26, 2020. https://www.transparency.org/en/cpi/2003.

Transparency International. "Corruption Perceptions Index 2010." Accessed August 26, 2020. https://www.transparency.org/en/cpi/2010.

Transparency International. "Corruption Perceptions Index 2016." Accessed August 26, 2020. https://www.transparency.org/en/cpi/2016/results.

Transparency International. "Corruption Perceptions Index—Tanzania." Accessed August 26, 2020. https://www.transparency.org/en/countries/tanzania.

Transparency International. *Integrity Pacts in Public Procurement: An Implementation Guide*. Berlin: Transparency International, 2013.

Ultracashmere House, Ltd v. Madison's of Columbus Inc 534 F.Supp. 542 (SDNY 1982).

UNCAC. *see* United Nations Convention against Corruption.

UNCITRAL Model Law on International Commercial Arbitration. Accessed August 26, 2020. https://uncitral.un.org/sites/uncitral.un.org/files/media-documents/uncitral/en/19-09955_e_ebook.pdf.

UNIAN. "Poroshenko Signs Law on Establishing High Anti-Corruption Court." June 26, 2018. Accessed November 28, 2021. https://www.unian.info/politics/10165775-poroshenko-signs-law-on-establishing-high-anti-corruption-court.html.

United Nations. "CICIG: International Commission against Impunity in Guatemala." Accessed August 26, 2020. https://dppa.un.org/en/mission/cicig.

United Nations Conference on Trade and Development (UNCTAD), *World Investment Report 2016*. Geneva: United Nations, 2016.

United Nations Convention against Corruption, October 31, 2003, 2349 UNTS 41.

United Nations Convention against Illicit Traffic in Narcotic Drugs and Psychotropic Substances, December 20, 1988, 1582 UNTS 95.

United Nations Convention against Transnational Organized Crime, December 12, 2000, 2225 UNTS 277.

United Nations Development Program. *Human Development Report*. New York: United Nations, 2001.

United Nations Office on Drugs and Crime, "United Nations Convention against Corruption: Signature and Ratification Status as of February 6, 2020." Accessed August 26, 2020. https://www.unodc.org/unodc/en/corruption/ratification-status.html.

United Nations. "Torture and Other Cruel, Inhuman or Degrading Treatment or Punishment." Accessed August 26, 2020. http://antitorture.org/wp-content/uploads/2012/07/V-Thematic-Report-Conditions-of-Detention-Children-in-Detention.pdf.

United Nations. "United Nations Convention against Transnational Organized Crime: Signature and Ratification Status as of August 26, 2020." Accessed August 26, 2020. https://treaties.un.org/pages/viewdetails.aspx?src=ind&mtdsg_no=xviii-12&chapter=18&lang=en.

United Nations. *United Nations Treaty Collection Treaty Reference Guide*. New York: United Nations, 1999.

"United States Code." *Office of the Law Revision Counsel, U.S. House of Representatives*. Accessed November 28, 2021. https://uscode.house.gov/.

United States ex rel. Pensacola Constr. Co v. St Paul Fire and Marine Ins. Co 705 F.Supp. 306 (WD La. 1989).

United States v. Liberty Reserve S.A. Indictment. SDNY. Accessed August 26, 2020. https://www.justice.gov/sites/default/files/usao-sdny/legacy/2015/03/25/Liberty%20Reserve%2C%20et%20al.%20Indictment%20-%20Redacted_0.pdf.

Universal Declaration of Human Rights. December 10, 1948. Accessed August 26, 2020. https://www.ohchr.org/EN/UDHR/Documents/UDHR_Translations/eng.pdf.

UNTOC. *see* United Nations Convention against Transnational Organized Crime.

USC. *see* United States Code.

U.S. Department of Justice. "About DOJ." Accessed November 1, 2020. https://www.justice.gov/about#:~:text=150%2C%2016%20Stat.,United%20States%20had%20an%20interest.

U.S. Department of Justice. "Former Mexican Federal Police Commander Arrested for Drug-Trafficking Conspiracy: Ivan Reyes Arzate Allegedly Received Hundreds of Thousands of Dollars in Bribes from Mexican Drug Cartels." January 24, 2020. https://www.justice.gov/usao-edny/pr/former-mexican-federal-police-commander-arrested-drug-trafficking-conspiracy.

U.S. Department of Justice. "History." July 25, 2019. https://www.justice.gov/criminal/history.

U.S. Department of Justice. "2015 National Drug Threat Assessment Summary." *Report No. DEA-DCT-DIR-008-16*. Washington, DC: Drug Enforcement Administration, 2015.

U.S. Department of Justice. "2017 National Drug Threat Assessment." *Report No. DEA-DCT-DIR-040-17*. Washington, DC: Drug Enforcement Administration, 2017.

U.S. Department of State. *International Narcotics Control Strategy Report: Volume 1—Drug and Chemical Control*. Washington, DC: Bureau for International Narcotics and Law Enforcement Affairs, 2017.

U.S. Department of the Treasury. "Specially Designated Nationals and Blocked Persons List (SDN) Human Readable Lists." August 25, 2020. https://www.treasury.gov/resource-center/sanctions/SDN-List/Pages/default.aspx.

U.S. Dep't of Treasury v. Haider, Civ. No. 15-1518, 2016 WL 107940 (D. Minn. Jan. 8, 2016).

U.S. Equal Employment Opportunity Commission. "Federal EEO Complaint Processing Procedures." Accessed August 26, 2020. https://www.eeoc.gov/eeoc/publications/fedprocess.cfm.

U.S. Joint Forces Command. *The 2008 Joint Operating Environment: Challenges and Implications for the Future Joint Force*. Suffolk, VA: U.S. Joint Forces Command, 2008.

us Swaleheen, Mushfiq, and Dean Stansel. "Economic Freedom, Corruption, and Growth." *Cato Journal* 27, no. 3 (2007): 343–358.

van der Does de Willebois, Emile, Emily M. Halter, Robert A. Harrison, Park Ji Won, and J.C. Sharman. *The Puppet Masters: How the Corrupt Use Legal Structures to Hide Stolen Assets and What to Do About It*. Washington, DC: The International Bank for Reconstruction and Development, 2011.

van de Walle, Nicolas. *African Economies and the Politics of Permanent Crisis, 1979–1999*. Cambridge: Cambridge University Press, 2001.

van de Walle, Nicolas. "The Politics of Non-Reform in Cameroon." In *Hemmed In: Responses to Africa's Economic Decline*, edited by Thomas Callaghy and John Ravenhill, 520–563. New York: Columbia University Press, 1993.

Vanguard. "Nwobike, SAN, Sent to Jail for Perverting Course of Justice." April 30, 2018. https://www.vanguardngr.com/2018/04/nwobike-san-sent-jail-perverting-course-justice/.

Vulliamy, Ed. *Amexica: War Along the Borderline*. New York: Farrar, Straus and Giroux, 2010.

Walker, Karen D., and Michael G. Tanner. "RICO Claims: The Challenge of Alleging the 'Pattern' Element." *The Florida Bar Journal* 76, no. 5 (2002): 34–39. https://www.floridabar.org/the-florida-bar-journal/rico-claims-the-challenge-of-alleging-the-pattern-element/.

Walker, Samuel, and Charles Katz. *The Police in America: An Introduction*. New York: McGraw-Hill, 2007.

Wang, Yunjong, and Deok Ryong Yoon. *Mechanisms of Regional Surveillance in East Asia and Its Prospects*. Tokyo: Institute for International Monetary Affairs-Kobe Research Project, 2002.

Warsh, David. "The Man Who Succeeded Gerschenkron." April 24, 2005. http://www.economicprincipals.com/issues/2005.04.24/145.html.

Weder, Beatrice, and Aymo Brunetti. "Another Tale of Two Cities: A Note on Institutions in Hong Kong and Singapore." *Journal of Institutional and Theoretical Economics-Zeitschrift Fur Die Gesamte Staatswissenschaft* 156, no. 2 (Jun 2000): 313–324.

WhatsApp. "Whatsapp Encryption Overview White Paper." December 19, 2017. https://scontent.whatsapp.net/v/t61.22868-34/68135620_760356657751682_6212997528851833559_n.pdf/WhatsApp-Security-Whitepaper.pdf?_nc_sid=41cc27&_nc_ohc=fLlLl2I4bncAX8ko-ZJ&_nc_ht=scontent.whatsapp.net&oh=a17937fd69583ffd5766f0adf2ba4924&oe=5F4820D3.

Whiting, Alex. "Is an International Anti-Corruption Court a Dream or a Distraction?" October 4, 2018. https://globalanticorruptionblog.com/2018/10/04/guest-post-is-an-international-anti-corruption-court-a-dream-or-a-distraction/.

Whitlock, Craig. "At War with the Truth: The Afghanistan Papers: A Secret History of the War." *The Washington Post*, December 9, 2019. https://www.washingtonpost.com/graphics/2019/investigations/afghanistan-papers/afghanistan-war-confidential-documents/.

Wickham-Crowley, Timothy P. *Guerrillas and Revolutions in Latin America*. Princeton, NJ: Princeton University Press, 1993.

Withnall, Adam. "The Brutal Central African Dictator Whose Playboy Son Faces French Corruption Trial." *Independent*, September 12, 2016. https://www.independent.co.uk/news/world/africa/teodoro-obiang-nguema-mbasogo-equatorial-guinea-french-corruption-trial-a7238501.html.

"Witness Protection: A Necessary Tool in Justice Administration." CICIG. September 27, 2011. http://www.cicig.org/index.php?page=0046-20110927E.

Wolf, Mark L. "The Case for an International Anti-Corruption Court." *Governance Studies*. Washington, DC: Brookings, 2014.

Wolf, Mark L. "The World Needs an International Anti-Corruption Court." *Daedalus* 147, no. 3 (2018): 144–156.

Wolf, Martin. *Why Globalization Works*. New Haven, CT: Yale University Press, 2005.

World Bank. "Anticorruption." Accessed August 27, 2020. https://tinyurl.com/yynbyckc.

World Bank. *Anticorruption in Transition: A Contribution to the Policy Debate*. Washington, DC: The World Bank, 2000.

World Bank. "Ending Impunity for Corruption: Global Knowledge for Local Impact." *Proceedings of the Third Biennial Meeting of the World Bank Group's International Corruption Hunters Alliance (ICHA)*, Washington, DC, December 8–10, 2014.

World Bank. *Fighting Corruption in Public Services: Chronicling Georgia's Reforms*. Washington, DC: The World Bank, 2012.

World Bank. *World Development Report 1997: The State in a Changing World*. New York: Oxford University Press, 1997.

Worthy, Ben. *The Politics of Freedom of Information: How and Why Governments Pass Laws That Threaten Their Power*. Manchester, UK: Manchester University Press, 2017.

Yeh, Stuart S. "An International Law Approach to End Money Laundering," *Journal of International Banking Law and Regulation* 35, no. 4 (2020): 148–163.

Yeh, Stuart S. "An International Treaty to Fight Money Laundering," *Journal of International Banking Law and Regulation* 35, no. 5 (2020): 190–207.

Yeh, Stuart S. "Anti-Corruption Inspections: A Missing Element of the IMF/World Bank Agenda?" *Journal of African Policy Studies* 18, no. 1 (2012): 1–41.

Yeh, Stuart S. "Application of a Model International Treaty to Money Laundering." *Journal of International Banking Law and Regulation* 35, no. 11 (2020): 443–462.

Yeh, Stuart S. "APUNCAC: An International Convention to Fight Corruption, Money Laundering, and Terrorist Financing." *Law and Development Review* 14, no. 2 (2021): 633–664.

Yeh, Stuart S. "Building a Global Institution to Fight Corruption and Address the Roots of Insurgency." *International Public Policy Review* 8, no. 1 (2014): 7–24.

Yeh, Stuart S. "Corruption and the Rule of Law in Sub-Saharan Africa." *African Journal of Legal Studies* 4, no. 2 (2011): 187–208.

Yeh, Stuart S. "Ending Corruption in Africa through United Nations Inspections." *International Affairs* 87, no. 3 (2011): 629–650.

Yeh, Stuart S. "Is an International Treaty Needed to Fight Corruption and the Narco-Insurgency in Mexico?" *International Criminal Justice Review* 22, no. 3 (2012): 233–257.

Yeh, Stuart S. "Poverty and the Rule of Law in Africa: A Missing International Actor?" *Poverty and Public Policy* 6, no. 4 (2014): 354–379.

Yeh, Stuart S. "Why UN Inspections? Corruption, Accountability, and the Rule of Law." *South Carolina Journal of International Law and Business* 11, no. 2 (2015): 227–260.

Yeh, Stuart S. "Why UN Inspections? The Accountability Gap in Sub-Saharan Africa." *International Public Policy Review* 7, no. 2 (2013): 1–29.

Zabokrytskyy, Ihor. "Transnational Civil Society Influence on Anti-Corruption Courts: Ukraine's Experience." *Global Jurist* 20, no. 1 (2020): 1–12.

Zucman, Gabriel. *The Hidden Wealth of Nations: The Scourge of Tax Havens.* Chicago: The University of Chicago Press, 2015.

Credits

Chapter 1 includes excerpts from Gary A. Haugen and Victor Boutros, *The Locust Effect: Why the End of Poverty Requires the End of Violence* (New York: Oxford University Press, 2014): xi, xiii, xiv, xvi, 43, 75, 81, 82, 83, 87, 92, 93, 94, 95, 135, 168, 169, 170, 181, 262. Copyright 2014 by International Justice Mission. Reproduced with permission of Oxford Publishing Limited (the Licensor) through PLSclear. All rights reserved. No part of the quoted material may be reproduced, stored in a retrieval system, or transmitted, in any form or by any means, without the prior permission in writing of Oxford University Press, or as expressly permitted by law, by license, or under terms agreed with the appropriate reproduction rights organization. Inquiries concerning reproduction should be sent to the Rights Department, Oxford University Press.

Chapter 2 is adapted from Stuart S. Yeh, "Ending Corruption in Africa through United Nations Inspections," *International Affairs* 87, no. 3 (2011): 629–50, doi:10.1111/j.1468-2346.2011.00994.x. Reprinted by permission of Oxford University Press on behalf of The Royal Institute of International Affairs. © 2011 The Royal Institute of International Affairs. All rights reserved. For permissions, please e-mail journals.permissions@oup.com.

Chapter 3 is adapted from Stuart S. Yeh, "Why UN Inspections? Corruption, Accountability, and the Rule of Law," *South Carolina Journal of International Law and Business* 11, no. 2 (2015): 227–60. Reprinted by permission of *South Carolina Journal of International Law and Business*.

Chapter 4 is adapted from Stuart S. Yeh, "Is an International Treaty Needed to Fight Corruption and the Narco-Insurgency in Mexico?," *International Criminal Justice Review* 22, no. 3 (2012): 233–57. Reprinted by permission of Sage.

Chapter 5 is adapted from Stuart S. Yeh, "Building a Global Institution to Fight Corruption and Address the Roots of Insurgency," *International Public Policy Review* 8, no. 1 (2014): 7–24. Reprinted by permission of *International Public Policy Review*.

Figure 5.1 is adapted from David Kilcullen, *Counterinsurgency* (New York: Oxford University Press, 2010), Figure 2.1, by permission of David Kilcullen.

Chapter 6 is adapted from Stuart S. Yeh, "Poverty and the Rule of Law in Africa: A Missing International Actor?," *Poverty and Public Policy* 6, no. 4 (2014): 354–79. Reprinted by permission of Policy Studies Organization, © 2014.

Chapter 7 is adapted from Stuart S. Yeh, "Corruption and the Rule of Law in sub-Saharan Africa," *African Journal of Legal Studies* 4, no. 2 (2011): 187–208. Reprinted by permission of *African Journal of Legal Studies* and the Africa Law Institute.

Chapter 8 is adapted from Stuart S. Yeh, "An International Treaty to Fight Money Laundering," *Journal of International Banking Law and Regulation* 35, no. 5 (2020): 190–207. Reprinted by permission of Thomson Reuters, trading as Sweet & Maxwell, 5 Canada Square, Canary Wharf, London, E14 5AQ.

Chapter 9 is adapted from Stuart S. Yeh, "An International Law Approach to End Money Laundering," *Journal of International Banking Law and Regulation* 35, no. 4 (2020): 148–63. Reprinted by permission of Thomson Reuters, trading as Sweet & Maxwell, 5 Canada Square, Canary Wharf, London, E14 5AQ.

Chapter 10 is adapted from Stuart S. Yeh, "Application of a Model International Treaty to Money Laundering," *Journal of International Banking Law and Regulation* 35, no. 11 (2020): 444–63. Reprinted by permission of Thomson Reuters, trading as Sweet & Maxwell, 5 Canada Square, Canary Wharf, London, E14 5AQ.

Chapter 11, chapter 12, and chapter 13 are adapted from Stuart S. Yeh, "APUNCAC: An International Convention to Fight Corruption, Money Laundering, and Terrorist Financing," *Law and Development Review* 14, no. 2 (2021): 633–664. Reprinted by permission of *Law and Development Review* and the Law and Development Institute.

Chapter 14 is adapted from Stuart S. Yeh, "APUNCAC and the International Anti-Corruption Court (IACC)," *Laws* 10, no. 1 (2021): 1–18. Reprinted by permission of *Laws* and MDPI.

Index

Page numbers followed with "n" refer to endnotes and italic page numbers refer to figures and tables.

About the Author

Professor Stuart S. Yeh was awarded a PhD degree from Stanford University. He led an initiative to promulgate changes in international law and international regulatory regimes for the purpose of fighting corruption and money laundering. This initiative culminated in the drafting of a model international anticorruption convention. Professor Yeh previously served as a Spencer Postdoctoral Fellow at Harvard University and as an invited expert at the OECD. He is currently a professor in the Department of Organizational Leadership, Policy, and Development at the University of Minnesota.

www.ingramcontent.com/pod-product-compliance
Lightning Source LLC
LaVergne TN
LVHW011702200926
848484LV00004B/1036
* 9 7 8 1 7 9 3 6 5 5 0 9 7 *